Energy Law in Germany

Energy Law in Germany

Third Edition

Henning Thomas

This book was originally published as a monograph in the International Encyclopaedia of Laws/Energy Law.

Founding Editor: Roger Blanpain
General Editor: Frank Hendrickx
Volume Editors: Kurt Deketelaere & Bram Delvaux

Wolters Kluwer

Published by:
Kluwer Law International B.V.
PO Box 316
2400 AH Alphen aan den Rijn
The Netherlands
E-mail: lrs-sales@wolterskluwer.com
Website: www.wolterskluwer.com/en/solutions/kluwerlawinternational

Sold and distributed by:
Wolters Kluwer Legal & Regulatory U.S.
7201 McKinney Circle
Frederick, MD 21704
United States of America
E-mail: customer.service@wolterskluwer.com

Printed on acid-free paper

ISBN 978-94-035-4843-2

e-Book: ISBN 978-94-035-4665-0
web-PDF: ISBN 978-94-035-4544-8

Printed in the United Kingdom.

The Author

Henning Thomas works as Lead Legal Counsel for Ørsted and is lecturer at the Professional School of the Leuphana University Lüneburg, Germany, in a Master's for sustainability law. Previously he worked in the field of renewable energy law at a law firm specialized in energy and infrastructure law. Born in Hamburg, Henning Thomas studied law in Hamburg and Münster with additional studies on the Common Law legal system. He wrote his doctoral thesis on sustainability of bioenergy. At the University of Leuven, Belgium he completed Master's in Energy and Environmental Law. During his legal education as well as his work as a lawyer, Henning Thomas worked *inter alia* in law offices in Sydney, Budapest, Brussels, and Birmingham as well as in the European Parliament. Henning Thomas published in particular on the topics of renewable energy law and law on energy storage.

The Author

Table of Contents

Table of Contents

Table of Contents

List of Abbreviations

ARegV	Verordnung über die Anreizregulierung der Energieversorgungsnetze, Anreizregulierungsverordnung, Ordinance on Incentive Regulation
BauGB	Baugesetzbuch, Construction Code
BBPlG	Bundesbedarfsplangesetz, Federal Requirements Plan Act
BGB	Bürgerliches Gesetzbuch, Civil Law Code
BGBl.	Bundesgesetzblatt, Federal Law Gazette
BGH	Bundesgerichtshof, Federal Court of Justice
BGHZ	*Decisions of the Federal Court of Justice*
BImSchG	Bundes-Immissionsschutzgesetz, Federal Immissions Control Act
BMWi	Federal Ministry for Economic Affairs and Climate Action
BNetzA	Bundesnetzagentur, Federal Network Agency
BT-Drs.	Bundestagsdrucksache, Parliamentary Material
BVerfG	Bundesverfassungsgericht, Federal Constitutional Court
BVerfGE	*Decisions of the Federal Constitutional Court*
BVerwG	Bundesverwaltungsgericht, Federal Administrative Court
BVerwGE	*Decisions of the Federal Administrative Court*
EC	European Community
ECJ	European Court of Justice
ECR	*European Court Reports*
EEG	Erneuerbare-Energien-Gesetz, Renewable Energy Sources Act
EEX	European Energy Exchange
EnWG	Energiewirtschaftsgesetz, Energy Industry Act
EnWZ	*Zeitschrift für das gesamte Recht der Energiewirtschaft*
EU	European Union
GasNZV	Gasnetzzugangsverordnung, Regulation on the Access to Gas Supply Grids
GG	Grundgesetz, German Basic Law

List of Abbreviations

IR	*InfrastrukturRecht*
kWh	Kilowatt hour
LKV	*Landes- und Kommunalverwaltung*
NABEG	Netzausbaubeschleunigungsgesetz Übertragungsnetz, Grid Expansion Acceleration Act
NJW	*Neue Juristische Wochenschrift*
NJW-RR	*Neue Juristische Wochenschrift Rechtsprechungs-Report*
NordÖR	*Zeitschrift für öffentliches Recht in Norddeutschland*
NVwZ	*Neue Zeitschrift für Verwaltungsrecht*
OJ	*Official Journal of the European Community*
OLG	Oberlandesgericht, Higher Regional Court
OVG	Oberverwaltungsgericht, Higher Administrative Court
RdE	*Recht der Energiewirtschaft*
RELP	*Renewable Energy Law and Policy Review*
TFEU	Treaty on the Functioning of the European Union
ZNER	*Zeitschrift für Neues Energierecht*
ZUR	*Zeitschrift für Umweltrecht*

Acknowledgements and Preface

The first and second editions of this monograph on Energy Law in Germany have been written by Dr Malte Petersen and Dr Henning Thomas together. Malte is taking a pause in this third edition of the monograph, and Henning has continued the work with many thanks to Malte for the good cooperation on the previous monographs – hoping that Malte will rejoin in one of the next revisions.

In light of the tremendous challenges resulting from climate change, the focus of this monograph is on the European and national energy law rules that shall enable the transformation of the energy sector in Germany to renewable energy sources and energy efficiency. While Germany has significantly progressed on these aims in recent years, the current decade needs to see unprecedented efforts to combat climate change. Besides this focus of the monograph, it aims to give a comprehensive overview on legal rules regarding all energy sources employed in Germany.

This description of Energy Law in Germany and comments expressed therein are strictly the personal view of the author and do not necessarily represent the views of his employer.

The information provided in this monograph has been verified with due diligence. However, the information cannot substitute any legal or practical advice in a particular case.

Lüneburg, May 2022 Henning Thomas

General Introduction

Chapter 1. General Background

§1. Geography and Population

1. Geographically, the Federal Republic of Germany is located in Central Europe. Covering a territory of 357,021 km^2, Germany shares borders with Denmark, Poland, the Czech Republic, Austria, Switzerland, France, Luxembourg, Belgium, and the Netherlands. Following France, Spain, and Sweden, Germany is the fourth largest country in the European Union (EU) in terms of territory. Germany has almost 2,400 kms of coastline along the Baltic and North Seas.

2. Since the reunification of the Federal Republic of Germany with the German Democratic Republic (East Germany), Germany's population has remained constant at over 80 million people. The next largest European countries are France and the United Kingdom with more than 60 million inhabitants each.

3. The capital and largest city is Berlin with a population of 3.7 million people. In 1999, many governmental institutions, ministries, and embassies were moved from Bonn, the former capital of Germany, to Berlin. Other large metropolitan areas in Germany include the Rhein-Ruhr area (approximately 10 million people), Frankfurt (approximately 5 million), Hamburg (approximately 4 million), Munich (approximately 3 million), and Leipzig (approximately 1.2 million people).[1]

4. Germany is a federal parliamentary republic divided into sixteen regions, the so-called Länder (Federal States). Germany has a bicameral parliament with a Federal Parliament (Bundestag) and Federal Council (Bundesrat). The 598 (plus members due to excess mandates) members of the Bundestag are elected by popular vote and serve four-year terms. The sixty-nine members of the Bundesrat are not elected, they are members of the state cabinets which can appoint and remove them. As a result, the composition of the Bundesrat changes whenever one of the sixteen Federal States holds an election.

5. Iron ore, coal, lignite, salt, nickel, potash, and natural gas are among the most significant natural resources.

1. Detailed figures are available on the webpage of the Federal Statistical Office, www.destatis.de.

6. In 2020, the Gross Domestic Product (GDP) during the COVID-19 crisis decreased by 5%[2] to an amount of EUR 3,330,2 billion. Germany has the largest national economy in Europe and the fourth largest by nominal GDP in the world. The service sector contributes around 70%, industry 23%, building industry 6%, and agriculture 1% to the total GDP.[3]

7. European Union legislation affects Germany's policies and legislation. In 2002, Germany introduced the common European currency (Euro) as part of the obligations under the European Monetary Union.

8. The government's policy fosters energy conservation and the use of renewable energy sources[4] such as solar, wind, biomass, hydroelectric, and geothermal energy. As a result of energy-saving measures, energy efficiency has been improving since the beginning of the 1970s.

§2. Legal and Political Structure

I. Germany's Territorial Organization

9. Germany is a Federal Republic consisting of sixteen States. In German these are known as *Länder* or *Bundesländer*. The area covered by the sixteen States is completely and solely the territory of Germany. The States are:

(1) Baden-Württemberg;
(2) Bayern (Bavaria);
(3) Berlin;
(4) Brandenburg;
(5) Bremen;
(6) Hamburg;
(7) Hessen;
(8) Mecklenburg-Vorpommern (Mecklenburg-Western Pomerania);
(9) Niedersachsen (Lower Saxony);
(10) Nordrhein-Westfalen (North Rhine-Westphalia);
(11) Rheinland-Pfalz (Rhineland-Palatinate);
(12) Saarland;
(13) Sachsen (Saxony);
(14) Sachsen-Anhalt (Saxony-Anhalt);
(15) Schleswig-Holstein; and
(16) Thüringen (Thuringia).

---

2. See information provided by the Federal Ministry of Economic Affairs and Climate Protection, available at www.bmwi.de, and by the Federal Statistical Office, available at www.destatis.de.
3. Statistical data is available at the webpage of the Federal Statistical Office. See, for instance, *Bruttoinlandsprodukt 2020 für Deutschland*, www.destatis.de.
4. See for more detail below Part V.

10. Being a Federal Republic there are two levels in the German political and legal system: the federal level and the state level. Each level has its own government bodies, legislation, executive, and judiciary (see section IV below). In addition, the German municipalities (*Gemeinden*) have rights to regulate all matters of the local community within their own responsibility.

II. Germany's Political Structure

11. In 1949, the Bundesrepublik Deutschland (Federal Republic of Germany) was founded through the announcement of the Grundgesetz (Basic Law). Fundamental aspects of the basic law are the protection of individual liberty and human rights. Moreover, it also ensures the separation of powers on the federal and state levels and that the judiciary is independent of the executive and the legislative branches.

12. Germany has a bicameral parliament with *Bundestag* (Federal Parliament) and *Bundesrat* (Federal Council). The *Bundestag* resides in the former *Reichstag* building in the capital city of Berlin. It consists of at least 598 members, which are elected in four-year terms. Members of the *Bundestag* are elected by popular election. Half of the members are elected directly from 299 constituencies, the other half are elected from the parties' land lists in a way to achieve proportional representation for the total Bundestag. In addition to the 598 members there might be additional – so-called – excess mandates.

13. The *Bundesrat* is a sixty-nine-member legislative body representing Germany's sixteen Federal States. The members of the *Bundesrat* are not elected, but are instead based on the composition of the sixteen regional state governments. They are members of the state cabinets that may appoint and remove them at any time. The individual States are not represented in the Bundesrat by an equal number of delegates. Rather, the population size of each state determines the number of votes. The composition of the *Bundesrat* changes whenever one of the sixteen *Länder* (States) holds an election.

14. The Federal President (*Bundespräsident*) is the head of state. According to the Basic Law, he is involved in the forming of the government. The Federal President, for instance, proposes the Chancellor (*Bundeskanzler*). However, it is important to note that the Chancellor is actually elected by the *Bundestag* according to a procedure set out in Article 63 of the Basic Law. Moreover, Federal Ministers are also appointed and dismissed by the Federal President upon proposal of the Chancellor. Furthermore, the Federal President appoints and dismisses *inter alia* federal judges, federal civil servants as well as commissioned and non-commissioned officers, except as otherwise foreseen by the law. However, the Federal President has only very restricted political powers. The Federal President is elected by the Federal Convention which consists of the members of the *Bundestag* and an equal number of members from the parliaments of the Federal States who are elected on the basis of proportional representation (in relation to the strength of the parties represented in the parliaments of the Federal States). The term of office is five years.[5]

15. The Federal Cabinet is made up by the Chancellor and the Federal Ministers. The Chancellor has a prominent position in the government. He or she has the right to form the cabinet and to determine who will be in the government. The Chancellor lays down general policy guidelines and bears responsibility for them (so-called principle of Chancellor policy guidelines). Pursuant to the principle of joint Cabinet decision-making, the Chancellor and the ministers decide jointly on matters of general political importance.[6]

III. Germany's Legal Structure

A. Division of Competences Between the Federation and the German States

16. It has been pointed out already that Germany is a Federal Republic formed by sixteen States. Hence, German law is strongly influenced by federalism, and the individual States each have their own responsibilities and particular laws. However, the German legal system is founded on the principles laid out by the Basic Law for the Federal Republic of Germany (*Grundgesetz*) which was created in the year 1949 after World War II as the German Constitution.[7] The Basic Law guarantees fundamental rights and regulates the organization of the state and the configuration of the bodies of government (like *Bundestag* and *Bundesrat* – Federal Parliament and Federal Council). It also regulates the procedure of legislation and the division of competences between the Federation and the German States. The States have constitutions of their own which have to be in accordance with the Basic law.

B. Legislation

17. The Basic Law for the Federal Republic of Germany contains regulations regarding the question whether the Federation or the States have the right to legislate on a certain matter. Pursuant to Article 70 of the Basic law, the States have the right to legislate insofar as the Basic Law does not confer legislative power to the Federation. There is a differentiation between the so-called exclusive legislative power of the Federation and the concurrent legislative powers.

18. On matters within the 'Exclusive legislative power of the Federation', the States shall have power to legislate only when and to the extent that they are

5. For an overview in English, see the webpage of the Federal President, www.bundespraesident.de.
6. For general information in English, see the webpage of the Federal Government, www.bundesregierung.de.
7. An official translation of the basic law (Grundgesetz) is available at: www.gesetze-im-internet.de/englisch_gg/index.html.

expressly authorized to do so by a federal law. Article 73(1) of the Basic Law contains an enumeration of matters under exclusive legislative power of the Federation:

1. foreign affairs and defence, including protection of the civilian population;
2. citizenship in the Federation;
3. freedom of movement, passports, residency registration and identity cards, immigration, emigration, and extradition;
4. currency, money and coinage, weights and measures, and the determination of standards of time;
5. the unity of the customs and trading area, treaties regarding commerce and navigation, the free movement of goods, and the exchange of goods and payments with foreign countries, including customs and border protection;

5a. safeguarding German cultural assets against removal from the country;

6. air transport;

6a. the operation of railways wholly or predominantly owned by the Federation (federal railways), the construction, maintenance, and operation of railroad lines belonging to federal railways, and the levying of charges for the use of these lines;

7. postal and telecommunications services;
8. the legal relations of persons employed by the Federation and by federal corporations under public law;
9. industrial property rights, copyrights, and publishing;

9a. protection by the Federal Criminal Police Office against the dangers of international terrorism when a threat transcends the boundary of one *land*, when responsibility is not clearly assignable to the police authorities of any particular land or when the highest authority of an individual *land* requests the assumption of federal responsibility;

10. cooperation between the Federation and the *Länder* concerning:
    a. criminal police work;
    b. protection of the free democratic basic order, existence, and security of the Federation or of a *land* (protection of the constitution); and
    c. protection against activities within the federal territory which, by the use of force or preparations for the use of force, endanger the external interests of the Federal Republic of Germany, as well as the establishment of a Federal Criminal Police Office and international action to combat crime.
11. statistics for federal purposes;
12. the law on weapons and explosives;
13. benefits for persons disabled by war and for dependents of deceased war victims as well as assistance to former prisoners of war;
14. the production and utilization of nuclear energy for peaceful purposes, the construction and operation of facilities serving such purposes, protection against hazards arising from the release of nuclear energy or from ionizing radiation, and the disposal of radioactive substances.

19. On matters within the concurrent legislative power, the States shall have the power to legislate as long as and to the extent that the Federation has not exercised its legislative power by enacting a law. Article 74(1) of the Basic Law contains an enumeration of matters under concurrent legislative powers:

1. civil law, criminal law, court organization, and procedure (except for the correctional law of pretrial detention), the legal profession, notaries, and the provision of legal advice;
2. registration of births, deaths, and marriages;
3. the law of association;
4. the law relating to residence and establishment of foreign nationals;
   4a. [repealed];
5. [repealed];
6. matters concerning refugees and expellees;
7. public welfare (except for the law on social care homes);
8. [repealed];
9. war damage and reparations;
10. war graves and graves of other victims of war or despotism;
11. the law relating to economic matters (mining, industry, energy, crafts, trades, commerce, banking, stock exchanges, and private insurance), except for the law on shop closing hours, restaurants, game halls, display of individual persons, trade fairs, exhibitions, and markets;
12. labour law, including the organization of enterprises, occupational health and safety, and employment agencies, as well as social security, including unemployment insurance;
13. the regulation of educational and training grants and the promotion of research;
14. the law regarding expropriation, to the extent relevant to matters enumerated in Articles 73 and 74;
15. the transfer of land, natural resources, and means of production to public ownership or other forms of public enterprise;
16. prevention of the abuse of economic power;
17. the promotion of agricultural production and forestry (except for the law on land consolidation), ensuring the adequacy of food supply, the importation and exportation of agricultural and forestry products, deep-sea and coastal fishing, and preservation of the coasts;
18. urban real estate transactions, land law (except for laws regarding development fees), and the law on rental subsidies, subsidies for old debts, home building loan premiums, miners' homebuilding and homesteading;
19. measures to combat human and animal diseases which pose a danger to the public or are communicable, admission to the medical profession and to ancillary professions or occupations, as well as the law on pharmacies, medicines, medical products, drugs, narcotics and poisons;
    19 a. the economic viability of hospitals and the regulation of hospital charges;
20. the law on food products including animals used in their production, the law on alcohol and tobacco, essential commodities and feedstuffs as well

as protective measures in connection with the marketing of agricultural and forest seeds and seedlings, the protection of plants against diseases and pests, as well as the protection of animals;

21. maritime and coastal shipping, as well as navigational aids, inland navigation, meteorological services, sea routes, and inland waterways used for general traffic;
22. road traffic, motor transport, construction and maintenance of long-distance highways, as well as the collection of tolls for the use of public highways by vehicles and the allocation of the revenue;
23. non-federal railways, except mountain railways;
24. waste disposal, air pollution control, and noise abatement (except for the protection from noise associated with human activity);
25. state liability;
26. medically assisted generation of human life, analysis, and modification of genetic information as well as the regulation of organ, tissue, and cell transplantation;
27. the statutory rights and duties of civil servants of the *Länder*, the municipalities and other corporations of public law as well as of the judges in the *Länder*, except for their career regulations, remuneration, and pensions;
28. hunting;
29. protection of nature and landscape management;
30. land distribution;
31. regional planning;
32. management of water resources; and
33. admission to institutions of higher education and requirements for graduation in such institutions.

20. It is important to note that there are some specific regulations with regard to concurrent legislative powers in Article 72 of the Basic Law. For instance, according to Article 72(3) of the Basic Law the States may enact laws at variance with the federal legislation with respect to certain matters such as protection of nature and landscape management, land distribution, regional planning, and the management of water resources even if the Federation has made use of its power to legislate. Hence, the division of powers between the Federation and the States is quite complicated.

21. The Basic Law for the Federal Republic of Germany does not contain a special chapter on energy. Since many legislative acts are important for the energy sector, various titles of the aforementioned regulations are relevant with regard to energy issues. However, Article 73(1) number 14 Basic Law states explicitly that the production and utilization of nuclear energy for peaceful purposes, the construction and operation of facilities serving such purposes, protection against hazards arising from the release of nuclear energy or from ionizing radiation and the disposal of radioactive substances fall within the exclusive legislative power of the Federation. And Article 74(1) number 11 Basic Law stipulates that the concurrent legislative power shall extend to the law relating to economic matters (including energy). Many legislative acts in the field of energy law covered in this monograph are based on this concurrent legislative power in Article 74(1) number 11 Basic Law.

C. *Executive*

22. As with regard to the legislative powers, the Basic Law for the Federal Republic of Germany contains a chapter on the execution of federal laws and the federal administration. Article 83 stipulates that the States shall execute federal laws in their own right insofar as the Basic Law does not provide or permit otherwise. Where the *Länder* execute federal law in their own right, they shall provide for the establishment of the required authorities and regulate their administrative procedures. If federal laws provide otherwise, the *Länder* may enact deviating regulations. More detailed regulations can be found in Article 84 of the Basic Law.

23. Article 85 Basic Law refers to the execution by the *Länder* on federal commissions (*Bundesauftragsverwaltung*). According to Article 85(1) Basic Law the establishment of the authorities shall remain the concern of the *Länder* – except insofar as federal laws enacted with the consent of the *Bundesrat* provide otherwise – where the *Länder* execute federal laws on federal commission.

24. Finally, there can be federal administration according to Article 86 Basic Law (*bundeseigene Verwaltung*). Where the Federation executes laws through its own administrative authorities or through federal corporations or institutions established under public law, the Federal Government shall, insofar as the law in question contains no special provision, issue general administrative rules.

D. *Public Law and Private Law*

25. In German law, there is a basic differentiation between private law (*Privatrecht*) and public law (*Öffentliches Recht*). Private law rules the relations between two private legal entities or two entities that act on the same level. This can also be the case, for instance, if an authority buys office equipment from a private company. In contrast to this, public law is to be applied whenever a state agency exercises sovereign power. In other words: public law rules the relations between a citizen or a private person and an official entity or between two official entities. With regard to energy matters, public law is relevant, for instance, if a permit is needed for a project or undertaking. But also regulatory law under which federal institutions like the Federal Network Agency (*Bundesnetzagentur*) exercise sovereign power over energy companies belongs to the area of public law.

26. The administrative work of the authorities is regulated by the Administrative Procedures Act (*Verwaltungsverfahrensgesetz*). A basic principle of this code is the so-called principle of investigation which obliges the authorities to examine the relevant facts of a case officially on their own accord. If somebody intends to force the authorities to take action – for instance to issue a permit – or if somebody wants to institute proceedings against administrative actions of an authority, the Administrative Courts Act (*Verwaltungsgerichtsordnung*) applies. It regulates different kinds of possible legal action and the stages of appeal.

IV. Sources of German Energy Law

27. Germany belongs to the continental law tradition which is characterized by its codified system of legal provisions, e.g., in the form of statutes. The sources of German Energy Law are the same as for German law in general: laws and other codifications, ordinances, statutes, court precedents, preparatory works, and customs. Moreover, it has to be pointed out that German law is greatly influenced by EU/EC law, which is especially true in the field of energy law. Of pivotal importance for the German energy sector have been, for instance, the EC electricity and gas directives (see below). Some brief remarks on the general hierarchy of German norms are given in the following section.

A. The Basic Law for the Federal Republic of Germany

28. The Basic Law for the Federal Republic of Germany deals with fundamental rights ('*Grundrechte*', particularly Articles 1–19 Basic Law) that fundamentally determine the relationship between individuals and the state. In addition to that, the Basic Law also regulates the organization and structure of the state and its institutions. Being the constitution of Germany, the Basic Law is the fundamental legal act in German law.

B. Statutes and Codes

29. In Germany, more or less all important legal issues are governed by comprehensive legislation in the form of statutes/acts and regulations. Legislative power is exercised by the German Federal Parliament (*Bundestag*), a parliament elected by German citizens.[8] The States take part in the legislative process by sending representatives to a federal chamber known as the Federal Council (*Bundesrat*).[9] The details of the legislative process are regulated in the Basic Law as well.[10]

30. As mentioned above, the legislative competence is allocated between the Federation and the States creating two levels in the legal system of Germany. It is important to note that the States also have legislative power with regard to certain

8. *See* Artt. 38–48 Basic Law.
9. Details are regulated in Artt. 50–53 Basic Law.
10. Articles 70–82 Basic Law.

issues and matters. Detailed rules about the division of powers between the Federation and the States can be found in the Basic Law. As a basic rule, it can be said that the States have the right to legislate insofar as the Basic Law does not confer legislative powers to the Federation. The extent to which the States have the right to legislate depends on whether the issue at stake falls into the exclusive legislative power of the Federation or rather into the so-called concurrent legislative power (see above). In case there should be a conflict between Federal law and State law, Article 31 Basic Law stipulates that Federal law shall take precedence over State law.

31. With respect to energy law, legislative competence lies principally with the Federation and not with the States. The most important legislative acts – such as the Energy Industry Act (*Energiewirtschaftsgesetz, EnWG*), the Renewable Energy Sources Act (*Erneuerbare-Energien-Gesetz, EEG*), and the more recent legal acts which have been enacted to implement European Directives – are Federal law. However, State law is relevant as well, especially with regard to procedural rules, participation of municipalities, the issuing of permits, etc.

C. *Ordinances*

32. In addition to legislative acts such as statutes and codes, regulations/ordinances (*Verordnungen*) are also important in German law. According to Article 80 Basic Law, the Federal Government, a Federal Minister or the governments of the Federal States may be authorized by a law to issue statutory instruments. The content, purpose, and scope of the authority conferred shall be specified in the law and each statutory instrument shall contain a statement of its legal basis.

33. In the field of Energy law, there are quite a number of highly relevant ordinances. Important ordinances include the Renewable Energy Ordinance (*Erneuerbare-Energien-Verordnung, EEV*), the Ordinance on Incentive Regulation (*Anreizregulierungsverordnung, ARegV*), the ordinances regarding network access (*Stromnetzzugangsverordnung, StromNZV* and *Gasnetzzugangsverordnung, GasNZV*), and the Electricity and Gas Grid Charges Ordinances (*Stromnetzentgeltverordnung, StromNEV* and *Gasnetzentgeltverordnung, GasNEV*).

D. *Statutes* (Satzungen)

34. Furthermore, municipalities have the right to issue statutes (*'Satzungen'*) with respect to regional and local issues.

E. Court Precedents

35. As mentioned above, Germany belongs to the continental law tradition, which means that the legal system is not first and foremost based on court precedents. Judgments or decisions of the courts are nevertheless relevant also with regard to subsequent legal disputes. They are used as guidance when it comes to interpreting an unclear provision or law. Thus, they often are a valuable point of reference for the interpretation of the law.

36. In principle, decisions of the courts do not formally bind other courts. In practice, however, principles laid down by higher courts often are closely adhered to by the lower courts. Hence, decisions of the German Federal Court of Justice (*Bundesgerichtshof*), Federal Administrative Court (*Bundesverwaltungsgericht*), Federal Finance Court (*Bundesfinanzhof*), Federal Social Court (*Bundessozialgericht*), Federal Labour Court (*Bundesarbeitsgericht*) and, last but not least, the Federal Constitutional Court (*Bundesverfassungsgericht*) are highly important for subsequent court decisions on related matters.

37. In general, the German judiciary has a good reputation, although the length of proceedings can be a problem, particularly if one party appeals against a judgment and higher courts get involved. Particularly for planning procedures and planning decisions, several legislative measures however have pursued to streamline procedures, e.g., by reducing the court instances that can decide upon a specific matter. An example is the 2006 Infrastructure Planning Acceleration Act[11] which has aimed at speeding up procedures. It is relevant *inter alia* for projects with regard to railway infrastructure, airports as well as electricity and gas lines. Sections 48 and 50 of the Administrative Procedures Act make the Federal Administrative Court and the Higher Administrative Courts (*Oberverwaltungsgerichte*) the court of first and last instance for certain projects.

F. EU Law

38. As a member of the EU, Germany is bound by the EU acquis communautaire. In the energy area, a large number of directives have been adopted by the European Union respectively the European Community which have been implemented into German law. EU energy policy in general influences German law to a large extent; this can be seen not only with respect to various amendments of the German Energy Industry Act (EnWG), but also with regard to a wide range of new laws and ordinances which have been adopted.

39. The Treaty of Lisbon has brought some changes with regard to the energy sector. The Treaty on the Functioning of the European Union (TFEU) contains explicit regulations about energy. Article 4 of the Treaty states that the European

11. Gesetz zur Beschleunigung von Planungsverfahren für Infrastrukturvorhaben, BGBl. I. 2833.

Union shall share competences with the Member States in the area of energy. Article 194 of the TFEU refers to energy as well. It states that European Union policy on energy shall aim – in the context of the establishment and functioning of the internal market and with regard for the need to preserve and improve the environment – in a spirit of solidarity between Member States, to:

(a) ensure the functioning of the energy market;
(b) ensure security of energy supply in the Union;
(c) promote energy efficiency and energy saving and the development of new and renewable forms of energy; and
(d) promote the interconnection of energy networks.

G. International Treaties

40. International treaties to which Germany is bound are not as such part of German law. In order to become part of the German hierarchy of norms, they have to be transformed into German law by an act of Parliament.

§3. Economic Characteristics

41. Germany's economic system has been described as social market economy (*soziale Marktwirtschaft*). The central idea of this concept is to maintain mechanisms of the free market whilst simultaneously fostering social contribution.

42. Market mechanisms function by balancing supply and demand. This balance determines market prices. In order to enable this balance, the state is responsible for a legal framework which establishes effective competition. At the same time, the state fosters the willingness and ability of individuals to take personal initiatives and to act independently. In order to compensate the downside of free markets, the concept of the social market economy includes a second principle: the principle of social equity. To foster social equity, the state may intervene in market processes by counteracting against destructive competition, excessive concentration of economic power, and socially inequitable impacts of market processes such as unemployment.[12]

43. Since it accounts for approximately 70% of GDP and the labour market, the service sector is a major driver of economic growth in Germany. It encompasses a vast spectrum of business activity including, for instance, trade, transport, communication, restaurants, etc. Business and personal services are experiencing the most rapid growth, whilst distribution services are tending to stagnate and social (state)

12. *See* the overview *Social market economy* on the webpage of the Federal Ministry for Economic Affairs and Climate Action, www.bmwi.de.

services are on the decline. The German government supports the efforts of technical service providers to cooperate with foreign partners, in order to help create greater opportunities for German companies in international markets.[13]

44. An important aspect of the German economic structure is export which accounts for more than one-third of national output. Between 2003 and 2008, Germany was the world's leading exporter of goods. However, it ceded the title of 'export world champion' to China in 2009. In 2019, Germany worldwide has been the third largest exporter of goods and exported goods worth a total of EUR 1,309.8 billion (1.7% more than in 2018), and its surplus of exports over imports tallied EUR 223.2 billion.[14]

§4. Social and Cultural Characteristics

45. The official language of Germany is German. The largest religion in Germany is Christianity, but the two largest churches – the Protestant Evangelical Church and the Roman Catholic Church – have lost significant numbers of members during the past years.

46. In 2021, approximately 83 million people live in Germany. The future development depends on three important demographic processes: the birth rate, the mortality rate, and the result of immigration and emigration. Until the early 1970s, Germany had a surplus in birth rates. Since then birth rates continuously have been at comparatively low levels. Despite the low birth rates, the population was nevertheless increasing in recent years due to an immigration surplus.[15]

---

13. Federal Ministry for Economic Affairs and Climate Action, *Service Industry*, available via www.bmwi.de.
14. Federal Ministry for Economic Affairs and Climate Action, *Strong Export Industry*, available at www.bmwi.de.
15. For figures, *see Bevölkerungsbilanz und Altersstruktur*, Federal Institute for Population Research, available at www.bib-demografie.de.

Chapter 2. Basic Principles of Energy Law

§1. General Background

47. The central goals of German energy policy are economic efficiency, security of supply, and environmental compatibility. In addition to these fundamental aims, the growing demand for energy, competition in supply, a global lag in investments in production, transport, and refinery capacities and, last but not least, challenges with regard to climate policy have to be taken into account as well. The fundamental aims of German Energy Law are also listed in section 1 EnWG (see Part I, Chapter 1 section 2 III. B).

48. German Energy Law is quite complex and a large number of different laws and ordinances are relevant when dealing with energy issues. The German energy sector is not regulated in one comprehensive legislative act, but fundamental regulations can be found in the Energy Industry Act (EnWG). These provisions are complemented not only by specific regulations concerning energy matters (such as the Ordinance on Incentive Regulation, etc.) but also by other legislative acts (such as the Federal Nature Conservation Act, the Federal Immissions Control Act, etc.) which are also relevant for the energy sector.

49. It is important to note that the legal provisions regarding the energy sector have changed considerably in recent years as the result of changes in global and European conditions. The developments in the EU have been of pivotal importance for German Energy Law. The fundamental aims of the EU in the field of energy are to set up a truly competitive internal market for gas and electricity in order to offer consumers a real freedom of choice at fair and competitive prices, to stimulate clean energy production to tackle climate change, and to improve security of supply. A large number of directives and EU-regulations have been implemented into German law and new legislative acts have been adopted. The EnWG has, for example, been amended various times in the past few years in order to bring the regulations in line with European requirements (see Part I, Chapter 1, section 2 below).

§2. Energy Scenario

50. Germany's energy sources consist of coal, nuclear energy, natural gas, wind power (offshore and onshore), solar energy, biomass, geothermal energy, hydrogen, hydropower, and petroleum. In 2020, the primary energy consumption was composed of 33.9% of oil, 7.6% of hard coal, 8.1% of lignite, 26.6% of natural gas, 6.0% of nuclear, and 16.8% of renewables.[16] It needs to be noted that there have been substantial reductions in demand by 8.7% in 2020 in comparison to 2013 due

16. AG Energiebilanzen, Energieverbrauch sinkt auf historisches Tief, Nr. 07 / 2020, 17 Dec 2020.

to the COVID-19 crisis. In 2013, the primary energy consumption was composed to 33.1% of oil, 12.7% of hard coal, 11.6% of lignite, 22.5% of natural gas, 7.6% of nuclear and 11.8% of renewables.[17]

51. Although the German hard coal consumption potentially could be covered by national resources, the utmost majority of the domestic demand is served by imports due to the high production costs in comparison to the world price.[18] Furthermore, the increase in imports results almost inevitably from the fact that the domestic reserves are limited. Rising demands in energy consumption will have to be almost entirely covered by rising imports. One example is the growing import of natural gas. The domestic production of natural gas in 2011 was 42.0% below the 1990 level, whilst imports increased by 40%, so that approximately 87% of the supply have been covered by imports.[19] In 2018, the domestic production of natural gas in Germany has been insignificant compared to gas imports.[20]

52. The share of nuclear power within the gross electricity production in Germany fell significantly since 2009. In 2000, the former government had negotiated an agreement with utilities regarding the tenure of nuclear power plants. According to the agreement made, nuclear power stations are to be shut down progressively. A complete shutdown of the plants was intended to occur by 2022.[21] In 2009, the change of government again initiated a national debate about the role of nuclear power in Germany's long-term fuel mix. A heated discussion took place and the then government consisting of *CDU* and *FDP* passed a law on longer running-times for nuclear power plants, abolishing the previous agreement (see Part I, Chapter 1, section 1). Following the nuclear accident of Fukushima, however, the Atomic Energy Act was amended again and eight nuclear power stations were already shut down in 2011 (see Chapter 7: The German *Energiewende*).[22] In 2013, the share of nuclear power of the gross electricity production fell by 8.2 TWh.[23] In 2020, the share of nuclear power in Germany's primary energy consumption has been at a level of 6.0%,[24] and the share of nuclear power in Germany's gross electricity production has been at 11.4%.[25]

---

17. Federal Ministry for Economic Affairs and Energy, *Primärenergieverbrauch in Deutschland 2013*. For information about the energy sector in Germany, also *see* Federal Ministry of Economics and Technology, *Energie in Deutschland, Trends und Hintergründe zur Energieversorgung*, February 2013, both available at www.bmwi.de.
18. *See* Federal Ministry for Economic Affairs and Energy, Energiedaten: Gesamtausgabe, October 2019 available at www.bmwi.de.
19. Federal Ministry of Economics and Technology, *Energie in Deutschland*, 15.
20. *See* Federal Ministry for Economic Affairs and Energy, Energiedaten: Gesamtausgabe, October 2019 available at www.bmwi.de.
21. For an overview in English, *see International Energy Agency, Energy Policies of IEA Countries* (2007), 8, available via www.iea.org.
22. Bundesnetzagentur / Bundeskartellamt, *Monitoringreport 2012*, p. 20, available in English at www-.bundesnetzagentur.de.
23. Bundesnetzagentur / Bundeskartellamt, *Monitoringreport 2013*, p. 15, available in English at www-.bundesnetzagentur.de.
24. AG Energiebilanzen, Energieverbrauch sinkt auf historisches Tief, Nr. 07 / 2020, 17 Dec 2020.
25. Destatis, Bruttostromerzeugung in Deutschland für 2018 bis 2020, available at www.destatis.de last access 1 May 2022.

53. During the past two decades, the share of renewable energy in primary energy consumption increased significantly. The share of wind energy, water, biomass, and solar energy increased from 1.3% in 1990 to 11.0% in 2011 and to 16.8% in 2020.[26]

§3. Relevant Legislative Acts

54. The fundamental legal act for the German energy sector – in particular for electricity and gas – is the EnWG (*Energiewirtschaftsgesetz*), which is supplemented by a number of additional laws and ordinances. Without going into detail, it can be said that German Energy Law is quite fragmented and complex. This needs to be seen together with constant amendments to the German energy legislation that seek to govern the German energy transition to energy efficiency and renewable energy sources, as well as to foster competition on the markets.

Of particular importance are the following[27]:

- Energy Industry Act (*Energiewirtschaftsgesetz, EnWG*)
- Renewable Energy Sources Act (*Erneuerbare-Energien-Gesetz, EEG*)
- Act on the Saving of Energy and the Use of Renewable Energies for Heat and Cold Generation in Buildings (*Gebäudeenergiegesetz, GEG*)
- Combined Heat and Power Act (*Kraft-Wärme-Kopplungsgesetz, KWKG*, can also be translated as Cogeneration Act)
- Offshore Wind Energy Act (*Windenergie-auf-See-Gesetz, WindSeeG*)
- Metering Point Operation Act (*Messstellenbetriebsgesetz, MsbG*)
- Energy Tax Act (*Energiesteuergesetz, EnergieStG*)
- Electricity Tax Act (*Stromsteuergesetz, StromStG*)
- Act on the Federal Network Agency (*Gesetz über die Bundesnetzagentur für Elektrizität, Gas, Telekommunikation, Post und Eisenbahnen, BEGTPG*)
- Federal Immissions Control Act (*Bundes-Immissionsschutzgesetz, BImSchG*)
- Fourth Ordinance to the Federal Immissions Control Act (*4. Bundes- Immissionsschutzverordnung, 4. BImSchV*)
- Environmental Impact Assessment Statute (*Gesetz über die Umweltverträglichkeitsprüfung, UVPG*)
- Greenhouse Gas Emissions Trading Act (*Treibhausgas-Emissionshandelsgesetz, TEHG*)
- Fuel Emissions Trading Act (*Brennstoffemissionshandelsgesetz, BEHG*)
- Atomic Energy Act (*Atomgesetz, AtG*)
- Coal-Fired Power Generation Termination Act, *Kohleverstromungsbeendigungsgesetz, KVBG*)
- Power Grid Expansion Act (*Energieleitungsausbaugesetz, EnLAG*)
- Grid Expansion Acceleration Act (*Netzausbaubeschleunigungsgesetz Übertragungsnetz, NABEG*)

---

26. Federal Ministry of Economics and Technology, *Energie in Deutschland*, 16; AG Energiebilanzen, Energieverbrauch sinkt auf historisches Tief, Nr. 07 / 2020, 17 Dec 2020.
27. Also *see* Part I Ch. 1 s. 2.

- Federal Requirements Plan Act (*Gesetz über den Bundesbedarfsplan, BBPlG*)
- Regional Planning Act (*Raumordnungsgesetz, ROG*)
- Federal Mining Law (*Bundesberggesetz, BBergG*)
- Renewable Energies Ordinance (*Erneuerbare-Energien-Verordnung, EEV*)
- Guarantees of Origin and Regional Guarantees of Origin Ordinance (*Herkunfts- und Regionalnachweis-Durchführungsverordnung, HkRNDV*)
- Ordinance on Grid Connection of Power Plants (*Verordnung zur Regelung des Netzanschlusses von Anlagen zur Erzeugung von elektrischer Energie – Kraftwerks-Netzanschlussverordnung, KraftNAV*)
- Regulation on General Conditions for the Grid Connection and Use for the Electricity Supply in Low Voltage (*Verordnung über Allgemeine Bedingungen für den Netzanschluss und dessen Nutzung für die Elektrizitätsversorgung in Niederspannung, NAV*)
- Regulation on General Conditions for the Universal Supply of Domestic Customers and the Substitute Supply with Electricity from the Low Voltage Grid (*Stromgrundversorgungsverordnung – StromGVV*)
- Ordinance on Incentive Regulation (*Anreizregulierungsverordnung, ARegV*)
- Ordinance on Concession Fees for Electricity and Gas (*Konzessionsabgabenverordnung, KAV*)
- Regulation on the Access to Gas Supply Grids (*Verordnung über den Zugang zu Gasversorgungsnetzen, GasNZV*)
- Regulation on the Access to Electricity Supply Grids (*Verordnung über den Zugang zu Elektrizitätsversorgungsnetzen, StromNZV*)
- Regulation on Remunerations for the Access to Gas Supply Grids (*Verordnung über die Entgelte für den Zugang zu Gasversorgungsnetzen, GasNEV*)
- Regulation on Remunerations for the Access to Electricity Supply Grids (*Verordnung über die Entgelte für den Zugang zu Elektrizitätsversorgungsnetzen, StromNEV*)
- Regulation on General Conditions for the Universal Supply of Domestic Customers and the Substitute Supply with Gas from the Low Pressure Grid (*Verordnung über Allgemeine Bedingungen für die Grundversorgung von Haushaltskunden und die Ersatzversorgung mit Gas aus dem Niederdrucknetz, GasGVV*)
- Regulation on General Conditions for the Universal Supply of Domestic Customers and the Substitute Supply with Electricity from the Low Voltage System (*Verordnung über Allgemeine Bedingungen für die Grundversorgung von Haushaltskunden und die Ersatzversorgung mit Elektrizität aus dem Niederspannungsnetz, StromGVV*)
- Regulation on General Conditions for the Grid Connection and Use for the Gas Supply in Low Pressure (*Verordnung über die Allgemeinen Bedingungen für den Netzanschluss und dessen Nutzung für die Gasversorgung in Niederdruck, NDAV*)

55. Furthermore, it has to be noted that with respect to regional and local issues, municipalities have the right to issue statutes (*Satzungen*).

§4. European Energy Packages

56. During the past two decades, German Energy Law has been influenced significantly by EU legislation. Various relevant legislative acts have been important for German legislation; the so-called energy packages have been of particular importance (see below Chapter 3 and Part I Chapter 1 section 2) and have led to amendments of the German laws.

§5. Fundamental Purposes of German Energy Law

57. Section 1 EnWG refers explicitly to purposes of German Energy Law. It is stated that the EnWG aims at a secure, low-cost, consumer-friendly, efficient, and environmentally compatible supply of the general public with electricity and gas which increasingly is based on renewable energy sources. Since it is more or less impossible to accomplish all these five goals at the same time, the enumeration of the purposes in section 1 EnWG is meant to highlight the objectives which are to be pursued as best possible.

58. Moreover, section 1 paragraph 2 EnWG highlights that the regulation of the electricity and the gas grids aims at securing efficient and undistorted competition with regard to electricity and gas supply and at securing a reliable and powerful operation of the grid in the long term. Furthermore, section 1 paragraph 3 EnWG stipulates explicitly that the purpose of the act is also the implementation and execution of European Union Law with respect to energy supplied by pipeline and cable.

59. Following amendments with the Electricity Market Act (see below Chapter 8), section 1 paragraph 4 EnWG sets out some more detailed aims of the Energy Industry Act. Accordingly, the Energy Industry Act shall in particular aim at strengthening the free pricing of electricity through competitive market mechanisms. Also, it shall enable the balancing of supply and demand for electricity in the electricity markets at all times. Further, generation facilities, electric energy storage facilities, and loads shall be used in the most environmentally sound, grid-compatible, efficient, and flexible manner to the extent necessary to ensure the security and reliability of the electric power system.

60. Section 1a paragraph 1 EnWG continues with additional principles for the electricity market. The price of electricity shall be formed freely on the market in accordance with competitive principles, and the level of prices for electricity on the wholesale market will not be restricted by regulation (section 1a paragraph 1 EnWG). The second paragraph underlines that the balancing group and balancing energy system is of central importance for ensuring the security of electricity supply, and that therefore, the balancing group managers' compliance and proper management of the balancing groups are to be ensured. Pursuant to section 1a paragraph 3 EnWG, a further aim is to work towards making supply and demand more flexible so that competition between efficient and flexible generation facilities, electrical energy storage facilities and loads, efficient coupling of the heat and transport sectors with the electricity sector, and the integration of charging infrastructure for electric vehicles into the electricity supply system are intended to reduce the cost of energy supply, enable the transformation to an environmentally compatible, reliable, and affordable energy supply system, and ensure security of supply.

61. Another central principle of German energy policy is individual responsibility of market participants. There is no state supervision of investments in energy infrastructure and, accordingly, investment decisions lie solely in the hands of private companies. Therefore, the general licensing procedures are relevant for the construction of power plants, gas storage sites, energy transmission lines, etc. Nevertheless, the government is responsible for creating conditions in which market forces can produce economically desirable outcomes. These conditions include, for instance, the regulation of natural monopolies (such as gas and electricity grids), the development of market-based instruments for climate change mitigation (e.g., emissions trading) and the provision of subsidies for certain technologies (such as renewables).

Chapter 3. Historical Background and Development of Energy Law

62. The first EnWG was adopted as early as 1935 and during the following decades many legislative acts have been adopted which are relevant for the energy sector. However, the most significant developments of German Energy Law have been triggered by legislation adopted on EU level during the past twenty years, and by beginning to transform the energy system to reduce carbon dioxide emissions.

63. The fundamental aims of the European Union for the energy sector according to Article 194 of the Treaty of the Functioning of the European Union are:

(a) ensure the functioning of the energy market;
(b) ensure security of energy supply in the Union;
(c) promote energy efficiency and energy saving and the development of new and renewable forms of energy; and
(d) promote the interconnection of energy networks.

64. Many measures of the European Union have been aimed at setting up a truly competitive internal market. European Energy policy in this area focuses *inter alia* on:

- access to the networks;
- unbundling;
- strengthening of regulators;
- cooperation of transmission system operators;
- reduction of possibilities for unfair competition; and
- encouragement of investment, etc.

65. The internal market for energy has been put in place gradually, starting more or less with Directive 96/92/EC which lays down rules for the internal market in electricity and Directive 98/30/EC which lays down rules for the internal market in natural gas. These directives introduced the distinction between the inevitably regulated part (transmission) and the potentially competitive parts (generation, purchase, and sales). In addition to the unbundling issue, the said directives promoted third-party access to networks and consumer choice (eligibility).

66. In a second step, further directives have been adopted – see the so-called Second Energy Package (consisting *inter alia* of Directives 2003/54/EC and 2003/55/EC) – which focused first and foremost on more regulation of the access to networks, on more effective regulation in general, and again on the unbundling issue.

67. In a third step, the Third Energy Package was adopted, which again consists of various directives and regulations (*inter alia* Directives 2009/72/EC and 2009/73/EC). For details see Part I Chapter 1 section 2.

68. On 14 June 2019, the European Union published several Acts of its so-called winter package on the energy markets – these are effectively a Fourth Energy Package.[28] This Fourth Energy Package also shows a focus on decarbonization of the energy sector with the intention to contribute to minimizing climate change. Also, strengthening consumer rights and security of supply are in the focus of the legislative amendments.

69. The implementation of all these directives has brought fundamental changes to German energy law and has led to amendments of the relevant Acts. A detailed overview of the relevant European legislation and its impact on German electricity law will be given in Part I Chapter 1.

28. *See* B. Scholtka & L. Keller-Herder, Die Entwicklung des Energierechts im Jahr 2019, *NJW* (2020): 890.

Chapter 4. Role of Government Institutions in the Shaping and Administration of Energy Law and Policy

§1. Overview

70. The main executive responsibilities for German energy policy lie with the Federal Ministry of Economic Affairs and Climate Action (*Bundesministerium für Wirtschaft und Klimaschutz,* until 12/2021 Federal Ministry of Economic Affairs and Energy, *Bundesministerium für Wirtschaft und Energie*). The Federal Ministry for the Environment, Nature Conservation, Nuclear Safety and Consumer Protection (*Bundesministerium für Umwelt, Naturschutz, nukleare Sicherheit und Verbraucherschutz*, BMUV) is, for instance, responsible for environmental regulations which affect the energy sector and also administers issues such as nuclear safety and repository projects. Repeatedly, there has been a discussion about whether the competences regarding energy issues should be concentrated within one ministry.[29] In 2013, the former Federal Ministry of Economics and Technology has been transformed to the Federal Ministry for Economic Affairs and Energy (now Federal Ministry of Economic Affairs and Climate Action). It is since then also responsible for renewable energies (i.e., the Renewable Energy Sources Act).

71. The Federal Network Agency (*Bundesnetzagentur für Elektrizität, Gas, Telekommunikation, Post und Eisenbahnen*, which took up its regulatory activity in the field of electricity and gas in 2005) and the Regulatory Authorities of the Federal States (*Landesregulierungsbehörden*) are responsible for the regulation of the gas and electricity networks. The legal framework for regulatory activities is the Energy Industry Act (*Energiewirtschaftsgesetz, EnWG*). It contains rules about the organization of the Federal Network Agency and about the cooperation between the Federal Network Agency and the Regulatory Authorities of the Federal States. It is important to note that the term 'regulatory authority' refers to the Federal Network Agency (*Bundesnetzagentur*) as well as to the Regulatory Authorities of the Federal States.

72. The Federal Cartel Office (*Bundeskartellamt*), the national authority for Competition Law matters, as well as the competition agencies in the Federal States are responsible for matters like monitoring possible abuses of a dominant position in the energy industry. The Federal Cartel Office is also responsible for overseeing mergers in the energy sector under Germany's Competition Act (*Gesetz gegen Wettbewerbsbeschränkungen*, GWB).

73. In the following chapter, an overview is provided on the government institutions involved in energy issues.

---

29. *See*, for instance, the comment of Krumrey, 'Kein neuer Kurs bei der Energie', *Energiewirtschaftliche Tagesfragen* (2009): Heft 12, 4; Kaiser, 'Auf dem Weg zu einem Energiewende Ministerium', *ZNER* (2013): 107.

§2. Regulatory Authorities (Bundesnetzagentur/ Landesregulierungsbehörden)

74. The competences of the regulatory authorities are set out in the EnWG. According to section 29 EnWG, for instance, the regulatory authorities are competent to decide upon terms and methods of grid access and connection to the grid by (administrative) decisions (*'Festlegungen'*). In addition to this, the regulatory authorities have extensive monitoring obligations (section 35 EnWG) and they are competent for proceedings with respect to (alleged) abusive or incorrect actions of network operators or other companies (these proceedings are quite relevant in practice, see below). It has been mentioned above already that the term 'regulatory authority' refers to the Federal Network Agency and to the Regulatory Authorities of the Federal States, see section 54 EnWG.

I. Federal Network Agency (Bundesnetzagentur)

75. One of the Federal Network Agency's fundamental tasks is to create the prerequisites for functioning competition in the upstream and downstream markets by unbundling and regulating the electricity and gas supply grids. Furthermore, the Federal Network Agency's range of regulatory tasks includes ensuring non-discriminatory network access and the approval of network charges levied by the network operators. The Agency's regulatory tasks also cover the supervision of abusive practices (*Missbrauchsverfahren*) and the system responsibility of the network operators.

76. The agency performs tasks and executes powers which under the EnWG have not been assigned to the Regulatory Authorities of the Federal States. These are responsible for regulating companies with fewer than 100,000 customers connected to their electricity or gas networks. The Regulatory Authorities of the Federal States are not responsible if the grid extends beyond a Federal State's borders (for details about the responsibilities of the Regulatory Authorities of the Federal States, see the next chapter).

77. Competences of the Federal Network Agency include further:

- Execution of energy-related EU law and fulfilment of tasks transferred by the EU Law, section 56 EnWG.
- Monitoring pursuant to section 35 EnWG to ensure market transparency and to fulfil tasks under the Coal-Fired Power Generation Termination Act, (*Kohleverstromungsbeendigungsgesetz*, *KVBG*). Monitoring deals *inter alia* with the rules for the management and the allocation of connecting capacity and the mechanisms to remove capacity bottlenecks. Also, there is monitoring with respect to terms and rates for the connection of new electricity generators.
- Cooperation with regulatory authorities of other EU Member States, section 57 EnWG.

- Publication of an annual report of its activities, the energy situation and the development of the market, section 63 EnWG.
- Prevention and removal of obstacles with regard to network access for suppliers and consumers.
- Standardizing processes for switching suppliers.
- Improving the conditions for connecting new power plants to the grid.[30]

78. Further, the Federal Network Agency has to fulfil tasks with respect to the expansion of the electricity grid infrastructure. An expansion of the grid has become necessary for various reasons: wind and solar energy are playing an increasingly important role in the energy mix, and Germany's electricity networks have been only partially equipped to transport large volumes of (renewable) energy. Many new renewable generation facilities have been constructed in the North and East of Germany, so that electricity needs to be transported to the centres of consumption. The transport of electricity generated in a decentralized way by many small generation facilities (in contrast to large nuclear, gas or coal-fired power plants) also may require an expansion of the grid. The legal basis for the Federal Network Agency's activities with regard to grid expansion are set out in the Grid Expansion Acceleration Act (NABEG; for more information, *see* Part I Chapter 1 section 2 IX. below).

79. The Federal Network Agency is a public agency created within the area of responsibility of the Federal Ministry for Economic Affairs and Climate Action (section 1 sentence 2 BEGTPG). It is separated from the ministry with regard to its organization, but the ministry has certain rights regarding supervision. Details concerning the organization of the Federal Network Agency are regulated in the Act on the Federal Network Agency (*Gesetz über die Bundesnetzagentur für Elektrizität, Gas, Telekommunikation, Post und Eisenbahnen, BEGTPG*).

80. The agency took up its regulatory activity in the field of electricity and gas – as did the Regulatory Authorities of the Federal States – with entry into force of the amended EnWG on 13 July 2005. At that time, a new department for energy regulation was established within the existing Regulatory Authority for Post and Telecommunications.

81. The Federal Network Agency has a president who represents the agency and who sets up rules of proceedings (*Geschäftsordnung*) regarding the organization and the distribution of tasks within the agency (section 3 paragraph 1 sentence 1 and 2 BEGTPG). The president and the vice-presidents of the Federal Network Agency are appointed by the government.

82. The decision-making bodies of the Federal Network Agency are the Ruling Chambers (*Beschlusskammern*, section 3 paragraph 1 sentence 3 and section 59 EnWG). The Ruling Chambers are collegiate bodies (*Kollegialorgan*) which consist of a chairman and two associates (*Beisitzende*), section 59 paragraph 2 EnWG.

30. For an overview in English *see* the webpage of the Federal Network Agency, www.bundesnetzagentur.de.

Section 59 paragraph 3 EnWG stipulates that members of the Ruling Chambers must neither hold or control a company of the energy industry nor can they be members of the management or the directorate of a company of the energy industry.

83. Decisions of the Ruling Chambers of the Federal Network Agency cannot be revoked by the Federal Ministry for Economic Affairs and Climate Action. However, it is possible to take action against decisions of the Ruling Chambers by filing a claim with civil courts (section 75 et seqq. EnWG).

84. Further bodies (*Gremien*) of the agency are the Advisory Council (*Beirat*) and the Federal States Committee (*Länderausschuss*). Pursuant to section 5 paragraph 1 sentence 1 BEGTPG, the Advisory Council consists of sixteen members of the German Parliament (*Bundestag*) and sixteen representatives of the *Bundesrat*. Responsibilities and tasks of the Advisory Council are regulated in section 60 EnWG. The Council is responsible for advising the agency with respect to the reports which have to be published according to section 63 paragraph 3 EnWG.

85. The Advisory Council is entitled to request information and statements from the Federal Network Agency. The agency is obliged to provide the requested information.

86. The Federal States Committee (*Länderausschuss*) consists of representatives of the Regulatory Authorities of the Federal States. Its main responsibility is to secure cooperation between the Federal Network Agency and the Regulatory Authorities of the Federal States on all questions of energy regulation. Thus, it aims at an alignment of the execution of the EnWG in Germany.

II. Regulatory Authorities of the Federal States

87. After the second act reforming the EnWG came into force on 13 July 2005, the Federal States also established Regulatory Authorities. These are responsible for the regulation of the electricity and the gas sector if less than 100,000 customers are connected to the respective grid. They are not responsible if the electricity and gas grid extends beyond the Federal States' borders.

88. Under these preconditions, section 54 paragraph 2 EnWG contains an enumeration of competences and responsibilities of the Regulatory Authorities of the Federal States. Among these are, for instance, the approval of fees for access to the grid, monitoring of compliance with unbundling regulations, the control of abusive practices (sections 30 et seq. EnWG), and decisions according to section 110 paragraph 2 and 4 EnWG with regard to the question whether the requirements of a *Geschlossenes Verteilernetz* (closed distribution system) are met. For issues not mentioned in section 54 paragraph 2 EnWG, the Federal Network Agency is responsible.

III. Division of Tasks

89. The responsibilities of the Federal Network Agency and the Regulatory Authorities of the Federal States are each clearly defined. The Regulatory Authorities of the Federal States are responsible if less than 100,000 consumers are connected to the respective electricity or gas grid, provided that the grid does not extend beyond the Federal States' borders. Also, the tasks must be explicitly mentioned in section 54 paragraph 2 EnWG.

90. The Federal Network Agency, however, is responsible if these requirements are not fulfilled, either because more than 100,000 customers are connected to the respective grid or because the grid extends beyond the Federal States' borders. In practice, the Federal Network Agency is always responsible as long as a task or responsibility is not expressly assigned to another public authority, section 54 paragraph 3 EnWG.

91. In spite of the fundamental subdivision of duties and responsibilities, the Federal Network Agency and the Regulatory Authorities of the Federal States have to cooperate and support each other. The exchange of information is in particular essential for the fulfilment of the regulatory tasks set out in the EnWG.

92. An important instrument to achieve sufficient coordination between the Federal Network Agency and the Regulatory Authorities of the Federal States is the so-called Committee of States/Federal States Committee (*Länderausschuss*) which consists of representatives from the Regulatory Authorities of the Federal States. Its main purpose is to assure alignment between the Federal Network Agency and the Regulatory Authorities of the Federal States to strive for a uniform execution of the EnWG in Germany (see section 60a EnWG).

IV. Abuse Proceedings According to the EnWG

A. Overview over Abuse Proceedings According to the EnWG

93. The EnWG provides for three different kinds of proceedings with respect to (alleged) abusive or incorrect behaviour of network operators or other entities:

–(1) 'specific abuse proceedings' pursuant to section 31 EnWG (*Besondere Missbrauchsverfahren*);
–(2) ex officio proceedings pursuant to section 65 EnWG (*Aufsichtsmaßnahmen*); and
–(3) ex officio proceedings pursuant to section 30 EnWG.

94. These proceedings are quite relevant; last but not least because entities whose interests are affected, for instance, by a network operator's behaviour can file applications with the regulatory authority for investigation of such behaviour. Each specific case must be checked against which proceedings apply because certain specifications of the different proceedings have to be taken into account.

95. If an entity considers the initiation of proceedings according to section 31 or section 65, said entity is required to establish that a concrete behaviour, action or measure was not in compliance with the law and significantly affected the entity's position or interests.

B. Basic Principles

96. The principle of judicial investigation (*Untersuchungsgrundsatz*) according to section 24 Administrative Procedure Act (*Verwaltungsverfahrensgesetz, VwVfG*) applies to investigations conducted by the regulatory authorities. The regulatory authorities therefore have extensive power to carry out investigations in order to be able to determine whether there is any abusive or incorrect behaviour.

97. In addition to this, section 68 EnWG explicitly states that regulatory authorities can lead enquiries and collect evidence. With regard to details, the EnWG refers to several regulations of the Code of Civil Procedure (*Zivilprozessordnung*) in section 68 EnWG.

98. Regulatory authorities can request information from entities and associations. They also have the power to review business documents during the normal working hours (see section 69 EnWG). The Federal Network Agency will request information by issuing a resolution (*Beschluss*). The Regulatory Authorities of the Federal States will do so by issuing a formal decision (so-called *Einzelverfügung*), section 69 paragraph 7 EnWG. Sequestration (*Beschlagnahmen*) and searches (*Durchsuchungen*) are also possible, if certain requirements are met.

99. With regard to the protection of business secrets, section 30 Administrative Procedure Act (*Verwaltungsverfahrensgesetz, VwVfG*) applies. This provision stipulates that the regulatory authority is not allowed to pass on business secrets to unauthorized persons. Section 71 EnWG contains additional regulations in this respect. To make sure that there is no breach of secrecy, an additional version of the respective documents has to be made available which covers up the sensitive information. If no information is marked as secret, the authority may be able to forward the documents to third persons or entities.

100. Section 72 EnWG stipulates that the regulatory authority also can take preliminary measures.

101. Regulatory authorities have to justify their decisions and have to give information on legal remedies available (*Rechtsbehelfsbelehrung*), section 73 EnWG.

102. With regard to enforcement, regulatory authorities have the power to execute their own decisions according to the rules of the Administrative Procedure Acts, section 94 EnWG. A penalty payment between EUR 1,000 up to EUR 10 million can be set.

103. Section 95 EnWG stipulates that some infringements against energy regulations constitute administrative offences (*Ordnungswidrigkeit*). Among these are, for instance, the operation of a network without permission and the disregard of the responsibility to provide information. The competence to avenge any administrative offences lies with the regulatory authorities (section 96 EnWG). They can decide on administrative fines up to EUR 5 million. If any profit was made in connection with the infringement, a higher fine can be set.

C. *Specific Abuse Proceedings Pursuant to Section 31 EnWG* (Besondere Missbrauchsverfahren)

104. According to section 31 paragraph 1 sentence 1 and 2 EnWG, entities whose interests are significantly affected by a network operator's behaviour can file an application with the regulatory authorities for the investigation of such behaviour. The regulatory authority investigates, in particular, whether the behaviour of the network operator is in compliance with the requirements regarding grid connection of sections 17 et seqq. EnWG and regarding grid usage in sections 20 et seqq. EnWG, the regulations (*Verordnungen*) based thereon or the provisions of section 29 paragraph 1 EnWG. The proceedings in the sense of section 31 EnWG are public proceedings and respective decisions are published by the regulatory authorities.

105. In case an application according to section 31 paragraph 1 sentence 1 EnWG is filed, the regulatory authority is obliged to carry out the respective investigations. There is no discretion to decide whether proceedings should be started or not.

106. Particularly with regard to the proceedings pursuant to section 31 EnWG, it is important to determine the precise complaint to be brought forward, as these proceedings have a restricted applicability.

107. Also, it is important to know that the regulatory authority has to decide over the application within two months after the submission of the complete application. A two-month extension is possible if the regulatory authority requests further information. Another extension requires approval by the adverse party.

D. *Proceedings Pursuant to Section 65 EnWG* (Allgemeines Aufsichtsverfahren)

108. According to section 65 paragraph 1 EnWG, the regulatory authorities are entitled to oblige an entity to refrain from a certain behaviour, which contravenes the provisions of the EnWG or the regulations which are based on the Act. Accordingly, the regulatory authorities are entitled to implement measures against entities to make them comply with the obligations under the EnWG or the respective regulations based thereon.

109. According to section 66 paragraph 1 EnWG, these proceedings are ex officio proceedings; i.e., the regulatory authorities are obliged to take action themselves if they have a good reason to believe that a non-compliance is likely to exist. An application by third parties is not necessary.

110. However, these proceedings can also be initiated by a third party according to the wording of section 66 paragraph 2 No. 1 EnWG. The proceedings pursuant to section 65 EnWG are non-public proceedings and are to be treated confidentially by the Federal Network Agency and the Regulatory Authorities of the Federal States.

111. Pursuant to section 67 paragraph 1 EnWG, the regulatory authority will hear the parties and all persons involved. The regulatory authority can also appoint a public hearing, section 67 paragraph 3 EnWG.

E. Proceedings Pursuant to Section 30 EnWG

112. According to section 30 EnWG, network operators are not allowed to abuse their market position, for example, by means of unreasonably constraining other entities directly or indirectly, by means of significantly affecting other entities' competition opportunities without justified reason or by means of treating similar entities (directly or indirectly) differently without justified reason. There are further scenarios which can constitute an abuse. In principle, the regulatory authorities have similar competences as the ones described above. In contrast to the proceedings according to section 65 EnWG, section 30 EnWG does not foresee the possibility for third parties to apply for the commencement of these proceedings by the regulatory authority. Still, if respective facts (with profound, substantiated evidence) are made known to the regulatory authority, the regulatory authority would (have to) become active itself.

F. Independence of National Regulatory Authority

113. In a judgment of 2 September 2021, the European Court of Justice has underlined the independency of the Federal Network Agency in specific matters regulated by European Directives.[31] The claim of the European Commission was directed against regulations in section 24 of the EnWG which allow the German

31. ECJ, judgment of 2 September 2021, C-718/18.

Federal Government to set out by ordinance (*Rechtsverordnung*) detailed provisions addressed to the Federal Network Agency. This legal provision allowed for setting detailed rules on the procedure and methods for determining network tariffs and conditions for network access. The European Court of Justice found this regulatory power for the German government to be in violation of several provisions of the Directives 2009/72 and 2009/73 which grant the national regulatory authorities various powers also in regards to fixing or approving transmission and distribution tariffs and their methodologies. Following the Advocate General, the European Court of Justice holds that 'the complete independence of NRAs from economic actors and public entities, be they administrative bodies or political bodies (and in the latter case, be they the holders of executive power or of legislative power) is instrumental in ensuring that the decisions taken by the NRAs are truly impartial and non-discriminatory, while the possibility of undertakings and economic interests connected with the government, the majority or political power being treated more favourably is excluded'.[32] This judgment will have significant implications for several detailed energy regulations in ordinances (*Rechtsverordnungen*) by the German government, and will enhance a Federal Network Agency acting independent from detailed regulative provisions in its core competencies.[33]

§3. Federal Ministry For Economic Affairs and Climate Action

114. The main responsibility for energy policy lies with the Federal Ministry for Economic Affairs and Climate Action (*Bundesministerium für Wirtschaft und Klimaschutz*). The ministry has the power to issue certain ordinances as foreseen in several powers to issue statutory instruments. As mentioned above, the Federal Ministry for the Environment, Nature Conservation, Nuclear Safety and Consumer Protection (*Bundesministerium für Umwelt, Naturschutz, nukleare Sicherheit und Verbraucherschutz*, BMUV), for instance, is responsible for environmental regulations that effect the energy sector. The Federal Ministry of Food and Agriculture (*Bundesministerium für Ernährung und Landwirtschaft*, BMEL) oversees biomass issues. The Federal Ministry of Finance and its subordinate agencies administer energy taxation.

115. As various ministries are involved in energy issues, there has been a discussion about whether the competences regarding energy issues should be concentrated within one ministry. Since 2013, the former Federal Ministry of Economics and Technology has been transformed into the Federal Ministry for Economic Affairs and Energy (since December 2021 Federal Ministry for Economic Affairs and Climate Action). It also became responsible for renewable energies in the electricity industry (i.e., the Renewable Energy Sources Act). The role of the ministry in the energy transition has been strengthened again in adding competencies on Climate Action when the government consisting of the Social Democratic Party (SPD), The Greens (Bündnis 90/Die Grünen) and the Free Democratic Party (FDP) came

---

32. ECJ, judgment of 2 September 2021, C-718/18, para. 112.
33. *See* R. Klahm & C. Fabritius, 'Das Aus für die normative Regulierung', ER (2021): 238.

into power in December 2021. Since that time the first Federal Minister for Economic Affairs from The Greens leads the ministry.

§4. Cartel Authorities

116. Cartel authorities are – depending on the extent of the market influence – either the Federal Cartel Authority (*Bundeskartellamt*) or the State Cartel Offices (*Landeskartellämter*). Unless a provision of the Act against Restraints of Competition (*Gesetz gegen Wettbewerbsbeschränkungen, GWB*) assigns competences for a particular matter to a particular cartel authority, the Federal Cartel Authority exercises the respective functions and powers if the effect of the influence on the market or of the restrictive or discriminatory conduct or of a competition rule extends beyond the territory of a Federal State. In all other cases, the supreme authority of the respective Federal State shall exercise these functions and powers (see section 48 GWB).

117. Decisions on cartels, mergers, and abusive practices of the Federal Cartel Authority are taken by Decision Divisions (*Beschlussabteilungen*) which are mainly organized according to the sectors of the economy. One of these divisions, which was set up in January 2008, deals exclusively with the prosecution of abusive practices and cartels in the energy sector. In the Decision Divisions, each case is decided upon by a collegiate body consisting of the division's chairman and two associate members. The Decision Divisions are autonomous and not subject to instructions in their decision-taking.

118. The tasks, activities, and organization of the Federal Cartel Authority are regulated in various legal provisions. However, of particular relevance for the energy sector is the GWB. Section 19 GWB, for instance, stipulates that a company which has a dominant position on the market is not allowed to abuse this position. The competence to execute antitrust provisions as stipulated in the GWB lies with the cartel authorities. Since the EnWG also contains regulations regarding abuse proceedings, the question arises how the competences of the respective authorities are defined.

119. Section 111 EnWG contains regulations about the relation of the EnWG to the GWB. According to this provision, some regulations of the GWB (e.g., section 19 GWB) are not applicable if the EnWG or respective ordinances have regulated a matter conclusively. According to this, for instance, there is an exclusive competence of the regulatory authorities with regard to grid operation. Insofar, the authority of the regulatory authorities concerning grid access and grid supply (sections 17 et seq. EnWG) overrides the competences of the cartel authorities. With respect to competition law, competences remain with the cartel authorities.

120. Responsibility for the administration and the control of abusive behaviour with regard to the operation of and access to the grid lies with the regulatory authorities (pursuant to sections 29 et seq. EnWG). In contrast to this, the cartel authorities are responsible for general matters like monitoring abuses in the energy industry. The cartel authorities remain, for instance, responsible for the control of abusive practices regarding energy prices – with the exception of network charges. As a general rule, it can be said that the regulatory authorities are responsible for the 'monopoly' with respect to the regulation of the grid, whereas the cartel authorities are responsible for competition regarding production and sales.[34] However, it is not always this easy to distinguish the respective competences as the EnWG assigns certain responsibilities explicitly to the regulatory authorities.

121. The EnWG contains regulations regarding the cooperation of the regulatory authorities and the cartel authorities in case both network operations and antitrust laws are affected (section 58 EnWG). In some cases, the Federal Network Agency requires approval of the Federal Cartel Authority – in other cases one authority has to hear the other authority before making a decision, section 58 paragraph 1 sentence 2 EnWG.

§5. Further Authorities

I. *Bundesamt für Strahlenschutz*

122. The Federal States are responsible for the approval and monitoring of the construction, operation, decommissioning, and dismantling of nuclear power plants. They are supervised and instructed by the Federal Ministry for the Environment, Nature Conservation, and Nuclear Safety and Consumer Protection. Several competencies in the field of radiation protection are assigned to the Federal Office for Radiation Protection (*Bundesamt für Strahlenschutz*, BfS), whereas several supervisory activities in this respect are performed by the individual Federal States.

II. DEHSt

123. The German Emissions Trading Authority (*Deutsche Emissionshandelsstelle, DEHSt*) at the Federal Environment Agency (*Umweltbundesamt*) is the national authority entrusted with the implementation of the European and national emissions trading as well as with project-based mechanisms of the Kyoto Protocol. Administration of emissions trading under the European emissions trading scheme as well as under the national emissions trading scheme and approval of Joint Implementation (JI) and Clean Development Mechanism (CDM) climate change projects under the Kyoto Protocol's flexibility mechanisms fall to the DEHSt. It is the designated national authority for JI and CDM in Germany.

124. Its mandate covers a broad range of activities defined in the EU Emissions Trading Scheme Directive, the Greenhouse Gas Emission Allowance Trading Act

34. *See* F. Hölscher in: G. Britz, J. Hellermann & G. Hermes, *EnWG, Energiewirtschaftsgesetz* (München: C.H. Beck, 3rd edn, 2015), s. 111 para. 12.

(*Treibhausgas-Emissionshandelsgesetz*, TEHG), the German Allocation Acts (*Zuteilungsgesetz*, ZuG 2007 and ZuG 2012), the Allocation Ordinance 2020 (*Zuteilungsverordnung*, ZuV 2020), in the national Fuel Emissions Trading Act (*Brennstoffemissionshandelsgesetz*, BEHG), and in the Project Mechanisms Act (*ProMechG*). The Emissions Trading Authority works in cooperation with the German Federal Ministry for Environment, Nature Conservation, Nuclear Safety and Consumer Protection, the Federal States, and the competent clean air authorities at the Federal State level. It is also the contact point for corporate entities whose installations are subject to EU or national emissions trading.

125. The pollution control authorities of the Federal States are responsible for the approval of Greenhouse Gas (GHG) emission allowances, these being an integral component of the approval procedures set out under pollution abatement law. The individual state administrations are also responsible for all issues concerning emissions monitoring and reporting.

126. The DEHSt is a provider of services to companies and businesses participating in European and national emissions trading, to verifiers, and public offices. This concerns the application procedure, the allocation of certificates, account management in the national registry, and annual emissions reporting.

III. *Deutsche Energie Agentur* (DENA)

127. The German Energy Agency (*Deutsche Energie Agentur*, DENA) is the federal government's centre for energy efficiency, renewable energy sources, and intelligent energy systems. It focuses on the development of sustainable energy systems which make optimum use of energy and integrate renewable energy sources. DENA was established in the autumn of 2000 and has its head office in Berlin. Shareholders in DENA are the Federal Republic of Germany and the KfW *Bankengruppe* (German Bank for Reconstruction).

IV. *Monopolkommission*

128. The Monopolies Commission (*Monopolkommission*) is a body of scientists and legal experts. Its main task is to evaluate competition in Germany and, *inter alia*, to publish biennial reports on competition trends in the gas and electricity markets. With its biennial reports, the Monopolies Commission prepares an opinion assessing the situation and the foreseeable development of business concentration in the Federal Republic of Germany, evaluating the application of the provisions concerning the control of concentrations, and commenting on other topical issues of competition policy. The Monopolies Commission submits its opinions to the Federal Government. The GWB contains explicit regulations about the organization and the mandate of the Monopolies Commission (see sections 44 et seqq. GWB).

129. The Federal Government may instruct the Monopolies Commission to prepare further opinions in addition to the above-mentioned reports. However, it is important to note that the Monopolies Commission is independent in pursuing its activities and is only bound by the mandate established by the GWB. Also, the Monopolies Commission may deliver opinions at its discretion.

130. The Monopolies Commission consists of five members who are required to have special knowledge and experience in the field of economics, business administration, social policy, technology or commercial law. Pursuant to section 45 GWB, the members of the Monopolies Commission shall not be members of the government or any legislative body of the Federation or a Federal State, or of the public service of the Federation, a Federal State or any other legal person under public law, except as university lecturers or staff members of a scientific institution. Moreover, they shall neither represent nor be bound by a permanent employment or service relationship to any industry association or an employers' or employees' organization. Furthermore, they shall not have held such a position during the year preceding their appointment to the Monopolies Commission.

Chapter 5. Role of Municipalities and Municipal Energy Supply Companies

131. The German municipalities used to and still play an important role in the German energy sector. With the breakup of the outdated regional monopolies and the closed energy supply areas, the role of the municipalities, however, changed. While the liberalization at first mainly led to a number of privatizations and fusions in the energy sector, today also other trends start to become visible – often discussed under the header 'remunicipalization'.

§1. Municipalities and the German Energy Markets

132. Energy supply is regarded to belong to the services of general interest. The municipalities have been considered as principally being in charge of fulfilling this task under their constitutional mandate (see Article 28 paragraph 2 of the Basic Law, GG).[35] A decisive feature for the municipalities is the conclusion of a so-called concession contract (*Konzessionsvertrag*). This contract allows an energy company the use of the public ways for laying electric cables belonging to the general supply.

133. While the conclusion of a concession contract used to determine the grid operator and the energy supply company in a certain area of energy supply, today it is of relevance mainly for the grid operation. With the entitlement to grid access, the supply of customers in other grid areas has been opened up for any other energy supply company as well. The basic supplier (*Grundversorger*), i.e., the company in charge of the general supply in a certain market area, is now determined empirical.[36] The municipalities thus still determine the person of the grid operator in the municipal area by the conclusion of a concession contract, but not the energy company for general supply.[37] Nevertheless, the municipalities still have an important role with the conclusion of concession contracts and with demanding the respective concession levies (*Konzessionsabgaben*).

134. Also, municipalities often are engaged in the operation of the grids or in the generation or the selling of energy. Municipalities may engage in the energy supply and energy distribution through their own establishments. These establishments may be departments set up under public law, being part of the municipality. However, municipalities may found energy supply companies and grid operators also in a private law form: either as a limited liability company (*Gesellschaft mit beschränkter Haftung*, GmbH) or as a stock corporation (*Aktiengesellschaft,* AG). The use of companies with limited liability is generally required by the municipality laws of the German Länder.

35. Christiane Nill-Theobald & Christian Theobald, *Grundzüge des Energiewirtschaftsrechts*, 3rd edn (München: C.H. Beck, 2013), 364 et seq.
36. *See* closer below Part I, Ch. 5, s. 3.
37. *See* H.G. Henneke & K. Ritgen, *Kommunales Energierecht* (Wiesbaden: Kommunal- und Schul-Verlag, 2010), 22 et seq.

§2. Legal Restrictions for Municipal Energy Supply Companies

135. Due to general concerns on the market participation of public companies, the role of municipal companies in the energy distribution and energy supply has been subject of controversial debates. With the mentioning of public undertakings in Article 106 TFEU, the existence of such public companies is acknowledged under European Law.[38] The extent to which public companies may participate in the market is subject to further provisions in Germany which shall thus briefly be introduced in the following.

136. For municipal companies (*Stadtwerke*) engaged in the energy distribution and/or supply, the general legal framework under the EnWG applies.[39] However, further legal restrictions for the economic activities of municipal companies originate from other provisions, particularly to be found in the municipal codes. These codes are adopted by the German *Länder*. The *Länder* may – insofar as admitted by the German Constitution – create further rules to restrict the economic activities of the municipalities. However, they may not protect municipal companies against competition with rules which favour municipal companies more than private companies.[40]

137. At first, the territorial scope of the protection of municipal activities under the German Constitution (Basic Law, *Grundgesetz*, GG) shall briefly be discussed. Article 28 paragraph 2 sentence 1 GG reads:

> Municipalities must be guaranteed the right to regulate all local affairs on their own responsibility, within the limits prescribed by the laws.

138. The activities of the municipalities are thus protected by the German Constitution insofar the municipalities are entrusted with local affairs. According to the German Constitutional Court, this comprises all affairs which root in the local community or those which have a specific reference to it.[41] This so-called locality principle (*Örtlichkeitsprinzip*) might result in a situation where municipal companies are only allowed to become active if such reference to the local community exists.

139. The municipal codes (*Gemeindeordnungen*) by the German *Länder* generally contain restrictions on the economic activities of municipalities. Such activities are often only allowed under the following conditions: first, a public end must require the economic activity of the municipality. Second, the economic activity

---

38. J. Wolff in: J.P. Schneider & C. Theobald, *Recht der Energiewirtschaft*, 5th edn (München: C.H. Beck, 2021), s. 5 paras 120–122.
39. Certain exemptions, however, may apply for smaller companies – independent of their public or private character – for example according to section 7 para. 2 EnWG.
40. *See* J. Wolff in: J.P. Schneider & C. Theobald, *Recht der Energiewirtschaft* (München: C.H. Beck, 5. Ed., 2021), s. 5 para. 122.
41. BVerfGE 50, 195, 201.

needs to stand in an appropriate relationship to the capacity of the municipality. Third, the public aim may not be fulfilled better and more economical by other enterprises.[42]

140. While this question has been long discussed and unevenly answered by the courts, private competitors under certain circumstances and dependent on the regulations and jurisdiction in the specific Federal State may have claims of protection against economic activities of the municipalities if their activity does not comply with the rules of the municipal code.[43] Moreover, the municipal codes may regulate the conditions on which municipalities may found private companies.[44] Contrary to private companies, municipal companies may generally not rely on the basic rights granted by the German Constitution.[45]

§3. Prospects

141. Concerns against the activities of municipal companies may be founded on the argument that the engagement of public companies may distort the free market. In how far municipal companies enjoy advantages in the markets is, however, questionable. Their activities are – in addition to the rules which apply under the general energy law – restricted by rules on economic activities in the specific municipal codes explained above section 2.

142. From a general perspective, an advantage of municipal companies may be that they contribute to the decentralization of energy generation and supply which is also promoted by the EU.[46] Moreover, municipal companies already play a role in diversifying the energy mix and in promoting energy production from renewable energy sources. In particular if municipal companies decide for an expansion of

---

42. *See*, for example, s. 107 para. 1 of the municipal code of North Rhine-Westphalia, Gemeindeordnung für das Land Nordrhein-Westfalen of 14 Jul. 1994. With a statutory amendment in 2010, the legislator introduced s. 107a GO NRW. According to this clause, economic activities of municipalities in North Rhine-Westphalia generally serve a public end if the activity takes place in the field of electricity, gas or heat supply. Also, s. 107a GO NRW clarifies under which conditions municipal companies may engage in economic activities in other regions or abroad. Rules are different in other municipal codes.
43. For North Rhine-Westphalia *see* OVG Münster, decision of 13 Aug. 2003, 15 B 1137/03, *NVwZ*, 2003, 1520.
44. *See* for example s. 108 GO NRW.
45. G. Britz in: J.P. Schneider & C. Theobald, *Recht der Energiewirtschaft* (München: C.H. Beck, 5th. edn, 2021), s. 5 para. 95. For private companies, the ability to rely on basic rights and the extent to which these rights may apply is governed by Art. 19 para. 3 GG.
46. *See*, for example, Recital 6 in the Directive 2009/28/EC of the European Parliament and of the Council of 23 Apr. 2009 on the promotion of the use of energy from renewable sources: 'The move towards decentralized energy production has many benefits, including the utilization of local energy sources, increased local security of energy supply, shorter transport distances, and reduced energy transmission losses.'

renewable energy, as a number of companies already do, this may be an important factor in the necessary restructuring of the energy industry.[47]

143. In recent years, a trend towards a remunicipalization became visible.[48] Much observed examples have been the founding of municipal companies taking over the electricity grids in Hamburg and in Berlin.[49] The development may insofar serve as an example since the town of Hamburg privatized the former public service company existing before.

47. *See* closer M. Altrock, 'Die Bedeutung der Erneuerbaren Energien in der kommunalen Wirtschaft', in *Kommunale Wirtschaft im 21. Jahrhundert, Festschrift für Dr Peter Becker* (VWEW: Frankfurt a.M., 2006), 303 et seq.
48. Grünewald & Schwettmann in: W. Danner & C. Theobald, *Energierecht* (München: C.H. Beck, 2008), XII GemEnW B 1 para. 82; H.G. Henneke & K. Ritgen, *Kommunales Energierecht* (Wiesbaden: Kommunal- und Schul-Verlag, 2010), 24 et seq.
49. *See* the information provided by Hamburg and Berlin on www.stromnetz-hamburg.de and www.berlin.de.

Chapter 6. Energy Concept 2010 and Phasing out of Nuclear Power

144. In 2010, the Federal Government of Germany reached an agreement on an Energy Concept which should pave the way for the development of the energy sector on a long-term basis, thinking up to 2050.[50] Before this no such concept existed in any official form.

145. The Energy Concept describes in nine sections the main future goals of the Federal Government for the further development of the energy sector. Renewable energy as a main element of the future energy supply is treated in the first section, while energy efficiency as a 'key issue' is discussed in the second section. Renewable energy shall make up for the majority share within the future energy mix.[51] The two topics can also be found throughout the Energy Concept. For example, the fourth section is engaged with an effective grid infrastructure for electricity being able to integrate renewable energy. The fifth section is concerned with energetic restoration of buildings and energy efficient building.

146. However, public discussion on the Energy Concept was, at least in prior, mainly restricted to the extension of running-times of the German nuclear power plants. In 2000, the former German government formed by a coalition of Social Democrats and Greens decided on the phasing out of nuclear power plants. But the coalition of Christian Democrats and Liberals, coming into power in 2009, aimed at extending the running-times.

147. After heavy discussions also within the coalition itself, the government at first agreed on an extension of running-times for nuclear power plants of – on average – twelve years. Running-times of older nuclear power plants (start of operation up to 1980) should have been extended by eight years, while the running-times of the plants which started operation from 1981 onwards should have been extended by fourteen years.[52]

148. Remarkably, there is not really a discussion in Germany on whether new nuclear power plants are required. Nowadays, also supporters mostly treat nuclear energy as a 'bridge technology'. One main argument of the supporters is that nuclear power would contribute to the ambitious German climate protection targets. Opponents, on the contrary, argue that nuclear power would obstruct the increased use of renewable energy. They also refer to the question on a final storage of nuclear waste.[53] Moreover, scandals on the storage for low- and medium-level radioactive waste in the former mine Asse resulted in severe concerns on the reliability of the

50. Energiekonzept für eine umweltschonende, zuverlässige und bezahlbare Energieversorgung, 28 Sep. 2010, BT-Drs. 17/3049. *See* closer P. Becker, 'Das Energiekonzept der Bundesregierung', *ZNER* (2010): 531 et seq.
51. Energy Concept, BT-Drs. 17/3049, 2.
52. Energy Concept, BT-Drs. 17/3049, 8.
53. *See* for the discussion on the effects on the use of renewable energy P. Focht & R. Köpke, 'Die Brücke der Unvereinbarkeit', *Energie & Management* 18, no. 10 (15 Sep. 2010): 1.

storage of nuclear waste. This mine has serious problems with its stability, groundwater found its way into the mine.[54] The public critics on the extension of the running-times have been immense and the already pacified conflict on the role of nuclear energy once again broke out.[55]

149. Things changed with the nuclear accident in Fukushima in March 2011. The decision to extend the running-times for nuclear power plants, taken just short time in advance, has been regarded even more critical in public under the impression of the accident in Japan. As a consequence of Fukushima, the German government ordered an examination of the security of the German nuclear power plants. The seven oldest German nuclear power plants had to stop the electricity generation during the duration of the security examinations.[56] But even more, the German government made a remarkable and immediate turnaround in its position towards nuclear energy: it decided to reverse the extension of running-times, and instead decided for phasing out of nuclear energy by 2022.

150. In the consequence, the German government developed an 'energy package' with the impetus to reach a faster end of nuclear energy generation in Germany (closer below Chapter 7).

151. The Energy Concept focused on renewable energy and energy efficiency. According to the German Energy Concept, conventional energy sources shall continuously be replaced by renewable energy sources.[57]

152. Also due to the increasing percentage of renewable energy, the focus more and more comes towards integrating them into markets and infrastructures. Thus, the Energy Concept named renewable energy together with energy efficiency, enforcing the energy grids and the construction of storage capacities.[58] The importance of energy storage for the expansion of renewable energy can be found throughout the concept.

153. Within the energy generation, the Energy Concept particularly names wind energy as a central pillar for 2050. As a consequence, an expansion of electricity grids and an increased construction and use of storage capacities became necessary to transport the increasing share of wind power. The Energy Concept also mentioned advantages of the use of bioenergy. These comprise that storage is easily possible and that biomass can be used as an energy source within all energy sectors, including in particular transport.[59]

---

54. *See* the webpage of the Federal Office of Radiation www.endlager-asse.de.
55. *See* Süddeutsche Zeitung, 'Massenprotest gegen Merkels Atompolitik', 8 Nov. 2010.
56. Federal Government, 'Sicherheit hat Vorrang', 16 Mar. 2011, available via www.bundesregierung.de, last access: 17 Mar. 2011.
57. Energy Concept, BT-Drs. 17/3049, 2.
58. Energy Concept, BT-Drs. 17/3049, 4.
59. Energy Concept, BT-Drs. 17/3049, 5 et seq.

Chapter 7. The German Energiewende in Energy Package 2011

154. One may say that the German *Energiewende* started after the nuclear accident of Fukushima (see above Chapter 6). In fact, there are good reasons however to argue that the real start of the *Energiewende* is much earlier. For instance, it might be traced back to the year of 1990 in which the first statute for the support of electricity from renewable energy sources has been agreed upon (see in more detail below Part V).[60] Nevertheless, after the nuclear accident of Fukushima, the German Parliament enacted a legislative package in 2011 which is known as *Energiewende* legislation and shall be introduced in this chapter. From this time on, the term 'German *Energiewende*' became more frequently used and shall describe the attempt of a thorough shift of the energy system from fossil to renewable energy sources.

155. The *Energiewende* legislation of 2011 consists of a number of statutory changes for the energy sector.[61] The German Bundestag accepted on 30 June 2011 with wide majority an amendment of the Atomic Energy Act under which the operating permits for nuclear power stations shall expire at the latest in end 2022.[62] In 2016, the Federal Constitutional Court (*Bundesverfassungsgericht*) holds that the phase-out of nuclear power by the Atomic Energy Act is in principle in accordance with the German Constitution. However, the Federal Constitutional Court also decided that the amendment of the Act would require a compensation in favour of the operators of nuclear power plants insofar as they have made investments based on their legitimate confidence in higher remaining production volumes which had been allocated to them under previous legislation.[63]

156. The energy package included a number of other statutory changes which should pave the way for replacing nuclear energy and other fossil energy by renewable energy sources and energy efficiency measures. In particular, the energy package included an amendment of the Renewable Energy Sources Act which came into force in 2012 (see in detail below Part V).[64] The Renewable Energy Sources Act 2012 contained more developed instruments for direct marketing of the electricity produced with the aim of a better market integration of electricity from renewable sources.[65]

60. D. Jacobs, 'The German *Energiewende* – History, Targets, Policies and Challenges', *RELP* (2012): 223, writes that the term '*Energiewende*' was first introduced in 1980.
61. For a detailed analyses *see* D. Jacobs, 'The German *Energiewende* – History, Targets, Policies and Challenges', *RELP* (2012): 223; C. Theobald & T. Gey-Kern, 'Das dritte Energiebinnenmarktpaket der EU und die Reform des deutschen Energiewirtschaftsrechts 2011', *EuZW* (2011): 896; B. Scholtka & S. Helmes, 'Energiewende 2011 – Schwerpunkte der Neuregelungen im Energiewirtschafts- und Energieumweltrecht', *NJW* (2011): 3185; D. Sellner & F. Fellenberg, 'Atomausstieg und Energiewende 2011 – das Gesetzespaket im Überblick', *NVwZ* (2011): 1025.
62. 13. Gesetz zur Änderung des Atomgesetzes, BGBl. 2011 I p. 1704. *See* BT-Drs. 17/6070, 17/6361.
63. BVerfG, judgment of 6 Dec. 2016, 1 BvR 2821/11 et al.
64. Gesetz zur Neuregelung des Rechtsrahmens für die Förderung der Stromerzeugung aus erneuerbaren Energien, BGBl. 2011 I p. 1634.
65. *See* G. Wustlich & D. Müller, 'Die Direktvermarktung von Strom aus erneuerbaren Energien im EEG 2012 – Eine systematische Einführung in die Marktprämie und die weiteren Neuregelungen

157. The legislative package also included an amendment of the EnWG[66] as well as a statute on the faster extension of the electricity grid[67]. With the amendment of the EnWG, the rules on unbundling in particular for transmission system operators have been designed anew, transposing the third energy package of the EU into national law (see below Part I Chapter 1 section 2 III. C.). Other rules concern topics like smart metering and the change of energy suppliers. The statute on the faster extension of the electricity grid (hereinafter: NABEG)[68] established a new planning system for grid projects that are determined to be high priority. Further measures of the legislative package of 2011 concerned the licensing regime for offshore wind parks, climate change provisions in the building law and a Special Fund for energy and climate.

---

zur Marktintegration', *ZNER* (2011): 380; W. Lehnert, 'Markt- und Systemintegration der Erneuerbaren Energien: Eine rechtliche Analyse der Regeln zur Direktvermarktung im EEG 2012', *ZUR* (2012): 4; T. Schomerus & A. Henkel, 'Die Marktprämie im EEG 2012 – eine erste Zwischenbilanz' *ER* (2012): 13; H. Thomas, 'Das EEG 2012 – Eine Darstellung nach Anspruchsgrundlagen', *NVwZ-Extra* (11/2012), 1.

66. Gesetz zur Neuregelung energiewirtschaftlicher Vorschriften, BGBl. 2011 I p. 1554.
67. Gesetz über Maßnahmen zur Beschleunigung des Netzausbaus Elektrizitätsnetze, BGBl. 2011 I p. 1690.
68. Netzausbaubeschleunigungsgesetz Übertragungsnetz of 28 Jul. 2011 (BGBl. I p. 1690).

Chapter 8. The Electricity Market Act 2016

158. Discussions in Germany have been ongoing on whether a new energy market design is necessary. The discussions included the (market) mechanisms under which power plants are to be financed. Many stakeholders agree that efficient and flexible power plants (and/or flexible consumption and storage facilities) will be necessary to balance the feed-in from – often intermittent – renewable energy sources. However, dispute exists as to whether capacity mechanisms are needed to finance the necessary amount of power plants or whether these plants will be economical under the existing market mechanisms (including the balancing markets). Further, if the necessity for capacity mechanisms is assumed, discussion continues as to if either a strategic reserve or a capacity market is the option to choose.[69]

159. In 2016, the German legislator addressed the discussions on the development of energy markets in the Electricity Market Act (*Strommarktgesetz*).[70] Prior to the adoption of this Act, the BMWi had conducted a consultation with the market participants on the future design of the electricity markets. This resulted in the White Paper of the BMWi on an Electricity Market for the *Energiewende* in 2015.[71] A core message of the White Paper is that instead of an introduction of a separate capacity market, the electricity market shall be developed further to an 'electricity market 2.0'. The BMWi regards this as being more cost-effective than an electricity supply system with an additional capacity market, and believes the electricity market 2.0 will enable innovation and sustainability. On contrast, the BMWi states capacity markets would be prone to regulatory failures and make it complicated to transform the power system. The BMWi continues that the electricity market 2.0 would not require intervention in market mechanisms and would therefore be less prone to error.

160. Following this political intention, the Electricity Market Act (*Strommarktgesetz*) foresaw changes to the Energy Industry Act in particular. Important amendments were designed to guarantee the free pricing on the electricity market and to support the incentives for keeping the balancing groups in which electricity is being delivered in balance. The new section 1 paragraph 4 Nr. 1 EnWG reads that the

69. There is an extensive literature of expert opinions and position papers to the future market design and capacity mechanisms, *see* for instance: EWI, 'Untersuchungen zu einem zukunftsfähigen Strommarktdesign, Endbericht', March 2012; Öko-Institut/LBD Beratungsgesellschaft/RAUE, 'Fokussierte Kapazitätsmärkte, Ein neues Marktdesign für den Übergang zu einem neuen Energiesystem', 8 Oct. 2012; ECOFYS, 'Notwendigkeit von Kapazitätsmechanismen, Endbericht', 14 Sep. 2012; BEE/ Greenpeace energy/ IZES, 'Kompassstudie Marktdesign', December 2012; Öko-Institut, 'Contribution to the consultation on generation adequacy, capacity mechanisms and the internal market in electricity', 7 Feb. 2013; EEX, 'Notwendigkeit und Design von Kapazitätsmechanismen', 5 Aug. 2013; Agora Energiewende, '12 Thesen zur Energiewende', November 2012.

70. Gesetz zur Weiterentwicklung des Strommarktes (*Strommarktgesetz*) of 26 Jul. 2016 (BGBl. I p. 1786).

71. Bundesministerium für Wirtschaft und Energie, Ein Strommarkt für die Energiewende, July 2015 www.bmwi.de last accessed 1 May 2022.

Energy Industry Act shall in particular aim at strengthening the free pricing of electricity through competitive market mechanisms. Section 1a paragraph 1 EnWG continues that the price of electricity shall be formed freely on the market in accordance with competitive principles, and that the level of prices for electricity on the wholesale market will not be restricted by regulation. Further, the Electricity Market Act aimed at strengthening the system of balancing groups (*Bilanzkreise*) and balancing energy (*Ausgleichsenergie*). The underlying idea on these changes is that the existing electricity market with such a system shall create sufficient price signals towards investors in energy installations which allow refinancing of generation and storage facilities at the existing electricity market (without need of establishing a separate capacity market). Accordingly, section 1a paragraph 2 EnWG now states that the balancing group and balancing energy system is of central importance for ensuring the security of electricity supply. Therefore, the balancing group managers' compliance and proper management of the balancing groups would need to be ensured.[72]

161. In seeking to support security of supply the legislator also implemented a so-called capacity reserve (*Kapazitätsreserve*) which shall be utilized in case the electricity market in itself does not ensure a sufficient balance between supply and demand.[73] According to section 13a paragraph 1 EnWG, the TSOs shall hold reserve capacity to compensate for power balance deficits resulting from the failure to fully balance supply and demand on the electricity markets in the German grid control system in the event of a threat to or disruption of the security or reliability of the electricity supply system. Importantly, the intention of the legislator is that the 'electricity market 2.0' sufficiently balances supply and demand. The capacity reserve shall only complement the electricity market for cases of a threat to or disruption of security of supply. Details for the capacity reserve are provided in the Capacity Reserve Ordinance (*Kapazitätsreserveverordnung, KapResV*).[74] The capacity reserve shall be procured by the transmission system operators in a competitive, transparent, and non-discriminatory tendering procedure, *see* sections 6 et seqq. KapResV. In principle generating plants, controllable load and storage facilities that meet the further preconditions of the Capacity Reserve Ordinance are entitled to participate in the tenders for capacity reserve. Section 3 of the Capacity Reserve Ordinance contains several principles to ensure that the capacity reserve ordinance operates outside the electricity market and therefore influences the electricity market as little as possible.[75] In particular, pursuant to section 3 paragraph 1 sentence 1 KapResV generation plants and storage facilities bound in the capacity reserve shall feed-in exclusively at the request of the transmission system operators. Further, the operator of a capacity reserve facility may not sell all or any portion of the output or work of its facility committed to the reserve in the electricity markets,

72. *See also* S. Kirschnick & D. Krappitz, 'Kernpunkte des Strommarktes 2.0 für Vertrieb, Erzeuger und Netzbetreiber', IR (2016): 266.
73. B. Scholtka & J. Martin, 'Die Entwicklung des Energierechts im Jahr 2016', NJW (2017): 932, 933: S. Kirschnick & D. Krappitz, 'Kernpunkte des Strommarktes 2.0 für Vertrieb, Erzeuger und Netzbetreiber', IR (2016): 266, 268.
74. Kapazitätsreserveverordnung of 28 Jan. 2019 (BGBl. I S. 58).
75. S. Kirschnick & D. Krappitz, 'Kernpunkte des Strommarktes 2.0 für Vertrieb, Erzeuger und Netzbetreiber', IR (2016): 266, 268.

section 3 paragraph 2 sentence 1 KapResV. In the auction for the first fulfilment period of the capacity reserve (1 October 2020 until 30 September 2022), the transmission system operators have allocated a capacity of 1.056 MW.[76] In addition to the provisions of the Capacity Reserve Ordinance, the transmission system operators have published standard conditions for capacity reserve installations which have been approved by the Federal Network Agency.[77]

76. Bundesnetzagentur, 'Kapazitätsreserve', www.bundesnetzagentur.de last accessed 1 May 2022.
77. Federal Network Agency, Approval decision (*Genehmigung*) 8121-19 Versorgungssicherheit of 23 Jul 2019.

Chapter 9. Enhanced Climate Change Policy and Legislation

162. On 11 December 2019 the European Commission published the "European Green Deal" as the Commission's central instrument for aiming to achieve climate neutrality for the European Union by 2050. The European Commission wants to increase the climate protection targets for 2030 to a reduction in greenhouse gas emissions of at least 55%. Particularly relevant for the (energy) industry is the Commission's statement that the climate protection measures with the Green Deal are to become Europe's 'new growth strategy'.[78] A further focus of the Commission is on guiding investments from a sustainability perspective.

163. Important policy documents on national level are the Climate Protection Plan 2050 (*Klimaschutzplan 2050*) and the Climate Protection Programme 2030 (*Klimaschutzprogramm 2030*). The Climate Protection Plan 2050 contains Germany's long-term strategy to reduce greenhouse gas emissions and sets out the ambition to essentially reach climate neutrality by 2050. It will require further updates also reflecting the developments on European level. The Climate Protection Programme 2030 sets out several measures that shall support reaching the climate protection targets for 2030. One important measure that has been introduced in 2021 pursuant to the Climate Protection Programme 2030 is the national emissions trading scheme for the sectors heat and transport not covered by the European emissions trading (see below Part VI Chapter 2 §3).

164. The Federal Climate Change Act (*Bundes-Klimaschutzgesetz*, KSG)[79] is the central national legislation on climate protection. Pursuant to section 3 paragraph 1, the Federal Climate Change Act aims at reducing emissions of greenhouse gases in comparison with their levels in 1990 by at least 65% by 2030, and by at least 88% by 2040. Section 3 paragraph 2 KSG further foresees that, by 2045, greenhouse gas emissions shall be reduced to the point of net greenhouse gas neutrality. After 2050, negative greenhouse gas emissions are to be achieved. To achieve the national climate targets, the Federal Climate Change Act provides that annual mitigation targets shall be set by stipulating annual emission budgets for several sectors, including energy, industry, and transport. Due to the significant reduction in its annual emission budget (see Annex 2 to the KSG), the energy sector has to reach the absolute highest reduction within the relevant sectors. The responsibility for reaching the annual emission targets rests with the competent Federal Ministry for each relevant sector.[80]

---

78. European Commission, The European Green Deal, Communication from the Commission of 11 Dec. 2019, COM(2019) 640 final, page 2.
79. Bundes-Klimaschutzgesetz of 12 Dec. 2019 (BGBl. I p. 2513).
80. W. Frenz, *Klimaschutzrecht* (Berlin: Erich Schmidt Verlag, 2021), § 4 KSG para. 60.

165. In 2021, the climate protection requirements within the Federal Climate Change Act have been enhanced following a much observed judgment of the Federal Constitutional Court.[81] Answering a claim directed against too lenient provisions within the Federal Climate Change Act, the Federal Constitutional Court held that the German Basic Law (*Grundgesetz*) obliges the safeguarding of freedom protected by fundamental rights over time and the proportionate distribution of opportunities for freedom across generations. Fundamental rights within the German Basic Law, as an inter-temporal safeguard of freedom (*intertemporale Freiheitssicherung*), would protect against a unilateral shift of the greenhouse gas reduction burden to the future. The protection of future freedom also would require that the transition to climate neutrality be initiated in good time. In the view of the Federal Constitutional Court, this requires the early formulation of transparent specifications for the further design of greenhouse gas reduction that provide orientation for the necessary development and implementation processes and give them a sufficient degree of development pressure and planning certainty. Following this judgment, the legislator promptly amended the Federal Climate Change Act and, in particular, foresaw a more ambitious climate protection target of minus 65% in 2030 (including enhanced reduction requirements for the relevant sectors until 2030), and more detailed greenhouse gas emission reduction requirements for the period post 2030.[82] Also, it will be interesting to see the implications of the detailed reasoning of the Federal Constitutional Court in future proceedings, possibly also in relation to disputes between private parties where indirect effects of fundamental rights of the German Basic Law may play a role.

81. BVerfG, decision of 24 Mar. 2021, 1 BvR 2656/18 et al.
82. Erstes Gesetz zur Änderung des Bundes-Klimaschutzgesetzes of 18 Aug. 2021 (BGBl. I p. 3905). *See* for more details the legislative reasoning in BT-Drs. 19/30230.

Chapter 10. Phase-Out of Coal

166. On 14 August 2020, the Act on the Reduction and Termination of Coal-Fired Power Generation (Coal-Fired Power Generation Termination Act, *Kohleverstromungsbeendigungsgesetz, KVBG*)[83] entered into force. The Coal-Fired Power Generation Termination Act provides for a gradual reduction of the coal-fired power generation in Germany up until 2038 against compensation for the operators (see in more detail below Part IV Chapter 1 § 5). The enactment of this law had been preceded by recommendations of the so-called coal commission (*Kohlekommission*) that has been introduced by the Federal Government in striving to achieve a broad social consensus on how to shape the structural change in Germany based on energy and climate policies. The final report of the coal commission set out a range of recommended measures with the first one being the gradual reduction and termination of coal-fired power generation.[84]

83. Kohleverstromungsbeendigungsgesetz of 8 Aug. 2020 (BGBl. I p. 1818).
84. Kommission Wachstum, Strukturwandel und Beschäftigung, Abschlussbericht, Jan 2019, www.bmwi.de last accessed 1 May 2022: 61 et seqq.

Chapter 11. Prospects

167. In the election campaign 2021, climate protection and related measures for the energy sector have been one of the key areas of discussion besides the COVID-19 crisis. In December 2021, a new government consisting of the Social Democratic Party (SPD), the Greens (Bündnis 90/Die Grünen) and the Free Democratic Party (FDP) which set itself ambitious targets in transforming and modernizing Germany on the path to climate neutrality, reaffirming the commitment to the 1.5-degree pathway. In the Coalition Agreement,[85] the parties state that the further expansion of renewable energies will be a core project of their government. The aim for the expansion of photovoltaics are 200 GW until 2030, for onshore wind energy 2% of the total area at land shall be assigned, and the capacities for offshore wind shall be substantially increased to at least 30 GW in 2030, 40 GW in 2035, and 70 GW in 2045. While accepting a higher electricity demand prognosis of 680–750 TWh, the parties state that 80% of the gross electricity consumption in 2030 shall be covered from renewable energy sources. The yearly tender amounts for renewable energy sources shall be adjusted accordingly. Instruments for expansion without financial support like power purchase agreements as well as the European wide trade with green certificates shall be strengthened. Planning and approval procedures as well as the expansion of electricity grids shall be accelerated. On new buildings for businesses, use of solar energy shall become coercive, on new private buildings it shall become the rule. Climate protection shall become a cross-sectional task, each legislative draft shall be checked on its compatibility with the national climate protection targets. The phase-out of use of coal for electricity generation shall be accelerated and 'ideally' succeed until 2030 already. The parties state that the construction of new gas fired power stations will be necessary for security of supply, but new installations shall be built in a way that they can be transformed to use climate neutral gases ('H2 ready'). A fast market ramp-up of hydrogen is aimed at, with using domestic generation based on renewable energy as first priority. The capacity for electrolysis shall reach around 10 GW in 2030. In the course of expansion of renewable energy, the parties intend working on a new electricity market design as well, and to allow economic use of electricity from renewable sources for sector coupling. Another focus is on socially just and competitive energy prices. One important measure announced in this context is that financing of the EEG levy shall be taken over by the state budget (see below Part V Chapter 2 §6).

168. In the beginning of 2022, several legislative amendments based on this agenda have been published (see closer below in Part V). Besides the items mentioned before, legislative measures also aimed at fostering security supply in light of the Ukraine-war.

85. SPD/GRÜNE/FDP, Mehr Fortschritt wagen, Bündnis für Freiheit, Gerechtigkeit und Nachhaltigkeit, Koalitionsvertrag zwischen SPD, BÜNDNIS 90/DIE GRÜNEN und FDP, Dec. 2021.

Part I. Regulatory Framework for Electricity

169. The following Part I gives an overview over the regulatory framework for electricity in Germany. It is divided into five chapters. Chapter 1 provides an overview of the electricity sector in Germany, including an overview over the relevant legislative acts. The current Energy Industry Act (EnWG) and further relevant legislative acts will be introduced. Furthermore, special attention is given to how Germany has dealt with the implementation of the European energy packages.

170. Chapter 2 refers to the production of electricity. In this chapter, the regime of authorizations and the regulations concerning the connection to the grid will be discussed. The focus with regard to grid connection lies not only on the fundamental provisions of the EnWG, but also on special regulations regarding the grid connection of power plants and offshore wind turbines.

171. Chapter 3 looks at plan approval procedures and other permits for electric wires/overhead lines. In addition to this, the use of roads/streets/infrastructure and concession agreements will be discussed.

172. Chapters 4 and 5 look at the German regulations on distribution and the consumption of electricity.

Chapter 1. General Introduction

§1. Electricity Sector in Germany

173. The electricity sector in Germany has experienced a number of fundamental changes since 1998. Of particular importance has been the liberalization of the market, the obligation of grid operators to guarantee non-discriminatory access to transmission and distribution grids, the establishment of regulatory authorities (Federal Network Agency – *Bundesnetzagentur* and the Regulatory Authorities of the Federal States) and the issuing of a number of new legislative acts. Another key area of development is the transition of the entire electricity system to the use of renewable energy sources to reduce greenhouse gas emissions of electricity production (see closer below Part V).

174. The fundamental law for the energy sector in Germany is the Energy Industry Act (*Energiewirtschaftsgesetz, EnWG*).[86] This Act, which has been amended various times during the past few years, required vertically integrated companies to unbundle their supply and trading business from the monopoly sides of their business, namely transmission and distribution. Responding to these requirements, *RWE* and *EnBW* outsourced their extra high voltage transmission grids to the subsidiaries *Amprion* GmbH and *EnBW Transportnetze AG*. To fulfil agreements reached with the European Commission, *E.ON* and *Vattenfall* sold their transmission network covering subsidiaries *Transpower* and *Vattenfall Europe Transmission GmbH* in their entirety.

175. The German electricity grid covers a length of around 1,920,700 km; it is divided into four voltage levels:

(1) low voltage (230 V or 400 V), 1,263,900 km;
(2) medium voltage (6–60 kV), 524,500 km;
(3) high voltage (60–220 kV), 94,800 km; and
(4) extra high voltage (220 and 380 kV) grid, 37,500 km.[87]

176. The Transmission Grid Operators (TSO) operating in Germany are *Tennet TSO GmbH, 50Hertz Transmission GmbH, Amprion GmbH, and TransnetBW GmbH*. The TSOs each operate transmission systems in four large zones in Germany. The four transmission system operators are obliged by the EnWG to provide non-discriminatory access to their networks.

177. Germany's network is linked to the neighbouring electricity grids via cross-border connections. In 2020, the cross-border trade totally amounted to 83 TWh.[88]

---

86. Gesetz über die Elektrizitäts- und Gasversorgung (Energiewirtschaftsgesetz – EnWG) of 7 Jul. 2005 (BGBl. I S. 1970, 3621).
87. Bundesnetzagentur / Bundeskartellamt, *Monitoringreport 2021*, Dec 2021, p. 39, available at www-.bundesnetzagentur.de
88. Bundesnetzagentur / Bundeskartellamt, *Monitoringbericht 2021*, Dec 2021, p. 12.

178. The low voltage grid to which the majority of consumers are connected is mainly owned by public utilities or other regional or local grid operators. On the regional and local level, electricity is distributed to end users by 872 network operators.[89] Some of them are limited to the territory of one municipality. They often also operate the infrastructure for natural gas, water and district heating.

179. German energy sources used for electricity generation consist of renewable energy sources (mainly wind onshore and offshore, solar energy, hydropower, biomass), coal (hard coal and lignite), nuclear energy, natural gas, and petroleum products. In 2020, the shares of these energy sources in the net electricity generation were as follows (whereas it needs to be noted that due to the COVID-19 crisis there has been a reduction in power consumption in 2020 with impact on these figures):

- renewable energy: 47.0%, (wind: 25.6%, photovoltaics: 9.0%, biogas: 6.0%);
- coal 24.8%;
- nuclear 12.1%;
- natural gas 13.6%;
- other conventional: 3%.[90]

180. Therefore, in 2020 wind energy detached coal as the most important source of electricity generation. Although the figures for 2020 have been influenced by the COVID-19 crisis, the trend clearly shows an increasing use of renewable energy in the electricity sector and reduction in the use of conventional fuels. This development also is a consequence of the so-called *Energiewende* Legislation which consists of various legislative acts. There is a strong governmental policy in Germany to foster the use of climate friendly electricity generation. This policy is showing results: a look at the total gross electricity generation shows that the importance of renewable energy is increasing rapidly (see Introduction Chapters 7, 9, 10, and 11 and below Part V). In 2020, the total electricity production in Germany fed into the grids amounted to 502.6 TWh.[91]

§2. Regulatory Framework Concerning Electricity in Germany

181. The basic or fundamental regulation on the electricity sector is the Energy Industry Act (*Energiewirtschaftsgesetz, EnWG*) of 7 July 2005.[92] The first version of the EnWG was adopted in Germany as early as 1935, and various modified and additional regulations concerning electricity have been issued since then. Also, further statutory sources exist which contain regulations about electricity, the relevant provisions are scattered and can be found in various legislative acts. German legislation with regard to electricity has experienced major reforms during the past

89. Bundesnetzagentur/Bundeskartellamt, *Monitoringreport 2021*, Dec 2021, p. 38.
90. Destatis, press release Nr. 101 of 5 Mar 2021, available at www.destatits.de.
91. Destatis, press release Nr. 101 of 5 Mar 2021, available at www.destatits.de.
92. Gesetz über die Elektrizitäts- und Gasversorgung (Energiewirtschaftsgesetz, EnWG) of 7 Jul. 2005 (BGBl. I S. 1970, 3621).

twenty-five years. During this time, the basic law regarding electricity regulation, the EnWG, has been amended several times, with major reforms implemented in 1998, 2003, 2005, 2011, and 2016. Also, further provisions and additional legislative acts with respect to the electricity sector have been adopted or amended fundamentally during the past two decades. These include, most notably, the Renewable Energy Sources Act (*Erneuerbare-Energien-Gesetz, EEG*, see in detail below Part V).

182. Therefore, the Germany electricity sector has more or less been given a new regulatory framework during the past twenty-five years. Main features of the amended legal framework relate to network access, grid connection, and separating network operation from the other activities of companies inside and outside of the energy sector as well as to the transition to a more climate friendly electricity generation mainly based on renewable energy sources.

183. Another relevant new aspect is that the enforcement of the electricity regulations lies with regulatory authorities. In 2005, the Federal Network Agency (*Bundesnetzagentur*) was established to regulate all network industries in Germany regarding electricity and gas (at that time, a new department for energy regulation was established at the previous Regulatory Authority for Posts and Telecommunications). See for more details on the Federal Network Agency above Introduction Chapter 4.

184. The following chapter provides an overview about the regulatory framework for electricity in ten parts. After a short overview of some of the relevant statutory acts (see I. below) and of the background of electricity regulation in Germany (see II. below), the focus lies on the regulations of the current EnWG (see III. below). This part will give a brief account on the content and some of the relevant provisions of this core regulation of German Energy Law. Special attention is given to the question how Germany has dealt with the implementation of the European Electricity and Gas Directives. The following sections provide a short overview of further relevant legislative acts, *inter alia* the Power Grid Expansion Act (see IV. below), the Ordinance on Network Connection of Power Plants (see V. below), the Regulation on General Conditions for the Grid Connection and Use for the Electricity Supply in Low Voltage (see VI. below), the Regulation on General Conditions for the Universal Supply of Domestic Customers, and the Substitute Supply with Electricity from the Low Voltage Grid (see VII. below), the Ordinance on Incentive Regulation (see VIII. below), and the Grid Expansion Acceleration Act (see IX. below).

I. Overview

185. As mentioned above, regulations concerning electricity can be found in various legislative acts. The basic law is the Energy Industry Act (*Energiewirtschaftsgesetz, EnWG*) which contains general principles and fundamental regulations concerning electricity and gas (for more details about the EnWG-regulations concerning the gas sector, see Part II below). The EnWG has been amended several times, *inter alia* in the course of the implementation of the European Electricity Directives 1996,[93] 2003,[94] 2009,[95] and 2019.[96]

186. In addition to the EnWG, various legislative acts determine the framework for the electricity sector in Germany. Of particular importance are (for a more comprehensive list of statutory acts concerning the energy sector see above Introduction, Chapter 2, § 3):

- Renewable Energy Sources Act (*Erneuerbare-Energien-Gesetz, EEG*).[97]
- Offshore Wind Energy Act (*Windenergie-auf-See-Gesetz – WindSeeG*).[98]
- Act against Restraints of Competition (*Gesetz gegen Wettbewerbsbeschränkungen, GWB*).[99]
- Combined Heat and Power Act (*Kraft-Wärme-Kopplungsgesetz, KWKG*).[100]
- Act on the Federal Network Agency (*Bundesnetzagenturgesetz, BEGTPG*).[101]
- Power Grid Expansion Act (*Energieleitungsausbaugesetz, EnLAG*).[102]
- Grid Expansion Acceleration Act (*Netzausbaubeschleunigungsgesetz Übertragungsnetz, NABEG*).[103]
- Federal Requirements Plan Act (*Gesetz über den Bundesbedarfsplan, BBPlG*).[104]

---

93. Directive 96/92/EC of the European Parliament and of the Council of 19 Dec. 1996 concerning common rules for the internal market in electricity, OJ 1997 L27/20. This Directive was part of the so-called First Energy Package. Part of the First Energy Package was as well Directive 98/30/EC of the European Parliament and of the Council of 22 Jun. 1998 concerning common rules for the internal market in natural gas, OJ 1998 L204/1.
94. Directive 2003/54/EC of the European Parliament and of the Council of 26 Jun. 2003 concerning common rules for the internal market in electricity and repealing Directive 96/92/EC, OJ 2003 L176/37. This Directive was part of the so-called Second Energy Package. The Second Energy Package also comprises a Regulation (EC) No. 1228/2003 of the European Parliament and of the Council of 26 Jun. 2003 on conditions for access to the network for cross-border exchanges of electricity, OJ 2003 L176/1, as well as a Directive and a Regulation on natural gas.
95. Directive 2009/72/EC of the European Parliament and of the Council of 13 Jul. 2009 concerning common rules for the internal market in electricity and repealing Directive 2003/54/EC, OJ 2009 L211/55. The Third Energy Package also comprises a Regulation (EC) No. 714/2009 on conditions for access to the network for cross-border exchanges in electricity and repealing Regulation (EC) No. 1228/2003, as well as a Directive and a Regulation on natural gas and a Regulation establishing an Agency for the Cooperation of Energy Regulators.
96. Directive 2019/944/EU of the European Parliament and of the Council of 5 Jun. 2019 on common rules for the internal market for electricity and amending Directive 2012/27/EU, OJ L 158/125. Together with other legislative acts this Directive has been enacted in the course of the so-called winter package published by the EU Commission in 2016.
97. Erneuerbare-Energien-Gesetz of 21 Jul. 2014 (BGBl. I p. 1066).
98. Windenergie-auf-See-Gesetz of 13 Oct. 2016 (BGBl. I p. 2258, 2310).
99. Gesetz gegen Wettbewerbsbeschränkungen in the version of the publication of 26 Jun. 2013 (BGBl. I p. 1750, 3245).
100. Kraft-Wärme-Kopplungsgesetz of 21 Dec. 2015 (BGBl. I p. 2498).
101. Gesetz über die Bundesnetzagentur für Elektrizität, Gas, Telekommunikation, Post und Eisenbahnen of 7 Jul. 2005 (BGBl. I p. 1970, 2009).
102. Gesetz zum Ausbau von Energieleitungen of 21 Aug. 2009 (BGBl. I p. 2870).
103. Netzausbaubeschleunigungsgesetz Übertragungsnetz of 28 Jul. 2011 (BGBl. I p. 1690).
104. Gesetz über den Bundesbedarfsplan of 23 Jul. 2013 (BGBl. I p. 2543).

– Ordinance on Grid Connection of Power Plants (*Verordnung zur Regelung des Netzanschlusses von Anlagen zur Erzeugung von elektrischer Energie, Kraftwerks-Netzanschlussverordnung, KraftNAV*).[105]
– Regulation on General Conditions for the Grid Connection and Use for the Electricity Supply in Low Voltage (*Niederspannungsanschlussverordnung, NAV*).[106]
– Regulation on General Conditions for the Universal Supply of Domestic Customers and the Substitute Supply with Electricity from the Low Voltage Grid (*Stromgrundversorgungsverordnung, StromGVV*).[107]
– Ordinance on Incentive Regulation (*Anreizregulierungsverordnung, ARegV*).[108]
– Regulation on Remunerations for the Access to Electricity Supply Grids (*Verordnung über die Entgelte für den Zugang zu Elektrizitätsversorgungsnetzen, StromNEV*).[109]
– Ordinance on Concession Fees for Electricity and Gas (*Konzessionsabgabenverordnung, KAV*).[110]
– Renewable Energies Ordinance *(Erneuerbare-Energien-Verordnung – EEV).*[111]
– Guarantees of Origin and Regional Guarantees of Origin Ordinance (*Herkunfts- und Regionalnachweis-Durchführungsverordnung – HkRNDV*).[112]
– Ordinance regulating the Procedure for the Procurement, Use and Settlement of a Capacity Reserve (*Kapazitätsreserveverordnung, KapResV*).[113]
– Ordinance on the Regulation of the Procurement and Provision of Installations in the Network Reserve (*Netzreserveverordnung, NetzResV*).[114]

187. Furthermore, it has to be noted that with respect to regional and local issues, municipalities have the right to issue statutes (*Satzungen*) on electricity/energy-related matters.

II. Background

188. Historically, the German electricity sector was decentralized and fragmented consisting of several thousand utilities – about 16,000 electricity supply utilities in 1936 – for decades. The majority of these were local municipal utilities

105. Verordnung zur Regelung des Netzanschlusses von Anlagen zur Erzeugung von elektrischer Energie of 26 Jun. 2007 (BGBl. I p. 1187).
106. Verordnung über Allgemeine Bedingungen für den Netzanschluss und dessen Nutzung für die Elektrizitätsversorgung in Niederspannung (Niederspannungsanschlussverordnung) of 1 Nov. (BGBl. I p. 2477).
107. Verordnung über Allgemeine Bedingungen für die Grundversorgung von Haushaltskunden und die Ersatzversorgung mit Elektrizität aus dem Niederspannungsnetz of 26 Oct. 2006 (BGBl. I p. 2391).
108. Verordnung über die Anreizregulierung der Energieversorgungsnetze of 29 Oct. 2007 (BGBl. I S. 2529).
109. Verordnung über die Entgelte für den Zugang zu Elektrizitätsversorgungsnetzen of 25. Jul. 2005 (BGBl. I p. 2225).
110. Verordnung über Konzessionsabgaben für Strom und Gas of 9 Jan. 1992 (BGBl. I p. 12, 407).
111. Erneuerbare-Energien-Verordnung of 17 Feb. 2015 (BGBl. I p. 146).
112. Herkunfts- und Regionalnachweis-Durchführungsverordnung of 8 Nov. 2018 (BGBl. I p. 1853).
113. Kapazitätsreserveverordnung of 28 Jan. 2019 (BGBl. I p. 58).
114. Netzreserveverordnung of 27 Jun. 2013 (BGBl. I p. 1947).

that distributed and supplied gas or power purchased from the large companies. In 1986, only about 1,000 electricity supply utilities remained.[115]

189. In the following, an overview on the development of the German electricity sector from the 1920s until the 1990s will be presented (see A. below). After this, a description of the developments on EU level will be presented which have had a fundamental influence on German Energy Law from the 1990s onward (see section B. below).

A. *Development of the German Electricity Sector*

190. Discussions to introduce a legislative act on the energy industry started as early as in the 1920s. At that time, the electricity sector experienced fundamental changes. Technological change (for instance, the development of more efficient long-distance transmission and cheaper, large-scale generation, etc.) prompted structural changes, such as larger private generators merging with smaller public utilities to form mixed public-private enterprises.[116]

191. After a few years and several drafts, a first EnWG was issued in 1935. Since then, the Act has been amended several times and remains to this day the fundamental legal act for the energy sector in Germany.

192. The EnWG of 1935, according to its preamble, was designed to 'avert the damaging effects of competition on the economy'. Another fundamental objective of the EnWG 1935 was to provide energy supply at secure and cost-effective prices. The EnWG 1935 was based on the assumption of a monopoly supplier system for each supply territory, and contained strong features of direct state control over the electricity industry.[117] In order to compensate for the absence of competition, the energy sector was subjected to increased regulation: the EnWG 1935 contained investment control and trading prohibition proceedings, and there were also special provisions on the control of abusive practices in the supply of energy in section 103 of the Act against Restraints of Competition (GWB). Nevertheless, government supervision could not prevent the energy markets from developing in a way typical for monopolized markets, and energy prices were relatively high.[118]

---

115. For information about origins and the development of the German electricity sector, *see* OECD, *Reviews of Regulatory Reform in Germany, Electricity, Gas and Pharmacies – Part 1* (2004), 8, available via www.oecd.org.
116. OECD Review, above, 10.
117. Also *see* K. Pritzsche et al., 'Part 3: Germany', in *R. Tudway, Energy Law & Regulation in the European Union* (London: Sweet & Maxwell, 1999): 3312.
118. For more information about the EnWG 1935, *see* C. Corino, *Energy Law in Germany and Its Foundations in International and European Law* (München: C.H. Beck, 2003), 47; Säcker in Säcker, *Energierecht* (Frankfurt: Fachmedien Recht und Wirtschaft, 3. Auflage, 2013), Einl. EnWG A. Rdnr. 15.

193. Although there is no doubt that the EnWG of 1935 was aiming to strengthen the German energy industry in the confrontational situation in Europe in the 1930s, it was not merely a product of the Nazi Government, but has rather to be seen against the developments and discussions in the 1920s. Hence, even though the EnWG had been enacted in 1935 under the Third Reich, the provisions were allowed to remain in force after 1945 because the material provisions did not conflict with the new 1949 German Constitution. This is based on Article 123 paragraph 1 of the Basic Law for the Federal Republic of Germany (*Grundgesetz*) which reads:

> Continued applicability of pre-existing law
>
> 'Law in force before the Bundestag first convenes shall remain in force insofar as it does not conflict with the Basic Law.'[119]

194. With respect to this regulation, the EnWG 1935 could remain in force after the end of the Third Reich.

195. Between 1945 and 1998, there were repeated attempts to reform the regulatory framework of the German EnWG 1935. Various attempts were made to provide for more competition within the existing regulations. In order to concentrate state supervision regarding the competition of energy supply, the German Parliament, for instance, requested the Federal Government to reform the EnWG while passing the GWB in 1957. However, it took until 1973 before a first ministerial draft for a new EnWG was set out. Not surprisingly, the industry was strongly opposed to any changes to the existing monopoly structures. The discussions regarding a reformed EnWG also have to be seen in the context of the 1970s oil crisis. At that time the supply industry evoked the threat of an energy supply deficit, which proved an effective argument to prevent reforms.[120]

196. In 1987, the federal government gave a mandate to an independent commission of experts, the Deregulation Commission, to examine prevailing regulations of economic activities and to make recommendations for the reduction of regulations which are inimical to market forces. The Commission delivered its report 'Opening of Markets and Competition' (*Marktöffnung und Wettbewerb*) in 1991. The report examined a wide range of the German economy and provided both general guidelines as well as specific recommendations for the electricity sector.[121]

---

119. Grundgesetz für die Bundesrepublik Deutschland of 23 May 1949 (BGBl. S. 1) (BGBl. I S. 944). A translation of the Grundgesetz is available at www.gesetze-im-internet.de/englisch_gg/index.html.
120. For further information about the development of the EnWG 1935, *see* W. Danner, in: Danner & Theobald, *Energierecht* (München, C.H. Beck, 78. Ergänzungslieferung, 2013), Einf., Rdnr. 31 ff.
121. For an overview in English, *see* OECD, Country Studies, *Germany – Regulatory Reform in Electricity, Gas and Pharmacies* (2004), 11 (available via www.oecd.org).

197. The Deregulation Commission presented specific recommendations for reforms of the electricity sector which aimed at the reliable and at the same time reasonably priced supply of electricity. For instance, it was suggested:

(a) to forbid agreements that restrict competition between electricity supply companies in the form of demarcation agreements and interconnection agreements and the exclusivity clause in concession agreements between supply companies and municipalities;
(b) to introduce a general obligation for network operators to transmit electricity;
(c) to make the maintenance of high voltage networks an independent service which should include the guarantee of network stability;
(d) to introduce uniform and load-dependent electricity prices for tariff customers;
(e) to gradually abolish concession fees.[122]

198. However, the monopoly structures on the energy market were not removed in the 1990s and it took a few more years to bring noteworthy changes to the electricity sector. For decades, many utilities and municipalities were strongly opposed to any changes because they had so far profited from the monopoly system. Although it was becoming increasingly clear that Germany would have to liberalize its electricity market, the most relevant steps were introduced in the context of the implementation of the European energy packages (see the next section).

B. European Influences

199. With regard to the reforms of the electricity sector, German legislation has been influenced to a large extent by the developments on EU level. European legislation has been a very important driver of the German reforms. The EnWG has been amended, in the course of implementing European legislation, most notably, in 1998, 2003, 2005, 2011, and 2021.

200. The following section is divided into ten parts. Following an introduction (1), the second part goes into the background of electricity sector reforms in Europe (2). In this context, the starting points of the reforms are examined. After that, the key elements of power sector restructuring will be discussed (3). Part (4) looks at competition in generation and supply. This part covers the access to the network for potential new suppliers and the way Europe is trying to introduce competition in generation. Part (5) focuses on the rules to introduce distinction between the networks and the generation as well as supply activities (unbundling). Part (6) attends to the opening of the market and the question whether customers are granted the right to choose their supplier. In part (7), it will be shown that the creation of a regulatory framework is a crucial but also difficult aspect of the power sector reform.

122. With respect to the findings and recommendations of the Deregulation Commission, *see* W. Danner, in: Danner & Theobald, *Energierecht* (München: C.H. Beck, 78. Ergänzungslieferung, 2013), Einführung, Rdnr. 47.

Part (8) treats the winter package of the EU Commission of 2016. Part (9) discusses impacts of the European Green Deal on electricity regulation.

201. After the developments on the European level have been presented (parts 1 to 9), the last part (10) will then provide a short overview over the influence which European legislation has had on German law.

1. Introduction

202. European influences have led to fundamental changes with regard to the German electricity sector. In order to understand these, a short overview of the most important steps and aspects of the electricity sector reform will be given.

203. Traditionally, the electricity sector had in its entirety been regarded as a naturally monopolistic industry. In order to ensure the maintenance of adequate energy supplies the task of energy supply was in various European countries assigned to (state-owned) vertically integrated corporations. One reason for this was the common belief that the introduction of competition would inevitably lead to macroeconomic shortcomings.[123] Another reason was that governments wanted to maintain their role as decision-makers concerning the politically sensitive energy sector.

204. Over the years, it became widely accepted that merely the transmission and distribution of electricity are natural monopolies, whereas the generation, purchase and sale of electricity are considered business activities of a competitive nature.[124] Accordingly, since the 1990s, power sector reform has been the focus of policy in European countries. Subsequently, power sector restructuring in European countries was not merely a matter of national legislation, but was strongly influenced by EU law.

205. Four so-called energy packages laid out the framework for national restructuring processes within the EU. Following the First Electricity Directive, 1996,[125] and the Second Electricity Directive, 2003,[126] further rules have been introduced with the adoption of the Third Energy Package in 2009 which took the restructuring

---

123. T. von Danwitz, 'Regulation and Liberalization of the European Electricity Market – A German View', *Energy Law Journal* 27 (2006): 425.
124. T. von Danwitz, above, 426.
125. Directive 96/92/EC of the European Parliament and of the Council of 19 Dec. 1996 concerning common rules for the internal market in electricity, OJ 1997 L27/20. Part of the First Energy Package was as well Directive 98/30/EC of the European Parliament and of the Council of 22 Jun. 1998 concerning common rules for the internal market in natural gas, OJ 1998 L204/1.
126. Directive 2003/54/EC of the European Parliament and of the Council of 26 Jun. 2003 concerning common rules for the internal market in electricity and repealing Directive 96/92/EC, OJ 2003 L176/37. Moreover, the Second Energy Package comprises a Regulation (EC) No. 1228/2003 of the European Parliament and of the Council of 26 Jun. 2003 on conditions for access to the network for cross-border exchanges of electricity, OJ 2003 L176/1, as well as a Directive and a Regulation on natural gas.

process of the electricity sectors of the Member States one step further, and in the course of the legislative acts developed following the so-called winter package 2016.

206. The Third Energy Package consisted of (for the winter package, see below 8.):

- Directive 2009/72/EC of the European Parliament and of the Council of 13 July 2009 concerning common rules for the internal market in electricity and repealing Directive 2003/54/EC.
- Directive 2009/73/EC of the European Parliament and of the Council of 13 July 2009 concerning common rules for the internal market in natural gas and repealing Directive 2003/55/EC.
- Regulation (EC) No. 713/2009 of the European Parliament and of the Council of 13 July 2009 establishing an Agency for the Cooperation of Energy Regulators.
- Regulation (EC) No. 714/2009 of the European Parliament and of the Council of 13 July 2009 on conditions for access to the network for cross-border exchanges in electricity and repealing Regulation (EC) No. 1228/2003.
- Regulation (EC) No. 715/2009 of the European Parliament and of the Council of 13 July 2009 on conditions for access to the natural gas transmission networks and repealing Regulation (EC) No. 1775/2005.

207. In the course of implementing European Directives, Germany has amended the EnWG several times since 1998,[127] thus abolishing old-fashioned monopolies and heading for a liberalization of the electricity sector.

2. Steps of Electricity Sector Reform in Europe

208. The reform process of the European Energy Sector can be characterized by three main features: the first refers to the abolition of the rights of monopolies (liberalization), and the second aspect (regulation) is to ensure competition whilst ensuring reliable energy supply for the welfare of the public.[128] The third, more recent driver for European reforms of the energy sector is the ambition to address the climate change impacts of electricity production, and in particular the transition to using an increased share of renewable energy sources (see below Part V Chapter

127. *See* in particular: 'Gesetz zur Neuregelung des Energiewirtschaftsrechts', BGBl. I (1998), 730; 'Erstes Gesetz zur Änderung des Gesetzes zur Neuregelung des Energiewirtschaftsrechts', BGBl. I (2003), 686; 'Zweites Gesetz zur Neuregelung des Energiewirtschaftsrechts', BGBl. I (2005), 1970; 'Gesetz zur Neuregelung energiewirtschaftsrechtlicher Vorschriften', BGBl. I (2011), 1554.
128. *See* only T. von Danwitz, above, 423.

1 §3). However, there are complex details and different ways of designing the manifold elements of an electricity reform. This becomes apparent when looking at the different steps by which the reform process has been pushed forward by the three European energy packages.[129]

209. The liberalization of the power sector has been on the EU agenda since the 1990s. The respective legislation was introduced in three steps, mainly through the Electricity Directives, which are part of the aforementioned energy packages. The First Electricity Directive triggered the European liberalization process in 1996, which was then enhanced with the Second Electricity Directive in 2003. The Third Energy Package and the winter package took the reform process further.

210. The first Directive introduced the distinction between the inevitably regulated part (transmission) and the potentially competitive parts (generation, purchase, and sale). Besides this unbundling issue, the Directive promoted third-party access to networks and consumer choice ('eligibility'). However, this Directive was just a first step towards liberalization[130] and was consequently substituted/enhanced by the Second Electricity Directive. The second Directive focused first and foremost on more regulation of the access to networks, on more effective regulation in general and on the unbundling issue.

211. Although these directives were aiming to establish a consistent and coherent power sector, the measures introduced were not sufficient to achieve a fully competitive European electricity market.[131] An energy sector inquiry conducted by the European Commission in 2007 showed that electricity markets at the wholesale level remained national in scope. The analysis also showed that the markets remained highly concentrated and that there was a high degree of vertical integration.[132]

212. With respect to further necessary steps, the Commission introduced the Third Energy Package with the aim to tackle the shortcomings of the liberalization and regulation rules introduced thus far. Primarily, the Third Energy Package referred to the fact that an internal market for electricity had not yet been established and that the vertical integration of incumbents still constituted a barrier for potential new players to enter the markets.[133]

---

129. For a detailed analysis, *see* M. Petersen, 'Restructuring the Electricity Sector in the EU and in Russia', *European Energy and Environmental Law Review* 18 (2009): 171.
130. *See* Recital 39 of the First Electricity Directive.
131. Explanatory Memorandum to the Third Energy Package, COM(2007) DRAFT, 19 Sep. 2007, 2. Also *see*, T. von Danwitz, above, 443.
132. Communication from the Commission: Inquiry pursuant to Art. 17 of Regulation (EC) No. 1/2003 into the European gas and electricity sectors (Final report), COM(2006) 851 final, 10 Jan. 2007, 5.
133. For the shortcomings of the situation before the adoption of the Third Energy Package, *see* P.D. Cameron, 'The Internal Market in Energy: Harnessing the New Regulatory Regime', *European Law Review* 30 (2005): 634.

213. With the provisions of the Third Energy Package, the Commission aimed at finally establishing a truly competitive energy market. Important aspects of the package are:

- to separate production and supply from transmission networks;
- more effective national regulators;
- the strengthening of consumer rights;
- to promote cross-border collaboration and investment;
- greater market transparency on network operation and supply.

214. The Third Energy Package also aimed to strengthen EU-wide cooperation through the development of a new EU Agency for the Cooperation of Energy Regulators.[134] The agency *inter alia* monitors the implementation of new interconnection projects and regional cooperation among transmission system operators.

215. Details have been set out in Regulation No. 713/2009 establishing an agency for the Cooperation of Energy Regulators. Pursuant to Article 2 number 1 of the Regulation, the agency shall be a Community body with legal personality. It shall issue opinions and recommendations addressed to transmission system operators, regulatory authorities, the European Parliament, the Council or the Commission. The agency furthermore shall take individual decisions in specific cases and shall submit non-binding framework guidelines to the Commission (see Article 4).

216. Furthermore, the Third Energy Package fostered a network called the 'European Network on Transmission System Operators for Electricity' (ENTSO-E). According to Article 4 of Regulation (EC) No. 714/2009, all transmission system operators shall cooperate at Community level through the ENTSO-E for electricity, in order to promote the completion and functioning of the internal market in electricity and cross-border trade and to ensure the optimal management, coordinated operation, and sound technical evolution of the European electricity transmission network.[135]

217. Germany has been following the development of the Third Energy Package with much interest, knowing that it would have a huge impact on further developments of the national electricity sector and on the German EnWG.[136]

---

134. For details about the proposal, *see* Explanatory Memorandum to the Third Energy Package, COM(2007) DRAFT, 19 Sep. 2007, 2–20.
135. Also *see*, Art. 4 of Regulation (EC) No. 715/2009 of the European Parliament and of the Council of 13 Jul. 2009 on conditions for access to the natural gas transmission networks and repealing Regulation (EC) No. 1775/2005.
136. *See e.g.*, G. Gerland & T. Helm, 'Übergang zum Übertragungsmodell (Ownership Unbundling) bei Energieversorgungsunternehmen – Wege aus dem Pachtmodell?', *Betriebs-Berater* (2008): 193–194. Also *see*, G. Hermeier, 'Die Zuständigkeitsverteilung bei der Regulierung des grenzüberschreitenden Stromhandels – Mehr Binnenmarkt durch mehr Zentralisierung?', *Recht der Energiewirtschaft* (2007): 249–255; B. Holznagel & P. Schumacher, 'ERGEGplus – Wieder der Versuch der Einführung eines Europäischen Regulierers durch die Hintertür', *Recht der Energiewirtschaft* (2007): 225–232; C. Kahle, 'Die Eigentumsrechtliche Entflechtung (Ownership Unbundling) der

3. Key Elements of the Restructuring Process

218. As the breaking up of traditional state-owned electricity companies constitutes a fundamental change for the electricity market, a complicated legal framework has been installed to ensure competition on the one hand and effective regulation on the other.

219. Key elements which form essentials of the power sector are:

(a) the creation of competition in generation and supply;
(b) unbundling;
(c) opening of the market;
(d) and the development of a regulatory framework.[137]

4. Competition in Generation and Supply

220. An important aspect of the liberalization of the electricity market and an important step towards the abolition of monopolies is to ensure competition in generation and supply activities.

221. With regard to European legislation, access to networks was already introduced to a certain degree through the First Electricity Directive in 1996, when potential new suppliers were granted access to the grid. According to the provisions of said Directive, Member States had the possibility to choose between three different alternatives for organizing access to the network: negotiated access, a regulated system of access, and a so-called single buyer procedure in which Member States would designate a legal entity to be a single buyer within the territory covered by the system operator.[138] However, even though in theory competition had thus been introduced, the provisions did not turn out to be very effective.

222. An important development could hence be seen between the First and the Second Electricity Directives.[139] The Second Electricity Directive limited the discretion of Member States with regard to the manner in which network access is established. According to the rules of the second Directive, Member States had to

---

Energieversorgungsnetze aus europarechtlicher und verfassungsrechtlicher Sicht', *Recht der Energiewirtschaft* (2007): 293–299; T. Mayen & U. Karpenstein, 'Eigentumsrechtliche Entflechtung der Energieversorgungsnetze – Verfassungs- und gemeinschaftsrechtliche Aspekte des Eigentumsschutzes', *Recht der Energiewirtschaft* (2008): 33–45.

137. With respect to the key elements of electricity sector restructuring and the aspects looked at in the following sections, also *see* M. Petersen, 'Restructuring the Electricity Sector in the EU and in Russia', *European Energy and Environmental Law Review* 18 (2009): 171.

138. *See* for more information about the three different alternatives for organizing access to operating systems, T. von Danwitz, above, 437.

139. For Germany, the requirement of regulated access to the network was probably the most important element of the Second Electricity Directive, *see* G. Kühne & C. Brodowski, 'Das neue Energiewirtschaftsrecht nach der Reform 2005', *Neue Zeitschrift für Verwaltungsrecht* (2005): 850.

introduce a regulated system of third-party access.[140] Member States have implemented these regulations into national law and Germany, as the only Member State which originally opted for the introduction of 'negotiated' access to network systems under the First Electricity Directive,[141] addressed the issue by providing for a statutory right for network access to non-discriminatory conditions in section 20 EnWG and in the Regulation on Access to Electricity Supply Grids (*Stromnetzzugangsverordnung, StromNZV*).[142]

223. The Third Energy Package also addressed the lack of transparency which still had been obstructing new entrants,[143] but the German rules regarding network access have not changed significantly in the course of the implementation of the Third Energy Package.[144]

5. Unbundling

224. Another important element of the energy packages was to introduce a distinction between transmission and distribution networks (the inevitably regulated parts of the energy sector) on the one hand and generation and supply (the potentially competitive parts) on the other hand. Although various aspects refer to fair access to networks, the so-called unbundling provisions are particularly aimed at an effective separation of network operations from generation and supply activities. This is based on the insight that the overall goal of having competitive markets has to be achieved by assigning the operation of transmission networks to a company active in neither the upstream market of energy production nor the downstream market of energy distribution.

225. In the First Energy Package, separate management and accounting rules were made mandatory in order to separate the network from generation and supply. Since this was insufficient to achieve a liberalized electricity market and to introduce effective competition, the Second Energy Package went one step further, requiring the legal separation between network operations and generation as well as supply activities.

226. Member States have complied with this requirement of 'legal unbundling' by applying different organizational structures: some Member States have required

140. *See* P.D. Cameron, above, 634.
141. *See* for more information about the previous system of negotiated access in Germany, T. von Danwitz, above, 440; G. Kühne & B. Scholtka, 'Das neue Energiewirtschaftsrecht', *Neue Juristische Wochenschrift* (1998): 1905–1906; Säcker in Säcker, *Energierecht* (Frankfurt: Fachmedien Recht und Wirtschaft, 3. Auflage, 2013), Einl. EnWG A Rdnr. 23.
142. Verordnung über den Zugang zu Elektrizitätsversorgungsnetzen of 25 Jul. 2005, BGBl. I, 2243. *See* for more information G. Kühne & C. Brodowski, 'Das neue Energiewirtschaftsrecht nach der Reform 2005', *Neue Zeitschrift für Verwaltungsrecht* (2005): 850–851.
143. Explanatory Memorandum to the Third Energy Package, COM(2007) DRAFT, 19 Sep. 2007, 16.
144. Säcker/Boesche in Säcker, *Energierecht* (Frankfurt: Fachmedien Recht und Wirtschaft, 3. Auflage, 2013), s. 20 EnWG Rdnr. 5.

a totally separate company for network operation, whereas others have required a legal entity within an integrated company.[145]

227. Germany introduced extensive unbundling regulations[146] and the issue was addressed in section 7 EnWG, requiring energy companies to ensure that operators of the grid are legally independent from other activities of energy supply.[147] According to German law, operators could choose whether they opt for transferring the entire ownership of the networks to independent entities ('ownership unbundling') or choose transfer of just the control of their networks to independent entities.[148] Since the latter went along with the leasing of the assets of the grid operation to a grid company it was called lease model ('*Pachtmodell*'). Many companies chose this latter model, last but not least because of tax advantages.[149]

228. The preferred option, particularly of the EU Commission, however, was complete ownership unbundling[150] which was made clear in the Third Energy Package.[151]

229. The Third Energy Package took into account the fact that the rules on legal and functional unbundling of TSOs as provided for in Directive 2003/54/EC and in Directive 2003/55/EC had not yet led to an effective separation of generation and supply of energy.[152] Accordingly, Directives 2009/72/EC and 2009/73/EC provided further rules with regard to unbundling.

230. The Directives of the Third Energy Package gave Member States a choice between three different models of unbundling:

(1) the ownership unbundling model;
(2) the Independent System Operator (ISO model); and
(3) the Independent Transmission Operator (ITO model).

---

145. Explanatory Memorandum to the Third Energy Package, COM(2007) DRAFT, 19 Sep. 2007, 4.
146. T. von Danwitz, above, 446.
147. For further information about the unbundling regulations of sections 7–10 EnWG after the implementation of the Second Energy Package, *see* G. Kühne & C. Brodowski, above, 854; S. Storr, Die Vorschläge der EU-Kommission zur Verschärfung der Unbundling-Vorschriften im Energiesektor, *Europäische Zeitschrift für Wirtschaftsrecht* (2007), 233.
148. The unbundling regulations of the German EnWG had become more strict in the course of implementing the Second Electricity Directive, *see* G. Kühne & C. Brodowski, above, 850.
149. For further information G. Gerland & T. Helm, 'Übergang zum Übertragungsmodell (Ownership Unbundling) bei Energieversorgungsunternehmen – Wege aus dem Pachtmodell?', *Betriebs-Berater* (2008): 192–196.
150. *See* for a discussion, D. Kennedy, 'Merger in the English Electricity Industry', *Energy Policy* 25 (1997): 393–399; Explanatory Memorandum to the Third Energy Package, COM(2007) DRAFT, 19 Sep. 2007, 4.
151. *See* for information about the question whether European Law provides the necessary legal basis for the introduction of ownership unbundling, C. Kahle, 'Die Eigentumsrechtliche Entflechtung (Ownership Unbundling) der Energieversorgungsnetze aus europarechtlicher und verfassungsrechtlicher Sicht', *Recht der Energiewirtschaft* (2007): 293–299.
152. This is highlighted *inter alia* in Recital 10 of Directive 2009/72/EC.

231. These models apply to transmission networks and provide for different degrees of structural separation of network operation from production and supply activities. However, all of them are expected to be effective in removing any conflict of interests between producers, suppliers, and transmission system operators.

232. Member States are basically free to choose one model, but certain certification procedures have to be followed. The ISO and ITO models can only be chosen for specific TSOs which belonged to a vertically integrated undertaking at the time the directives entered into force.[153] It is not possible to change from a situation of ownership unbundling to an ISO or an ITO if the transmission system did not belong to a vertically integrated undertaking when the directives entered into force.[154]

233. Article 9 of Directive 2009/72/EC laid down rules on ownership unbundling: Member States had to ensure that from 3 March 2012 each undertaking which owns a transmission system acts as a transmission system operator and that the same person or persons are neither entitled:

(a) directly or indirectly to exercise control over an undertaking performing any of the functions of generation or supply, and directly or indirectly to exercise control or exercise any right over a transmission system operator or over a transmission system; nor
(b) directly or indirectly to exercise control over a transmission system operator or over a transmission system, and directly or indirectly to exercise control or exercise any right over an undertaking performing any of the functions of generation or supply.

234. Under ownership unbundling, the same person should not be entitled to appoint members of the managing boards of a transmission system operator or a transmission system and to exercise control or any right over generation or supply undertaking. For more detailed information about the ownership unbundling model, see the Commission Working Paper 'Interpretative Note on Directive 2009/72/EC concerning common rules for the internal market in electricity and Directive 2009/73/EC concerning common rules for the internal market in natural gas – The Unbundling Regime'.[155]

235. As alternatives to ownership unbundling, the ISO and ITO options allow energy companies to retain the ownership of their transmission networks. Under the ISO option, Member States can oblige integrated energy companies to hand over the technical and commercial operation of their transmission networks to a separate

153. Article 9 Directive 2009/72/EC and Directive 2009/73/EC.
154. European Commission, Commission staff working paper, Interpretative Note on Directive 2009/72/EC concerning common rules for the internal market in electricity and Directive 2009/73/EC concerning common rules for the internal market in natural gas – The Unbundling Regime (22 Jan. 2010), 5.
155. European Commission, Commission staff working paper, *The Unbundling Regime* (22 Jan. 2010), 5, *see* above.

body – the ISO. Under Article 13 Electricity Directive, the ISO is proposed by the owner of the transmission system concerned; it is approved and designated as an ISO by the respective Member State under the condition that it has been certified by the regulatory authority as having complied with the specific requirements.[156]

236. Under the third option – the ITO model – the TSO may remain part of a vertically integrated undertaking. But in this case the integrated company is obliged by certain rules to ensure that the two sections of the company operate independently in practice. In this respect, the following aspects have to be taken into account:

(a) the overall management structure and the corporate statues of the ITO should provide for a decision-making structure and rules ensuring effective independence of the ITO;
(b) the ITO has to establish and implement a compliance programme setting out the measures taken in order to ensure that discriminatory conduct is excluded;
(c) the compliance programme has to be approved by the regulatory authority;
(d) a compliance officer is to be appointed by the supervisory body, subject to approval by the regulatory authority;
(e) management staff is not allowed to work for the supply and generation company for three years before and for four years after being employed with the transmission operator (mandatory 'cooling-off periods').[157]

237. With respect to unbundling it can be concluded that Europe has approached the issue step by step, starting off with rules regarding separate management, pushing forward with legal unbundling and then trying to complete this element with ownership unbundling and the ISO and ITO options. Germany has implemented three options into German law in the course of the reform of the EnWG 2011 (see below III. C.).

6. Opening of the Market

238. Another essential element of the European energy packages is the opening of the market. Granting consumers the right to choose their supplier ('eligibility') is particularly important in order to ensure that they will benefit from competition between suppliers in the end.

239. The First Electricity Directive introduced eligibility by granting large customers the right to choose their supplier. In 2003, the Second Electricity Directive went one step further, requiring Member States to ensure that from 1 July 2004 onward all non-household customers and from 1 July 2007 all customers would

---

156. For details, *see* European Commission, Commission staff working paper, *The Unbundling Regime* (22 Jan. 2010), 10.
157. With respect to details regarding the ITO, *see* Commission staff working paper, *The Unbundling Regime*, 17.

have the possibility to choose their supplier.[158] This did not have a far-reaching impact on German law, because Germany had already introduced market opening into national law.[159]

240. It can be said that the EU, after a restrained approach,[160] completed the opening of the electricity market with the Second Electricity Directive to the extent that all households are now freely entitled to choose their supplier.

However, the Third Energy Package brought further changes with regard to consumer rights. New rules *inter alia* focused on:

- the implementation of intelligent metering systems;
- consumer information of actual electricity/gas consumption and costs frequently enough to enable them to regulate their own electricity/gas consumption;
- providing customers with all relevant gas and electricity consumption data in an easily understandable harmonized format;
- consumer rights to change their gas and electricity suppliers within three weeks and free of charge;
- providing customers with a choice between different payment methods.[161]

241. Moreover, Member States must ensure that the roles and responsibilities of energy undertakings, *inter alia* transmission and distribution system operators and suppliers, are defined with respect to contractual arrangements, commitment to customers, data exchange and settlement rules, data ownership, and meter responsibility.[162]

7. Development of a Regulatory Framework

242. The introduction of competition into generation and supply activities as well as unbundling and the opening of the market are key elements of power sector restructuring. All these instruments have been designed to break up vertically integrated monopolies and to establish a competitive electricity sector. But, in addition to these elements some form of regulation is not only a result of, but rather a necessary accompaniment to market liberalization.[163] Accordingly, the regulation of the restructured electricity market is by way of necessity a major issue in Europe.

158. *See* Art. 21 Directive 2003/54/EC of the European Parliament and of the Council of 26 Jun. 2003 concerning common rules for the internal market in electricity and repealing Directive 96/92/EC.
159. H. Lecheler & J. Gundel, 'Ein weiterer Schritt zur Vollendung des Energie-Binnenmarktes: Die Beschleunigungs-Rechtsakte für den Binnenmarkt für Strom und Gas', *Europäische Zeitschrift für Wirtschaftsrecht* (2003): 621, 624.
160. T. von Danwitz, above, 435.
161. With regard to the respective amendments of the German EnWG, *see* K. W. Lange, 'Verbraucherschutz im neuen EnWG', *RdE* (2012): 41.
162. Article 41 Directive 2009/72/EC, Art. 45 Directive 2009/73/EC.
163. T. von Danwitz, above, 423.

243. The First and the Second Electricity Directives required Member States to establish regulatory authorities. Germany, in the course of implementing the Second Electricity Directive, declared the Federal Network Agency (*Bundesnetzagentur, BNetzA*) responsible for the regulation of the electricity sector.[164] It should be noted that there are in addition also Regulatory Authorities in the Federal States; for information on their responsibilities, see Introduction, Chapter 4, section 2.

244. Country reviews carried out by the Commission showed that in some Member States regulatory authorities had become well-established bodies with substantial powers and resources and are thus able to ensure proper market regulation. However, in other Member States the established regulatory authorities were still relatively weak.[165] With regard to these findings, the Third Energy Package aimed at improving these shortcomings and strengthening the powers of the regulatory authorities in various respects: first, their market regulation power should be strengthened in particular with regard to promoting effective competition, monitoring compliance with third-party access rules and unbundling obligations. Second, regulators were to be provided with (more complete) access to information on the operational decisions of the companies. And last but not least, the package aimed at improving the cooperation between regulators on a European level.[166]

245. Accordingly, Directives 2009/72/EC and 2009/73/EC introduced a new set of rules with respect to the national regulatory authorities with the aim to enhance their independence. Under the amended legislation – see Article 35 of the Electricity Directive and Article 39 of the Gas Directive – each Member State were to designate a single national regulatory authority. Member States should guarantee the independence of the regulatory authorities and shall ensure that these exercise their powers impartially and transparently.[167]

246. Without going into detail, it can be said that the independence of the German Federal Network Agency already met said requirements of the Third Energy Package mentioned above. It was not considered necessary to change the German system – for example, the fact that there are Regulatory Authorities of the Federal

164. Section 54 EnWG. For more information about regulation of the electricity market in Germany, *see* G. Kühne & C. Brodowski, above, 855; C. Schalast, 'Das EU-Energiepaket 2007 – Wettbewerb, Binnenmarkt und Umweltschutz', *InfrastrukturRecht* (2007): 75.
165. Comprehensive Country reviews carried out by the Commission stated a lack of uniformity and in many cases the weakness of the regulatory authority, *see* Explanatory Memorandum to the Third Energy Package, COM(2007) DRAFT, 19 Sep. 2007, 8.
166. Explanatory Memorandum to the Third Energy Package, COM(2007) DRAFT, 19 Sep. 2007, 7–9.
167. For details, *see* European Commission, Commission staff working paper, *Interpretative note on Directive 2009/72/EC concerning common rules for the internal market in electricity and Directive 2009/73/EC concerning common rules for the internal market in natural gas – The Regulatory Authorities* (22 Jan. 2010), 3, 4.

States in addition to the Federal Network Agency. However, there was an assessment whether any changes with regard to the organization of the Regulatory Authorities of the Federal States would be necessary in order to comply with the rules of the Third Energy Package.[168]

8. Winter Package 2016

247. In 2016, the European Union initiated a process for several legislative amendments on energy regulation to foster a 'clean and fair energy transition' with the so-called winter package. The legislative amendments on the energy markets – effectively a Fourth Energy Package – have been published on 14 June 2019.[169] This legislative package comprises in particular the following acts:

- Regulation 2019/943/EU of 5 June 2019 on the internal market for electricity, OJ L 158/54.
- Directive 2019/944/EU of 5 June 2019 on common rules for the internal market for electricity and amending Directive 2012/27/EU, OJ L 158/125.
- Directive 2018/2001/EU of 11 December 2018 on the promotion of the use of energy from renewable sources, OJ L 328/82.

248. The directly applicable Regulation 2019/943/EU contains important principles for the day ahead, intraday and balancing markets. For instance, Article 8 paragraph 4 of Regulation 2019/943/EU requires that the imbalance settlement period shall be fifteen minutes in principle. Also, the regulation sets out rules to strive for redispatching of generation, energy storage, and demand response on basis of objective, transparent and non-discriminatory criteria (Article 13 of the Regulation). Article 14 provides for a process of bidding zone review.

249. Directive 2019/944/EU builds on many of the established principles of Directive 2009/72/EC, and brings in selective new aspects. A focus on the amendment has been on strengthening consumer rights. Chapter III of the Directive sets out rules on 'Consumer Empowerment and Protection'. Member States need to ensure that final consumers receive the basic contractual rights listed in Article 10 Directive 2019/944/EU towards their suppliers. National regulation shall enable suppliers to offer, and under further conditions final customers to request, dynamic electricity price contracts. According to Article 15 of the Directive, Member States shall ensure that final customers are entitled to act as 'active customers', in particular in regards to self-generation of electricity.

250. A further focus of the Fourth Energy Package is on decarbonization of the energy sector with the intention to contribute to minimizing climate change. The

168. Bundesministerium für Wirtschaft und Technologie, *Eckpunkte zur EnWG-Novelle 2011* (27 Oct. 2010), 8.
169. *See* B. Scholtka & L. Keller-Herder, Die Entwicklung des Energierechts im Jahr 2019, *NJW* (2020): 890.

Renewable Energy Directive 2018/2001/EU, in principle, leaves the right to design the support schemes for renewable electricity with the Member States. Also, the revised renewable energy Directive provides for enhanced rights on self-generation from renewable energy sources.

9. The European Green Deal

251. On 11 December 2019 the European Commission published the 'European Green Deal' as the Commission's central instrument for aiming to achieve climate neutrality for the European Union by 2050.[170] The European Commission wants to increase the climate protection targets for 2030 to a reduction in greenhouse gas emissions of at least 55%.

252. In 2021, the European Climate Law for establishing the framework for achieving climate neutrality has been enacted.[171] The European Climate Law provides for the general aim that Union-wide greenhouse gas emissions and removals regulated in Union law shall be balanced within the Union at the latest by 2050, thus reducing emissions to net zero by that date (section 2(1) of the Regulation). For 2030, the Union sets a binding climate target to reduce net greenhouse gas emissions by at least 55% compared to 1990 levels (section 4(1) of the Regulation).

253. In its "Fit for 55" communication, the EU Commission explained several measures by which it intends achieving the goal for 2030.[172] The suggested measures include in particular:

- Changes to the EU emission trading system, including applying emissions trading to new sectors (e.g., maritime sector shall be included in the EU Emissions Trading Scheme, start applying emissions trading from 2026 for road transport and buildings)
- New requirements for industry to decarbonize production processes, and support mechanisms
- Increase the renewable energy target from 32% to at least 40% of renewables in the EU energy mix by 2030
- Increase energy efficiency goals in a revised Energy Efficiency Directive

170. European Commission, The European Green Deal, Communication from the Commission of 11 Dec. 2019, COM(2019) 640 final, page 2.
171. Regulation 2021/1119/EU of 30 Jun. 2021 establishing the framework for achieving climate neutrality and amending Regulations (EC) No 401/2009 and (EU) 2018/1999 ('European Climate Law'), ABl. L 243/1.
172. European Commission, 'Fit for 55': delivering the EU's 2030 Climate Target on the way to climate neutrality, Communication from the Commission of 14 Jul. 2021, COM(2021) 550 final.

10. Developments with Regard to the Electricity Sector in Germany

254. As mentioned above, the German EnWG has been amended various times in the course of the implementation of the European energy packages. In 1998, the EnWG of 12 April 1998 came into force which *inter alia* implemented the regulations of the First European Electricity Directive (Directive 96/92/EC) into German law.[173] The 1998 amendments of the EnWG *inter alia* required electricity companies to separate the accounting for their different activities (production, transmission, distribution), and to separately manage electricity transmission. Furthermore, the amendments reduced entry barriers and introduced provisions to promote non-discriminatory access to the electricity supply system. The amendments focused on the implementation of Directive 96/62/EC concerning common rules for the internal market in electricity into German law.

255. The regulations of Directive 98/30/EC of 22 June 1998 concerning common rules for the internal market in natural gas (*Gas Directive, Erdgasbinnenmarktrichtlinie*) were implemented into German law through an amendment of the EnWG in 2003. The next amendment of the EnWG in 2005 gave rise to a new energy policy framework and marked a further turning point. With regard to the implementation of the Third Energy Package, the Federal Ministry of Economics and Technology presented a benchmark paper (*'Eckpunkte zur EnWG-Novelle 2011'*) on 27 October 2010.[174] The following further amendment of the EnWG took place in 2011 focusing *inter alia* on the implementation of the Third Energy Package.[175] Directive 2019/944/EU as part of the so-called winter package has been transposed into national law particularly by an Act of 2021 which also introduced rules on hydrogen grid infrastructure.[176] Details of the current EnWG will be presented in the following section.

III. Energy Industry Act (*Energiewirtschaftsgesetz* (EnWG))

A. Content/Overview

256. The full title of the EnWG reads as follows: 'Law on Electricity Supply and Gas Supply' (*Gesetz über die Elektrizitäts- und Gasversorgung, Energiewirtschaftsgesetz*). It contains – as the heading implies – regulations regarding the German electricity and gas sectors and, following recent amendments, also the hydrogen sector being under development. It aims to ensure effective competition and the efficient and reliable operation of energy supply networks in the long term.

173. For an overview in English, *see* OECD, Reviews of Regulatory Reform – Regulatory Reform in Germany, Electricity, Gas and Pharmacies – Part 1 (2004), 135.
174. Bundesministerium für Wirtschaft und Technologie, Eckpunkte zur EnWG-Novelle 2011.
175. J. Kühling/R. Pisal, 'Die Umsetzung der EU-Entflechtungsvorgaben im EnWG 2011', *Energiewirtschaftliche Tagesfragen* (2012): 127; Säcker in Säcker, *Energierecht* (Frankfurt: Fachmedien Recht und Wirtschaft, 3. Auflage, 2013), Einl. EnWG A para. 33.
176. Gesetz zur Umsetzung unionsrechtlicher Vorgaben und zur Regelung reiner Wasserstoffnetze im Energiewirtschaftsrecht of 16 Jul. 2021, BGBl. I p. 3026.

257. The EnWG is divided into ten parts:

(1) Part 1: General Provisions;
(2) Part 2: Unbundling;
(3) Part 3: Regulation of Grid Operation;
(4) Part 4: Energy Supply to End Consumers;
(5) Part 5: Plan Approval Procedure/Use of Infrastructure;
(6) Part 6: Security and Reliability of Energy Supply;
(7) Part 7: Authorities;
(8) Part 8: Procedure and Legal Protection in the event of overlong Court Proceedings;
(9) Part 9: Additional Provisions;
Part 9a: Transparency;
(10) Part 10: Evaluation; Concluding Provisions.

On the following pages, an overview of some of the relevant regulations will be presented.

B. General Provisions

258. Part One of the EnWG highlights the fundamental aims of the Act. According to section 1 paragraph 1 EnWG, the Act aims at a supply of electricity, gas, and hydrogen which is as secure, low-cost, consumer-friendly, efficient, and environmentally friendly as possible in the interest of society as a whole. The sentence continues stating that the supply increasingly shall be based on renewable energies. Section 1 paragraph 2 EnWG emphasizes that the regulation of electricity and gas grids shall secure efficient and undistorted competition and, pursuant to section 1 paragraph 3 EnWG, the EnWG aims at the implementation and execution of European law. The latter becomes apparent in particular if one keeps in mind that major amendments of the EnWG undertaken in the last decades served the purpose of implementing European Directives into national law. Section 1 paragraph 4 EnWG sets out some more detailed aims. Accordingly, the Energy Industry Act shall in particular aim at strengthening the free pricing of electricity through competitive market mechanisms. Also, it shall enable the balancing of supply and demand for electricity in the electricity markets at all times. Further, generation facilities, electric energy storage facilities, and loads shall be used in the most environmentally sound, grid-compatible, efficient, and flexible manner to the extent necessary to ensure the security and reliability of the electric power system. Section 1a paragraph 1 EnWG continues with additional principles for the electricity market (see above Introduction, Chapter 2, § 5).

259. Section 3 EnWG contains a number of definitions which are relevant for the energy sector. According to section 3 number 14 EnWG, for instance, the term 'energy' covers electricity, gas, and hydrogen used in the supply of energy via supply lines. Further definitions refer, for instance, to the terms 'energy facilities', 'supply companies' (*Energieversorgungsunternehmen*), and 'network operators'

(*Netzbetreiber*). Furthermore, there are legal definitions of the terms 'end consumer' (*Letztverbraucher*), 'direct line' (*Direktleitung*), etc.

260. Section 4 EnWG makes clear that the operation of an energy grid requires an authorization by the responsible authority. The authorization may only be refused if the applicant does not have the personnel, technical and economic capacity and reliability to guarantee network operation in the long term in accordance with the provisions of the EnWG (*see* section 4 paragraph 2 sentence 1 EnWG). On contrast, the supply of electricity by an energy supply company to customers in Germany as such, unlike in some other EU Member States, does not require an authorization. In case of energy supply to domestic customers (*Haushaltskunden*), however, section 5 requires that energy supply companies must notify the regulatory authority without delay of the commencement and termination of the activity as well as changes to their company. Domestic customers are final consumers who purchase energy mainly for their own household consumption or for their own professional, agricultural or commercial consumption not exceeding an annual consumption of 10,000 kilowatt-hours (see section 3 Nr. 22 EnWG).

C. *Unbundling*

261. Part Two of the EnWG contains regulations regarding unbundling. The Act distinguishes between different unbundling regulations:

262. Following general unbundling provisions (sections 6–6d EnWG), regulations concerning the unbundling of distribution network operators (*Verteilnetzbetreiber*) are found in sections 7 et seqq. EnWG.

263. With respect to transmission system operators (TSOs, *Transportnetzbetreiber*), unbundling is regulated in sections 8 et seqq. EnWG:

- *Eigentumsrechtliche Entflechtung* (Ownership unbundling, section 8 EnWG);
- *Unabhängiger Systembetreiber* (Independent System Operator, section 9 EnWG); and
- *Unabhängiger Transportnetzbetreiber* (Independent Transmission Operator, section 10 et seqq. EnWG).

264. These regulations transformed the aforementioned unbundling models of the Third Energy Package into national law. Ownership unbundling according to section 8 EnWG requires that the TSO, per direct ownership or indirect ownership through shares, is owner of the grid. Moreover, there are requirements for staff unbundling between the grid company and any supply/generation company (section 8 paragraph 2 EnWG).

265. In Germany, Tennet TSO GmbH and 50 Hertz Transmission GmbH have opted for ownership unbundling while Amprion GmbH and TransnetBW GmbH (former EnBW Transportnetze GmbH) have chosen the ITO model. The Federal

Network Agency initially refused the certification of TenneT TSO GmbH because TenneT was unable to provide the necessary proof of having the financial means to fulfil the expansion obligations (offshore connection), but the necessary certification has been granted subsequently in 2015.[177]

D. Regulation of Grid Operation

266. Part Three of the EnWG refers to the regulation of grid operation. This part of the Act is subdivided into four chapters: Chapter One focuses on obligations of grid operators, Chapter Two contains provisions about grid connection, Chapter Three comprises provisions regarding grid access, and Chapter Four deals with competences of the regulatory authorities. Further, Chapter 3a contains specific provisions in the context of cross-border electricity lines, and Chapter 3b on the regulation of hydrogen grids.

267. Pursuant to Part Three Chapter One of the EnWG, grid operators are required to operate, expand, and enhance the grid in order to ensure a safe, reliable, and efficient operation (section 11 EnWG). Sections 12 et seq. set out special obligations for transmission grid operators. They have to take all necessary measures to ensure the safety and reliability of the grid (for details, see section 13) and have certain obligations with respect to the expansion of the transmission grid (sections 12a et seqq., see NABEG, IX. below).

268. Provisions on system responsibility with regard to the security of supply are set out in sections 13–13j et seq. EnWG. If the security or reliability of the electricity supply system in the respective control area is endangered or disrupted, the transmission system operators are entitled and obliged to take grid-related measures or market-related measures, section 13 paragraph 1 EnWG. Market-related measures cover in particular, as the practically most important instruments of the TSOs, the use of balancing energy (*Regelenergie*) and redispatch measures according to section 13a EnWG.

269. The framework for the provision of balancing energy is closer defined in section 22 EnWG and in sections 6–9 of the Regulation on Access to Electricity Supply Grids (*StromNZV*) as well as in several detailed decisions of the Federal Network Agency. Balancing energy is procured by the German TSOs via a tender mechanism in the forms frequency containment reserve (FCR, or primary control reserve, *Primärregelleistung, PRL*), frequency containment reserve with automatic activation (aFRR, or secondary control reserve, *Sekundärregelleistung, SRL*), and frequency containment reserve with manual activation (mFRR, or minute reserve, *Minutenreserve, MRL*). The tenders for balancing energy take place via the common platform of the TSOs on www.regelleistung.net. Potential providers of balancing energy products need to provide evidence that they meet the requirements

177. BNetzA, BK6-12-047, available at www.bundesnetzagentur.de.

necessary to ensure security of supply for the provision of the different types of balancing energy, see section 6 paragraph 5 StromNZV. Fulfilment of these requirements is verified in a so-called prequalification procedure, following which a framework agreement with the TSO on the provision of balancing energy will be concluded in order to allow participation in the balancing energy markets.

270. Whereas the provision of balancing energy therefore is organized in balancing energy markets in which potential providers can submit offers, the TSOs are entitled to take measures to adjust active or reactive power generation towards operators of installations for the generation or storage of electrical energy with a rated output of 100 kW or more or which can be remotely controlled. This redispatch regime set out in section 13a EnWG has been amended with effect from 1 October 2021 to cover all types of generation (so-called Redispatch 2.0), whereas previously a separate so-called feed-in management regime applied for installations generating electricity based on renewable energy sources. With exceptions for smaller installations, the principle of cost efficiency is the decisive criterion for the selection decision towards which installation measures are to be taken if redispatch becomes necessary, see section 13 paragraph 1 sentence 2 EnWG. If there are several equally suitable measures, the one that is likely to cause the lowest overall costs for the system as a whole is to be selected. However, for renewable energy installations section 13 paragraphs 1a to 1c EnWG establish a system of imputed costs for the selection decision which shall ensure a feed-in priority of renewable energy installations. The Federal Network Agency has set the so-called minimum factor for installations on basis of renewable energy to 10 in a decision of 30 November 2020.[178] This means that the feed-in priority for renewable energy installations factually continues to exist since a feed-in management towards such installations is only permissible in case a multiple of conventional power installations would need to be dispatched.[179]

271. Redispatch measures need to be appropriately financially compensated between the transmission system operator and the operator of the installation for the generation or storage of electrical energy. The general principle set out, but further explained in, section 13a paragraph 2 EnWG is that the financial compensation shall be appropriate if it places the operator of the installation neither better nor worse off economically than it would have been without the measure. Besides this, one important feature of the new redispatch regime is that the balancing group responsible person has a direct claim for balancing group compensation towards the TSO under section 13a paragraph 1a EnWG.

272. As a further step within the measures available to the TSO, if other instruments are not sufficient to ensure secure system operation it can make use of additional reserves, section 13 paragraph 1 sentence 1 Nr. 3 EnWG. One of these

178. BNetzA, decision of 30 Nov. 2020, PGMF-8116-EnWG § 13j.
179. H. Weyer/T. Iversen, 'Grundzüge des Redispatch 2.0', Recht der Energiewirtschaft (2021): 1 (7).

reserves is the grid reserve (*Netzreserve*) under which the TSOs can contract installations only for the purpose of ensuring system security and reliability, and allowing management of grid bottlenecks and possible restoration of the grid operation in particular. The capacity reserve (*Kapazitätsreserve*) is designed to compensate for power balance deficits resulting from incomplete balancing of supply and demand. The Federal Network Agency carries out a continuous review of the security of supply and available power plants.[180]

273. Chapters Two and Three of Part Three of the EnWG contain regulations about grid connection and grid access. Basically, the EnWG stipulates that the terms and conditions of connection and access to the grid need to be adequate, non-discriminatory, transparent, and not less favourable than those applied by the grid operator in comparable cases either within the vertically integrated undertaking to which it belongs or to affiliated or associated companies.

274. Section 17 EnWG contains a general obligation for grid operators to guarantee grid connection to non-discriminatory conditions.[181] In addition to this fundamental regulation, section 18 EnWG contains a special provision concerning the grid connection of end consumers in low voltage. Pursuant to this provision, respective grid operators need to make the general conditions for grid connection and grid use of end customers public. Moreover, they are required to connect all consumers to the electricity grid according to these conditions.

275. The federal government is entitled to issue ordinances in order to regulate details with respect to grid connection and it has done so for instance by issuing an 'Ordinance on Grid Connection of Power Plants' (*Verordnung zur Regelung des Netzanschlusses von Anlagen zur Erzeugung von elektrischer Energie, Kraftwerks-Netzanschlussverordnung, KraftNAV*). Hence, it has to be kept in mind that regulations concerning grid connection can be found not only in the EnWG but also in additional regulations.

276. Grid connection and grid access can only be denied under certain circumstances. According to section 17 paragraph 2 EnWG and section 20 paragraph 2 sentence 1 EnWG, grid connection and grid access can be denied if granting connection or access is impossible or unacceptable for operational, or other technical or commercial reasons, taking into consideration the statutory aims of the EnWG. For details regarding the regulations about grid connection, see Part I, Chapter 2, §2.

277. Part Three Chapter Four of the EnWG contains regulations regarding the competences of regulatory authorities. Regulatory Authorities are the Federal Network Agency and the Regulatory Authorities of the Federal States (section 54 paragraph 1 EnWG). Whereas the Federal Network Agency is responsible for regulating

---

180. *See* for example Bundesnetzagentur / Bundeskartellamt, Monitoringreportbericht 2021, Dec 2021, available at www.bundesnetzagentur.de.
181. For details, *see* Part I, Ch. 2, s. 2 II.

power supply companies with more than 100,000 customers connected to the electricity network, the Regulatory Authorities of the Federal States are responsible for the regulation of the electricity (and the gas) sector if less than 100,000 customers are connected to the grid. For details regarding the competences and responsibilities of the Federal Network Agency versus those of the Regulatory Authorities of the Federal States, see Introduction, Chapter 4, section 2.

278. Of particular importance with respect to Chapter Four of Part Three of the EnWG are the abuse proceedings which are regulated in sections 30 and 31 EnWG. Pursuant to section 31 paragraph 1 sentence 1 EnWG, persons and entities whose interests are significantly affected by a network operator's behaviour can file an application with the competent regulatory authority for investigation of such behaviour. In the course of such abuse proceedings, the authority might investigate, for instance, whether the behaviour of a network operator is in compliance with the requirements of section 17 EnWG. It is important to note that third parties have the possibility to trigger such proceedings by an application to the regulatory authority. However, it is also important to determine the precise complaint to be brought forward. In principle, the regulatory authority has to decide over the application within two months after the filing of the application.

279. The proceedings pursuant to section 31 EnWG are called 'specific abuse proceedings' (*Besondere Missbrauchsverfahren*) and have to be distinguished from the proceedings pursuant to section 30 EnWG. Section 30 EnWG stipulates that network operators may not abuse their market position, for example, by means of unreasonably constraining other entities directly or indirectly, by means of significantly affecting other entities' competition opportunities without unjustified reason. In contrast to the specific abuse proceedings, proceedings according to section 30 EnWG cannot be initiated by an application by third parties.[182]

280. For the sake of completeness with regard to the competences of regulatory authorities, it should be mentioned that the EnWG also provides for additional proceedings in section 65 EnWG. The regulatory authorities are, for instance, entitled to oblige an entity to refrain from a certain behaviour which contravenes the provisions of the EnWG. These proceedings are ex officio proceedings but can also be initiated by a third party.

E. Energy Supply to End Consumers

281. The EnWG contains regulations about the supply of energy to end consumers in Part Four which comprises sections 36–42a EnWG. In this part of the Act it is explicitly foreseen that energy supply companies must issue general conditions and general prices for electricity supplied to domestic customers in low voltage in areas where they take care of the basic supply of domestic customers public. Moreover, respective supply companies are obliged to supply any domestic customer

---

182. For details *see* Introduction, Ch. 4, s. 2.

with electricity to these conditions. This obligation to provide basic supply (*Grundversorgungspflicht*) is regulated in section 36 paragraph 1 sentence 1 EnWG (see for more details below Chapter 5, § 3).

282. Section 38 EnWG addresses end customers who consume electricity over the energy grid of general supply in low voltage without a supply contract. The EnWG stipulates that the electricity consumed shall be regarded as electricity supplied by the energy supply company which is the basic supplier according to section 36 EnWG. It should be noted that more detailed regulations about the obligation to basic supply are set out in a Regulation on General Conditions for the Universal Supply of Domestic Customers and the Substitute Supply with Electricity from the Low Voltage Grid (*Stromgrundversorgungsverordnung – StromGVV*). As the title implies, the Ordinance also covers the substitute supply in terms of section 38 EnWG.

283. It also merits mentioning that the provisions with regard to energy supply to end consumers of Part Four EnWG also apply to the supply of gas; for more information see below Part II.

F. Plan Approval Procedure/Use of Infrastructure

284. The EnWG furthermore contains regulations about plan approval procedures and the use of infrastructure in Part Five.

285. According to section 43 EnWG, the construction and operation of high voltage overhead power lines with a voltage of at least 110 kV requires a plan approval procedure (*Planfeststellungsverfahren*). This is a special form of licensing procedure. It is characterized by the fact that the official planning approval – if granted – comprises all permits and licensing procedures which are required for the realization of a project (for details see below Chapter 3, § 1). It has to be noted that in addition to this, specific rules regarding the expansion of the transmission grid have been introduced with the NABEG (Grid Expansion Acceleration Act) in 2011 (see section IX. below).

286. Furthermore, the EnWG contains regulations on the use of public streets and infrastructure and about concession agreements. Section 46 paragraph 1 EnWG requires municipalities to make their public infrastructure available by contract for the installation and operation of networks for the supply of energy to end consumers in a non-discriminating way. Section 46 paragraph 2 EnWG refers to concession agreements which are special public law agreements for the installation and operation of entire networks for the public supply ('*Energieversorgungsnetze der allgemeinen Versorgung*' – see the definition in section 3 number 17 EnWG). Importantly, with regard to these agreements the EnWG stipulates a limitation of the term of such concession agreements to twenty years (for details see Chapter 3, § 3).

G. Authorities

287. In Part Seven, the EnWG contains regulations about authorities. In this part, provisions about the Federal Network Agency, the Regulatory Authorities of the Federal States and about the cooperation of the regulatory authorities and the cartel authorities (section 58 EnWG) can be found.

H. Procedure

288. In sections 65–108, the EnWG contains regulations about procedures, competences and procedural rules. Of particular importance are the ex officio proceedings in section 65 EnWG. Pursuant to section 65 EnWG, the regulatory authority is entitled to oblige an entity to refrain from a certain behaviour which contravenes the provisions of the EnWG. However, these proceedings need to be distinguished from the proceedings according to section 30 EnWG and the specific abuse proceedings pursuant to section 31 EnWG (*Besondere Missbrauchsverfahren*); for more information see Introduction, Chapter 4, § 2, IV.

IV. Power Grid Expansion Act (*Energieleitungsausbaugesetz* (*EnLAG*))

289. In order to maintain a high level of energy supply security, an increased investment in networks and an expansion of the transmission networks must be fostered. Expansions of the grid have become necessary *inter alia* because of the increasing transportation distances and the increased use of renewable energy sources.

290. The Power Grid Expansion Act (*Energieleitungsausbaugesetz, EnLAG*) dated 21 August 2009 aims to foster the necessary expansion measures by focusing on certain projects which are listed in an annex to the Act.[183] The necessity and urgent need with regard to these grid expansion measures is decided as per this act with consequences for the relevant planning procedures. Main features of the Act include that the procedure itself is shortened and the right to appeal is limited to one instance.[184] Furthermore, the Power Grid Expansion Act also supports the application of underground cables for several pilot high voltage power transmission lines (380 kV). Grid operators are entitled to add the respective costs to electricity prices.[185]

183. With regard to criticism about the Act and with respect to possible alternative solutions, *see* Holznagel & Nagel, 'Verfahrensbeschleunigung nach dem Energieleitungsausbaugesetz – Verfassungsrechtliche Grenzen und Alternativen', *DVBl.* (2010): 669–677.

184. For a discussion of the EnLAG, *see* Schirner, 'Das Gesetz zur Beschleunigung des Ausbaus der Höchstspannungsnetze', *DVBl.* (2010): 1349.

185. *See* BT-Drs. 16/10491 for information about the draft of the Power Grid Expansion Act and its motivation.

V. Ordinance on Grid Connection of Power Plants (*Kraftwerks-Netzanschlussverordnung* (*KraftNAV*))

291. The Ordinance on Grid Connection of Power Plants (Verordnung zur Regelung des Netzanschlusses von Anlagen zur Erzeugung von elektrischer Energie, Kraftwerks-Netzanschlussverordnung, KraftNAV) dated 26 June 2007 applies to power generation facilities with at least 100 MW nominal capacity and it provides regulations on the procedure for the connection of power plants to high voltage grids. The KraftNAV foresees a certain procedure for the grid connection process. It begins upon receipt of a qualified inquiry which is then followed by the assignment and preparation of a feasibility study, a connection commitment and the conclusion of a grid connection contract. Furthermore, grid operators are obliged to disclose grid load figures, and signalize actual or expected grid congestion.[186]

VI. Regulation on General Conditions for the Grid Connection and Use for the Electricity Supply in Low Voltage (*Niederspannungsanschlussverordnung* (*NAV*))

292. The Regulation on General Conditions for the Grid Connection and Use for the Electricity Supply in Low Voltage (Verordnung über Allgemeine Bedingungen für den Netzanschluss und dessen Nutzung für die Elektrizitätsversorgung in Niederspannung -Niederspannungsanschlussverordnung, NAV) of 1 November 2006 applies to connections to the low voltage electricity grid. In the regulation, details about the grid connection relationship are set out and relevant terms such as connection taker (*Anschlussnehmer*) and connection user (*Anschlussnutzer*) are defined. Furthermore, the NAV provides for clauses which shall guarantee a smooth operation of the grid (see, for instance section 19 NAV). Accordingly, consumer devices must be operated by the connection taker or connection user in such a way that interference with other persons and disruptive effects on the grid operator's or third parties' equipment are excluded.

VII. Regulation on General Conditions for the Universal Supply of Domestic Customers and the Substitute Supply with Electricity from the Low Voltage Grid (*Stromgrundversorgungsverordnung* (*StromGVV*))

293. The Regulation on General Conditions for the Universal Supply of Domestic Customers and the Substitute Supply with Electricity from the Low Voltage Grid contains provisions for the basic supply of energy (*Grundversorgung*) in accordance with section 36 EnWG. It also refers to the substitute supply (*Ersatzversorgung*) in the sense of section 38 EnWG (see for more details below Chapter 3, § 3).

186. Also *see* Ch. 2, § 2, IV.

294. It merits mentioning that the StromGVV is automatically regarded as a contractual agreement between the basic supplier and the domestic customer. Agreements deviating from the regulation generally change the domestic customer into a special customer.

VIII. Ordinance on Incentive Regulation (*Anreizregulierungsverordnung* (*ARegV*))

295. In 2007, the Ordinance on Incentive Regulation (*Verordnung über die Anreizregulierung der Energieversorgungsnetze, Anreizregulierungsverordnung, ARegV*) came into effect. The incentive regulation shall motivate grid operators to an efficient operation of supply grids. It is a governmental regulatory instrument to reduce the charges for the use of electricity (and gas) networks. Incentive regulation does not mean that fixed prices or revenues of a company are set. Instead, a 'revenue cap' limits the maximum revenues for the grid operators in a certain regulation period. The incentive regulation shall allow efficient companies higher returns whereas inefficient companies shall only be allowed lower returns.

296. The Ordinance sets out a certain timeline for incentive regulation. In order to relieve the process of auditing, different timelines are foreseen for electricity and gas. With regard to electricity, in 2012 the audit of costs of 2011 (sample year for the second regulation period) took place for benchmarking in 2013. Grid operators were obliged to submit detailed information and data on capital costs, operating and maintenance costs, structural parameters, etc., which are analysed by the regulatory authority. The revenue cap is determined according to a specific formula which takes into account *inter alia* non-influenceable costs, efficient costs, and inefficient costs that must be reduced. Basically, it can be said that the revenue cap is adjusted (reduced) over the course of time. For extensions and restructuring measures it is possible to apply for investment budgets and further instruments, such as an expansion factor, can be relevant as well.[187]

IX. Grid Expansion Acceleration Act (*Netzausbaubeschleunigungsgesetz Übertragungsnetz* (*NABEG*))

297. In the course of the German *Energiewende* various legislative acts such as the Grid Expansion Acceleration Act (*Netzausbaubeschleunigungsgesetz Übertragungsnetz, NABEG*)[188] were adopted.[189]

---

187. For further information, *see* B. Holznagel/R. Schütz, *Anreizregulierungsrecht*, 2. ed. 2019.
188. Netzausbaubeschleunigungsgesetz Übertragungsnetz of 28 Jul. 2011 (BGBl. I p. 1690).
189. For a discussion of the NABEG, *see* for instance M. Appel, 'Neues Recht für neue Netze – das Regelungsregime zur Beschleunigung des Stromnetzausbaus nach EnWG und NABEG', *UPR* (2011): 406; W. Durner, 'Die "Bundesfachplanung" im NABEG – Dogmatischer Standort, Bindungswirkung, Prüfprogramm und infrastrukturpolitische Modellfunktion', *DVBl.* (2013): 1564; K. J. Grigoleit/C. Weisensee, 'Das neue Planungsrecht für Elektrizitätsnetze', *UPR* (2011): 401; C. Moench/M. Ruttloff, 'Netzausbau in Beschleunigung', *NVwZ* (2011): 1040.

298. The adoption of the NABEG has to be seen in connection with various developments that have made an expansion and reinforcement of the transmission grid necessary: the share of coal and gas fired power plants in electricity generation is decreasing. In addition to this, most nuclear power plants have been shut down in the course of the *Energiewende,* and a shutdown of the few remaining reactors is foreseen by end of 2022. This decrease of power plants is being replaced by a rapid expansion of renewables which may rely on intermittent energy sources such as wind and solar radiation. This also means that electricity generated from an increasing number of facilities (wind, solar power, biomass, etc.) needs to be collected and transported to where it is consumed. This development constituted a challenge for the transmission and distribution grids. Moreover, it has to be noted that fossil and nuclear power plants had traditionally been built in areas where the electricity was consumed (especially in western and southern Germany) whereas renewable energy production has a focus in northern (and eastern) Germany. Accordingly, the average distance between generation and consumption has been increasing and (more) transport over long distances is required. The transmission grid has to cope with these challenges, and the NABEG shall contribute to reach the necessary expansion.[190]

299. The NABEG and the respectively amended sections 12a et seqq. EnWG set out a certain procedure for the expansion of the transmission grid[191]: transmission grid operators have to draft a so-called Scenario Framework (*Szenariorahmen*) biannually which contains a description of the expected developments within at least the next ten years. The framework has to cover at least three possible development scenarios and it has to be approved – after a public consultation – by the Federal Network Agency. Subsequently, the transmission grid operators are obliged to prepare a Grid Development Plan (*Netzentwicklungsplan*) on the basis of the approved Scenario Framework. The Federal Network Agency can demand amendments regarding the Grid Development Plan (section 12c EnWG) and will confirm the plan after respective amendments have been made. The Grid Development Plan will then be submitted as a draft Federal Requirements Plan (*Bundesbedarfsplan*) to the Federal Government at least once in a period of four years. It contains a list of projects which are regarded as necessary and urgent. The German Parliament (*Bundestag*) has to adopt the Federal Requirements Plan in a legislative process. After this has been finalized with the adoption of a *Bundesbedarfsplangesetz,*[192] the Federal Network Agency is the competent authority for planning activities as part of the Federal Sectoral Planning process and for laying down the exact routes for the power lines.

190. With regard to the question whether the planning procedure as foreseen in the NABEG is in accordance with the Constitution, *see* W. Durner, 'Die aktuellen Vorschläge für ein Netzausbaubeschleunigungsgesetz (NABEG) – Bewertung der Verfassungsmäßigkeit und des Beschleunigungspotentials', DVBl. (2011): 853.
191. Information about the grid expansion procedure is available in English at www.netzausbau.de.
192. A first Bundesbedarfsplangesetz has been adopted on 23 Jul. 2013 (BGBl. I S. 2543), and has been amended subsequently with further projects for which the necessity and urgency are determined.

Chapter 2. The Production of Electricity

300. The construction and operation of larger facilities for electricity generation, i.e., power plants, etc., requires a permit under German law. Most facilities (with photovoltaics being an important exception, see below Part V.) require a permit according to the Federal Immissions Control Act (*Bundes-Immissionsschutzgesetz, BImSchG*). The BImSchG and a number of Federal Immission Control Ordinances set out detailed rules about the regime of authorization. In addition to a BImSchG-permit, licences according to German water law might be required as well. For some installations – i.e., in cases when no BImSchG-permit is necessary – a building licence is required. The authorization regime is presented in more detail in Part II, but the following chapter will provide a short overview relevant for the electricity sector.

301. Also in this chapter, the German regulations for grid connection will be explained. The focus in this respect will lie not only on the fundamental provisions of the EnWG, but also on special regulations with respect to the grid connection of power plants and offshore wind turbines. Special regulations apply for the construction of power lines (section 43 EnWG, EnLAG, NABEG), see Chapter 3 below.

§1. Regime of Authorizations

302. Of great importance for electricity generation facilities is the comprehensive licensing regime set out in the Federal Immissions Control Act (*BImSchG*). In general, it can be said that the construction, operation and also (substantial) alterations of many large facilities relevant for the electricity sector require a permit according to the BImSchG (one important exception are offshore wind installations, see Part V Chapter 3 § 1 II.).

303. Section 4 BImSchG stipulates that facilities which are 'on the basis of their constitution or their operation suitable to a special extent to cause harmful environmental influences or to endanger, disadvantage or substantially disturb the general public or the neighbourhood' require a permit according to the Federal Immissions Control Act. In this respect, it is important to note that the Fourth Federal Immissions Control Ordinance (*4. Bundes- Immissionsschutzverordnung, 4. BImSchV*) provides in its annex a detailed list of facilities which fall under the licensing regime.

304. A permit according to the Federal Immissions Control regulations includes – almost all – other permits necessary for the construction and operation of the facility. This feature of the BImSchG permit is called 'concentration effect' and is regulated in section 13 BImSchG.

305. Many different licensing provisions and regulations can be relevant for energy installations. In addition to the BImSchG, the Atomic Energy Act, Water

Law, Nature Protection Law, and Building Law should be mentioned. Also, regulations with regard to health and safety, such as the Code on Product Safety (*Produktsicherheitsgesetz, ProdSG*) and, for instance, the Ninth Statutory Ordinance to the Code on Product Safety (by which the Machinery Directive 2006/42/EC has been implemented into German law) should be mentioned.

306. Last but not least, it should be noted that not only federal law but also the legislation of the Federal States can be relevant for authorization procedures. With regard to Building Law, for instance, provisions issued on state level – such as the building codes (*Bauordnungen*) – set out the applicable rules.

§2. Grid Connection

I. Introduction

307. The following chapter discusses the provisions of the EnWG regarding grid connection. The respective legal provisions can be found in Part Three of the EnWG which is subdivided into four sections: section one refers to obligations of grid operators, section two contains regulations about grid connection, section three refers to grid access, and section four comprises provisions regarding competences of the regulatory authorities. The following chapter focuses on grid connection (sections 17 et seqq. EnWG) and in particular on the obligation of grid operators to connect end consumers, networks as well as generation and storage facilities to the system.

308. Section 17 EnWG contains the general obligation of grid operators to guarantee grid connection to non-discriminatory conditions. This provision will be discussed in detail in the following chapter. In addition to this fundamental rule, there is also a special provision regarding the grid connection of end consumers in low voltage (section 18 EnWG) which refers specifically to grid operators who operate energy grids for the general supply of end consumers. Section 18 EnWG stipulates that these grid operators have to publish general conditions for the grid connection and grid use of end consumers publicly and that they have to connect everyone to the energy grid on these conditions.

309. With regard to grid connection, it is important to note that the Federal Government is entitled to issue ordinances in order to regulate details and conditions of the required grid connection (see section 17 paragraph 3 EnWG). Hence, the EnWG is not the only relevant act with respect to grid connection. Of particular importance in this respect is the Ordinance on Grid Connection of Power Plants (*KraftNAV*, see below IV.) which was issued in 2007.

310. The following section gives an overview over the basic structures and requirements of grid connection in Germany. Special attention lies on the fundamental obligation of grid operators to guarantee grid connection (section 17

EnWG). Also, some particularly interesting issues regarding the grid connection of offshore wind parks and power plants will be presented below III. and IV.

311. The section is divided into four parts. Following this introduction, section II. provides a short overview of section 17 EnWG and the fundamental regulations regarding network connection. Section III. looks at the network connection of offshore wind turbines. In section IV. the grid connection of power plants will be discussed. In this part, the Ordinance on Grid Connection of Power Plants, which was issued in 2007, will be presented.

II. Section 17 Energy Industry Act

312. According to section 17 EnWG, grid operators have to connect end consumers (*Letzverbraucher*), equal or downstream electricity and gas supply networks or lines, charging points for electric vehicles as well as generation and storage facilities to the grid on technical and economic conditions which are reasonable, transparent and non-discriminatory.

313. The grid connection can be refused according to section 17 paragraph 2 EnWG only if the grid operator proves that granting connection to the grid is impossible or unacceptable for operational, or other technical or commercial reasons, taking into consideration the statutory aims of the EnWG (for the aims of the EnWG see above Introduction, Chapter 2, § 5). It is important to note that the burden of proof rests with the grid operator.[193] The assessment whether granting connection to the grid is economically reasonable or not should not be based on the overall economic situation of the grid operator, but on the balance of service and return between the grid operator and the connection taker.[194]

314. If a grid connection is refused, the grid operator has to give reasons for the refusal in text form (see section 17 paragraph 2 sentence 2 EnWG). There is a legal definition for the term 'text form' in section 126b Bürgerliches Gesetzbuch (BGB) which becomes relevant when 'text form' is prescribed by law as it is for instance the case with section 17 paragraph 2 sentence 2 EnWG. Text form means that the declaration must be made on a durable medium suitable for its permanent reproduction. Moreover, the person making the declaration must be named.

315. If the reason for a refusal is capacity shortage, the reasons given for the refusal have to comprise information regarding what needs to be done to realize the grid connection (network expansion, costs, etc.).[195] According to this information the connectee can then agree to bear the necessary costs of a network expansion.

---

193. Hartmann/Wagner in Theobald & Kühling, *Energierecht* (München: C.H. Beck, 112. EL, 2021), EnWG s. 17 Rdnr. 142.
194. Hartmann/Wagner in Theobald & Kühling, *Energierecht* (München: C.H. Beck, 112. EL, 2021), EnWG s. 17 Rdnr. 151.
195. BT-Drs. 613/04, 105.

However, there is no general obligation for the grid operator to provide such information. There is only an obligation to provide such information if the applicant asks for it (see section 17 paragraph 2 sentence 3 EnWG).

III. Grid Connection of Offshore Wind Turbines (Sections 17a et seqq. EnWG)

316. The regulations concerning the grid connection of offshore wind turbines were amended fundamentally in 2011. The former provision, section 17 paragraph 2a EnWG, has been replaced by more detailed regulations in sections 17a et seqq. EnWG.

317. According to these, the grid connections of offshore wind farms are planned in a multistage process which involves the Federal Maritime and Hydrographic Agency (*Bundesamt für Seeschifffahrt und Hydrographie*), the Federal Agency for Nature Conservation (*Bundesamt für Naturschutz*), the Transmission Grid Operators, the coastal Federal States, and the Federal Network Agency.

318. The Transmission Grid Operators are obliged to construct the necessary connections set out in the Offshore Grid Development Plan (section 17d paragraph 1 EnWG). The TSOs have to construct the necessary connections as set out in the Grid Development Plan (*Netzentwicklungsplan*) and the Site Development Plan (*Flächenentwicklungsplan*), see closer below Part V, Chapter 3, §1, II. Detailed obligations of the TSOs that shall provide for a timely construction of the offshore grid connection are set out in section 17d paragraph 2 EnWG. The grid connections for the offshore wind farms are provided by TenneT TSO GmbH and 50Hertz Transmission GmbH; TenneT TSO GmbH is responsible for grid connections in the North Sea and 50 Hertz Transmission GmbH is responsible for those in the Baltic Sea. In 2021, the legislator introduced a separate regime of obligations for the TSOs to construct the grid connection for offshore wind installations within the territorial sea (*Küstenmeer*) in section 17d paragraphs 6 to 9.[196]

319. In case the grid connection is delayed, the operator of offshore wind turbines is entitled to demand a compensation payment from the Transmission System Operator which is calculated on the basis of a detailed regulation set out in section 17e EnWG.

IV. Grid Connection of Power Plants

320. It has already been mentioned above that the Federal Government is entitled to issue ordinances in order to regulate details and conditions of the required grid connection (section 17 paragraph 3 EnWG). Of particular importance in this

---

196. *See* closer T. Kirch, 'Die Netzanbindung von Windenergieanlagen auf See im Küstenmeer', *IR* (2021), 221.

respect is the Ordinance on Grid Connection of Power Plants (*Verordnung zur Regelung des Netzanschlusses von Anlagen zur Erzeugung von elektrischer Energie, Kraftwerks-Netzanschlussverordnung, KraftNAV*).[197]

321. The Ordinance on Grid Connection of Power Plants entered into force on 30 June 2007. Its aim is to ensure greater planning safety for all parties involved in power plant and network investment. The objective of the Ordinance is to relieve power plant investors from procedural obstacles and costs as well as to create greater transparency for all market players.

322. Pursuant to section 1 paragraph 1 KraftNAV, the Ordinance applies to power generation facilities with at least 100 MW nominal capacity and it provides regulations on the procedure for the connection of conventional power plants. Note that special other rules apply for grid connection of offshore wind installations (see above III.) and for other renewable energy facilities (see below Part V.).

323. Pursuant to the KraftNAV, important steps of the grid connection process are *inter alia*:

- grid connection request by the interested party;
- advance payment of 25% of the expected costs for the review;
- review of the grid connection request, feasibility study, etc.;
- connection authorization;
- reservation commitment/payment of the reservation fee;
- negotiation timetable (‘*Verhandlungsfahrplan*’);
- conclusion of a grid connection contract;
- realization timetable (‘*Realisierungsfahrplan*’);
- realization of the grid connection.

324. However, further important steps are:

- conclusion of a grid use contract;
- conclusion of a contract regarding planning and construction of the respective connection lines; and
- further services, maintenance, etc.

325. A party interested in a network connection has to begin the connection process by submitting a network connection request (see section 3 paragraph 2 sentence 1 KraftNAV). The request/application has to contain sufficient data and information to enable the grid operator to carry out the required review of the grid connection. On receipt of the application and the respective documents, the grid operator is required by the KraftNAV to inform the applicant within two weeks not only about the necessary steps to carry out the review but also about the costs for the grid connection review.

197. Kraftwerks-Netzanschlussverordnung of 26 Jun. 2007 (BGBl. I p. 1187).

326. In the next step of the connection procedure, the applicant is obliged to pay an advance payment of 25% of the expected costs for the review of the grid connection request, section 3 paragraph 3 sentence 1 KraftNAV. On receipt of this payment, the grid operator has to start the review of all necessary aspects of the desired grid connection. During this phase of the grid connection procedure, various investigations will be carried out and a feasibility study will be conducted.

327. It is quite important that section 3 paragraph 3 sentence 5 KraftNAV stipulates that the applicant needs to be informed about the results of the review within three months. In case the investigation cannot be completed within three months, the grid operator has to demonstrate that the review procedure is taking longer due to special circumstances. However, in practice the grid operator and the applicant might agree upon a longer timeframe for the review procedure.

328. If the review procedure leads to a positive result, the party applying for the grid connection will be granted authorization to reserve the requested grid connection capacity at the technically most suitable network connection point. At that time, the applicant is required to pay a reservation fee to ensure that the grid connection authorization becomes effective. Pursuant to section 4 paragraph 1 sentence 4 KraftNAV, the reservation fee (EUR 1,000 per MW of network connection capacity) has to be paid within one month after the granting of the authorization.

329. If the grid connection is realized, the reservation fee will be taken into account/set off when the total costs for the connection are calculated. If the grid connection cannot be realized, the reservation fee will be paid back to the applicant provided that the applicant is not responsible for the failure (see section 4 paragraph 1 sentence 5 KraftNAV).[198]

330. According to section 4 paragraph 2 sentence 1 KraftNAV, the grid operator and the applicant are obliged to cooperate in order to ensure an efficient preparation of the grid connection contract. In addition to this general obligation, section 4 paragraph 2 sentence 3 KraftNAV states explicitly that the grid operator and the party to be connected have to draw up a negotiation timetable (so-called *Verhandlungsfahrplan*) as soon as the reservation fee has been paid. The '*Verhandlungsfahrplan*' sets out the required steps towards concluding the grid connection contract.[199] It will comprise a schedule for the preparation of the contract and the connection and further details regarding the conclusion of the grid connection contract. Section 4 paragraph 2 sentence 3 KraftNAV stipulates that the parties shall agree on a grid connection contract within twelve months after the payment of the reservation fee.

331. Together with the conclusion of the network connection contract, an implementation timetable ('*Realisierungsfahrplan*') shall be agreed upon which sets out

198. For details, *see* M. Weise/C. de Wyl/T.C. Hartmann, 'Gescheiterte Großkraftwerksprojekte und Verfall der Reservierungsgebühr', *Energiewirtschaftliche Tagesfragen* (2011): 83.
199. Lück in: Säcker (ed.), *Berliner Kommentar zum Energierecht*, vol. 1, 2nd edn (2010), Anh. s. 17 EnWG, s. 4 KraftNAV para. 5.

the details of the realization of the grid connection. The timetable will comprise specifications regarding time sequence and responsibilities for the setting up of the power plant and the network connection. A schedule for the required planning procedures and the construction phase should be included as well.

332. Apart from the details of the grid connection procedure and the application process, it has to be kept in mind that various permits are required to finalize a power plant project. The most important steps and licences which have to be coordinated are:

- potentially a regional planning procedure (*Raumordnungsverfahren*);
- permit for the power plant according to the Federal Immissions Control Act (BImSchG); possibly an advance notice (*Vorbescheid*) or various partial licences according to the Federal Immissions Control Act;
- plan approval procedure for overhead lines;
- plan approval procedure for a gas pipeline in case of a gas and steam power plant;
- grid connection process.

333. Hence, although the Ordinance on Grid Connection of Power Plants provides some timelines for the grid connection process, coordination with the other permitting processes is necessary. And with respect to the timelines of the Kraft-NAV, it has to be stated that they leave considerable room for negotiations and delay.

334. With regard to a timely realization of the project, it should furthermore be kept in mind that third parties (land owners, neighbours, environmental associations, etc.) might file a claim against a permit and thus can cause a delay.

Chapter 3. Transport

335. The construction of power lines has recently been in the focus of the European and German energy discussions. Particularly the necessity to take off high amounts of energy from renewable sources and the increasing amount of electricity transport within Europe render an expansion of the power lines necessary. The European Commission announced an expansion of the power lines which would make high investments necessary and thus would also affect electricity prices.[200] The German Energy Concept is also concerned with the expansion of power lines, particularly for integrating electricity from offshore wind parks.[201] Also, the topic of storage facilities and hydrogen facilities is receiving more importance also in connection with the expansion of power lines.

336. However, building new power lines as well as reinforcing existing lines often leads to conflicts with various stakeholders affected by the project such as immediate neighbours to construction sites, interested citizens, and associations/interest groups. The legislator has continuously tried to accelerate and streamline the licensing procedures for power grids. In contrast, also the rights of private citizens as well as the so-called higher interests – particularly of environmental protection – need to be taken into account. Such demands are a result in particular from Constitutional as well as European Laws.

337. The German transmission grids are operated by 50Hertz Transmission GmbH[202] (before: Vattenfall Europe Transmission GmbH), Amprion GmbH (before: RWE Transportnetz Strom GmbH), TransnetBW GmbH (before: EnBW Transportnetze AG), and TenneT TSO GmbH[203] (before: E.ON Netz GmbH, transpower stromübertragungs GmbH). The distribution grids are operated by a number of often regional and local grid operators.

338. There is no single German statute governing the construction and operation of power lines. In the EnWG, the legislator has stipulated a plan approval procedure (*Planfeststellungsverfahren*) for certain larger power lines in section 43 EnWG. This particular form of licensing procedure applies in particular for high voltage open wires with a rated voltage of at least 110 kV. One main feature of the plan approval procedure is that it comprises all licences and licensing procedures which would otherwise be necessary for the project. Due to the high relevance of these larger high voltage open wires for the future expansion of the power lines, the scope and content of section 43 EnWG will be explained in more detail in § 1 below.

339. It merits mentioning that the 2009 EnLAG (Power Grid Expansion Act, see Chapter 1, § 2, IV. above) contains special regulations which are relevant for an

---

200. Handelsblatt, *Oettinger: Netzausbau treibt Strompreise* (9 Feb. 2011).
201. Energy Concept, BT-Drs. 17/3049, 4.
202. Since 2010, the Belgium transmission system operator Elia holds the majority shares of 50Hertz.
203. In 2010, transpower, the former subsidiary of E.ON, was sold to the Dutch TenneT under pressure of the European Commission in a Cartel proceeding against E.ON.

expansion of the transmission grid. Furthermore, elaborated rules for the public planning of energy lines for the transmission grid have been introduced with the Grid Expansion Acceleration Act (NABEG, see in more detail above Chapter 1, § 2, IX.). Transmission grid operators have to develop a common scenario (*Szenariorahmen*) every second year with at least three possible development scenarios for at least the next ten years, section 12a EnWG. On this basis, the transmission grid operators also have to develop a Grid Development Plan (*Netzentwicklungsplan*). This Grid Development Plan needs to be confirmed by the Federal Network Agency which can also demand changes within the Grid Development Plan, sections 12b and 12c EnWG. With these rules, the grid expansion – necessary for the German *Energiewende* to happen – finds a much more detailed framework and structural planning. However, there is still concern whether the expansion of the grids is taking place at the pace necessary.

340. For other electric wires, the necessary licences and the procedures which apply differ according to the concrete effects and the location of the planned installation. Typical norms which apply for these installations will briefly be mentioned in § 2.

341. Of high relevance for the operation of power lines is the fact that municipalities have to make their public infrastructure available for the installation and operation of networks for the supply of energy to end consumers (section 46 EnWG). The respective so-called concession agreements are explained in § 3 below.

§1. Electric Wires Subject to a Plan Approval Procedure, Section 43 EnWG

342. A plan approval procedure is necessary for high voltage open wires with a rated voltage of at least 110 kV, high voltage wires for grid connection of offshore wind installations and other wires listed in section 43 paragraph 1 EnWG. The plan approval concentrates all preconditions for the construction and operation in a single procedure. Contrary to the usually 'simply' affirmative or negative decision under administrative law, the plan approval involves elements of planning and forming in the decision. The decision has the function of determining the location of the power line as well as of deciding on the – final – admissibility of the project.[204]

I. Scope of Section 43 EnWG with Regard to Power Lines

343. Construction and operation as well as alterations of the high voltage wires mentioned above require a plan approval by the competent state authority (section 43 EnWG). The open wire power lines subject to the plan approval procedure under section 43 paragraph 1 Nr. 1 EnWG comprise voltages of 110 kV, 220 kV, 380 kV,

204. G. Hermes in: G. Britz, J. Hellermann & G. Hermes, *EnWG, Energiewirtschaftsgesetz* (München: C.H. Beck, 3rd edn., 2015), s. 43 para. 10.

and more. Under Nr. 2, electric wires which shall connect offshore wind power installations via submarine cable and – on land – open wire or earth-laid wire to the next connection point also have to conduct a plan approval procedure (see closer below Part V, Chapter 3, section 1). A plan approval procedure also applies for specific earth-laid high voltage wires listed in the *Bundesbedarfsplan*, see section 43 paragraph 1. Nr. 4 EnWG.

344. The plan approval procedure is necessary for construction and operation as well as changes of these high voltage open wires. The plan approval order (*Planfeststellungsbeschluss*) allowing the high voltage line thus needs to exist before the construction works start.[205] Insignificant changes or extensions may be approved by means of a notification procedure instead of the planning approval procedure, see section 43f EnWG.

345. Legislative changes with the intention to accelerate and simplify the licensing procedure for larger installations are incorporated in the current version of section 43 EnWG. This includes in particular a statute from 2006 for the Acceleration of Planning Procedures for Infrastructure Projects.[206] The aim is to improve the procedural conditions which apply for major infrastructure projects. One main issue for electricity wires is, for instance, the necessary extension of high voltage open wires for the connection of (offshore) wind parks.

346. For the realization of a project falling within the scope of section 43 EnWG as well as for other projects serving the purpose of energy supply, an expropriation may be conducted (see section 45 EnWG and its further conditions). Under section 44b EnWG, the operators may also reach an early possession of the property to guarantee that such projects can practically be realized without substantive delay. In which cases such measures are urgently required by public interests, is subject to controversial court decisions.[207]

II. Plan Approval Procedure and Plan Approval Order

347. Section 43 paragraph 4 EnWG declares sections 72–78 of the Administrative Procedure Act (*Verwaltungsverfahrensgesetz, VwVfG*) applicable on the plan approval procedure. It thus refers to the general rules on such administrative procedures. However, sections 43a–45b of the EnWG contain additional and modifying provisions. The Environmental Impact Assessment procedure is integrated in the plan approval procedure.[208]

---

205. T. Leidinger, *Energieanlagenrecht* (Stuttgart: Richard Boorberg Verlag, 2007), 336.
206. Gesetz zur Beschleunigung von Planungsverfahren für Infrastrukturvorhaben vom 9 Dec. 2006 (BGBl. 2006, I p. 2833).
207. References at M. Maslaton, 'Die Entwicklung des Rechts der Erneuerbaren Energien 2007/2008', *LKV* (2009): 152, 158.
208. G. Hermes in: G. Britz, J. Hellermann & G. Hermes, *EnWG, Energiewirtschaftsgesetz* (München: C.H. Beck, 3rd, edn, 2015), s. 43 para. 30.

348. Although the plan approval order is also an 'administrative act',[209] the plan approval procedure follows another scheme for decisions than the normal conditional administrative norms. The plan approval is an instrument for the planning administration, leaving an area of discretion and formation to include all the diverse interests affected by the project and to bring them into a possibly optimal balance.

349. A major procedural step in the course of the plan approval is the hearing procedure (section 73 VwVfG in conjunction with section 43a EnWG). The applicant needs to hand in the plan (drawings and explanations) to the hearing authority. Due to the aim of providing the authority with the necessary information to decide about the project, the plan needs to facilitate an overall assessment of the project (section 73 paragraph 1 sentence 2 VwVfG). Also, third parties need to be able to raise founded objections against the project on the basis of this documentation. The public hearing shall in particular provide procedural protection for the public affected.[210]

350. The hearing authority needs to initiate that the plan is displayed by the municipalities in which the project has an effect on any third parties. Section 43a number 1 EnWG limits the period in which the municipalities need to display the plan to only two weeks within the receipt of the plan. The hearing authority also asks for official opinions of any administration whose area of competency is affected by the project.

351. Anybody who might be affected in his interests by the project can raise objections until two weeks after the period of display expires (section 73 paragraph 4 VwVfG). The period of display lasts for one month (section 73 paragraph 3 VwVfG). Most importantly, any objections are precluded after the period for objections expires. The precluded third parties neither participate in the further procedure, nor need their material interests be regarded in the course of the proceedings.[211] They are generally also precluded from taking legal action against the project on grounds of objections which have not been raised within the procedure.

352. Generally speaking, the hearing authority will then conduct a hearing according to section 73 paragraph 6 VwVfG. A notification of the authorities, the project proponents and the parties who raised objections needs to take place (the notification of third parties can be replaced by public announcement if many persons are affected). However, section 43a number 3 EnWG allows for waiving the hearing in restricted cases.

353. The planning authority is entitled to take the decision upon the admissibility of the project by issuing the plan approval order (section 74 paragraph 1 VwVfG). According to section 74 paragraph 2 VwVfG, it particularly decides about

209. *Verwaltungsakt*, pursuant to s. 35 Administrative Procedure Act.
210. T. Leidinger, *Energieanlagenrecht* (Stuttgart: Richard Boorberg Verlag, 2007), 340.
211. T. Leidinger, *Energieanlagenrecht* (Stuttgart: Richard Boorberg Verlag, 2007), 341.

the objections on which no agreement could be reached during the course of the hearing procedure. The decision shall impose the obligation upon the project developer to take measures or to erect and maintain structures or facilities necessary for the general good or to avoid detrimental effects on the rights of others (sentence 2). Only where these measures are impracticable or irreconcilable with the project, a monetary compensation needs to be paid to the person affected instead (see below section IV.).

354. The plan approval order needs to be delivered to the project developer and to the people whose objections have been dealt with in particular. It needs to contain an instruction on the right on legal remedies available.

III. Overview on the Material Requirements

355. In the plan approval, the affected public and private concerns need to be taken account of in a balancing decision (section 43 paragraph 3 EnWG). Briefly summarized, the plan approval needs first to determine whether a justification for the concrete planning exists (*Planrechtfertigung*), and as second step it needs to balance all interests in a final process of balancing.

356. The necessity of a project is often determined by the energy companies themselves and may to some extent be verified in the administrative decision. However, in the Act on the Expansion of Power Lines (EnLAG),[212] the Bund decided on the necessity of certain priority projects of grid expansion (see closer above Chapter 1, § 2, IV.). For these projects, the necessity and priority are determined binding by law (see section 1 paragraph 2 sentence 2 EnLAG). As far as a prior examination of the necessity on state level did not take place, both the elements of the necessity as well as of the balancing are incorporated in the final decision.[213]

357. The balancing requires that all relevant interests are determined and incorporated into the balancing process. They may also not be balanced in a way disproportional to their objective relevance.[214] However, this still leaves discretion for the authority in deciding on the project.

358. Which public and private concerns are comprised in this balancing process needs to be determined in relation to the concrete project, in particular its possible effects. The private interests concerned will often be property and personal health, but the balancing is not limited to these interests. In determining the public concerns, the general aims of the EnWG in its section 1 are of high importance.[215]

212. Energieleitungsausbaugesetz of 21 Aug. 2009 (BGBl. I p. 2870). *See* G. Hermes in: G. Britz, J. Hellermann & G. Hermes, *EnWG, Energiewirtschaftsgesetz*, 3rd edn (München: C.H. Beck, 2015), s. 43 para. 6a.
213. T. Leidinger, *Energieanlagenrecht* (Stuttgart: Richard Boorberg Verlag, 2007), 357 et seq.
214. G. Hermes in: G. Britz, J. Hellermann & G. Hermes, *EnWG, Energiewirtschaftsgesetz*, 3rd edn (München: C.H. Beck, 2015), s. 43 para. 25a with references.
215. T. Leidinger, *Energieanlagenrecht* (Stuttgart: Richard Boorberg Verlag, 2007), 346 et seq.

Comprised are also such areas as spatial planning law, construction law, building law, nature protection law, and aviation law.[216] Section 49 EnWG provides for requirements on the technical safety of energy installations.

359. Under Nature Protection Law, interferences may be prohibited in particular with regard to protected species or protected habitats. Of high importance are particularly the Habitats and the Birds Directives of the European Community and their transposition into national law.[217] Also if interferences should be allowed in the specific case, they need to be restricted to the necessary minimum. Any remaining interference of nature and landscape may need to be compensated.

360. The Twenty-sixth Ordinance on the Implementation of the Federal Immission Control Act (Ordinance on Electromagnetic Fields, hereinafter: 26. BImSchV)[218] provides in its annex limit values for the strength of the electric and magnetic fields for the particular frequency range. The main material conditions are stipulated in sections 2 to 4 of the 26. BImSchV. Accordingly, for the protection against harmful effects on the environment, the facilities have to be constructed and operated in a way that the limit values of the annex may not be transgressed. Certain short-term transgressions or transgressions at a small local scale may be neglected.

IV. Legal Effects of the Plan Approval Order

361. The plan approval order generates legal effects which go beyond the mere admission of the project. With regard to the wide scope of the material conditions verified and the formal plan approval procedure, the plan approval results in a so-called concentration effect. This means that the plan approval generally includes all other permits necessary for the project, and concentrates also all the related admission procedures. Section 75 paragraph 1 sentence 1 second clause VwVfG regulates that no other administrative decisions, in particular public law licences, grants, permits, authorizations, agreements or planning approvals are required. Due to the non-restricted wording of this clause, also permits under the Water Law and licences under the Federal Immissions Control Act are comprised. According to the second sentence of section 75 paragraph 1 VwVfG, the plan approval regulates legally binding all relationships under public law between the project developer and those affected by the project. The decision, thus, generates constitutive legal effects for these persons.

---

216. *See* closer G. Hermes in: G. Britz, J. Hellermann & G. Hermes, *EnWG, Energiewirtschaftsgesetz*, 3rd edn (München: C.H. Beck, 2015), s. 43 paras 18a et seqq.
217. G. Hermes in: G. Britz, J. Hellermann & G. Hermes, *EnWG, Energiewirtschaftsgesetz*, 3rd edn (München: C.H. Beck, 2015), s. 43 paras 21 et seqq.
218. Verordnung über elektromagnetische Felder in the version of the publication of 14 Aug. 2013 (BGBl. I p. 3266).

362. Moreover, the plan approval provides a predestination for a later expropriation (*enteignungsrechtliche Vorwirkung*). This is governed by section 45 paragraph 2 EnWG; it is decided in the plan approval upon the admissibility of an expropriation concerning a property necessary for the realization of the project. The plan approval needs to be taken as a basis for the expropriation procedure and it is binding for the authority deciding on the expropriation. This means that this authority does not verify whether the project itself is necessary or lawful. Instead, it has been determined with binding effect that this project contributes to the collective good and generally allows for expropriations. The expropriation authority merely has to control whether the expropriation of the particular property is necessary to realize the project, see section 45 paragraph 1 EnWG.[219]

363. Most important are section 75 VwVfG and section 43e EnWG which provide for a number of far-reaching clauses which shall secure the continuous existence of a plan if it was once approved. In fact, a plan once approved can hardly successfully be challenged in front of court with the aim of cancellation. If legal proceedings are successful, they will often merely lead to a supplementation of the plan or a supplement procedure, taking account of the failures within the plan.

364. Section 75 paragraph 1a VwVfG states that defects in the balancing of the public and private interests affected by the project are only relevant if they were obvious and had an impact on the result of the balancing process. The norm continues that even relevant defects (as well as mistakes in the procedure or form) will lead to a cancellation of the plan approval only if they cannot be removed by a supplementation of the plan or a supplement procedure.

365. If the plan approved once became incontestable, section 75 paragraph 2 VwVfG precludes claims to stop the project, to remove or alter structures or to stop their use. In case of non-foreseeable effects of the project or plan occurring only after the plan became incontestable, the party affected is, however, entitled to demand measures excluding these detrimental effects. However, a claim may be made only for monetary compensation if these measures are impracticable or irreconcilable with the project.

366. The plan becomes invalid in case its realization does not begin within ten years after the plan became incontestable (section 43c number 1 EnWG). This period can be expanded by the competent authority for up to five years.

V. Plan Approval Permit

367. Instead of the plan approval order, a plan approval permit (*Plangenehmigung*) with lower requirements but similar legal effects to the plan approval order can be issued in certain cases. A plan approval permit is possible if rights of others are not or only marginally impaired (section 74 paragraph 6 VwVfG).

---

219. T. Leidinger, *Energieanlagenrecht* (Stuttgart: Richard Boorberg Verlag, 2007), 362.

368. The provisions on the planning approval procedure and thus on the specific public participation in the hearing procedure do not apply for the plan approval permit (section 74 paragraph 6 sentence 2 second clause VwVfG). Under the general provisions of the Administrative Procedure Act, the plan approval permit has the legal effects of the plan approval. The plan approval permit may also form the basis of a later expropriation (section 45 paragraph 1 number 1 EnWG). This needs to be seen together with the possibility to issue a plan approval permit also if rights of third parties are only marginally impaired.

VI. Legal Protection for Parties Affected by the Plan Approval

369. When bringing forward a legal claim against a plan approval, parties affected will need to overcome a number of obstacles. First, any party who did not raise objections against the project in time is precluded from taking further legal steps against the plan according to section 73 paragraph 4 VwVfG. Otherwise, all persons whose rights might have been violated by the decision, in particular parties whose legal interests have been regarded in the balancing decision, are entitled to sue.[220]

370. Second, the rules for maintenance of the plan will often restrict the claim against the plan to a claim towards supplementary measures or a supplementary procedure (section 75 VwVfG). Consequently, to avoid unnecessary cost risks, third parties challenging the project will have to deliberate whether they file an application for cancellation of the plan, or merely for taking supplementary measures.

371. Moreover, section 43e EnWG contains further restrictions in particular for the provisional legal protection. According to its paragraph 1, a rescission action (*Anfechtungsklage*) against a plan approval has no suspensive effect. This is changing the general rule under which objection and rescission action generally have such a suspensive effect (section 80 paragraph 1 VwGO). The general rule under administrative law is therefore that the permit or plan may not be executed for the time it is challenged in front of the courts. Since this rule is changed for actions against a plan approval for electric wires, third parties will have to file an application for reaching provisional legal protection to the administration or to the courts (section 80 paragraph 4 or 5 in conjunction with section 80a VwGO). Section 43e paragraph 1 sentence 2 EnWG further requires generally a filing and reasoning of such an application within one month after the plan approval has been delivered.[221] The administration or the court may order the suspensive effect if a provisional decision on the case reveals that the claim will presumably be successful. All in all, the legal protection against a plan approval contains considerable burdens for parties affected. They need to become active and they need to comply with a number of strict requirements and deadlines.

---

220. T. Leidinger, *Energieanlagenrecht* (Stuttgart: Richard Boorberg Verlag, 2007), 363.
221. If the facts demanding the suspensive effect only occur later, the application may be filed within one month after reaching notice of these facts (s. 43e para. 2 EnWG).

§2. Electric Wires Not Subject to a Plan Approval Procedure

372. Electric wires not within the scope of section 43 EnWG are subject to the material preconditions as well as licensing procedures of the relevant statutes applying in the particular case. A building permit for electric wires for public supply is often not necessary. Most of the *Länder* relieved the wires from the necessity of applying for such a permit.[222] For the related masts, the scope of the construction laws by the *Länder* generally applies. However, due to the far-reaching rules on relieving projects from a permit under the construction law, also the masts will often not require such a permit.[223] Importantly, this does not exempt the wires from the necessary compliance with the material requirements of construction law.

373. Electric wires generally do not require a licence under the Federal Immissions Control Act (BImSchG). However, transformer stations with a high-end voltage of 220 kV or more, including the switch bays, are subject to a licence under the BImSchG, see number 1.8 of Annex 1 to the 4. BImSchV. Indoor transformer stations are excluded from this licensing requirement.

§3. Use of Infrastructure: Concession Agreements

374. Regulations about the use of public streets and infrastructure and about concession agreements are found in section 46 EnWG.

I. Use of Infrastructure

375. Section 46 paragraph 1 EnWG requires municipalities to make their public infrastructure available for the installation and operation of networks for the supply of energy to end customers by contract in a non-discriminatory way. Such agreements have to be distinguished from agreements in the sense of section 46 paragraph 2 EnWG (see next section).

376. Details with respect to the rates are specified in section 48 EnWG and in the Ordinance on Concession Fees (*Konzessionsabgabenverordnung*).

II. Concession Agreements

377. Section 46 paragraph 2 EnWG refers to concession agreements which are special public law agreements for the installation and operation of entire networks

222. *See* for example s. 1 para. 2 no. 3 BauO North Rhine-Westphalia (Nordrhein-Westfalen); s. 1 para. 2 no. 3 LBauO Rhineland-Palatinate (Rheinland-Pfalz). For a further list *see* H. Loibl & T. Becker in: C. Germer & H. Loibl, *Energierecht, Handbuch,* 2nd edn (Berlin: Erich Schmidt Verlag, 2007), 549.
223. H. Loibl & T. Becker in: C. Germer & H. Loibl, *Energierecht, Handbuch,* 2nd edn (Berlin: Erich Schmidt Verlag, 2007), 549 et seq.

for the public energy supply (*'Energieversorgungsnetze der allgemeinen Versorgung'* – see the definition in section 3 number 17 EnWG). In concession agreements, municipalities grant grid companies a concession to use public property. At the same time, the concessionaire is required to lay and operate the local energy distribution networks.

378. In order to enable competition also with regard to energy grids and an occasional change of concessionaire, section 46 paragraph 2 EnWG sets the term for such concession agreements to a maximum of twenty years. Since the time limit was originally introduced in 1990, many terms expired around 2010 or in the following few years. Because of the practical relevance, the issue has been the subject of extensive discussions from that time onwards.[224]

379. The EnWG provides a few regulations concerning the procedures and formal requirements which have to be followed when a concession agreement is about to expire. At least two years before a concession agreement expires, for instance, the expiry has to be published in the – electronic – Federal Gazette (*Bundesanzeiger*), section 46 paragraph 3 EnWG. In case the network supplies more than 100,000 customers in a municipality, the expiry has to be published in the Official Journal of the EU. These regulations are meant to enable interested energy suppliers to submit an offer and to obtain the concession.

380. With respect to formal requirements, it should be noted that the formal German public procurement law does not have to be followed when concluding (new) concession agreements. However, it is important to make sure that all interested parties are treated equally and in a non-discriminatory way. Furthermore, it is crucial to complete the procedures in a transparent way.

381. Across Germany, municipalities have been considering, and in quite some cases conducted a remunicipalization (*Rekommunalisierung*) of the networks (see above Introduction, Chapter 5, § 3). The question whether or not a remunicipalization is the favoured option is usually assessed by means of a feasibility study before publishing the expiry of the respective concession agreement.

382. On 15 December 2010, the Federal Cartel Office and the Federal Network Agency published a joint guideline for new electricity and gas concession agreements (*Gemeinsamer Leitfaden von Bundeskartellamt und Bundesnetzagentur zur*

224. *See*, for instance, Theobald, 'Auslaufende Konzessionsverträge Strom und Gas: Was ist seites der Kommunen zu tun?', *DÖV* (2009): 356; Thomale & Kießling, 'Anforderungen an den (Neu-) Abschluss von Konzessionsverträgen', *N&R* 4 (2008): 166; Byok, 'Neuabschluss und Verlängerung von Konzessionsverträgen –Anforderungen an Bekanntmachung und Durchführung desAuswahlverfahrens', *RdE* (2008): 268; Reck, 'Pflichten der Kommunen bei auslaufenden Konzessionsverträgen in der Energieversorgung', *KommJur* (2009): 401.

Vergabe von Strom- und Gaskonzessionen und zum Wechsel des Konzessionsnehmers).[225] Although the guideline is not legally binding, it sets out various details *inter alia* with regard to the procedure which has to be followed when a new concession agreement is concluded.

383. Pursuant to the joint guideline, German and European antitrust law is applicable as municipalities engage in commercial activities when granting concessions. Any abuse of the dominant position which municipalities hold in the local market must be prevented. The joint guideline gives examples for activities which are considered an abuse of a dominant position:

(a) granting a concession without prior publication according to section 46 paragraph 3 EnWG;
(b) demanding illegal return services of payments which are not in accordance with the Ordinance on Concession Fees;
(c) influencing sale activities of bidders or the prior concessionaire;
(d) not providing all interested parties with the necessary information about the network (level playing field);
(e) favouring individual bidders without substantive reason;
(f) etc.

384. With regard to expiring concession agreements, a certain time plan should be followed in order to enable all necessary assessments and to ensure that the required procedures are observed.[226]

385. A very important issue is the fact that the operator of an electricity or gas network is required to transfer the ownership of the network to the new company after the concession agreement has expired, see section 46 paragraph 2 sentence 2 EnWG. According to the EnWG as amended in 1998, there was only an obligation to relinquish ('*überlassen*') the network. This led to a discussion about whether the ownership had to be transferred or not.[227] However, this issue has meanwhile been clarified by an amendment of section 46 EnWG in 2011. The wording of the provision now explicitly requires a transfer of the ownership ('*übereignen*').

III. Concession Fees

386. Regulations on concession fees can be found in section 48 EnWG and also in the Ordinance on Concession Fees for Electricity and Gas (*Verordnung über Konzessionsabgaben für Strom und Gas, Konzessionsabgabenverordnung, KAV*). The Ordinance was issued in 1992 and it is based on an authorization pursuant to

225. Available via the webpage www.bundesnetzagentur.de. A second updated edition of the guideline has been published 21 May 2015.
226. An example is given by Theobald, 'Auslaufende Konzessionsverträge Strom und Gas: Was ist seitens der Kommunen zu tun?', *DÖV* (2009): 363.
227. *See*, for instance, BGH, 29 Sep. 2009, EnZR 14/08 and EnZR 15/08.

the EnWG.[228] The Ordinance lays down rules about the levying of concession fees and regulates the assessment and the permissible amounts of concession fees.

387. Section 48 paragraph 2 sentence 2 EnWG stipulates that maximum fees have to be determined in cents per kWh (and not any more in form of a percentage of the energy supply companies' gross revenue).[229] Accordingly, section 2 paragraph 2 KAV sets out maximum fees per kWh for supplying tariff customers and section 2 paragraph 3 KAV contains maximum fees per kWh for supplying special-contract customers (*Sondervertragskunden*). Hence, it becomes clear that the ordinance differentiates between tariff and special-contract customers. The maximum concession fee for tariff customers is many times higher than the fee that may be charged to special-contract customers.

228. *See* s. 48 para. 2 EnWG.

229. For more information in English, *see* C. Corino, *Energy Law in Germany and Its Foundations in International and European Law* (München: C.H. Beck, 2003), 92; also *see* Theobald in: Danner & Theobald, *Energierecht* (München: C.H. Beck, 79. Ergänzungslieferung, 2013), s. 48 EnWG Rdnr. 25.

Chapter 4. Distribution

388. Traditionally, the electricity sector can be subdivided into four different stages: generation, transmission, distribution, and supply. Whereas competition is fostered with regard to the production of electricity (generation), there is nowadays little doubt that the high voltage transport of electricity over long distances in a transmission grid has to be considered a natural monopoly. The same applies to distribution networks which aim at transporting electricity at low voltages to final customers.

389. The EnWG sets out various regulations not only concerning transmission networks but also distribution grids. These have to be seen – as the whole EnWG – against the background of European legislation with regard to unbundling, etc.

390. The EnWG distinguishes between various different definitions with regard to grids and grid operators (see section 3 EnWG) and sets out regulations about obligations of grid operators in sections 11 et seqq. EnWG.

391. With respect to distribution networks, section 14 EnWG explicitly sets out responsibilities and rules for distribution network operators. Many regulations apply to transmission system operators and to distribution system operators alike (see in particular the references in section 14 paragraph 1 EnWG to sections 12, 13 to 13c EnWG) such as, for instance, the obligation to ensure reliable and secure supply of electricity. However, pursuant to section 14 EnWG there are few special requirements with respect to distribution grid operators. Sections 7 et seq. set out specific rules regarding the unbundling of distribution network operators.

Chapter 5. Consumption

392. The following chapter discusses legal provisions governing the relations between electric supply companies and their customers as well as grid operators and their customers, particularly domestic customers. Liberalization of the energy markets had an enormous impact on these relationships.

393. Before, the relation between electric companies and their 'tariff customers' was governed by the Regulation on General Conditions for the Electricity Supply of Tariff Customers (*Verordnung über Allgemeine Bedingungen für die Elektrizitätsversorgung von Tarifkunden*, hereinafter: AVBEltV). Up to the amendment of the EnWG in 2005, the underlying basis for this regulation has been the duty under section 10 of the EnWG of 1998. Accordingly, energy companies generally needed to publish general conditions and tariffs for the supply in low voltage and to connect and supply everyone to these conditions and tariffs. This applied for areas in which the energy companies were responsible for the general supply of end customers.

394. With the duty to unbundle power supply and grid operation, liberalization rendered necessary to reflect this approach also in the relation towards the customers.[230] Based on provisions in the new EnWG, the government decided on four new regulations for the grid connection and use as well as for universal service obligations in the electricity as well as in the gas sector. In the electricity sector, these regulations are the Regulation on General Conditions for the Universal Supply of Domestic Customers and the Substitute Supply with Electricity from the Low Voltage Grid (*Stromgrundversorgungsverordnung*, hereinafter: StromGVV)[231] and the Regulation on General Conditions for the Grid Connection and Use for the Electricity Supply in Low Voltage (*Niederspannungsanschlussverordnung*, hereinafter: NAV).[232]

§1. Domestic Customers and Special Customers

395. For the further explanation of these regulations and their effects on the energy supply contracts, the basic distinction between domestic and special customers needs to be explained.

396. Domestic customers are all end consumers who buy energy predominantly for their own consumption in the household, or for their own consumption not

230. C. De Wyl, J. Eder & T.C. Hartmann, *Netzanschluss- und Grundversorgungsverordnungen* (Frankfurt a.M.: VWEW Energieverlag, 2008), 1; F.R. Groß, 'Die neuen Netzanschluss- und Grundversorgung sverordnungen im Strom- und Gasbereich', *NJW* (2007): 1030, 1031.

231. Verordnung über Allgemeine Bedingungen für die Grundversorgung von Haushaltskunden und die Ersatzversorgung mit Elektrizität aus dem Niederspannungsnetz, Stromgrundversorgungsverordnung of 26 Oct. 2006 (BGBl. I p. 2391).

232. Verordnung über Allgemeine Bedingungen für den Netzanschluss und dessen Nutzung für die Elektrizitätsversorgung in Niederspannung, Niederspannungsanschlussverordnung of 1 Nov. 2006 (BGBl. I p. 2477).

exceeding a yearly consumption of 10,000 kWh for professional, agricultural or commercial purposes (section 3 number 22 EnWG). Thus, the term 'domestic customer' is not restricted to the use of the energy for the household. Instead, other ends are also included in case the yearly consumption of 10,000 kWh is not exceeded. Domestic customers are, generally speaking, only interested in a full supply of their unsteady and hardly predictable demand. The energy supply generally takes place on basis of an all-inclusive-contract being a standard form contract by the supplier.[233]

397. Without a positive legal definition of special customers, they basically need to be defined negatively in contrast to domestic customers. Importantly, the universal service obligation in section 36 EnWG does not apply to special customers. However, provisions of the StromGVV/NAV are often included also in the energy supply contracts with special customers by an explicit reference to these provisions.

398. Energy supply contracts are treated as purchase contracts under German civil law.[234] Consequently, the general provisions of sections 433 et seqq. of the Civil Law Code (BGB) apply to these contracts.

§2. Grid Connection and Use in Low Voltage

I. Section 18 EnWG

399. The duty to connect end consumers to the grid (section 18 EnWG) is a special rule for the grid connection of end consumers in low voltage.[235] It supplements the general obligation to guarantee grid connection to non-discriminative conditions in section 17 EnWG (see above Chapter 2, section 2). According to section 18 paragraph 1 EnWG, grid operators, who operate energy grids for the general supply of end consumers, need to make public general conditions for the grid connection and grid use of end consumers in low voltage or low pressure. They also have to connect everyone to their energy grid on these conditions and to allow for the use of the connection for the offtake of energy.

II. NAV

400. The Regulation on General Conditions for the Grid Connection and Use for the Electricity Supply in Low Voltage (*Niederspannungsanschlussverordnung, NAV*) stipulates in more detail the rules for the grid connection and use. Unlike

233. Christiane Nill-Theobald & Christian Theobald, *Grundzüge des Energiewirtschaftsrechts*, 3rd edn (München: C.H. Beck, 2013), 136 et. seq.
234. Christiane Nill-Theobald & Christian Theobald, *Grundzüge des Energiewirtschaftsrechts*, 3rd edn (München: C.H. Beck, 2013), 155 with further references.
235. C. De Wyl, J. Eder & T.C. Hartmann, *Netzanschluss- und Grundversorgungsverordnungen* (Frankfurt a.M.: VWEW Energieverlag, 2008), 31.

under the former AVBEltV, the rules in section 18 EnWG and in particularly in the NAV distinguish between the grid connection and the use of this connection.

401. The connection taker (*Anschlussnehmer*) is defined in section 1 paragraph 2 NAV. Connection taker is anyone (in the sense of section 18 paragraph 1 sentence 1 EnWG) on behalf of whom a property or building is connected to the low voltage grid. Moreover, every owner or leaseholder (*Erbbauberechtigter*) of a property or building which is connected to the low voltage grid is also regarded as a connection taker. The relationship between grid operator and connection taker comprehends the connection of the electrical installation via the grid connection as well as its operation (section 2 paragraph 1 NAV).

402. Second, the connection user (*Anschlussnutzer*) is any end consumer using a connection to the low voltage grid for the offtake of electricity. In particular, any lessee, though not being connection taker, is a connection user.[236] This relationship comprises the right to use the grid connection for the offtake of electricity (section 3 paragraph 1 sentence 1 NAV). The second sentence of this norm highlights that the use of the connection does neither cover the supply of the connection user with electricity, nor the access to the electricity grid (according to section 20 EnWG). Most often, this latter relationship comes into existence by the conclusion of a contract at the latest at the time of the first take-off of electricity. It can also come into existence automatically, i.e., without the conclusion of contract (see closer below section 3).

403. In both relationships of grid connection and use, the provisions of the NAV are automatically part of the relationship between grid operator and connection taker, respectively connection user (section 1 paragraph 1 sentence 2 NAV). The relationship of grid connection is governed by the second part of the NAV, the use of this connection by the third part. Part Four provides for a number of common provisions.

404. With regard to the grid connection relationship, the NAV determines the location of the grid connection (section 5 NAV). The grid connection starts at the branch-off point of the low voltage grid and ends with the house connection fuse. In the following, the NAV regulates in particular how the grid connection is established and who needs to bear the costs. Generally speaking, the grid operator is responsible for establishing the grid connection (section 6 NAV) and will demand the costs from the connection taker (section 9 NAV) by making use of lump sum payments. Moreover, the grid operator may demand a partial payment of the building costs for the establishment or enforcement of the local distribution facilities, including low voltage transformer stations. These partial payments may at most sum up to 50% of these costs (section 11 paragraph 1 sentence 2 NAV).

---

236. C. De Wyl, J. Eder & T.C. Hartmann, *Netzanschluss- und Grundversorgungsverordnungen* (Frankfurt a.M.: VWEW Energieverlag, 2008), 40.

405. The NAV also provides for clauses which shall support grid operators in their task of operating the grids. For example, connection takers (if property owners) are under section 12 NAV – subject to further conditions and exceptions – obliged to allow for the installation and relocation of cables or other installations across their properties free of charge. The installations need to serve purposes of the local energy supply via the low voltage or the medium voltage grid. As a consequence of this toleration, the property owner may demand a relocation of the installation on costs of the grid operator if it becomes unacceptable at the old place (section 12 paragraph 3 NAV).[237]

406. In the relationship of using the grid connection, the grid operator generally needs to provide for the use to the designated extent at any time (section 16 NAV). Most important are the rules on the limitation of liability for grid operators in section 18 NAV. Liability is restricted to (at least) gross negligence in some cases of financial damages (whereby gross negligence, however, may be presumed to exist). Moreover, certain maximum limits of liability are provided.

§3. Universal Services

407. The duty of energy supply companies to supply domestic customers is regulated in section 36 EnWG and in the Regulation on General Conditions for the Universal Supply of Domestic Customers and the Substitute Supply with Electricity from the Low Voltage Grid (*Stromgrundversorgungsverordnung*, *StromGVV*). The substitute supply (*Ersatzversorgung*) set forth in section 38 EnWG has also been included in the StromGVV and will therefore also briefly be treated in this section.

I. Sections 36 and 38 EnWG

408. Energy supply companies need to make public general conditions and general prices for the supply of domestic customers in low voltage or low pressure for grid areas in which they are responsible for the basic supply (*Grundversorgung*) of domestic customers (section 36 paragraph 1 EnWG). They are also obliged to supply any domestic customer to these conditions and prices with energy. An exception of these duties is provided for if the supply is not economically reasonable for the energy company.

409. The second paragraph of section 36 EnWG defines which energy supply company is the basic supplier (*Grundversorger*). Accordingly, the basic supplier is the energy supply company which supplies most of the domestic customers in a grid area of general supply. The basic supplier is therefore determined on an empirical basis. The energy supply company being basic supplier is determined every three years by the grid operator of the grid of general supply.

---

237. *See* on contrast s. 1023 BGB.

410. The term of 'energy supply grids of general supply' is defined in section 3 number 17 EnWG. However, how to determine the scope of an area of the grid is not at all regulated precisely and can lead to controversies in the particular case. The concession can at least be taken as an indication for determining the relevant grid area.[238]

411. The substitute supply in section 38 EnWG shall clarify what happens if an end consumer uses energy over the energy grid of general supply in low voltage without any energy supply contract. In these cases, the energy consumed is regarded as energy supplied by the basic supplier (in terms of section 36 paragraph 1 EnWG).

II. StromGVV

412. The StromGVV contains provisions for the basic supply in accordance with section 36 EnWG and for the substitute supply as set forth in section 38 EnWG. Both domestic customers as well as end consumers in the case of substitute supply are defined as customers within the terms of the regulation (section 1 paragraph 2 StromGVV).

413. Like the NAV, the StromGVV is automatically regarded as contractual agreement between the parties. Under the StromGVV, this concerns the basic supplier and the domestic customer (section 1 paragraph 1 sentence 2 StromGVV). Agreements deviating from the StromGVV generally change the domestic customer into a special customer. However, amendments are only allowed as far as the content of the StromGVV is not coercive.[239]

414. At first, section 2 StromGVV gives requirements for the conclusion of the contract between the basic supplier and the customer. The basic supply contract (*Grundversorgungsvertrag*) shall be concluded in text form. That means that the declaration must be made in a document or in another manner suitable for its permanent reproduction in writing in which the person making the declaration is named (section 126b Civil Law Code, BGB). If the contract has been concluded in another way, the basic supplier needs to confirm the conclusion of the contract in text form. The basic supplier needs to provide any new customer with the general conditions before the conclusion of the contract (section 2 paragraph 4 StromGVV).

415. The customer is generally obliged to supply his complete demand of electricity over the grid from the basic supplier during the duration of the basic supply

238. C. De Wyl, J. Eder & T.C. Hartmann, *Netzanschluss- und Grundversorgungsverordnungen* (Frankfurt a.M.: VWEW Energieverlag, 2008), 18.
239. C. De Wyl, J. Eder & T.C. Hartmann, *Netzanschluss- und Grundversorgungsverordnungen* (Frankfurt a.M.: VWEW Energieverlag, 2008), 22; Christiane Nill-Theobald & Christian Theobald, *Grundzüge des Energiewirtschaftsrechts*, 3rd edn (München: C.H. Beck, 2013), 150 et seq.

contract (section 4 StromGVV).[240] In general, the basic supplier is obliged to supply the electricity demand of the customer for the duration of the supply contract and up to the extent envisaged in the contract at any time (section 6 StromGVV). Paragraph 3 of this clause relieves the basic supplier from its duty of supply in particular in cases of an interruption due to failures in the grid operation.

416. In its Part Three, the StromGVV contains provisions on measuring devices and the admission to the property of the customer. Part Four is concerned with the accounting of the electricity supply. Section 17 paragraph 1 StromGVV provides that any bills fall due at the earliest two weeks after receipt of the demand bill. Any objections against the bills, however, justify a delay or refusal of payment only under certain conditions. Also, the customer may charge up against claims of the basic supplier only with undisputed or legally binding counterclaims (section 17 paragraph 3 StromGVV).

417. The supply of the customer may only be interrupted on certain grounds (section 19 StromGVV). In the important case of non-fulfilment of payment obligations, the basic supplier may only four weeks after announcement cut off the basic supply. The customer also needs to have outstanding payment obligations of at least EUR 100 (whereas the minimum amount may be higher depending on the specific customer). Disputes on the appropriateness of prices may not justify for an interruption.[241]

418. Importantly, section 20 StromGVV gives the right to terminate the basic supply contract with a period of only two weeks. The termination needs to be in text form, and the basic supplier shall confirm the termination without delay. Any fees for the termination of the contract or the change of supplier may not be demanded. This section shall thus safeguard for an easy change of supplier – a cornerstone for competition in the energy markets.

419. Section 3 StromGVV declares a number of provisions dealing with basic supply applicable also for the substitute supply. In effect, this assures that also cases of energy supply for which no contractual agreement seems to exist can be dealt with in similar ways as if an agreement with the basic supplier existed.

§4. Standard Business Terms

420. The law on the general terms and conditions plays an important role for the protection of customers in case standard form contracts are used. The relevant provisions can be found in sections 305 et seqq. of the Civil Law Code (BGB).

240. Excluded is for example the consumption from own installations for the generation of electricity from renewable sources.
241. F.R. Groß, 'Die neuen Netzanschluss- und Grundversorgungsverordnungen im Strom- und Gasbereich', *NJW* (2007): 1030, 1034.

421. Section 305 BGB governs which clauses are standard business terms and therefore subject to an intensified legal review. Section 305c BGB prohibits any surprising and ambiguous clauses. General provisions securing the reasonableness of standard business terms are provided in section 307 BGB. Sections 308 and 309 BGB provide for more specific contents being regarded as unreasonable. According to section 307 paragraph 1 BGB, provisions in standard business terms are ineffective if, contrary to the requirement of good faith, they unreasonably disadvantage the other party to the contract. Such an unreasonable disadvantage may also arise from the provision not being clear and comprehensible.

422. Section 310 paragraph 2 BGB might exclude contracts for the supply of electricity, gas, and district heating for special customers to some extent from the application of sections 308 and 309 BGB. However, the general provision of section 307 BGB still may apply and provide courts with the possibility of an intensified legal review of standard business terms.

§5. Measuring

423. The installation and operation of metering points has traditionally been the task of the grid operators. In the process of liberalization, measuring has been opened up by allowing other market participants to operate metering points. Also, the regulatory regime seeks to equip at least certain metering points with modern metering devices and intelligent metering systems.

424. Initially, the relevant rules have been provided in sections 21b to 21i EnWG and a Measuring Access Regulation (*Messzugangsverordnung, MessZV*) of 2008 which are now out of force. Section 21b paragraph 1 EnWG in the former version already allowed the operation of metering points as well as the measuring of the energy supplied to be fulfilled by third persons under further conditions.

425. In 2016, the Metering Point Operation Act (*Messstellenbetriebsgesetz, MsbG*)[242] came into force. This Act is building on the free right to decide for a metering point operator, but even more it seeks to create a framework for the introduction of modern metering devices and intelligent metering systems. A modern metering device is a metering device that reflects the actual electricity consumption and the actual time of use and can be securely integrated into a communication network via a Smart-Meter-Gateway (section 2 Nr. 15 MsbG). An intelligent metering system is a modern metering device integrated into a communication network via a Smart-Meter-Gateway, the latter being the communication unit of the metering device (see section 2 Nr. 7 and 19 MsbG). With the Metering Point Operation Act, the roll out of these intelligent metering systems has been started.

426. The metering point operation as a general rule is the task of the basic metering point operator (*grundzuständiger Messstellenbetreiber*), section 3 paragraph 1

242. Messstellenbetriebsgesetz of 29 Aug. 2016 (BGBl. I p. 2034).

MsbG. This basic metering point operator is the grid operator, who however can transfer the basic responsibility for the metering point operation to another company pursuant to section 43 MsbG. Also, the Metering Point Operation Act upholds the principle that a third person, a competitive metering point operator, can be chosen for the metering point operation. Sections 5 and 6 MsbG provide how the connection user (or the connection taker) can exercise this right.

427. The basic meter point operator is responsible to roll out intelligent metering systems in particular for final consumers with a relatively high consumption of above 6.000 kWh per year and for operators of renewable energy and cogeneration installations with an installed capacity above 7 kW, section 29 paragraph 1 MsbG. The obligations to use intelligent metering systems are conditioned to being technically possible and economically justifiable, whereas sections 30 and 31 MsbG provide further details. Germany therefore chose a model for roll out of intelligent metering systems based on a cost-benefit analysis. According to section 30 sentence 1 MsbG, the equipment of metering points with an intelligent metering system is technically possible if at least three independent companies offer intelligent metering systems on the market. This is analysed by the Federal Office for Information Security (*Bundesamt für Sicherheit in der Informationstechnik*) and published on its webpage.[243] Certification of the third company offering intelligent metering systems has been granted in December 2019, so that the roll out could be started in February 2020.[244] The roll out of intelligent metering systems on a broader scale therefore has been started.[245]

§6. Energy Storage

428. Due to the increasing relevance of intermittent renewable energy sources in the electricity system (see closer below Part V), the topic of energy storage becomes more and more important. Together with the required expansion of the energy grids, demand side management, and the use of flexible power plants, energy storage will play a role in integrating renewable energies into the system.

429. For the operation of an energy storage installation and in particular in respect of possible exemptions from grid fees, the question of how the process of energy storage is treated in legal terms is of high importance. In the jurisdiction of the Federal Court of Justice (BGH), the offtake of electricity from the grid for the pump procedure within a pumped storage hydro power station is regarded as 'final consumption' of this electricity. As a consequence, the BGH is of the opinion that a duty to pay grid fees in principal also exists if electricity is taken from the grid for

243. www.bsi.bund.de.

244. A. Bartsch in: J.P. Schneider & C. Theobald, *Recht der Energiewirtschaft*, 5th edn (München: C.H. Beck, 2021), § 18 para. 21.

245. For delays in the roll out also caused by court proceedings *see* the statements of the Federal Government in BT-Drs. 19/29925 of 19 May 2021 and Bundesnetzagentur / Bundeskartellamt, *Monitoringreport 2021*, Dec 2021, p. 33 et seq., available at www.bundesnetzagentur.de.

the operation of the pumps in a pumped storage hydro power station.[246] In the legal literature, some authors criticize this approach, in particular taking account of the overall process in which the offtake of the electricity merely aims at a later reconversion and feed-in of the stored electricity into the energy grids.[247] Indeed, following the view of the Federal Court of Justice, grid fees in principle would have to be paid twice – first for the offtake of electricity for the energy storage installation and second when the stored electricity is (after reconversion) delivered to a final consumer via the electricity grids.

430. However, to ease the consequences of the judgment of the Federal Court of Justice and to enable the use of storage facilities, the legislator created far-reaching (partly) exemptions for the electricity take-off for energy storage installations with regard to grid fees and other charges and levies, in particular for the EEG surcharge which so far had to be paid to allocate the overall costs for the support of renewable energy. According to section 118 paragraph 6 sentence 1 EnWG, storage installations newly constructed after 31 December 2008 and going into operation within fifteen years from 4 August 2011 may be exempted from grid fees for the electricity consumed from the grid for a period of twenty years.[248] The exemption is only granted if the electric energy for storage is taken off the transmission or distribution grid in an electrical, chemical, mechanical or physical electricity storage and if the electric energy which is reconverted for the output is – with timely delay – fed into the same grid, section 118 paragraph 6 sentence 3 EnWG. Also, an exemption from grid fees for duration of ten years may be available for pumped storage hydro power installations in case their pump capacity, turbine output or storable energy amount has been increased by certain degrees after 4 August 2011.[249] Sentences 7 and 8 make clear that the exemption in section 118 paragraph 6 sentence 1 EnWG also applies for certain power-to-gas installations.[250] The provisions in section 61l EEG seek to avoid a double payment of the EEG surcharge in case of using a storage installation (see for more details on the EEG surcharge and the changes in financing the EEG support below Part V).

431. While these clauses allow for a (partly) exemption from grid fees and EEG surcharge, this does not in itself make the use of storage installations economical. Support for first storage projects using new storage technologies often has been and may be available by research and development funds.[251] Also due to cost decreases in energy storage, more storage installations have been used in the German market at least in specific applications.

246. BGH NVwZ-RR 2010, 431; OLG Düsseldorf, ZNER 2008, 380.
247. *Krebs*, RdE 2012, 19; *Salje*, EEG, 6. Ed. 2012, s. 37 para. 60. *See also Wieser*, ZUR 2011, 240 (243).
248. Closer *Lehnert/Vollprecht*, ZNER 2012, 356 (360 et seq.).
249. Section 118 para. 6 sentence 2 EnWG.
250. *See* BT-Drs. 17/6365, p. 14.
251. *See* as example a common press release of Federal Ministry of Economics and Technology, Federal Ministry for the Environment and Federal Ministry of Education and Research, 'BMWi, BMU und BMBF geben Startschuss für Leuchtturmprojekte der Speicherinitiative' of 11 Jul. 2012.

432. Several of the provisions on energy storage also take account of production of hydrogen, in particular of producing hydrogen from renewable energy sources in an electrolysis. In 2020, the German government published the National Hydrogen Strategy. Whereas so far hydrogen projects have been largely supported by R&D support, the ambition of the National Hydrogen Strategy is to enable a market ramp up for hydrogen generation, with a focus of hydrogen based on renewable energy sources.[252]

252. Bundesregierung, Die Nationale Wasserstoffstrategie, Juni 2020.

Part II. Regulatory Framework Concerning Gas

433. Chapter 1 of this part provides an overview of the importance of the gas sector in the energy supply of Germany. Chapter 2 is dedicated to gas production and elaborates on the central statute governing the installation and operation of larger gas fired plants: the Federal Immissions Control Act. This statute also applies to large power plants that run on a different energy source (with the exception of nuclear power plants). The explanations provided in Chapter 2 are equally important and applicable to these power plants. The third chapter on exploitation briefly touches upon the Federal Mining Statute, which is explained in more detail in Part IV, Chapter 2, section 2. Chapter 4 is dedicated to the topic of transport and pays special attention to the rules on the construction of large gas pipelines. The central rules on competition in the gas markets are summarized in Chapter 5, though it is important to note that they are of significance to other parts of the value-added chain as well. The special rules on gas grid access and use for biogas plants are also discussed in this chapter. Finally, Chapter 6 provides an overview on the rules for gas consumption, in particular on those governing the protection of small customers.

434. The rules on liberalization and regulation in the energy markets as well as on their historic development have been introduced in the Introduction and Part I. Since the central EnWG covers both electricity and gas, these explanations often likewise apply for the gas sector.

Chapter 1. General Introduction

435. In Germany, gas accounted for approximately 22% of primary energy consumption in 2009, 22.3% in 2013 and 27% in 2021.[253] The share of gas in total electricity generation was 11.9% in 2009 and 15.4% in 2021.[254]

§1. Import of Gas

436. Most of the natural gas that is used in Germany is imported. Domestic resources and reserves being very low, Germany is dependent on gas imports. Germany's most important gas suppliers are Russia, Norway, and the Netherlands, with import from Russia in 2020 accounting for considerably more than half of the imports.[255] The amount of gas supplied to Germany by each of these countries exceeds German domestic gas production. The sourcing is usually based on long-term supply contracts.[256]

437. Large gas pipeline projects are an import route for gas to Europe as a whole, and Germany in particular. A large part of the gas transported through these pipelines comes from Russia. For instance, the Nord-Stream-Pipeline is running straight through the Baltic Sea, and transports gas from Russia. Already at the time of its construction, this project has been controversial due to the location of the route of the pipeline. The pipeline allows for the transportation of gas from Russia to Germany while entirely bypassing neighbouring countries along the Baltic Sea, which have objected to the project. Also, environmental concerns against a pipeline through the Baltic Sea have been raised. Another project, the Nabucco Pipeline, was designed to allow for gas supply of the EU from countries around the Caspian Sea and should have contributed to a diversification of Europe's gas supply. However, the project was stopped in 2013 due to the competing Trans-Adria-Pipeline.[257]

438. Extensive controversies in particular with the United States accompanied the construction of the Nord Stream 2 pipeline which shall expand the import capacity from Russia through the Baltic Sea. It has been criticized for again increasing dependency on gas imports from Russia.

---

253. Federal Ministry of Economy and Energy, 'Primärenergieverbrauch nach Energieträgern', statistical data available via the webpage www.bmwi.de, 9 Aug. 2010 and 11 Sep. 2014. Umweltbundesamt, Primärenergieverbrauch, statistical data available via the webpage www.umweltbundesamt.de, 4 Feb. 2022.
254. Federal Ministry of Economy and Technologies, *Energie in Deutschland, Trends und Hintergründe zur Energieversorgung in Deutschland* (August 2010), 21; Destatis, Bruttostromerzeugung in Deutschland, statistical data available via the webpage www.destatis.de, 4 Feb. 2022.
255. Bundesnetzagentur / Bundeskartellamt, *Monitoringreport 2021*, Dec 2021, p. 353 et seq., available at www.bundesnetzagentur.de.
256. H.W. Schiffer, *Energiemarkt Deutschland,* 10th edn (Köln: TÜV Media, 2008), 172, 173.
257. Frankfurter Allgemeine Zeitung of 26 Jun. 2013, *Nabucco ist gescheitert*, available via www.faz.net (last access 20 Feb. 2014).

439. The difficulties for security of supply due to high dependency on importing gas from Russia have become apparent during the Ukraine-war beginning of 2022. Whereas the share of gas from Russia in 2021 amounted to around 55% of the imports, the German government aimed at reducing the dependency on gas from Russia. End of April 2022, it stated that the share would only amount to 35% of the imports anymore.[258] The permitting procedure for Nord Stream 2 has been stopped in February 2022 until further notice.[259] The gas imports shall be diversified further, in particular by using gas in the form of Liquefied Natural Gas (LNG).

440. Transporting gas in the form of LNG constitutes an alternative to gas transportation in pipelines. Germany is connected to an LNG distribution point through the major LNG terminal in Zeebrugge (Belgium).[260] While there were intentions to construct LNG terminals in Germany, so far Germany did not have an own LNG terminal. Driven by the Ukraine-war, Germany now wants to install an own LNG infrastructure. In an initial phase, several Floating Storage and Regasification Units (FSRU) shall be constructed, the first of which in Wilhelmshaven shall be commissioned until end of 2022.[261]

§2. Market Structure

441. On the German gas markets, essentially three groups of players are active: the first group, larger gas companies are also entrusted with imports of gas from abroad. The second group, regional gas companies, often buy gas from the supra-regional gas companies and sell it to local gas companies. They basically do not import gas. On the third regional and local level, smaller companies – often municipal companies (*Stadtwerke*) – supply and distribute gas.[262]

§3. Competition

442. Much like the electricity market, the gas market and by extension the gas supply is fundamentally grid bound. It is therefore subject to the same competition-related difficulties as the electricity market. During the liberalization process of the past decades, German gas markets have gradually opened up to competition. Inspired by EU provisions on the matter, the German legislator has enacted statutes

258. Tagesschau news, 'Wie abhängig Deutschland von Russland ist', 27.4.2022, www.tagesschau.de/wirtschaft/weltwirtschaft/gas-stopp-faq-101.html, last access 1 May 2022.
259. ZEIT ONLINE, 'Pipeline Nord Stream 2 wird gestoppt', 22.2.2022, www.zeit.de/politik/ausland/2022-02/nord-stream-2-wird-gestoppt?utm_referrer=https%3A%2F%2Fwww.google.de%2F, last access 1 May 2022.
260. H.W. Schiffer, *Energiemarkt Deutschland,* 10th edn (Köln: TÜV Media, 2008), 188.
261. ZDF heute news, 'LNG-Terminals: Startschuss in Wilhelmshaven', 5.5.2022, www.zdf.de/nachrichten/wirtschaft/lng-terminal-wilhelmshaven-ukraine-krieg-russland-100.html, last access 1 May 2022.
262. Monopolies Commission, Special Report, *Strom und Gas 2009 – Energiemärkte im Spannungsfeld von Politik und Wettbewerb*, BT-Drs. 16/14060, 46; H.W. Schiffer, *Energiemarkt Deutschland,* 10th edn (Köln: TÜV Media, 2008), 168.

and regulations aiming at enhancing effective competition and giving new players the opportunity to enter the market freely. These rules will be further explained in Chapter 5.

443. The German gas sector has been divided into several market areas. In the light of enhancing competition on the gas market, the Monopolies Commission advocated a further reduction in number of market areas.[263] During recent years, the number of market areas has been already reduced significantly. From 1 April 2011 onwards, only three market areas existed; this already reached a significant reduction of market areas. On 1 October 2011, two of these market areas fused so that only two market areas (GASPOOL and NetConnect Germany (NCG)) remained. Market areas traditionally existed for H-Gas (High Gas) and L-Gas (Low Gas), but then also combined the qualities of High Gas and Low Gas.

444. From 1 October 2021, the two market areas have been consolidated into a common market area 'Trading Hub Europe (THE)'.[264] The Regulation on the Access to Gas Supply Grids (*Gasnetzzugangsverordnung, GasNZV*)[265] was a key driver in bringing the number of market areas further down (see below Chapter 5).

445. Competition in the gas market benefits from the possibility to trade gas over the European Energy Exchange (EEX) and the trading points in the market area. New rules like the just mentioned GasNZV, but also decisions by the Federal Network Agency like GABi Gas have supported this trade option to enhance competition.[266] As a result, competition on the gas markets has been increased significantly. For example, end consumers increasingly started to make use of the option to change suppliers.[267] Also the reduction of market areas significantly added to competition on the markets.

§4. Prospects

446. Gas has taken on an important role in the German energy markets and is – or at least has been – often viewed as a 'transitional fuel' in the process towards more sustainable energy supply. This is due to natural gas having advantages compared to other fossil fuels as it produces less GHG. Moreover, gas may facilitate the

263. Monopolies Commission, Special Report, *Strom und Gas 2009 – Energiemärkte im Spannungsfeld von Politik und Wettbewerb*, BT-Drs. 16/14060, 86.
264. *See* Bundesnetzagentur / Bundeskartellamt, *Monitoringreport 2021*, Dec 2021, p. 403 et seq., available at www.bundesnetzagentur.de.
265. Verordnung über den Zugang zu Gasversorgungsnetzen, Gasnetzzugangsverordnung of 3 Sep. 2010, BGBl. I p. 1261.
266. *See* closer M. Bandulet, W. Elsenbast & M. Krug, 'Wettbewerbsprobleme und aktuelle Regulierungsansätze im deutschen Gasmarkt', *InfrastrukturRecht* (2010): 245 et seq.
267. P. Focht, 'Wettbewerb lernt langsam laufen', *E&M* (15 Mar. 2011): 1.

integration of renewable energy in the electricity markets since the intermittent electricity fed-in from wind and solar energy plants can be complemented with electricity generated by gas fired power plants. Due to their flexibility the latter are well suited to cover the peak demand.[268]

447. However, in the course of the Ukraine-war the risks for security of gas supply have become apparent, and gas prices have increased substantially. In the short term, the German government seeks to diversify sources for gas imports. But the concerns around security of gas supply – together with the need to decarbonize – also raise new questions around which role gas can and shall play in the energy transformation.

448. So far, politics have aimed at biogas playing an increasingly important role in future gas markets. In Germany, there are several regulations in place to foster the development and the integration of this renewable fuel. These relate particularly to the access and use of the natural gas grid for biogas installations.

449. Further, other innovative options may be promoted. For instance, green hydrogen might be produced from electricity generated from renewable sources in order to store this electricity in the gas grids. In future, the enormous capacity of the existing gas grids thus could also be used as a storage facility to solve the storage problems of electricity (particularly from renewable sources). The regulatory regime has been updated to reflect opportunities of power to gas and hydrogen.

268. Federal Ministry of Economy and Technologies, *Energie in Deutschland, Trends und Hintergründe zur Energieversorgung in Deutschland* (August 2010), 19.

Chapter 2. Production

450. This chapter will focus on the licensing regime for gas fired power plants under the Federal Immissions Control Act (*Bundes-Immissionsschutzgesetz, BImSchG*).[269] Which type of construction and operation licence the operator needs depends on the constitution and size of the facility. Most important is the licence under the Federal Immissions Control Act which – due to its so-called concentration effect – generally covers all permits necessary under public law for the construction and operation of a facility. Excluded from this concentration effect are permits that fall within the scope of the Federal Water Resources Act.

451. The licensing regime of the Federal Immissions Control Act applies only to a predefined list of facilities. This list comprises all 'classic' power plants that exceed a certain capacity. For smaller facilities, other licensing regimes particularly under construction law apply.

452. The Federal Immissions Control Act is therefore the central statute regulating the authorization of major power plants (excluding nuclear power plants) and of other large industrial facilities. The first part of the statute (sections 1–3 BImSchG) sets out the aim and scope of the BImSchG, and specific terms are defined. The important second part of the statute relates to licence admission of power plants (as well as to other facilities), and deals with the construction and the operation of these facilities.

453. This chapter also contains more general remarks on the Federal Immissions Control Act since this statute is the central licensing regime for all other larger power plants. Other parts of this monograph will refer to this section.

454. An important influence on the location of a plant results from the determinations under planning law (briefly introduced in Part IV, Chapter 1, section 1). The preconditions of the planning law need to be respected in granting a licence under the Federal Immissions Control Act.[270]

§1. Federal Immissions Control Act: Regulatory Mechanism and Definitions

455. The second part of the BImSchG regulates the construction and operation of facilities. The term 'facility' (*Anlage*) is defined in the general provisions of section 3 paragraph 5 BImSchG as 'operating sites' or 'other stationary installations'.

269. Gesetz zum Schutz vor schädlichen Umwelteinwirkungen durch Luftverunreinigungen, Geräusche, Erschütterungen und ähnliche Vorgänge, Bundes-Immissionsschutzgesetz in the version of the publication of 17 May 2013 (BGBl. I p. 1274). Translations of the clauses of the BImSchG have often been taken from an English translation of this statute which can be found on the webpage of the Federal Ministry for the Environment, www.bmu.de.

270. For a more detailed introduction into planning law *see* G. Hermes in: J.P. Schneider & C. Theobald, *Recht der Energiewirtschaft*, 5th edn (München: C.H. Beck, 2021), § 8.

However, machines and other devices or properties that can cause emissions can also be classified as facilities in terms of the Federal Immissions Control Act. It can therefore be said that the definition of the term is very broad.

456. The Federal Immissions Control Act clearly differentiates between immissions and emissions in section 3 paragraphs 2 and 3 BImSchG. Immissions are defined as air pollution, noises, percussions, light, heat, radiation, and similar occurrences that have an impact on humans, animals and plants, the ground, the water, the atmosphere or cultural, and other factual goods. Emissions are understood as such occurrences which emanate from a facility. The decisive factor is therefore whether the same incidents are observed and measured at the point of impact (immissions) or at the point of exhaustion (emissions). In line with this distinction, the Act sets different limit values for immissions and emissions. As the title of the Federal Immissions Control Act suggests, the statute originally aimed to regulate immissions and therefore to set immission limit values. However, until today emission-related protection became increasingly important. The statute now aims to reduce both immissions and emissions.[271] As will be explained below section 8, the differentiation between these two is of high importance, in particular for the legal protection of people affected by a certain facility.

457. In order to come to a full understanding of the Federal Immissions Control Act, it is crucial to be aware of the several accompanying ordinances (*Rechtsverordnungen*) and administrative regulations (*Verwaltungsvorschriften*).[272] These are often more specific provisions, though below the status of a formal statute, are most decisive in particular to determine the relevant limit values for a certain substance in a certain area. While the Federal Immissions Control Act contains the basic rules and principles, the accompanying ordinances provide details on how immissions and emissions should be measured and they set the maximum amount allowed for each substance. Particularly relevant for power plants are the following:

- Fourth Ordinance for the Implementation of the Federal Immission Control Act (Ordinance on Installations Requiring a Permit – 4. BImSchV).[273]
- Ninth Ordinance for the Implementation of the Federal Immission Control Act (Ordinance on the Licensing Procedure – 9. BImSchV).[274]
- Twelfth Ordinance for the Implementation of the Federal Immission Control Act (Major Accidents Ordinance – 12. BImSchV).[275]

271. H.D. Jarass, 'Grundstrukturen des Immissionsschutzrechts', *Juristische Schulung* 7 (2009), 610.
272. There are forty-four legal ordinances to concretize the general provisions of the Federal Immissions Control Act, some of them already out of force.
273. Vierte Verordnung zur Durchführung des Bundes-Immissionsschutzgesetzes, Verordnung über genehmigungsbedürftige Anlagen, 4. BImSchV (BGBl. I p. 1440).
274. Neunte Verordnung zur Durchführung des Bundes-Immissionsschutzgesetzes, Verordnung über das Genehmigungsverfahren, 9. BImSchV, in the version of the publication of 29 May 1992 (BGBl. I p. 1001).
275. Zwölfte Verordnung zur Durchführung des Bundes-Immissionsschutzgesetzes, Störfall-Verordnung – 12. BImSchV, in the version of the publication of 15 Mar. 2017 (BGBl. I p. 483).

– Thirteenth Ordinance for the Implementation of the Federal Immission Control Act (Ordinance on Major Combustion and Gas-Turbine Facilities – 13. BImSchV).[276]
– Seventeenth Ordinance on the Implementation of the Federal Immission Control Act (Ordinance on Waste Incineration and Co-Incineration – 17. BImSchV).[277]

§2. Necessity of a Permit

458. The just explained regulatory mechanism of the Federal Immissions Control Act already applies for the decision of whether a permit is necessary for the construction and operation of a certain facility. The second part of the BImSchG differentiates between the different types of facilities that require a permit, and provides rules for these facilities in the first chapter, sections 4–21 BImSchG. In the second chapter, sections 22–25a BImSchG address facilities that do not require a permit.

459. Section 4 paragraph 1 sentence 1 BImSchG contains, however, only a very general description of facilities requiring a permit under the Federal Immissions Control Act. This section refers to facilities that are 'on the basis of their constitution or their operation suitable to a special extent to cause harmful environmental influences or to endanger, disadvantage or substantially disturb the general public or the neighbourhood'.[278] Since this definition merely offers a broad guideline, the facilities requiring a permit are regulated in detail in the Ordinance on Installations Requiring a Permit (hereinafter: 4. BImSchV). With this Ordinance, the Federal Government implemented an exclusive catalogue of facilities that require a permit under the Federal Immissions Control Act. It was entitled to set out this catalogue by section 4 paragraph 1 sentence 3 BImSchG.[279]

276. Dreizehnte Verordnung zur Durchführung des Bundes-Immissionsschutzgesetzes, Verordnung über Großfeuerungs-, Gasturbinen- und Verbrennungsmotoranlagen of 6 Jul. 2021 (BGBl. I p. 2514).
277. Siebzehnte Verordnung zur Durchführung des Bundes-Immissionsschutzgesetzes, Verordnung über die Verbrennung und die Mitverbrennung von Abfällen – 17. BImSchV, of 2 May 2013 (BGBl. I p. 1021, 1044, 3754).
278. The term 'harmful environmental influences' is defined in s. 3 para. 1 BImSchG as immissions which are suitable to cause dangers, substantial disadvantages or substantial disturbances for the general public or the neighbourhood according to their character, extent or duration. Since this definition thus essentially refers to immissions, this text will use the term 'immissions' in the following instead of the term 'harmful environmental influences'.
279. Such an authorization of the government is necessary according to Art. 80 para. 1 of the German Basic Law (*Grundgesetz*) which also contains material conditions for the definiteness of an authorization. The described regulatory mechanism requires the Federal Immissions Control Act to contain a high number of such authorizations to entitle the government to set out more specific rules.

460. The Fourth Federal Immissions Control Ordinance and in particular its annex have been revised by transposing Directive 2010/75/EU on industry emissions into national law.[280] While the structure of the annex to the Fourth Federal Immissions Control Ordinance has been changed quite extensively to reflect European legislation, there have been only few material changes.[281] Of high importance for the immissions protection law will be, in particular, the enhanced duties to align with the best available techniques.

461. Annex 1 of the Fourth Federal Immissions Control Ordinance contains an extensive catalogue of facilities. The catalogue is relevant to the applicable licensing procedure (more details below section 4). Generally speaking, facilities listed with a 'V' may be subject to a simplified licensing procedure, while the facilities listed with a 'G' require a normal procedure with advanced public participation. In addition, facilities according to Article 10 of Directive 2010/75/EU on industry emissions are marked with an 'E' as specific immission protection provisions may apply for these installations.

462. The most important provisions for facilities in the energy sector can be found in the first number of the 4. BImSchV under the heading 'heat generation, mining, and energy'. In this section of the monograph, only the numbers relevant for gas fired power plants are listed; relevant numbers for other plants are listed in the related sections.

463. Number 1.1 of Annex 1 of the 4. BImSchV reads:

> Installations for the generation of electricity, steam, hot water, process heat or hot waste gas by use of fuels in a combustion facility (such as a power plant, combined heat and power plant, heating plant, gas-turbine plant, stationary internal combustion engine, other combustion installation), including related steam boilers, with a rated thermal input of 50 megawatts or higher.

464. Accordingly, these facilities require a permit under the Federal Immissions Control Act and need to hold an official authorization, to be obtained following the normal licensing procedure. They also are facilities according to Article 10 of Directive 2010/75/EU on industry emissions. The next provisions in number 1.2 are listed with a 'V', meaning that the facilities in this provision also require a permit. However, this permit is easier to obtain since it may be granted through the simplified licensing procedure. Here, several installations for the generation of electricity, steam, hot water, process heat or hot waste gas by use of – for instance – gaseous fuels are listed.

---

280. Directive 2010/75/EU on industrial emissions (integrated pollution prevention and control), OJ L 334/17. For the transposition *see inter alia* Gesetz zur Umsetzung der Richtlinie über Industrieemissionen of 8 Apr. 2013, BGBl. I p. 734.

281. J. Betensted & R. Grandjot & S. Waskow, 'Die Umsetzung der Richtlinie 2010/75/EU über Industrieemissionen (IE-Richtlinie) im Immissionsschutzrecht', *ZUR* (2013): 395 (396).

465. Number 1.4 of Annex 1 of the 4. BImSchV sets forth the necessity of a permit for certain stationary internal combustion engines for the drive of machines or for the generation of electricity, steam, hot water, process heat, and hot waste gas using specifically listed fuels, such as gaseous fuels.

466. The extent of the necessary licence is determined by section 1 paragraphs 2–5 of the 4. BImSchV. Due to section 1 paragraph 2 number 1, first of all the parts of installations or process stages which are required for the operation of the installations are subject to a licence, the 'core' of the facility. In the case of power plants, this principle is applicable to all parts of the facility and procedural steps that are usually connected with such facilities. In most cases, it even comprises the whole operating site.[282]

467. Also auxiliary facilities associated with parts of installations and process stages which may be relevant for the emission characteristics of the facility or for the occurrence of other risks are encompassed (number 2 of section 1 paragraph 2 of the 4. BImSchV). Under section 1 paragraph 3, permit requirements apply to common facilities as well. These are defined as several facilities of the same kind, closely linked in terms of location and operation.

§3. Material Prerequisites for a Licence

468. Section 6 paragraph 1 number 1 BImSchG stipulates that a licence needs to be granted when it is certain that all duties set out in section 5 BImSchG (the so-called operator's duties), as well as any ordinance issued under section 7 BImSchG will be complied with. Moreover, the construction and operation of the plant (number 2) may not be in conflict with any other provision under public law or with any occupational safety and health concerns. The scope of the legal requirements that need to be fulfilled in order to gain the licence is thus very broad, since it covers all other provisions of public law as well. However, the advantage of this wide assessment for the operator is first a right of the operator to gain a permit in case he complies with all provisions. Contrary to other provisions in German Public Law, section 6 BImSchG leaves no discretion to the administration to decide on whether or not to issue a licence when the material preconditions are fulfilled. However, it may not be disregarded that some more detailed provisions which need to be complied with might in certain cases factually give leeway to the administration. The second main advantage for the operator is that the licence under the BImSchG comprises basically all other permits that would otherwise have been necessary (the so-called concentration effect, see in detail below section 5).

469. The binding character of the licence limits the opportunities to examine alternative plans for the project throughout the course of the licensing procedure. At

282. C. Franzius in: M. Appel & M. Ohms & J. Saurer, *BImSchG* (Berlin: Erich Schmidt Verlag, 2021), § 4 para. 79.

this point of the procedure, the authority has no legal measures to influence the location or the concept of a power plant; it can only oversee and control the fulfilment of the legal requirements.[283]

470. In the following, the material requirements for a (gas fired) power plant arising of the Federal Immissions Control Act will be addressed. According to the regulatory mechanism of this statute, the 'operator's duties' set forth in section 5 BImSchG are only of a general nature. These provisions can only be applied to concrete cases by taking the more detailed provisions in legal ordinances and administrative regulations into account. These will also be summarized in this section. However, given the scope of this monograph only an overview of the extensive provisions can be offered.

I. Principle of Protection

471. Section 5 paragraph 1 number 1 BImSchG contains the so-called Principle of Protection. In order to ensure a high level of protection for the environment as a whole, this principle states that facilities subject to licensing need to be constructed and operated in such a way that harmful effects on the environment or any other hazards, significant disadvantages and significant nuisances to the general public and the neighbourhood are avoided.

472. It would be difficult to apply these general terms to concrete, practical cases, if other legal provisions did not prescribe any limit values. Such concrete limit values for the control of air pollution (and therefore concerning the energy sector) are provided by the Technical Instructions on Air Quality Control (*Technische Anleitung zur Reinhaltung der Luft, TA Luft*).[284] These Technical Instructions as well as other Technical Instructions affecting noise protection (Technical Instructions on Noise Protection, *Technische Anleitung zum Schutz gegen Lärm, TA Lärm*) are treated as 'norm-concretizing administrative regulations' (*Normkonkretisierende Verwaltungsvorschriften*) in the jurisdiction of the Federal Administrative Court.[285] This means that these provisions shall in general provide binding rules and values, implying that courts shall apply these provisions in the same way as if these rules were contained in a statute or an ordinance. In atypical cases, these regulations lose their otherwise binding effect. Third parties can also argue that new scientific evidence would require stricter values than the values provided by these regulations.

283. K. Hoffmann & A. Fridrich in: C. Germer & H. Loibl, *Energierecht, Handbuch,* 2nd edn (Berlin: Erich Schmidt Verlag, 2007), 397.
284. Neufassung der Ersten Allgemeinen Verwaltungsvorschrift zum Bundes-Immissionsschutzgesetz, Technische Anleitung zur Reinhaltung der Luft, of 18 Aug. 2021. These rules can be found on the webpage of the Federal Ministry of the Environment, www.bmu.de.
285. BVerwG, judgment of 20 Dec. 1999, 7 C 15/98, *NVwZ,* 2000, 440. The older jurisdiction treated these Technical Instructions as 'anticipated expert opinions' with similar legal effects, *see* BVerwG, judgment of 17 Feb. 1978, 1 C 102/76, *BVerwGE,* 55, 250, 256 et seq.

473. The inherent problem of this legal classification must briefly be mentioned. The provision in section 5 BImSchG concerning the operator's duties is very general and does not offer a clear guideline. Therefore, the relevant decisions on immission values and ultimately on the lawfulness of the operation of a plant are often taken in the Technical Instructions, the point at which the immission values are specified. However, the executive rather than the parliament enacts these Technical Instructions. This conflicts with the general principle of the German Constitutional Law, which states that essential decisions must be taken within a formal statute. Contrary to legal ordinances, administrative regulations generally do not require a legal basis in a statute and merely constitute rules for the internal administration system. Generally speaking, they do not create rights and duties for citizens. One of the underlying reasons for the jurisdiction to give more legal weight to these Technical Instructions is that they are allowed for in section 48 BImSchG. Moreover, a high number of experts and institutions are involved in the process of the definition of the provided values. Since this regulatory mechanism is similar to the one applicable to legal ordinances, and since the duties of the operator are hardly applicable in the absence of more precise values, the approach of the jurisdiction is understandable. However, it must be mentioned that the European Court of Justice decided that European Directives cannot be transferred into national law based on Technical Instructions alone, due to the generally non-binding character of administrative regulations.[286] To comply with this judgment, immission values are therefore regulated in more detail also by legal ordinance. Nevertheless, the rules and limit values of the TA Luft are still of high practical relevance.

474. Section 4 of the Technical Instructions on Air Quality Control provides immission values for the protection of the environment against harmful effects. Particularly relevant for energy plants are the immission values for the protection against human health hazards, as set forth under number 4.2 of the Technical Instructions.

475. Important are the additional clauses in the Technical Instructions on Air Quality Control, which address the situation of several sources being responsible for immissions. The clauses provide details how to take the pre-existing load and the additional load into account. Number 4.2.2 regulates:

> If the total load of an air pollutant listed under 4.2.1, which is determined in compliance with 4.7, exceeds the immission value at any evaluation parcel, a license may not be refused on the grounds of such excess value provided that, with regard to the respective pollutant,
>
> a) the indicator for the additional load caused by emissions from the facility at this evaluation parcel does not exceed 3.0 per cent of the annual immission value and if it is ensured by imposed obligation that further measures for clean-air maintenance, including, in particular, measures which reach beyond the best available techniques, are carried out, or

286. ECJ, judgment of 30 May 1991, C-361/88, *NVwZ*, 1991, 866.

b) it is ensured by imposed condition that, as a general rule no later than 12 months after the commissioning of the facility, remediation measures (dismantling, closing down, alteration) or other measures which ensure the observation of the immission values pursuant to 4.2.1 are carried out at existing facilities of the applicant or third parties, or
c) compliance with the immission value is to be expected after a transitional period by means of measures within the framework of a clean air plan.

476. The underlying reasoning for this provision is that the concrete immission value in a given area of exposure of a facility is the sum of the emission of this facility, as well as of all other air pollutants that can be measured at this location. The immission value provides the total value of all air pollutants at a certain location; therefore, it does not precisely reveal the share of a certain facility in this value. For instance, a facility could cause hardly any emissions and therefore barely contribute to the total immission value. In this case it is not reasonable to deny this facility a licence, despite the fact that the absolute immission value at this location exceeds the preset limits. Number 4.2.2 consequently declares that a licence may not be refused if the additional emissions by the facility do not exceed 3.0% of the total annual immission value in a certain area. In this case the emissions of the facility are therefore not considered to be the cause for the immission value in a legal sense. However, the clause allows the authority to demand stricter measures for emission control that go beyond the best available techniques. Although this concerns the principle of precaution under section 5 paragraph 1 number 2 BImSchG, this provision is still lawful. It applies only in the case a licence was granted to a facility even though immission values were exceeded in this specific area (as long as the facility did not contribute to this excess in a manner that is relevant enough to deny a licence).

477. Similarly, the Technical Instructions on Air Quality Control provide for other immission values and also allow for licensing in case these values are exceeded under certain circumstances or with specific further requirements for the operator. The Technical Instructions also contain detailed rules on the measurement of immissions and on the estimated geographical area that needs to be taken into account.

II. Principle of Precaution

478. The Principle of Precaution in section 5 paragraph 1 number 2 BImSchG requires that precautions are taken to prevent any harmful effects to the environment or any other hazards, significant disadvantages or significant nuisances, in particular by such measures as are appropriate according to the best available techniques. While the principle of protection is designed to avoid concrete dangers, the principle of precaution takes a preventive approach and requires the operator to take on an active role in taking precautionary measures. These must be taken well before a potential danger could arise, even when no concrete knowledge about the effects of a substance on the environment is available. One of the inherent justifications for the principle of precaution is also the long-distance transport of harmful substances. Since the principle of precaution applies already before a certain danger can be determined, the prevailing jurisdiction and literature are of the opinion that this clause does not provide rights to third parties and consequently cannot be enforced by such persons in court proceedings (more details in section 8).

479. Carbon dioxide emissions have so far been excluded from the principle of precaution by section 5 paragraph 2 BImSchG. These are – in principle – governed by the Greenhouse Gas Emissions Trading Act (*Treibhausgas-Emissionshandelsgesetz, TEHG*) alone (see on this Act below Part VI Chapter 2). Limitation requirements on GHG emissions are only admissible in case they aim to ensure compliance with the Protection Principle of section 5 paragraph 1 number 1 BImSchG (closer below Part IV, Chapter 1, section 4).

480. The measures necessary to comply with the principle of precaution have a close connection to the 'best available techniques' (*Stand der Technik*) which are taken into account by section 5 paragraph 1 number 2 BImSchG. Section 3 paragraph 6 BImSchG gives a definition of the best available techniques, describing them as:

> the state of development of advanced processes, establishments or modes of operation which is deemed to indicate the practical suitability of a particular technique for restricting emission levels to air, water or soil, for guaranteeing installations safety or for preventing or reducing any effects on the environment with a view to achieve a high level of protection of the environment as a whole.

The Annex to the Federal Immissions Control Act further defines criteria to determine the best available techniques, taking the general principle of proportionality into account, as well as of the principles of prevention and precaution.

481. The standard of best available techniques practically requires a guarantee that a certain technique has the ability to reduce emissions, and it is dynamic so as to capture technological improvements.[287] In contrast to the rather absolute principle of protection, the standard of best available techniques is – according to the criteria in the annex – limited by the principle of proportionality, which asks for a balance between effort and use. It consequently does not require measures as far-reaching as the comparatively higher standard of 'state of the art of science and technology', which often applies in the Atomic Energy Act for instance.

---

287. C. Bickenbach in: M. Appel & M. Ohms & J. Saurer, *BImSchG* (Berlin: Erich Schmidt Verlag, 2021), § 3 para. 116 et seqq.; K. Hoffmann & A. Fridrich in: C. Germer & H. Loibl, *Energierecht, Handbuch*, 2nd edn (Berlin: Erich Schmidt Verlag, 2007), 390.

482. While the Principle of Protection relates to immissions, the Principle of Precaution deals mostly with emissions. A precautionary approach requires a preset limit to emission values, even if a concrete hazard for humans or the environment cannot yet be determined. Concrete emission limit values are provided *inter alia* by the Ordinance about Major Combustion and Gas-Turbine Facilities (*Verordnung über Großfeuerungs- und Gasturbinenanlagen, 13. BImSchV*) and the Ordinance on Waste Incineration and Co-Incineration (*Abfallverbrennungsverordnung, 17. BImSchV*).

483. The 13. BImSchV provides emission limit values for any combustion facilities. These include gas turbine facilities, as well as gas turbine facilities that power machines, with a rated thermal input of 50 MW or higher, using any kind of combustibles. The relevant emission limit values are provided in sections 5 to 12 of the 13. BImSchV. The emission values of the 13. BImSchV are of an absolute nature. However, section 23 of the 13. BImSchV allows for exceptions in case a disproportional effort is required to comply with the limit values, and is subject to further conditions. On the contrary, the 13. BImSchV is not conclusive as to the obligations of installation operators, so that the authority can also impose additional requirements (*see* section 24 of the 13. BImSchV).[288]

484. The 17. BImSchV is of particular relevance for waste-to-energy plants. Section 8 contains emission limit values and is thus closely linked to the Principle of Precaution in section 5 paragraph 1 number 2 BImSchG. It also provides obligations for the delivery and interim storage of input materials, combustion requirements, requirements for co-incineration plants or for heat recovery.

485. For smaller facilities, emission values are provided in the Technical Instructions on Air Quality Control. These provisions contain emission standards requiring emissions to be reduced or, if possible avoided entirely, using the best available techniques. They also contain requirements that comply with the best available emissions reducing techniques.

III. Principle of Waste Avoidance and Clearance

486. Section 5 paragraph 1 number 3 BImSchG requires that waste in general is avoided, unavoidable waste is recovered and non-recoverable waste is disposed of without impairing the public welfare. Moreover, the section refers to the Act for the Promotion of Closed Substance Cycle Waste Management (*Kreislaufwirtschaftsgesetz, KrWG*), which basically provides that waste is avoided and, if that is not possible, is recycled. As a last resort waste can be disposed of, but only if recycling is not an option.

---

288. H. Wöckel in: M. Appel & M. Ohms & J. Saurer, *BImSchG* (Berlin: Erich Schmidt Verlag, 2021), § 7 para. 72.

IV. Principle of Effective Use of Energy

487. The fourth requirement for operators in section 5 paragraph 1 number 4 BImSchG is to ensure an economical and efficient use of energy. This principle aims at a high standard of energy efficiency in every type of facility that requires a permit.

V. Maintenance

488. Section 5 paragraph 3 BImSchG requires the operator of a facility that is subject to licensing to ensure that 'no harmful effects to the environment or no other hazards, significant disadvantages and significant nuisances to the general public and the neighbourhood may be caused' even after the facility ceases to operate. Moreover, existing wastes need to be recovered in an orderly and safe fashion, or be disposed of without impairing the public welfare. Finally, the restoration of the site to proper condition needs to be guaranteed.

489. These continuing duties can already become relevant at the construction stage or operation phase of a plant. Already at this point in time, the competent authority may take preventive actions if it feels that measures taken after cessation of the plant's operations would be less effective.[289]

VI. Other Material Preconditions

490. Additionally, section 6 paragraph 1 number 2 BImSchG demands that the construction and operation of a facility does not conflict with any other provisions under public law or any occupational safety and health concerns. As a consequence, applicants must be in compliance with all other requirements of the complete public law if they wish to obtain a licence under the Federal Immissions Control Act. This covers public law provisions of the Bund as well as of the Länder. Section 6 also covers material provisions that are reviewed in a separate licensing procedure, as well as those provisions that are not subject to a separate licensing regime.[290] The provisions that will be reviewed are *inter alia* norms of construction law, waste law, nature protection law, and soil protection law.

491. The Major Accidents Ordinance (Twelfth Ordinance for the Implementation of the Federal Immission Control Act, *Störfall-Verordnung, 12. BImSchV*) shall

289. H.D. Jarass, *BImSchG*, 8th edn (München: C.H. Beck, 2010), s. 5 para. 115; K. Hoffmann & A. Fridrich in: C. Germer & H. Loibl, *Energierecht, Handbuch*, 2nd edn (Berlin: Erich Schmidt Verlag, 2007), 404.

290. However, if a separate licence under the Water Balance Statute is necessary, the authority competent for the licence under the BImSchG will orientate itself on this other decision. If such a licence is not yet issued, it often will not conduct a detailed review but refer in the BImSchG licence to the still necessary permit under the other statute. *See* M. Fehling & C. Schings in: J.P. Schneider & C. Theobald, *Recht der Energiewirtschaft*, 5th edn (München: C.H. Beck, 20021), § 9 para. 115.

ensure the operating safety of facilities subject to licensing. According to its section 1 paragraph 1, it applies to facilities where dangerous substances are present in quantities that exceed the maximum limits specified in a substance list annexed to the 12. BImSchV.

492. The Ordinance further differentiates between facilities that are subject to 'basic obligations' as provided in sections 3–8 and facilities to which also extended obligations under sections 9–12 apply. Once more the substance list specifies the quantities of dangerous substances that need to be dealt with in order to fall under the basic or the extended obligations.

493. Section 3 paragraph 1 of the 12. BImSchV provides that the operator shall take such precautions as are necessary to prevent major accidents with regard to nature and extent of the potential hazards. The necessary precautionary measures are further specified in the subsequent articles that contain requirements for the prevention of major accidents, as well as requirements that limit the effects of major accidents. The Ordinance also provides a high number of reporting obligations, which increase for facilities that fall under the extended obligations. These facilities have to issue safety reports in addition to alarm and emergency plans.

§4. Licensing Procedure

494. Facilities that require a permit under the Federal Immissions Control Act face different licensing procedures, which depend on whether the facility is listed with a 'G' or with a 'V' in Annex 1 to the 4. BImSchV. Section 2 paragraph 1 of the 4. BImSchV stipulates that the normal licensing procedure (according to section 10 BImSchG) shall be carried out for facilities listed with a 'G' in Annex 1, facilities consisting of facilities listed with a 'G' and a 'V' in Annex 1 and finally for facilities listed with a 'V' in Annex 1 that require an environmental impact assessment (under the Statute about the Environmental Impact Assessment). The simplified procedure according to section 19 BImSchG shall be carried out generally for facilities listed with a 'V' in Annex 1.

495. Facilities subject to a formal licensing procedure require an environmental impact assessment if they are listed in Annex 1 to the Environmental Impact Assessment Statute (*UVPG*).[291] However, if these facilities are subject to an environmental impact assessment, this assessment is conducted as a dependent part of the formal licensing procedure according to section 1 paragraph 2 of the licensing procedure ordinance (*9. BImSchV*). In this case, the 9. BImSchV governs the environmental impact assessment, as prescribed by the second sentence of section 1 paragraph 2.

---

291. Gesetz über die Umweltverträglichkeitsprüfung, in the version of the publication of 18 Mar. 2021 (BGBl. I p. 540).

496. As a result, three kinds of licensing procedures must be distinguished: the formal licensing procedure with an environmental impact assessment, the formal licensing procedure without an environmental impact assessment, and the simplified licensing procedure under section 19 BImSchG. Since most major power plants need to conduct an environmental impact assessment as a dependent part of the formal licensing procedure, only the first and the third type of procedure will be discussed in the following paragraphs.

I. Formal Procedure under Section 10 BImSchG

497. The formal licensing procedure is regulated in section 10 BImSchG and is further detailed in the Ordinance on the licensing procedure (*9. BImSchV*). The public authority shall advise the applicant on the filing of the application, as soon as the applicant informs the authority about the planning of the facility (section 2 paragraph 2 of the 9. BImSchV). During the consultation the necessary documents to file an application will be specified. In case an environmental impact assessment needs to be conducted, this consultation is called 'scoping' and it will mark the scope of the anticipated examination, section 2a of the 9. BImSchV.

498. In the next step, the applicant has to submit his application in written form and with all documents necessary for the examination of the licensing preconditions. Sections 4–4e of the 9. BImSchV provide more specific guidelines on the necessary documents for the application. The competent authority will acknowledge receipt of the documents and verify whether the documentation is complete (sections 6 and 7).

499. The main element of the procedure is a public participation, which takes place in the course of the formal licensing procedure. According to section 10 paragraph 3 BImSchG, the competent authority must give public notice of the project in its official gazette and, additionally, either on the Internet or in local daily newspapers that are widely read in the area where the facility will be constructed. Following this public announcement, the application and attached documents containing information about the effects of the facility on the neighbourhood and the general public have to be displayed, and the owner must allow any interested person to inspect the facility. If any other official documents containing information about the effects of the facility on the neighbourhood and the general public are available, these have to be displayed as well.

500. Everybody now has the opportunity to raise objections against the project. It is crucial to note that this is not merely a right for any interested person. Any person who misses this opportunity to object to the facility will not be able to do so in a possible subsequent court procedure at a later point in time. This is stipulated by the rather hidden clause in section 10 paragraph 3 sentence 5 BImSchG, which states: 'At the end of the objection period, no further objections shall be admissible unless they are based on special titles under civil law.'

501. The authority competent to issue the final decision will initiate another participation for other public authorities whose field of responsibility is affected by the facility. The authority now 'may' organize a public consultation involving all persons who raised objections during the procedure, section 10 paragraph 6 BImSchG. This had been an obligatory step before. Now, the initiation of such a consultation is under the discretion of the competent authority. It is often of mutual interest to the parties involved to conduct this consultation at a stage in the procedure where solutions and settlements are still possible.

502. When the facility is subject to an environmental impact assessment, the competent authority has to sum up and assess all possible effects the construction and the operation of the facility could have on the subjects of protection that are listed in section 1a of the 9. BImSchV. These are human health, animals, plants, biological diversity, soil, water, air, climate, landscape, culture, and other factual goods, as well as any reciprocal effects. They are further detailed in a description, in accordance with section 20 paragraph 1a, 1b of the 9. BImSchV. The authority has to take this assessment into account in its decision 'according to the provisions that apply for this purpose'.

503. Therefore, the final decision about the licence is regulated by the material conditions explained above. The environmental impact assessment mainly offers a procedural strengthening of environmental protection, since it does not alter the material preconditions.[292] According to section 20 paragraph 1 of the 9. BImSchV, the decision needs to be taken without delay after all relevant factors have been reviewed. Section 10 paragraph 6a BImSchG provides that the authority must take a decision regarding the application within seven months after the latter was filed. In the case of the simplified procedure this period is shortened to three months.

II. Simplified Procedure

504. The requirements of the simplified licensing procedure are set forth in section 19 BImSchG in conjunction with section 24 of the 9. BImSchV. As described above, the simplified procedure can only be applicable if the facility in question does not need an environmental assessment, since this would render a formal licensing procedure necessary.

505. Section 19 paragraph 2 BImSchG as well as section 24 of the 9. BImSchV regulate that many provisions of the formal procedure do not apply for the simplified procedure. Most of all, the entire public participation, meaning the public announcement, the special possibility to raise formal objections and the public consultation, do not apply to the simplified procedure. Moreover, the simplified procedure allows for objections to be raised during the course of the normal hearing of affected parties as well, but these objections do not have the same special form and

292. M. Fehling & C. Schings in: J.P. Schneider & C. Theobald, *Recht der Energiewirtschaft*, 5th edn (München: C.H. Beck, 2021), § 9 para. 77.

consequences of the formal extensive procedure. Consequently, the preclusion of non-raised objections in section 10 paragraph 3 sentence 5 BImSchG does not apply. The licence also does not exclude private claims under section 14 BImSchG (see below section 5 III.).

§5. Legal Effects of a Permit

506. If the operator complies with the licence requirements under the Federal Immissions Control Act, section 6 BImSchG leaves no discretion to the authority to issue such a permit. Moreover, this licence has some other far-reaching effects. The most important ones are the concentration effect and the exclusion of private claims, which offer a high grade of legal certainty to the operator. These effects will be described in more detail in the following paragraph. The standards for environmental protection under the Federal Immissions Control Act are regulated in a particularly dynamic way. They leave room for the authorities to issue subsequent measures under certain predefined conditions, with the purpose of reaching the optimal level of environmental protection.

I. Approval for Construction

507. The licence removes the principal prohibition to construct and operate a facility. The extent to which the construction and operation are now allowed is mainly determined by the operative provisions and the other documents referred to in the licence. If the licence contains collateral clauses – and it usually does – the permit serves as a burden for the operator at the same time. As a result, the operator can take legal measures against the collateral clauses. The final legal effect is only provided when the licence becomes non-appealable.

II. Concentration Effect

508. According to section 13 BImSchG, the licence includes basically all other permits necessary for the construction and the operation of a facility. These several necessary permits can be said to be concentrated in this single licence under the Federal Immissions Control Act. This concentration effect also covers the relevant procedures for other permits.[293] The typical permits covered by the concentration effect are the building licence, the necessary exceptions under the construction law, the permit under the industrial safety ordinance, and the exceptional permits under nature protection law.

509. However, section 13 BImSchG excludes certain types of approval from the concentration effect. These are namely planning approvals, approvals of operation plans under mining law, official decisions based on nuclear law and permits and

293. BVerwG, decision of 17 Dec. 2002, 7 B 119/02, *NVwZ*, 2003, 750.

authorizations that fall under water law. In particular, applications for permits and approvals under the Federal Water Resources Act (which are often relevant for power plants) follow a separate procedure. Permits that refer to criteria within the person of the operator, rather than to the operation of the plant, are also not included.[294]

510. It must also be kept in mind that the concentration effect does not absolve the licence from the material preconditions set by other areas of public law. As described above (section 3), the scope of examination of the licence under the Federal Immissions Control Act generally extends to all fields of public law.

III. Exclusion of Private Claims

511. Section 14 sentence 1 BImSchG reads:

> Nobody shall have the right to request cessation of operation at any installation on grounds of civil-law claims to protection against the detrimental impacts emanating from a piece of land on neighboring premises, if the civil-law claims are not based on specific titles and the license for the installation has become final; it shall only be admissible to insist on precautionary measures to prevent the detrimental impacts.

512. This provision substantially adds to the right of continuance for the operator of a facility since it excludes private claims against the facility in a manner that goes beyond other permits granted under public law. Civil claims, in particular under section 1004 in conjunction with section 906 of the Civil Law Code (BGB), that otherwise allow the neighbour to intervene against any harmful effects on his property which he need not tolerate, are generally excluded by this provision of the Federal Immissions Control Act. In such cases, the neighbour is restrained to ask for precautionary measures and, if these are not technically feasible or economically viable, to demand compensation (section 14 sentence 2 BImSchG).

IV. Subsequent Measures

513. It is important to note that the Federal Immissions Control Act allows the authority to issue subsequent orders with further requests for the operator of a plant, even after the licence has been granted under the BImSchG, and the plant is already in operation. This authorization best demonstrates the dynamic character of the operator's duties under the Federal Immissions Control Act. In order to ensure a high protection level for the environment, later knowledge of new hazards and

294. D. Sellner, O. Reidt & M.J. Ohms, *Immissionsschutzrecht und Industrieanlagen*, 3rd edn (C.H. Beck, 2006), 191.

advanced legal requirements for the operation of plants resulting thereof may be demanded from an operative plant also if it is in possession of a valid permit.

514. These new requirements need to be applied to the plant in question by a subsequent order that is to be issued by the authority. Section 17 paragraph 1 sentence BImSchG reads: 'In order to ensure that the obligations resulting from this Act or from any ordinance issued hereunder are met, orders may be issued following the granting of the licence or an alteration notified under section 15 paragraph 1.' Sentence 2 provides that such a subsequent order shall be issued if the protection of the general public or the neighbourhood turns out to be inadequate after the issue of such a licence or after an alteration. In these cases, the competent authority is generally obliged to issue a subsequent order and may only in atypical cases refrain from such an order.

515. At first, these provisions appear to leave remarkable discretion to the authority, enabling it to intervene with the licensed operation of a plant. However, further paragraphs of section 17 constrain this power of intervention in order to provide the plant operator with sufficient legal certainty. According to section 17 paragraph 2, the competent authority may not issue subsequent orders if such orders would lack proportionality, and above all if the effort needed to comply with the order is not commensurate with the desired effect (so-called operator's protection clause).[295] This clause thus refers to the general principle of proportionality and provides further aspects that must be balanced if a subsequent order is issued. However, section 17 paragraph 2 sentence 2 specifies that the licence may be revoked by the authority in case of disproportionality of a subsequent order, and if the additional conditions of section 21 paragraph 1 numbers 3–5 are fulfilled. In case a licence is revoked, the authority in certain cases must indemnify the financial loss suffered by the operator as a result of his trust in the continued validity of the licence, if his trust is worthy of protection (see section 21 paragraph 4 BImSchG). Overall, it can be said that the licence under the BImSchG leads to a restricted right of continuance.[296]

516. Section 21 BImSchG allows for the revocation of a lawfully issued licence. The right of continuance is protected by allowing this revocation only under the specified conditions in numbers 1–5 of section 21 paragraph 1 BImSchG. Number 3, for example, allows the revocation only if subsequently occurred facts show that the licensing authority was entitled to refuse to grant the licence, and if non-revocation might put the public interest at risk. Number 5 entitles the authority to revoke the licence if this helps to prevent or eliminate any serious impairments of the public welfare. Even if these material conditions are fulfilled, the authority must still exercise discretion and balance other aspects that are not explicitly specified in the clause, should the authority want to revoke the licence.

---

295. K. Hoffmann & A. Fridrich in: C. Germer & H. Loibl, *Energierecht, Handbuch*, 2nd edn (Berlin: Erich Schmidt Verlag, 2007), 416.
296. K. Hoffmann & A. Fridrich in: C. Germer & H. Loibl, *Energierecht, Handbuch*, 2nd edn (Berlin: Erich Schmidt Verlag, 2007), 398.

517. Section 20 paragraph 1 BImSchG entitles the authority to prohibit the operation of a facility in case of non-compliance with certain material conditions specified in this clause. These material conditions may arise out of an additional condition, an enforceable subsequent order or a definitive obligation ensuing from an ordinance issued under section 7. Furthermore, the second paragraph of section 20 requires that the authority shall order the closing down or the dismantling of a facility that operates without the correct required licence. This formal illegality, meaning the lack of a required licence, constitutes sufficient reason to close down a facility. The facility does not need to be in conflict with other material legal preconditions.[297] Finally, the third paragraph entitles the authority to prohibit the operation of a plant in case the operator in charge turns out to be unreliable. In this case, factual evidence must suggest the operator has not shown sufficient competence or reliability to operate the facility in compliance with the legal requirements.

§6. Special Forms of a Licence

518. Some special forms of licensing with high practical importance will now briefly be explained. In several steps these special licences help to proceed in the long licensing procedure; offering the possibility to start construction of the plant even before the final licence has been granted. Profound changes to an already existing facility are rendered possible through the licence for major alterations.

I. Partial Licence

519. The partial licence (*Teilgenehmigung*) under section 8 BImSchG allows a separate licence for construction and operation of a part of the whole facility, or to construct but not yet operate the whole facility. This special form of a licence thus renders possible the start of construction for (part of) the facility, even before a final decision for the whole installation has been taken. The partial licence corresponds to a normal licence in its legal effects, in particular with regard to the concentration effect of section 13 BImSchG.

520. A main additional precondition is a legitimate interest in granting a partial licence, which in case of a major power plant will easily be fulfilled. Furthermore, to obtain the licence the owner must make sure the part of the facility he wishes to operate already fulfils certain material conditions, and a preliminary assessment must show that there are no fundamental, irremovable obstacles to the construction and the operation of the entire installation. This positive preliminary assessment serves as the main protection for the operator to obtain a licence for the whole facility at a later point in time. According to the second sentence of section 8 BImSchG, the positive preliminary assessment results in a binding effect upon the competent authority to issue the licence for the whole facility. However, this is only the case

297. M. Fehling & C. Schings in: J.P. Schneider & C. Theobald, *Recht der Energiewirtschaft,* 5th edn (München: C.H. Beck, 2021), s. 8 para. 122.

if no changes in the factual and legal situation occur, and if no individual assessment results in an outcome that differs from the positive provisional assessment. By filing a detailed application for the whole facility already at this point in time, the operator can minimize the risk of not getting the final licence for the entire facility.

II. Advance Notice

521. Certain singular preconditions of a licence or the choice of a site for the facility can be decided on a provisional basis with the advance notice (*Vorbescheid*) under section 9 BImSchG. The aim of this advance notice is to create security upon single conditions for the facility at an early point in time. The questions presented are decided with a final and thus binding character for the subsequent licensing procedure for the facility. Requirements for an advance notice are that the implications resulting from the installation can be adequately assessed and that there is a legitimate interest to gain such a notice.

522. Contrary to the partial licence, the advance notice does not entitle the operator to start with the construction of the facility. Furthermore, the application for the advance notice requires almost the same information as the application for a licence of the entire plant, without having the legal effects of a licence.

III. Permission of Early Start

523. When the licensing procedure for the entire facility has been initiated, the operator can apply for permission to already get started with the construction of the facility under section 8a BImSchG. This measure *inter alia* requires that the applicant can expect a favourable decision, and that he has a legitimate interest in starting the construction early. Though this permission allows for a faster construction of the facility, the authorities retain the right to revoke it at any time. It generally does not offer any binding effect for the later decision. In practice, the authorities often dislike this permit and try to reach a certain level of detail in their examination before granting one.[298]

IV. Major Alterations

524. In practice, the licence necessary for major alterations of an existing facility is of major importance. This permit is obligatory in case of any alteration of the location, nature or operation of a facility subject to licensing, if the alteration may lead to adverse effects of potential relevance to the operator's duties (section 16 paragraph 1 BImSchG). The alteration licence becomes mandatory if the extension or the alteration reaches the capacity limits set out in the 4. BImSchV. A licence is

---

298. D. Sellner & O. Reidt & M.J. Ohms, *Immissionsschutzrecht und Industrieanlagen,* 3rd edn (C.H. Beck, 2006), part 2, para. 215.

not necessary if the adverse effects of the alteration are obviously minor and the fulfilment of the obligations arising from the principle of protection under section 5 paragraph 1 number 1 BImSchG can be guaranteed (section 16 paragraph 1 sentence 2 BImSchG).

525. Alterations at least need to be notified to the competent authority in written form under section 15 BImSchG, at least one month prior to the alteration. The competent authority needs to examine without delay whether the planned alteration requires a licence. Once the authority notifies the operator that no licence is necessary, or in case the authority does not react within the specified time limit, the operator can proceed with his alteration plans. A facility subject to licensing that is planning to terminate operations must also notify this to the authorities, according to section 15 paragraph 3.

§7. Material Preconditions for Facilities not Subject to a Licence

526. In case a facility does not fall under the conditions of the 4. BImSchV and therefore does not require a licence under the BImSchG, the Federal Immissions Control Act also provides material preconditions. These duties are provided for in section 22 paragraph 1 BImSchG, which regulates that facilities not subject to licensing:

> shall be constructed and operated in such a way that
>
> 1. harmful effects on the environment which are avoidable with the use of the best available techniques are prevented;
> 2. harmful effects on the environment which are unavoidable with the use of the best available techniques are kept to a minimum and
> 3. wastes produced during the operation of such installations can be properly disposed of.

527. Section 22 BImSchG is restricted to avoiding harmful effects on the environment and thus to exclude concrete dangers to human health, animals, and plants. However, this duty of avoidance is not absolute either; it is subject to the use of the 'best available techniques'. If harmful effects cannot be avoided by using such techniques, section 22 paragraph 1 number 2 BImSchG only orders to keep them to a minimum, not to avoid them entirely.

528. Since these facilities are not subject to a licence under the BImSchG, the authorities only have *ex post* measures at their disposal to control them. Under section 24 BImSchG, the authority may issue orders to ensure compliance with the just described duties; finally section 25 BImSchG entitles the authority to prohibit the operation of a facility as a last resort.

§8. LEGAL PROTECTION

I. Legal Protection for the Operator against Denial of the Licence or Detrimental Collateral Clauses

529. If the authority denies the licence under the BImSchG, the applicant can take action by bringing the case before the administrative courts. The action to issue an administrative act (*Verpflichtungsklage*) is permissible under section 42 paragraph 1, 2. alternative to the Administrative Courts Procedures Act (VwGO).[299]

530. It is generally obligatory to conduct an objection procedure (*Widerspruchsverfahren*) according to sections 68 et seqq. VwGO prior to the proceedings before administrative courts. The operator must raise the objection within one month after the original decision is announced (section 70 VwGO). This objection procedure provides an internal administrative review of the authority's decision. This process is usually advantageous for the operator, since it provides him with additional opportunity to review the challenged decision.

531. Legal action must be taken within one month after the decision has been served to the operator (section 74 VwGO). If the operator has a legal claim to receive the desired licence, the objection procedure will end in his favour (section 113 paragraph 5 VwGO). Since section 6 paragraph 1 BImSchG leaves no discretion to the authority, the court will decide in favour of the applicant if all material preconditions for the licence are fulfilled. Generally the point in time of the last hearing is decisive in the judgment on the material conditions (contrary to rescission actions).[300]

532. In case the administration does not decide about an objection or about the application to take a decision without a sufficient reason within a reasonable period, the operator may take action to have the licence issued anyway based on the administration's failure to act following the proper objection procedure (see section 75 VwGO). Under the Federal Immissions Control Act, the 'reasonable period' in which a decision must be taken might even be shortened compared to the general applicable period of three months in section 75 VwGO, if special circumstances require a shorter period of time (section 14a BImSchG).

---

299. Verwaltungsgerichtsordnung on the version of the publication of 19 Mar. 1991 (BGBl. I p. 686).
300. K. Hoffmann & A. Fridrich in: C. Germer & H. Loibl, *Energierecht, Handbuch*, 2nd edn (Berlin: Erich Schmidt Verlag, 2007), 418.

533. Moreover, under certain circumstances requiring urgent measures, provisional legal protection under section 123 VwGO may be possible. However, the provisional permit to construct and operate a facility is in conflict with the principle according to which no de facto final decisions should be made before taking a decision about the main issue.[301]

534. Often the desired licence will be granted, but accompanied by collateral clauses. Such clauses are permissible under section 12 paragraph 1 BImSchG if this is necessary to warrant compliance with the licensing conditions referred to in section 6 BImSchG. While the legal protection against collateral clauses is still debated in jurisdiction and literature, it can generally be said that these clauses can be challenged on an individual basis in front of the courts.[302] Generally speaking, the operator is therefore not limited to legal action to obtain the licence, but he could initiate a rescission action against the detrimental clause. However, under the jurisdiction of the Federal Administrative Court, in the end such a claim will only be successful if the licence can legally exist without the challenged collateral clause.[303] Therefore, if an isolated revocation is not possible, the operator may only take legal action for an issuance of a licence without the detrimental collateral clause.[304]

II. Legal Protection for Third Parties

535. Section 42 paragraph 2 VwGO restricts the possibilities of third parties to take rescission actions against licences, granted under the Federal Immissions Control Act (as well as under other acts). Accordingly, claimants need to plead that the administrative act violates their rights to render their claim admissible. So far, this clause has been interpreted rather narrowly by the German jurisprudence, following the reasoning that legal protection is only permissible if so-called subjective rights might be infringed. Such rights evolve from a norm that was designed to protect specific third parties (so-called theory of protective norms). The system of individual legal protection is contrasted by the system of popular action, which the German legislator did not intend.

536. In order to take an admissible action, the neighbour thus needs to claim a violation of his rights provided to him by a legal clause, the clear intention of which

---

301. K. Hoffmann & A. Fridrich in: C. Germer & H. Loibl, *Energierecht, Handbuch,* 2nd edn (Berlin: Erich Schmidt Verlag, 2007), 419; M. Fehling & C. Schings in: J.P. Schneider & C. Theobald, *Recht der Energiewirtschaft,* 5th edn (München: C.H. Beck, 2021), § 9 para. 213.
302. The collateral clauses need however be distinguished from such orders which change the substantial content of the licence itself. Since in such cases the isolated revocation of such clauses is logically excluded – the licence would be granted existence without parts it necessarily needs to regulate – the operator can only raise an action for the issue of a licence with the desired content, but not take isolated rescission action against the clause itself.
303. BVerwG, judgment of 19 Jan. 1989, 7 C 31/87, *BVerwGE,* 81, 185.
304. M. Fehling & C. Schings in: J.P. Schneider & C. Theobald, *Recht der Energiewirtschaft,* 5th edn (München: C.H. Beck, 2008), § 9 para. 209.

is to protect the neighbour's legal rights. Such a clause is undisputedly the principle of protection in section 5 paragraph 1 number 1 BImSchG. Harmful effects need to be prevented for the 'neighbourhood' in general as well under this principle, which demonstrates that the legislator has taken these particular interests into account. This requires a territorial definition of neighbourhood to see who falls within the protection of the clause, and is therefore entitled to take legal measures. Generally speaking, the definition covers the whole area of exposure, meaning the area in which harmful effects might take place. A certain specified spatial area around the planned facility is therefore necessary to take legal action.

537. Contrary to the principle of protection, the principle of prevention is generally seen to not provide any rights to third parties (under section 5 paragraph 1 number 2 BImSchG). While this principle was designed to avoid long-distance transport of hazardous substances and to take a preventive approach against harmful effects on the environment, it does not deal with concrete dangers to human health. Therefore, it generally does not contain legal protection for the persons located within the area of exposure of the facility.[305] However, the opportunities of third parties to evoke section 5 paragraph 1 number 2 BImSchG in administrative proceedings have been improved. Part of this development can be attributed to the growing influence of European Law on the German system of legal protection. Under the principle of prevention, limit values on emissions shall be protective for the entire neighbourhood if no sufficient immission values for the protection against hazards exist.[306]

538. Similarly, the protection of procedural rights of third parties could and can hardly be enforced before the courts, even though the procedural norms on the participation of third parties are designed to protect the rights of the latter. Section 44a VwGO states that mistakes in the procedure can only be challenged in conjunction with legal actions against the objective matter. Moreover, sections 45 and 46 of the Administrative Procedure Code (VwVfG)[307] give the authorities the possibility to rectify mistakes in the procedure, or also declare certain mistakes in the procedure not grave if these mistakes obviously did not influence the decision on the matter. However, European Law as well as the special right of participation of environmental organizations renders certain procedural mistakes relevant to the final decision.[308]

539. If a third party objects to a facility or takes legal action before the courts, the licensing decision is suspended under section 80 paragraph 1 VwGO (so-called

305. BVerwG, judgment of 18 May 1982, 7 C 42.80, *BVerwGE*, 65, 313, 320; M. Fehling & C. Schings in: J.P. Schneider & C. Theobald, *Recht der Energiewirtschaft*, 5th edn (München: C.H. Beck, 20218), § 9 para. 222.

306. BVerwG, judgment of 11 Dec. 2003, 7 C 19/02, *NVwZ*, 2004, 611; M. Fehling & C. Schings in: J.P. Schneider & C. Theobald, *Recht der Energiewirtschaft*, 5th edn (München: C.H. Beck, 2021), § 9 para. 222.

307. Verwaltungsverfahrensgesetz in the version of the publication of 23 Jan. 2003 (BGBl. I p. 102).

308. *See* closer M. Fehling & C. Schings in: J.P. Schneider & C. Theobald, *Recht der Energiewirtschaft*, 5th edn (München: C.H. Beck, 2021), § 9 para. 224 et seqq.

suspensive effect of objection and legal action). Nevertheless, the authority may order the immediate execution of the decision under section 80 paragraph 2 number 4 VwGO. The operator can also file for a decision to grant immediate execution of the permit in front of the courts under section 80a paragraph 3 in conjunction with paragraph 1 number 1 VwGO.

540. If a third party desires *ex post* measures under section 24 and 25 BImSchG against a facility that is not subject to a permit, it needs to take action for the issuance of an administrative act.

Chapter 3. Exploitation

541. As has been explained above, Germany essentially relies on imports of gas. However, domestic production of natural gas can still be found in Germany. Some figures and central legal rules for gas exploitation as provided in the Mining Law are discussed below.

§1. Figures: Domestic Production and Import of Gas

542. Based on figures of the State Authority for Mining, Energy and Geology (LBEG) of Lower Saxony, ten active exploration wells for petroleum and natural gas exploration had been active in Germany in 2008. The number of field development wells drilling amounted to twenty-one, the footage drilled accounted for 57,481 m. The annual gas production amounted to 16.4 billion m^3 in field quality. Natural gas reserves (proven and probable) had been estimated at to be around 194 billion m^3.[309]

543. The annual production of natural gas in Germany further declined to 5.6 billion m^3 in 2020. The remaining domestic natural gas reserves have been calculated with only 43.2 billion m^3 in 2020.[310]

544. Whether unconventional fracking should be used to produce shale gas in Germany, and whether it can be gained in an efficient and economically feasible manner, has been a much-disputed topic. With legislative measures of 2016 and 2017, Germany has implemented a far-reaching prohibition for any activities of unconventional fracking for shale gas, effectively leading to fracking for shale gas not being admissible in Germany until further notice.[311] This led to no applications for fracking having been made until mid-2021, and also no test drillings with fracking technology have been made during that period.[312]

309. State Authority for Mining, Energy and Geology (LBEG) of Lower Saxony, *Jahresbericht Erdöl und Erdgas in der Bundesrepublik Deutschland, Summary,* available at: www.lbeg.niedersachsen.de/master/C38213918_N38202288_L20_D0_I31802357, last access: 26 Feb. 2011.

310. State Authority for Mining, Energy and Geology (LBEG) of Lower Saxony, *Jahresbericht Erdöl und Erdgas in der Bundesrepublik Deutschland 2020, Summary,* available at: www.lbeg.niedersachsen.de, last access: 1 May 2022.

311. Gesetz zur Änderung wasser- und naturschutzrechtlicher Vorschriften zur Untersagung und zur Risikominimierung bei den Verfahren der Fracking-Technologie of 4 Aug. 2016 (BGBl. I p. 1972).

312. Bericht des Bundesministeriums für Wirtschaft und Energie des Bundesministeriums für Umwelt, Naturschutz und nukleare Sicherheit des Bundesministeriums für Bildung und Forschung, Evaluierung des „Regelungspakets Fracking", 21 Jun. 2021, available at www.bmwi.de, last access 1 May 2022.

§2. Mining Law

545. The mining law will be discussed in detail in Part IV, Chapter 2, section 2 in connection with the coal mining sector in Germany. At this stage, some general remarks on the Mining Law and special remarks for the gas sector will be provided.

546. Section 3 paragraph 1 of the Federal Mining Law (*Bundesberggesetz, BBergG*)[313] states that gases generally belong to the natural resources governed by this statute. They most often fall into the category of freely minable resources, which are listed in section 3 paragraph 3 BBergG. This clause names all substances that fall into this group. It also claims that gases belong to the group of freely minable resources if they accrue while hydrocarbons are exploited, or if they accrue during the exploitation of black coal or brown coal. Gases can also fall within the group of freehold resources listed under section 3 paragraph 4 BBergG, since section 2 comprises all resources that do not fall within the explicitly listed groups (as long as they are explored or exploited under the surface).

547. The Federal Mining Law generally requires the possession of a mining right for the exploration and exploitation of freely minable resources like natural gas (section 6 BBergG). These mining rights are subdivided into an exploration licence, a production licence, and the mining proprietorship. However, concrete mining activities may only be conducted based on so-called operating plans (*Betriebspläne*), approved by the competent authorities. These operating plans can be *inter alia* framework operating plans that provide a general overview of the mining operation. Framework operating plans also connect the more detailed operating plans, main operating plans that are generally necessary for the operation of a mine, special operation plans for certain projects that render an additional plan necessary, and final operating plans that must be prepared in case a mining activity is ceased. The main material prerequisites are verified in the approval procedure for operating plans as stipulated in sections 54 et seqq. BBergG.

548. In case the project is listed in the Ordinance on the Environmental Impact Assessment for Mining Projects (hereinafter: *UVP-V Bergbau*)[314] an environmental impact assessment must be conducted, and a framework operating plan must be proposed under the Federal Mining Statute. In section 1 number 2, the UVP-V Bergbau lists the exploitation of natural gas for commercial purposes with a delivery volume of more than 500,000 m^3 of natural gas per day. Moreover, the construction and operation of offshore platforms in coastal waters or around the continental shelf is listed in section 1 number 2 b) UVP-V Bergbau. These projects thus need in any case to conduct an environmental impact assessment and to propose framework operating plans, in addition to other operating plans required by the Federal Mining Law.

---

313. Bundesberggesetz of 13 Aug. 1980 (BGBl. I p. 1310).
314. Verordnung über die Umweltverträglichkeitsprüfung bergbaulicher Vorhaben, UVP-V Bergbau, of 13 Jul. 1990 (BGBl. I p. 1420).

Chapter 4. Transport

549. Like for the electricity grids, the planning procedures for gas grids and the required permits depend on the size of the pipeline. As is the case for certain high voltage open wires, section 43 EnWG stipulates the necessity of a plan approval procedure for any gas supply line that has a calibre of more than 300 mm. The requirements applicable to gas pipelines generally cover underground pipelines as well. Both the material conditions and the planning procedures for gas pipelines are similar to those for electricity grids (see explanations above in Part I, Chapter 3). The important topic of use of public streets in particular by concession contracts and of the respective concession levies is also explained in the said chapter.

550. The following sections will, however, discuss some of the special features that apply to gas pipelines specifically.

§1. Ordinance on High-Pressure Gas Pipelines

551. Essential technical requirements to guarantee the safeness of gas pipelines are contained in the Ordinance on High-Pressure Gas Pipelines (hereinafter: *GasH-DrLtgV*).[315] This Ordinance applies in particular to all high-pressure gas pipelines for the public gas supply with an overpressure of more than sixteen bar (section 1 paragraph 1 GasHDrLtgV).

552. High-pressure gas pipelines generally need to be constructed and operated in compliance with the provisions in sections 3 and 4 of the Ordinance on High-Pressure Gas Pipelines. For instance, high-pressure gas pipelines must be able to withstand the operational demands and must remain leakproof. They must also be laid in protection strips, which need to be clearly marked.

553. The planned construction of a high-pressure gas pipeline must be notified to the competent authority in order to ensure compliance with these technical requirements. According to section 5 GasHDrLtgV, this must be done at least eight weeks before the beginning of the construction works. This notification must be submitted together with all relevant documentation to assess the safety of the installation. A report of an expert stating compliance with the material demands of sections 2 and 3 of the Ordinance must be included in the paperwork. Moreover, an expert has to examine the leak tightness and the existence of the necessary protection measures before commissioning (see section 6 GasHDrLtgV). He has to issue a certificate stating that no safety-related arguments can be made against the commissioning of the pipeline.

---

315. Gashochdruckleitungsverordnung of 18 May 2011 (BGBl. I p. 928).

§2. Environmental Impact Assessment

554. The pipeline must be in compliance with the material conditions arising from environmental protection law, whether or not an environmental impact assessment is carried out. If an environmental impact assessment is deemed necessary, various data must be collected and the project's effect on the natural environment has to be assessed.

555. Number 19 of the Annex 1 to the Environmental Impact Assessment Statute (*UVPG*) contains the criteria that determine whether or not an environmental impact assessment is necessary.[316] Number 19.2 of the annex lists the construction and operation of gas supply lines (excluding lines that do not run beyond factory premises) but differentiates based on their length and calibre. For instance, a gas supply line with a length of more than 40 kms and a calibre of more than 800 mm will always require an environmental impact assessment. A gas supply line with a length of more than 40 kms and a calibre from 300 mm up to 800 mm and a line with a length from 5–40 kms and a calibre of more than 300 mm, these lines would both require a general preliminary examination. The decision to carry out an environmental impact assessment will be based on this examination. For gas supply lines with a length of less than 5 kms and a calibre of more than 300 mm, a site-related preliminary examination needs to be conducted.

316. Gesetz über die Umweltverträglichkeitsprüfung, in the version of the publication of 18 Mar. 2021 (BGBl. I p. 540).

Chapter 5. Distribution

556. The following chapter highlights the rules for the regulation of the gas sector in Germany. Since the EnWG applies to both the electricity and the gas sector, the basic structures of gas regulation are similar to those in the electricity sector (explained above in Part I, Chapters 1 and 2). For these reasons, this chapter will attempt to identify and clarify particularities of the gas sector.

§1. Overview and History of Gas Regulation

557. A decisive step towards liberalization was made on the EU's internal natural gas market with the implementation of Directive 98/30/EC.[317] In Germany, rules for grid access have been developed in a number of Association Agreements which have been concluded between the associations in the energy markets. The EnWG enacted in 2003 transposed the requirements of Directive 98/30/EC.

558. However, in that same year the European Community enacted Directive 2003/55/EC on the internal market in natural gas, repealing the former Directive 98/30/EC.[318] Like Directive 2003/54/EC for the electricity sector, Directive 2003/55/EC rendered regulated grid access obligatory by eliminating the option of contract-based grid access. As a consequence, the German EnWG 2005 drew up several amendments to transpose the European standards into German national law.

559. The European framework has been developed further with Directive 2009/73/EC, which needed to be transposed into national law by 3 March 2011.[319] The rules of this Third Energy Package have been transposed into national law by an amendment of the EnWG in particular (see in detail above Introduction, Chapter 7 and Part I, Chapter 1, section 2, II. B.)

560. The 'winter package' of the European Union of 2016 as such did not contain a comprehensive amendment of the Gas Directive 2009/73/EC. However, in 2021 the European Commission initiated a process to amend the European Gas Directive and the Gas Regulation 715/2009. The focus of the legislative amendments is to create a framework for renewable and low-carbon gases, in particular for hydrogen and biomethane.[320] The proposals in particular aim at establishing a

317. Directive 98/30/EC of the European Parliament and of the Council of 22 Jun. 1998 concerning common rules for the internal market in natural gas, OJ L 204, 21 Jul. 1998, 1–12.
318. Directive 2003/55/EC of the European Parliament and of the Council of 26 Jun. 2003 concerning common rules for the internal market in natural gas and repealing Directive 98/30/EC, OJ L 176, 15 Jul. 2003, 57–78.
319. Directive 2009/73/EC of the European Parliament and of the Council of 13 Jul. 2009 concerning common rules for the internal market in natural gas and repealing Directive 2003/55/EC, OJ L 211, 14 Aug. 2009, 94–136.
320. *See* European Commission, Commission proposes new EU framework to decarbonize gas markets, promote hydrogen, and reduce methane emissions, 15 Dec. 2021; European Commission, Proposal

hydrogen infrastructure complementing the network for natural gas, and at progressively replacing fossil gas by other low-carbon sources.

561. The rapid pace at which legal provisions are drafted and implemented demonstrates the liberalization trend, which now becomes more and more outperformed by the intention of decarbonizing the gas markets. In the following, main elements of the EnWG and its subsequent regulations transposing the European provisions will be summarized. As new European rules on renewable and low-carbon gases are still in the process of being enacted, the focus of the following sections is on the already implemented rules for liberalization of the gas markets.

§2. Unbundling

562. The following section shall briefly mention the rules on unbundling in the EnWG. These also apply to gas companies. Most of the unbundling rules apply to vertically integrated energy supply companies. These companies are, in the gas sector, engaged with at least one of the activities associated with long-distance transport, distribution, operation of an LNG facility or storage, and with at least one activity in the field of the production or the sale of natural gas (section 3 number 38 EnWG). However, the scope of the unbundling provisions may differ. For example, the duties on financial accounting and on the internal bookkeeping of section 6b EnWG apply to vertically integrated energy supply companies generally. Special rules for transport grid operators have been implemented in sections 8 to 10e EnWG, following the requirements of the Third Energy Package (see in detail above Part I, Chapter 1, section 2, II. B. 5.).

563. Legal unbundling under section 7 EnWG requires vertically integrated energy supply companies to ensure that distribution grid operators who are associated with the company are organized in a legal form independent from the other business operating areas of the company. An exception applies to small vertically integrated companies that have less than 100,000 customers directly or indirectly connected to their gas supply grids (section 7 paragraph 2 EnWG). No duty of a full ownership unbundling currently exists. Such an obligation would render a separation of the assets necessary.

564. With the operational unbundling in section 7a EnWG, independence between the grid operation and the other business activities of the company shall be ensured. Persons working for the grid operator must be separated from the other business activities of a vertically integrated company, subject to the provisions in section 7a paragraphs 2–4 EnWG. For example, companies have to take appropriate measures to ensure the independence of persons entrusted with leading jobs by the grid operator (paragraph 2 and 3). Vertically integrated companies must ensure that grid operators enjoy real decision authority regarding the assets necessary for

---

for a Directive on common rules for the internal markets in renewable and natural gases and in hydrogen of 15 Dec. 2021, COM(2021) 803 final.

the operation, maintenance, and expansion of the grid under section 7a paragraph 4 EnWG. It is important to note that the provisions on operational unbundling are not mandatory for small vertically integrated companies with less than 100,000 customers directly or indirectly connected to their gas supply grids (section 7a paragraph 7 EnWG).

565. Moreover, vertically integrated companies have to ensure the confidentiality of economically sensitive information they acquired during their activities as grid operator (section 6a EnWG). Section 6b EnWG contains further rules on financial accounting and internal bookkeeping. Companies associated with a vertically integrated company are obliged to keep separate accounts for certain activities, such as long-distance transport of gas, gas distribution, and gas storage.

§3. Access to the Grid

566. Section 20 paragraph 1 EnWG obliges operators of gas grids to grant grid access to any interested party based on justified and non-discriminatory conditions, as discussed in Part I of this monograph. Section 20 paragraph 1b EnWG stipulates conditions on the access to gas supply grids, which will be further explained below. These conditions are regulated in more detail in the Regulation on the Access to Gas Supply Grids (*Gasnetzzugangsverordnung, GasNZV*).[321] On the European Level, Regulation 715/2009 on conditions for access to the natural gas transmission networks provides for directly applicable provisions on access to gas transmission networks.[322]

I. Grid Access According to Section 20 Paragraph 1b EnWG

567. According to section 20 paragraph 1b EnWG, the access to gas supply grids is based on the conclusion of contracts for gas feed-in as well as for gas offtake. Access to the gas grid is therefore granted based on a so-called entry-exit system. Operators of gas supply grids are obliged to offer feed-in and offtake capacities, allowing for grid access without the transport path being determined or dependent on the transaction. Moreover, the feed-in and offtake capacities must be useable and tradable independent of each other. Sentence 10 of the clause gives a legal definition of the entry-exit system by stating that operators of gas transmission networks are obliged to arrange for reserved capacities in a way as to entitle the transport customer, generally speaking, to supply gas at every entry point of the gas grid to every exit point within the grid. In practice, the DSOs are also included in this form of entry-exit system.

321. Verordnung über den Zugang zu Gasversorgungsnetzen, Gasnetzzugangsverordnung of 3 Sep. 2010, BGBl. I p. 1261.
322. Regulation (EC) No. 715/2009 of the European Parliament and of the Council of 13 Jul. 2009 on conditions for access to the natural gas transmission networks and repealing Regulation (EC) No. 1775/2005, OJ L 211/36.

568. Generally it is therefore not necessary to agree on a certain transport path. However, with fees depending on the transport distance, the use of a certain physical transport path was required before the new legal provisions came into force.[323] Under the previous Association Agreement Gas II, the model for the access to the gas grids was based on a contract-dependent path (point-to-point model), which did not lead to sufficient competition.[324] The entry-exit model has largely resolved this competition issue; seen together with the reduction of market areas (see below II, C).

569. The entry-exit system requires for a feed-in contract to be concluded with the grid operator in whose grid the feed-in shall take place. An offtake contract can be signed with the grid operator in whose grid the offtake shall take place (section 20 paragraph 1b sentences 2 and 3 EnWG). Sentences 5–9 of section 20 paragraph 1b EnWG demand the cooperation of the grid operators, which is necessary to allow a manageable transport via the gas networks. This includes the duty to confer the booked feed-in and offtake capacities in case the supplier changes and the new supplier cannot otherwise fulfil his supply obligation (which must be well-founded, *see* sentence 9 of section 20 paragraph 1b EnWG). The obligation for grid operators to cooperate has led to a system of 'cooperation agreements' with high practical relevance for the grid access.[325]

570. The access to the gas networks allowed for by section 20 paragraphs 1 and 1b EnWG may be denied under the restrictive conditions in section 20 paragraph 2 EnWG. To legitimately deny access under section 20, grid operators need to prove that granting of the grid access is impossible or unreasonable due to operational or other grounds. Grid access denial must be reported to the Network Agency; therefore, such a measure is likely to be subject to controls by the authorities.

II. Regulation on the Access to Gas Supply Grids (GasNZV)

571. Grid access conditions that grid operators must comply with are further specified in the Regulation on the Access to Gas Supply Grids (*GasNZV*). This regulation has been enacted anew in a substantially amended version in 2010. The earlier version of the GasNZV did not sufficiently match the entry-exit model.

323. H.W. Schiffer, *Energiemarkt Deutschland*, 10th edn (Köln: TÜV Media, 2008), 203. The introduction of the entry-exit model also goes back to the so-called Marathon-Procedure conducted by the European Commission against several transmission network operators.
324. Christiane Nill-Theobald & Christian Theobald, *Grundzüge des Energiewirtschaftsrechts*, 2nd edn (München: C.H. Beck, 2008), 277; J. Müller-Kirchenbauer, C. Thole & P. Stratmann in: F.J. Säcker, *Berliner Kommentar zum Energierecht*, 2nd edn (Frankfurt a.M.: Verlag Recht und Wirtschaft, 2010), s. 20 EnWG para. 160; F. Arndt in: G. Britz, J. Hellermann & G. Hermes, *EnWG*, 2nd edn (München: C.H. Beck, 2010), s. 20 para. 127.
325. *See* C. de Wyl, & C. Thole & A. Bartsch in: J.P. Schneider & C. Theobald, *Recht der Energiewirtschaft*, 5th edn (München: C.H. Beck, 2021), § 17 paras 409 et seqq.

Discussions on the model for grid access were still ongoing until the very moment it was meant to enter into force, and some rapid last-minute changes had to be made.[326]

572. Two main drawbacks identified and addressed by the revised GasNZV at that time were the lack of gas capacities available to competitors due to the long-term booking of the capacities, and the practical difficulties resulting from the existence of several market areas. The latter has been problematic when gas transports cover more than one market area. The GasNZV addresses these issues in order to improve capacity management by setting limits to the share in capacities that can be booked on a long-term basis, for instance. It also successfully aimed at reducing the market areas. Furthermore, with regard to the necessary capacities in the grid for such projects, the GasNZV intends to provide security of investment in storage facilities as well as in gas fired power plants.[327]

A. Overview of the Rules on Access to the Gas Grid

573. Transport customers of gas can be wholesale dealers, gas suppliers, and final consumers (section 3 number 31d EnWG). For the grid access under the GasNZV, they are entitled and obliged to conclude feed-in and offtake contracts.[328] If a transport customer only intends to deal at the virtual point of trade, he will need to conclude at least a grid balance contract with the person responsible for the market area (section 3 paragraph 1 sentence 2 GasNZV). The virtual point of trade is a point in the market area at which gas can be transferred between balancing groups (*Bilanzkreisen*), without corresponding to a real physical feed-in and offtake point (section 2 number 15 GasNZV). The conclusion of a grid balancing contract (*Bilanzkreisvertrag*) is necessary since it provides rules for the balancing and accounting of differences in the feed-in and offtake amounts.[329] The content of grid balancing contracts is to a high degree determined by the rules of the 'GABi Gas 2.0' set forth by the Federal Network Agency.[330]

574. TSOs must offer standardized feed-in and offtake contracts (section 3 paragraph 3 GasNZV) to transport customers. Whereas the feed-in contract allows the transport customer to use the grid from the point of feed-in up to the virtual point of trade, the offtake contract allows the transport customer to use the grid from this virtual point down to the point where the gas is taken out of the grid again; most

326. F. Arndt in: G. Britz, J. Hellermann & G. Hermes, *EnWG*, 2nd edn (München: C.H. Beck, 2010), s. 20 para. 130.
327. Reasons of the Regulation, BR-Drs. 312/10, 1 et seq.
328. *See* s. 3 GasNZV.
329. BT-Drs. 312/10, 59.
330. Bundesnetzagentur, decision of 19 Dec. 2014, BK7-14-020.

often a DSO system. Section 4 GasNZV further elaborates on the minimum specifications in the standard terms of feed-in and offtake contracts. Transport customers must be registered at the grid operator with whom they intend to conclude contracts (section 6 GasNZV).

575. Section 8 GasNZV specifies how the issue of grid access needs to be handled. According to paragraph 1, all grid operators are obliged to transfer the amount of gas supplied by the transport customer at a point of feed-in to the point of offtake appointed by the transport customer, and to deliver gas with the same energy content. The obligation of transmission network operators to offer freely assignable capacities allowing for feed-in and offtake without determination of a transport path is regulated in more detail in section 8 paragraph 2 GasNZV. Accordingly, it must be possible for transport customers to book feed-in and offtake capacities independent of each other, in different amounts and at variable times. The rights on the booked capacities (so-called capacity rights) entitle the transport customer to provide gas within their capacity rights at any booked point of feed-in for offtake at any booked point of offtake within the market area. The flexibility targeted by the entry-exit system shall thereby be ensured.[331] Grid operators had to agree on a Cooperation Agreement (*Kooperationsvereinbarung*) on the processing of transports that cross the borders of networks, pursuant to section 8 paragraph 6 GasNZV.[332] The cooperation agreements have a high relevance for practice. They contain *inter alia* rules on contracts (feed-in, offtake and grid balance contracts), on market areas, regulating energy and on balancing.

B. Capacity Management

576. The subsequent provisions of the GasNZV contain rules on capacity management with the aim of providing a more effective access to capacities and thus for an enhanced competition. A decision procedure with regard to capacity management (*Festlegungsverfahren*) started by the Federal Network Agency in 2010 lead to the decision called ‘KARLA’ which shall in particular help to avoid capacity shortages.[333]

577. Transmission network operators need to determine their technical capacity, according to the rules in section 9 GasNZV. Section 11 GasNZV names minimum capacity products that transmission network operators must be able to offer.[334]

331. BT-Drs. 312/10, 63.
332. The Cooperation Agreements, including the current Cooperation Agreement XII effective from 1 Oct. 2021, can be found on the webpage of the Bundesverband der Energie- und Wasserwirtschaft, www.bdew.de.
333. Bundesnetzagentur, Decision BK7-10-001; further information can be found via on www-.bundesnetzagentur.de. *See* also the addition BK7-18-087 of 6 Dec. 2018.
334. BT-Drs. 312/10, 67.

578. As for the allocation of feed-in and offtake capacity, transmission network operators are required to operate a common platform, section 12 GasNZV. The allocation of feed-in and offtake capacities must be organized according to the rules contained in section 13 GasNZV in a transparent and non-discriminating procedure. Paragraph 3 of this clause clarifies that capacity allocation in the form of tenders does not apply to offtake capacities that connect to final consumers. It does not apply to biogas plants either.[335] These other capacities (still) are allocated according to a principle of priority ('first-come-first-serve').

579. Section 15 GasNZV generally obliges transport customers to nominate the intended use of feed-in and offtake capacities according to hourly amounts in kilowatt-hours (kWh) to the transmission network operator. Until this point of nomination, transport customers are obliged to offer unused definite capacities on a separate platform or to provide them to the transmission network operator under the more detailed rules of section 16 GasNZV. The second paragraph generally obliges the transmission network operator to offer the capacities that are not nominated by the transport customer for the day ahead as definite capacities.

C. Reduction of Market Areas

580. From 1 October 2011 on, only two market areas existed in the German market (GASPOOL and NetConnect Germany (NCG)). Before, from 1 April 2011 onwards, three market areas existed in Germany; one market area already combined the qualities of H-gas and L-gas. In November 2010, all gas consumers still fell within one of six market areas for gas supply in Germany. These market areas could not be regarded as completely separate, since they often overlapped each other.[336] The transmission network operators establish the market areas, and assign a person responsible for the market area. This person in particular needs to operate the virtual point of trade of the market area, handle the grid balance (*Bilanzkreisabwicklung*), and procure and control the use of balancing energy, section 20 GasNZV.

581. From 1 October 2021, the two market areas have been consolidated into a common market area 'Trading Hub Europe (THE)'.[337] Over the course of more than ten years, the number of market areas thus has been significantly reduced. This reduction of the number of market areas has always been regarded as an important measure for enhanced competition.[338] The GasNZV has been one main driver behind the further reduction of market areas. At last, it foresaw in section 21 paragraph 1 sentence 2 GasNZV to form one market area out of the remaining two market areas latest until 1 April 2022.

---

335. BT-Drs. 312/10, 71.
336. H.W. Schiffer, *Energiemarkt Deutschland,* 10th edn (Köln: TÜV Media, 2008), 204.
337. *See* Bundesnetzagentur / Bundeskartellamt, *Monitoringreport 2021*, Dec 2021, p. 403 et seq., available at www.bundesnetzagentur.de.
338. Monopolies Commission, Special Report, *Strom und Gas 2009 – Energiemärkte im Spannungsfeld von Politik und Wettbewerb*, BT-Drs. 16/14060, 86.

D. Balancing

582. Rules on balancing (*Bilanzierung*) and on the use of balancing energy (*Regelenergie*) can be found in the fifth part of the GasNZV (sections 22 et seqq. GasNZV). Deviations between the feed-in and the offtake of gas amounts by transport customers are balanced out by a so-called balancing group (*Bilanzkreis*) as set out in section 22 paragraph 1 GasNZV. The rules in the GasNZV have largely been based on the 28 May 2008 decision of the BNetzA concerning the balancing and regulating of energy.[339] With this decision, the Federal Network Agency standardized and concretized the rules for the balancing of gas by providing a standard grid balancing contract (*Bilanzkreisvertrag*). It also set forth rules on regulating energy and balancing within the gas sector in Annex 2 to the said decision, the so-called GABi Gas.

583. According to the rules in the GABi Gas (now GABi Gas 2.0)[340], the relevant period for balancing is one day, the so-called gas day. Section 23 GasNZV defines the length of the gas day reaching from 6.00 am to 6.00 am of the following day. As for the allocation of offtake amounts of final consumers, distribution grid operators use standard load profiles (*Standardlastprofil*) up to a maximum hourly offtake of 500 kWh per hour and up to a maximum yearly offtake of 1.5 million kWh (section 24 paragraph 1 GasNZV). The surplus and the shortfall between the allocated amounts and the real offtake of the final consumer count as supplied by the offtake grid operator. The differences are therefore settled between the grid operator and the transport customer (section 25 paragraph 1 GasNZV).

584. To compensate for fluctuations of the grid load, balancing energy is used in accordance with the rules in sections 27 et seqq. GasNZV. The costs for the purchase of regulating energy may be apportioned in particular via the balancing groups, see closer section 29 GasNZV.

E. Storage, LNG and Production Facilities

585. The GasNZV also provides rules that shall allow for a more effective access to capacity for storage, LNG, and production facilities with the aim to provide more investment security for their construction. Under section 38 GasNZV, operators of storage, LNG, and production facilities that have been connected to the grid after the GasNZV came into force now generally enjoy a right to reserve offtake capacity for the transmission gas network within the technically available capacity. This right does not exist if the reservation results in the technical capacity designated being exceeded, taking into account the share of the technical capacity of the transmission system concerned that has already been booked. The provision shall encourage operators to invest in such facilities. With the demands in the second paragraph of

---

339. BNetzA, decision of 28 May 2008, File Number: BK7-08-002. *See* the reference of the reasoning to the GasNZV to this decision in BT-Drs. 312/10, 83.
340. Bundesnetzagentur, decision of 19 Dec. 2014, BK7-14-020.

section 38 GasNZV, the future operator of the facility shall ensure that its investment is sufficiently concretized so that operators may not reserve a 'stock' of capacities.[341]

586. If a reservation of capacity fails, operators could even have a claim to expand the existing capacity according to the rules in section 39 GasNZV. An exception applies if the capacity expansion is economically non-feasible for the transmission grid operator. An expansion is deemed economically feasible if the capacity is booked with the transmission grid operator on a long-term basis (see closer section 39 paragraph 1 sentence 2 GasNZV). This is intended to protect the transmission grid operator against stranded investments.[342] The operator of the facility who wants to connect to the grid has to elaborate a 'realization roadmap' for the capacity expansion together with the transmission grid operator (section 39 paragraph 2 GasNZV).

587. In light of the Ukraine-war and to foster security of supply, sections 35a et seqq. EnWG foresee fill level specifications (*Füllstandsvorgaben*) which shall lead to defined fill levels in the period from 1 October of a calendar year to 1 February of the subsequent year. The operator of a gas storage facility shall include contractual provisions defining the respective framework conditions for achieving these filling level requirements.

F. Change of Supplier and Role of the Federal Network Agency

588. Sections 41 et seqq. GasNZV provide rules on the change of the supplier. The change of supplier constitutes a singularly important tool for competition, which is underlined by the reasoning in the GasNZV.[343] Grid operators need to offer nationwide uniform procedures on supplier change, that are suitable for high-volume business. The new supplier may under certain conditions demand the transfer of the feed-in and offtake capacities booked by the former supplier in accordance with the 'backpack-principle' in section 42 GasNZV.

589. Section 50 GasNZV gives the Federal Network Agency a broad number of authorizations to take further decisions on the topic of grid access. These rules shall guarantee that the system of grid access is capable of learning.[344]

590. The Ruling Chamber of the Federal Network Agency (*BNetzA*) competent for the regulation of access to gas grids is the seventh Ruling Chamber. Decisions

341. BT-Drs. 312/10, 97.
342. BT-Drs. 312/10, 99.
343. BT-Drs. 312/10, 99.
344. BT-Drs. 312/10, 103.

taken by the BNetzA are most relevant to the gas sector in practice. The undertakings concerned are allowed to participate in the proceedings of the Ruling Chamber. The decisions of the Ruling Chambers can be found on the webpage of the BNetzA.[345]

III. Grid Fees, Incentive Regulation

591. The amount of grid fees (*Netzentgelte*) is of high importance for the competition on the gas markets. Grid fees in Germany are subject to regulation. Cost control is carried out *ex ante* in the regulated market, which is contrasted by the control of the cartel authorities, which is usually carried out *ex post*. Following the European Directives of 2003, with the EnWG 2005 grid fees started to become regulated. First, a cost-orientated regulation of the grid fees according to section 21 paragraph 2 EnWG was undertaken. This system of cost-orientated control of the grid fees has been changed into a model of 'incentive regulation' (*Anreizregulierung*).

592. Based on section 21a EnWG, the details of the incentive regulation are to be found in the Incentive Regulation Ordinance (*Anreizregulierungsverordnung, ARegV*).[346] From 1 January 2009, grid fees are determined by means of this incentive regulation (section 1 paragraph 1 ARegV).

593. The incentive regulation aims at demanding higher effectiveness of the companies concerned and thus to converge to market conditions. The incentive regulation modifies the cost-orientated regulation pursuant to section 21 paragraph 2 EnWG. The key element is the determination of a 'revenue cap' being the admissible total revenue resulting from the grid access fees for a grid operator, see section 4 paragraph 1 ARegV.[347] The revenue caps are determined by the Regulatory Authorities. They are calculated pursuant to sections 4 et seqq. ARegV and to the rather complicated 'regulation formula' in Annex 1 of the ARegV.[348]

594. In principle, the revenue caps shall allow for a compensation of the grid costs and an appropriate equity yield rate.[349] But costs shall be lowered to an efficient level. The revenues allowed are for certain periods of times uncoupled from the approvable costs. Consequently, an additional reduction of costs leads to a

345. www.bundesnetzagentur.de.
346. Verordnung über die Anreizregulierung der Energieversorgungsnetze, Anreizregulierungsverordnung of 29 Oct. 2007 (BGBl. I p. 2529).
347. Closer R. Ruge, 'Die neue Anreizregulierungsverordnung (ARegV) – Systemwechsel bei der Regulierung der Netzentgelte im Energiebereich', *DVBl* (2008): 956 et seq.
348. *See* in more detail H. Weyer in: J.F. Baur, P. Salje & M. Schmidt-Preuß, *Regulierung in der Energiewirtschaft* (Köln: Carl Heymanns Verlag, 2011), 1226 et seq.
349. H. Weyer in: J.F. Baur, P. Salje & M. Schmidt-Preuß, *Regulierung in der Energiewirtschaft* (Köln: Carl Heymanns Verlag, 2011), 1221.

higher rate of return, working as an incentive to become more efficient. Any inefficiency shall be minimized during the so-called regulation periods. Such a regulation period generally lasts five years (section 3 paragraph 2 ARegV). Overall, the incentive regulation shall compensate for the lack of competition in the (gas) grids.[350]

§4. Biogas

595. There is no exclusive statute for the promotion of biogas in Germany. Instead, the existing framework that fosters the use of biogas is spread over a number of legal statutes and ordinances. The feed-in of biogas into the natural gas grid in particular is promoted by rules on the connection and offtake of biogas facilities.

I. Rules Promoting the Use of Biogas

596. The rules that apply to the promotion of biogas depend on the end use of the biogas. If biogas is used for the generation of electricity, the electricity fed-in into the electricity grid may under further conditions be promoted by the Renewable Energy Sources Act (*Erneuerbare-Energien-Gesetz, EEG*). Under the provisions of the EEG, financial support paid by the grid operator for the electricity from biogas that is fed into the grid may be available (see closer below Part V, Chapter 5, section 2). Biomass installations with an installed capacity of more than 150 kW generally must successfully participate in a tender procedure to accrue a claim for financial support.

597. One of the preconditions for this promotion is that the biogas counts as biomass to fall under the definitions contained in the Biomass Ordinance (*Biomasseverordnung*, hereinafter *BiomasseV*).[351] According to section 2 BiomasseV, biomass within the meaning of the Ordinance means fuels made of phytomass and zoomass, also including products, by-products, residues, and waste from phytomass and zoomass whose energy content comes from phytomass and zoomass. Gas produced from biomass by gasification or pyrolysis and all resulting products and by-products are regarded as biomass (section 2 paragraph 2 number 5 BiomasseV). However, section 3 of the Ordinance in particular lists substances that are not regarded as biomass.

598. The Renewable Energy Sources Act contains further preconditions for the right to claim financial support, which are treated in detail below in Part V, Chapter 2. As a general rule, the facility that generates electricity from renewable sources must use renewable energy sources exclusively in order to be entitled to the remuneration, section 19 paragraph 1 EEG.

---

350. H. Weyer in: J.F. Baur, P. Salje & M. Schmidt-Preuß, *Regulierung in der Energiewirtschaft* (Köln: Carl Heymanns Verlag, 2011), 1219, 1221 et seq.
351. Verordnung über die Erzeugung von Strom aus Biomasse of 21 Jun. 2001 (BGBl. I p. 1234).

599. The heat sector constitutes another possible area of application of biogas. Here, the Act on the Saving of Energy and the Use of Renewable Energies for Heat and Cold Generation in Buildings (*Gebäudeenergiegesetz, GEG*)[352] prescribes a minimum share of renewable energy in the supply of thermal energy demand of buildings (closer below Part V, Chapter 7). The use of gaseous biomass meets the obligation to reach a certain share of renewable energy if at least 50% of the thermal energy demand is covered by this source (or 30% if used in a cogeneration unit), section 40 paragraph 2 GEG.

600. Moreover, biogas also benefits from the quotas that target a certain share of biofuels within the transport sector. The minimum share of biofuels in the transport sector are set forth in section 37a Federal Immissions Control Act (*BImSchG*), while section 37b of this Act regulates that in particular biomethane may count as a biofuel to fulfil the targets (see closer below Part III, Chapter 5, section 2).

II. Connection with the Grid and Grid Access for Biogas

601. The above-named support mechanisms for the use of biogas do not only apply if biogas is directly consumed at the point of its production. Instead, biogas can also be fed into the natural gas grid and be used elsewhere. For the support mechanism under the Renewable Energy Sources Act, this is foreseen in section 44b paragraph 4 EEG. Accordingly, gas withdrawn from a gas network is deemed to be biomethane where the thermal equivalent of the withdrawn quantity of such gas at the end of a calendar year corresponds to the quantity of gas from biomass fed into the gas network elsewhere, within the territorial application of the Act. Also, mass balance systems must be used for the entire transportation and distribution of the gas, from its production or generation, feed into the natural gas network and its transportation within the natural gas network through to its withdrawal from the natural gas network.

602. The German government wants to foster the feed-in of biogas into the natural gas network. This shall facilitate the transportation of biogas to the place where consumption is most reasonable by making use of the existing infrastructure. The government has also provided rules on the connection of biogas plants to the natural gas grid and the offtake of biogas by the grid operator in the Regulation on the Access to Gas Supply Grids (*GasNZV*).[353] In 2010, this regulation was amended, resulting in better rules on grid access and use for biogas plants and an enhanced promotion of the feed-in of biogas. Together with the EEG 2014, previous concrete aims for the volume of biogas feed-in have been abolished since they are not realistic, given the reduced support for new biogas installations from the EEG 2014 onwards.[354]

---

352. Gebäudeenergiegesetz of 8 Aug. 2020 (BGBl. I p. 1728).
353. *See* in more detail M. Altrock & C. Helbach in: H. Loibl et al., *Biogasanlagen im EEG,* 4th edn (Berlin: Erich Schmidt Verlag, 2016), 869 et seq.
354. BT-Drs. 18/1891, p. 3.

603. Section 33 GasNZV obliges grid operators to offer a preferential connection to their natural gas grids to biogas plants. The norm contains detailed rules on the procedure of establishing a connection to the natural gas grid. If an assessment of the possible connection with the gas grid is positive, the grid operator needs to offer a contract for the connection and feed-in, which includes the assurance of a certain guaranteed minimum feed-in capacity. The revised version of the clause from 2010 further states that plant operators and grid operators will agree on a 'realization roadmap' (section 33 paragraph 7 GasNZV).

604. Importantly, section 33 paragraph 1 GasNZV also contains a standard by which the costs for the connection of the biogas plant to the gas grid are shared between the plant and the grid operator. As a general rule, the natural gas grid operator must bear 75% of the costs for the connection. In case the connecting pipe has a length of up to 1 km, the plant operator only needs to bear costs of up to EUR 250,000. However, the plant operator must bear the additional costs if a connecting pipe exceeds a length of 10 kms.

605. Operators of the natural gas grids are obliged to conclude contracts on the feed-in and output preferentially with transport customers of biogas and to transport biogas preferentially, section 34 GasNZV. An exception of their duty to take off the biogas is made in the second paragraph of this clause, but only if the feed-in is technically impossible or economically unreasonable. The Regulation on the Access to Gas Supply Grids also contains special balancing rules with regard to biogas and prescribes minimum quality requirements biogas must meet if it is to be fed into the natural gas grid.

606. Moreover, a flat remuneration for transport customers of biogas is stipulated by section 20a of the Regulation on Remunerations for the Access to Gas Supply Grids (*Gasnetzentgeltverordnung, GasNEV*). The operator of the gas grid needs to pay transport customers of biogas EUR 0.007 per kWh for avoided net costs for ten years. Any remuneration under the Renewable Energy Sources Act is available for electricity generated from the biogas in addition.

607. Regarding grid connection and take-off obligation, the existing rules can be deemed sufficient. However, due to the high costs connected with biogas production (as compared to wind energy and solar energy after the prices for panels went down) and also due to the ongoing questions on the sustainability of biomass as an energy source, the revised Renewable Energy Sources Act 2014 only provided for a narrow path for expansion of bioenergy. Waste and residues have been promoted as input substances. Following these legislative changes, during recent years there has been only a moderate increase in capacity of installations feeding in biomethane into the natural gas grid.[355]

---

355. Deutsche Energie Agentur, Branchenbarometer Biomethan 2021, 07/2021, available at www.dena.de, last access 1 May 2022, p. 4.

§5. National Emissions Trading

608. From 2021 onwards, the Fuel Emissions Trading Act (*Brennstoffemissionshandelsgesetz, BEHG*) creates a system of national emissions trading in addition to the European emissions trading scheme. This national emissions trading is of particular relevance for the gas sector as it applies also for the distribution of natural gas. The national emissions trading scheme is explained closer below in Part VI, Chapter 2, §3.

Chapter 6. Consumption

609. Before the beginning of liberalization in the energy sector, the relation between gas companies and their 'tariff customers' was governed by the Regulation on General Conditions for the Gas Supply of Tariff Customers (*Verordnung über Allgemeine Bedingungen für die Gasversorgung von Tarifkunden*, hereinafter: *AVBGasV*). Until the amendment of the EnWG in 2005, the underlying basis for this regulation has been the duty under section 10 of the EnWG of 1998. Accordingly, energy supply companies had to publish general conditions and tariffs for the gas supply in low pressure, and to connect and supply everyone to these conditions and tariffs in their area. The latter was defined as the territory in which a given energy company is responsible for the general supply of end consumers.

610. This approach needed to be remodelled, especially in terms of customer relations, in the light of the liberalization process and the unbundling of the supply and the grid operation.[356] Based on provisions in the revised EnWG, the government decided on four new regulations for grid connection and grid use, as well as for the universal service obligation in the electricity and gas sector. In the gas sector, these new regulations were the Regulation on General Conditions for the Universal Supply of Domestic Customers and the Substitute Supply with Gas from the Low Pressure Grid (*Gasgrundversorgungsverordnung, GasGVV*)[357] and the Regulation on General Conditions for the Grid Connection and Use for the Gas Supply in Low Pressure (*Niederdruckanschlussverordnung, NDAV*).[358]

611. Both gas-related regulations resemble the regulations for the electricity sector, which have been explained above in Part I, Chapter 5. The following paragraphs will therefore briefly explain some of the provisions of the GasGVV and the NDAV.

§1. Grid Connection and Use in Low Pressure

612. The Regulation on General Conditions for the Grid Connection and Use for the Gas Supply in Low Pressure stipulates in more detail the rules for the grid connection and use in low pressure, which are generally provided by section 18 EnWG. Contrary to the AVBGasV, the rules in section 18 EnWG and in the NDAV in particular, distinguish between the grid connection and the use of this connection.

356. C. De Wyl, J. Eder & T.C. Hartmann, *Netzanschluss- und Grundversorgungsverordnungen* (Frankfurt a.M.:VWEWEnergieverlag, 2008) 1; F.R. Groß, 'Die neuen Netzanschluss- und Grundversorgungsverordnungen im Strom- und Gasbereich', *NJW* (2007): 1030, 1031.

357. Verordnung über Allgemeine Bedingungen für die Grundversorgung von Haushaltskunden und die Ersatzversorgung mit Gas aus dem Niederdrucknetz, Gasgrundversorgungsverordnung of 26 Oct. 2006 (BGBl. I pp. 2391, 2396).

358. Verordnung über Allgemeine Bedingungen für den Netzanschluss und dessen Nutzung für die Gasversorgung in Niederdruck, Niederdruckanschlussverordnung of 1 Nov. 2006 (BGBl. I pp. 2477, 2485).

613. In line with the rules of the NAV for the electricity sector, the NDAV also differentiates between the connection taker (*Anschlussnehmer*) in section 1 paragraph 2 NDAV and the connection user (*Anschlussnutzer*) in section 1 paragraph 3 NDAV. The relationship between grid operator and connection taker comprehends the connection of the gas installation via the grid connection as well as its operation, section 2 paragraph 1 NDAV. In contrast, the relationship with the connection user includes the right to use the grid connection for the offtake of gas, section 3 paragraph 1 sentence 1 NDAV. The second sentence of this norm highlights that the use of the connection neither covers the supply of the connection user with gas, nor the access to the gas grid (according to section 20 EnWG). This relationship is usually established through the conclusion of a contract at the latest at the time of the first offtake of gas. This relationship can also be established automatically, i.e., without the conclusion of a contract.

614. Both relationships of grid connection and use automatically include the provisions of the NDAV as part of the arrangement between grid operator and connection taker or user (section 1 paragraph 1 sentence 2 NDAV). The relationship of grid connection is governed by the second part of the NDAV, the use of this connection in the third part, while Part Four provides for a number of common provisions.

615. The NDAV sets out the location of the grid connection in section 5 with regard to the grid connection relationship. Connecting the grid for the general supply with the gas installation of the connection taker, the grid connection comprises the grid connection pipe, a blocking installation outside the building if such installation exists, insulating piece, main blocking installation, and house pressure control device. The provisions on the grid connection are also applicable to a pressure control device, if the control device is installed behind the end of the grid connection within the area of the customer installation. In the following, the NDAV regulates how the grid connection is established and who must bear the costs. Generally speaking, the grid operator is responsible for establishing the grid connection (section 6 NDAV) and will demand the costs from the connection taker (section 9 NDAV) using lump sum payments. Moreover, the grid operator may demand a partial payment of the building costs for the establishment or enforcement of the local distribution facilities. These partial payments may not be more than 50% of the building costs, section 11 paragraph 1 sentence 2 NDAV.

616. In the relationship of grid connection use, it is usually the grid operator who must provide for the use to previously designated extent at any given time, section 16 NDAV. The rules on the limitation of liability in section 18 NDAV are most relevant in this respect. In certain cases of financial damages, liability is first restricted to at least gross negligence, whereas gross negligence may be presumed to exist. Moreover, certain maximum limits of liability are provided.

§2. Universal Services

617. The duty of certain energy supply companies to supply domestic customers is regulated in section 36 EnWG and the Regulation on General Conditions for the Universal Supply of Domestic Customers and the Substitute Supply with Gas from the Low Pressure Grid (*GasGVV*).

I. Sections 36 and 38 EnWG

618. Energy supply companies have to set general public conditions and general prices for the supply of domestic customers in low voltage or low pressure, in those grid areas in which they conduct the basic supply (*Grundversorgung*) of domestic customers, section 36 paragraph 1 EnWG. They are also obliged to supply any domestic customer using these conditions and energy prices. An exception of these duties is possible if the energy company can demonstrate that the energy supply is not economically reasonable.

619. The second paragraph of section 36 EnWG defines the energy supply companies as the basic supplier (*Grundversorger*) and subject to these duties. Accordingly, the basic supplier is the energy supply company that supplies most of the domestic customers in a grid area of general supply. Every three years, the grid operator of the grid of general supply re-evaluates and determines which energy supply company is the basic supplier in a given area.

620. The substitute supply in section 38 EnWG clarifies what happens if an end consumer consumes energy over the energy grid of general supply in low voltage, without any energy supply contract. In these cases, the energy consumed is regarded as energy supplied by the basic supplier in accordance with section 36 paragraph 1 EnWG.

II. GasGVV

621. Consequently, the GasGVV also contains provisions for the basic gas supply in line with section 36 EnWG and for the substitute supply as set forth in section 38 EnWG. Both domestic customers as well as end consumers (in the case of substitute supply) are defined as customers within the terms of the regulation in section 1 paragraph 2 GasGVV.

622. Like the NDAV, the GasGVV is automatically regarded as a contractual agreement between the parties, in this case between the basic supplier and the domestic customer (section 1 paragraph 1 sentence 2 GasGVV). Section 2 GasGVV provides requirements for the conclusion of the contract between the basic supplier and the customer. The basic supply contract (*Grundversorgungsvertrag*) shall be concluded in text form, see closer section 126b BGB.

623. In general, the customer is obliged to supply his complete demand for gas over the grid from the basic supplier for the duration of the basic supply contract, section 4 GasGVV. Excluded from this obligation is consumption from own installations for the generation of gas from renewable sources. The basic supplier concludes the necessary contracts with the grid operator to ensure and enforce the basic gas supply. At any time, he is – with closer defined exceptions – obliged to supply the customer's gas demand for the duration of the supply contract, up to the defined extent of the contract (section 6 GasGVV). Paragraph 3 of this clause relieves the basic supplier from his supply duty, in particular in case of interruption due to failures in the grid operation.

624. Part Three of the GasGVV contains further provisions on measuring devices, the admission to the property of the customer and in Part Four on the accounting of the gas supply. Importantly, section 20 GasGVV gives the customer the right to terminate the basic supply contract with a period of only two weeks. Section 3 GasGVV declares a number of provisions dealing with basic supply to be applicable to substitute supply as well. Special cases of energy supply for which no contract currently exists can therefore be dealt with in a similar manner as an agreement with a basic supplier that is governed by a contract.

Part III. Regulatory Framework Concerning Petrol

625. Mineral oil is still the dominant energy source in Germany with regard to primary energy sources. In 2009, mineral oil had a share of 34.9% in the primary energy consumption by energy sources. In 2013, this value amounted to 33.1%, and in 2021 the share of mineral oil in the primary energy consumption still amounted to 32%.[359] However, this share decreased from a percentage of over 50% in the 1970s.[360] Mineral oil still is of high relevance for the transport sector and heating sector in particular. The use of mineral oil in the heating sector, however, has decreased significantly in recent years.[361] For the electricity generation, the use of mineral oil usually is between 1 and 2%.[362]

626. Germany is dependent on oil imports, the domestic oil exploitation adds only insignificantly to the fulfilment of the demand.

359. Umweltbundesamt, 'Primärenergieverbrauch', statistical data available via the webpage www.umweltbundesamt.de, last access 1 May 2022.
360. Federal Ministry of Economy and Climate Action, 'Mineralöl und Kraftstoffe', available at www.bmwi.de, last access: 1 May 2022.
361. Destatis, Deutscher Rohöl-Import 2018 auf Tiefstand seit 1992, Pressemitteilung Nr. 369 vom 20. September 2019, available at www.destatis.de, last access: 1 May 2022.
362. Umweltbundesamt, Erneuerbare und konventionelle Stromerzeugung, available at www.umweltbundesamt.de, last access 1 May 2022.

Chapter 1. Production

627. Chapter 1 will briefly introduce some provisions of the Federal Immissions Control Act (*BImSchG*) under which a permit may be necessary if oil is used as a charge material. Under the Federal Immissions Control Act explained above in Part II, Chapter 2, a permit is necessary for a facility using oil if it falls within the Fourth Ordinance for the Implementation of the Federal Immission Control Act (4. *BImSchV*). With this Ordinance, the Federal Government provided an exclusive catalogue of facilities which are in need of a permit under the Federal Immissions Control Act. The Fourth Federal Immissions Control Ordinance and in particular its annex have been revised by transposing Directive 2010/75/EU on industry emissions into national law, however with only few material changes.[363]

628. Relevant for large petroleum fired power plants is the provision in number 1.1 of Annex 1 of the 4. BImSchV, see above Part II, Chapter 2, section 2. More specific licensing requirements for the energy production using petroleum can be found in number 1.2.3 of Annex 1. Accordingly, installations for the generation of electricity, steam, hot water, process heat or hot waste gas by use of extra light fuel oil, methanol, ethanol, untreated vegetable oils or vegetable oil methyl esters, untreated natural gas, liquid gas, gases from public gas supply or hydrogen may require a permit depending in particular on the rated thermal input of the installations. For these facilities the simplified licensing procedure may apply.

629. Also, number 1.4 of Annex 1 is of relevance for the petroleum sector. Under this clause, in particular (but not exclusively) stationary internal combustion engines or gas turbine plants for the drive of machines with use of extra light fuel oil, diesel fuel, methanol, ethanol, untreated vegetable oils or vegetable oil methyl esters may be subject to a permit. For these facilities, the general or the simplified procedure under the BImSchG may apply dependent on the rated thermal input of the facility.

630. Also facilities for refining or processing petroleum are subject to a licence under the BImSchG according to number 4.4 Annex 1 of the 4. BImSchV. This provision comprehends installations for the distillation or refining or further processing of crude oil or crude oil in mineral oil, waste oil or lubricant refineries, in petrochemical plants or during paraffin production as well as gas refineries. The regular licensing procedure under the Federal Immissions Control Act applies for these facilities because they are listed with a 'G' in Annex 1 to the 4. BImSchV.

631. The licensing procedures and the material preconditions for the granting of a licence are explained in more detail above in Part II, Chapter 2, section 4.

---

363. J. Betensted & R. Grandjot & S. Waskow, 'Die Umsetzung der Richtlinie 2010/75/EU über Industrieemissionen (IE-Richtlinie) im Immissionsschutzrecht', *ZUR* (2013): 395 (396).

Chapter 2. Exploitation

632. According to figures provided by the LBEG of Lower Saxony, there have been ten active exploration wells for petroleum and natural gas exploration in Germany in 2009. The number of field development wells drilling amounted to twenty-three, the footage drilled accounted for 66,201 m. The annual oil production declined to 2.8 million metric tonnes in 2009. The proven and probable reserves of oil have been estimated at 41 million tonnes.[364] In 2020, the domestic oil production further decreased to 1.9 million tonnes.[365]

633. The Federal Mining Law (BBergG) will be discussed in detail in Part IV, Chapter 2, section 2 due to its particular relevance for the coal mining in Germany. At this stage, some special remarks for the petroleum sector shall be given.

634. Petrol belongs to the freely minable resources which are listed in section 3 paragraph 3 BBergG.[366] The Federal Mining Law generally requires the possession of a mining right for the exploration and exploitation of freely minable resources like natural gas, section 6 BBergG. These mining rights are divided into an exploration licence, a production licence, and the mining proprietorship. However, concrete mining activities may only be conducted on the basis of the so-called operating plans (*Betriebspläne*) approved by the competent authorities. Operating plans are *inter alia* framework operating plans which provide a general overview on the mining operation. Framework operating plans also connect the more detailed operating plans, the main operating plans (generally necessary for the operation of a mine), the special operation plans (applying for certain projects), and the final operating plans (for the case of mining activities being ceased). The main material preconditions are verified in the approval procedure for operating plans stipulated in sections 54 et seqq. BBergG.

635. A duty to conduct an environmental impact assessment as well as to propose a framework operating plan under the Federal Mining Statute arises in case the project is listed in the Ordinance on the Environmental Impact Assessment for Mining Projects (UVP-V Bergbau). In section 1 number 2, the UVP-V Bergbau lists the exploitation of petroleum for commercial purposes with a delivery volume of more than 500 tonnes of petroleum per day. Moreover, the construction and operation of offshore platforms in the area of coastal waters or the continental shelf is listed in

---

364. State Authority for Mining, Energy and Geology (LBEG) of Lower Saxony, *Jahresbericht Erdöl und Erdgas in der Bundesrepublik Deutschland, Summary,* available at: www.lbeg.niedersachsen.de/master/C38213918_N38202288_L20_D0_I31802357, last access: 28 Mar. 2011.

365. State Authority for Mining, Energy and Geology (LBEG) of Lower Saxony, *Jahresbericht Erdöl und Erdgas in der Bundesrepublik Deutschland 2020,* p. 24, available at: www.lbeg.niedersachsen.de, last access: 1 May 2022.

366. U. Büdenbender, W. Heintschel von Heinegg & P. Rosin, *Energierecht I, Recht der Energieanlagen* (Berlin/New York: Walter de Gruyter, 1999), para. 127.

section 1 number 2 b) UVP-V Bergbau. These projects thus in any case need to conduct an environmental impact assessment and to propose framework operating plans in addition to other operating plans necessary under the Federal Mining Law.

Chapter 3. Transport (German Petroleum Stockpiling Act)

636. Mineral oil is transported to Germany mainly by oil tankers and pipelines. Afterwards, most of the mineral oil products are refined in Germany.[367] The transport of the mineral oil products within the country is often conducted through pipelines. Also, there exists a large capacity for refined mineral oil storage. More than 50% of this storage capacity is used by the German National Petroleum Stockpiling Agency, whose function shall be explained in this chapter.[368]

637. As it has been demonstrated above, Germany's supply with petroleum is nearly exclusively based on imports from abroad. The high share of imported petroleum results in concerns on the security of oil supply, especially since the oil crisis in the 1970s. Concerns around security of supply have been increased again with the beginning of the war in Ukraine. In order to secure the supply with petroleum for a certain period of time, Germany enacted the German Petroleum Stockholding Act (hereinafter: *ErdölBevG*) in 1978.[369]

638. Under this Act, the German National Petroleum Stockpiling Agency has been founded as a corporation under public law.[370] This agency is responsible for the stockpiling of petroleum and petroleum products in accordance with the provisions of the ErdölBevG. Sections 3 and 4 ErdölBevG specify the product groups and the required quantity of the stockpile. They oblige the Petroleum Stockpiling Agency to keep stocks of the petroleum products listed. The stocks must reach the amount with which the specified products have been imported to and produced in Germany during the last three years on average within the course of ninety days.

639. The means necessary to fulfil this task are provided by fees of the members to the Petroleum Stockpiling Agency. In this way, an equal sharing of the costs of the stockpiling among producers and importers of petroleum products shall be achieved.[371] Member is, as a general rule with a number of exceptions and specifications, anyone who commercially or within the course of commercial undertakings imports petroleum products or produces them in Germany on his own account (section 13 ErdölBevG).

640. In the course of the Ukraine-war, the German government released a part of the national reserve to contribute to relieving oil markets.[372]

---

367. Bundeskartellamt, *Sektorenuntersuchung Kraftstoffe*, B8-100/07, Zwischenbericht, June 2009, 10.
368. Bundeskartellamt, *Sektorenuntersuchung Kraftstoffe*, B8-100/07, Zwischenbericht, June 2009, 13.
369. Now Erdölbevorratungsgesetz of 16 Jan. 2012 (BGBl. I p. 74).
370. Further information is available on the webpage of the German National Petroleum Stockpiling Agency, www.ebv-oil.org.
371. German National Petroleum Stockpiling Agency, *Mineralölpflichtbevorratung in der Bundesrepublik Deutschland* (2008), available on www.ebv-oil.org, last accessed 1 May 2022.
372. Die Bundesregierung, 'Bundesregierung gibt Teil der Ölreserve frei', 3 Mar. 2022, available at www.bundesregierung.de, last access 1 May 2022.

Chapter 4. Distribution

641. In a report to its review of the fuel sector in Germany, the *Bundeskartellamt* (the German Federal Competition Authority) assessed that an important drawback for enhanced competition in the fuel markets would be the high degree of vertical and horizontal concentration. Namely, the five companies of BP/Aral, ConocoPhilips/Jet, ExxonMobil/Esso, Shell, and Total together would constitute a dominant oligopoly on the petrol station market and would be integrated over all steps of the mineral oil economy.[373] Thus, the Bundeskartellamt announced that it would be necessary to stop a further concentration process by a restrictive merger control. It also states that the merger between Total and OMV concerning the Eastern German petrol station network of OMV was prohibited due to these reasons. The merger Shell/Lomo could have only been granted on the basis of a collateral clause. In particular, further mergers between the five companies named above would generally not be possible or if only under conditions.[374]

373. Bundeskartellamt, *Sektorenuntersuchung Kraftstoffe*, B8-200/09, Abschlussbericht, May 2011, 19.
374. Bundeskartellamt, *Sektorenuntersuchung Kraftstoffe*, B8-200/07, Abschlussbericht, May 2011, 34 et seq.

Chapter 5. Consumption (Renewable Energy in the Transport Sector)

642. This chapter is concerned with the promotion of renewable energy in the transport sector. Biofuels and renewable fuels of non-biological origin as an alternative for gasoline and diesel are discussed. However, the general discussion has shifted towards using electricity from renewable sources or green hydrogen or other innovative renewable fuels for the drive of electric vehicles. Also on the European level, the European Directive 2009/28/EC and its successor Directive 2018/2001/EU on the promotion of the use of energy from renewable sources already support 'E-Mobility' and renewable liquid and gaseous transport fuels of non-biological origin like green hydrogen.

643. Within the transport sector, the utilization of biofuels and in particular biodiesel increased significantly in the first decade of the twenty-first century. Biofuels may be used as a pure substitute for petrol or in a blend together with fossil fuels. The share of biofuels in the sector of transport fuels reached 6.2% in 2008, the share of biodiesel in the diesel sector even 8.2%.[375] In 2009, around 2.8 billion litres of biodiesel and around 1.1 billion litres of bioethanol have been sold in Germany.[376] However, since then the share of biofuels used in the German transport sector more or less remained static. In 2013, the share of biofuels amounted to 5.3%.[377] Also in 2019, the share of biofuels in the entire German fuel mix remained at a level of around 5%, and 2.4 billion tonnes of biodiesel and 1.2 tonnes of bioethanol have been used.[378]

644. With regard to the measures taken against climate change as well as due to the increasing concerns on security of supply, the EU and Germany initially have been striving for an increased use of biofuels for transport. In principle, benefits for combating climate change as well as for security of supply may be achieved by using biofuels. However, the contribution of biofuels to tackle climate change has been questioned in recent years. The principal GHG reduction potential of biofuels may be offset in case of forests being cleared or in case of other environmentally valuable land being used for the growth of energy plants. An intense debate also developed on land-use conflicts between food and energy crops. It has also been proposed to use biomass mainly within the electricity sector since it reaches a more favourable efficiency there.[379] The concerns on the environmental performance of

375. Federal Ministry of Economy and Technologies, *Energie in Deutschland, Trends und Hintergründe zur Energieversorgung in Deutschland* (August 2010), 22.
376. BT-Drs. 17/2861, 3 et seq.
377. Agentur für Erneuerbare Energien, press release of 24 Apr. 2014.
378. Bundesministerium für Ernährung und Landwirtschaft, Wissenswertes rund um Biokraftstoffe, available at www.bmel.de, last access 1 May 2022.
379. Sachverständigenrat für Umweltfragen, *Klimaschutz durch Biomasse, Sondergutachten* (Berlin: Erich Schmidt Verlag, July 2007), 101.

biofuels have been addressed in particular by a Regulation on Requirements for a Sustainable Production of Biofuels (Biofuels-Sustainability Ordinance, hereinafter: *Biokraft-NachV*).[380]

645. That is one key reason why the focus of debate on reducing greenhouse gas emissions in the transport sector meanwhile shifted to the use of electro-mobility and renewable liquid and gaseous transport fuels of non-biological origin. Biofuels and other renewable transport fuels are promoted by the European Directive 2018/2001/EU as well as by the biofuel quota obligations under national law. These legal measures will be explained subsequently.

§1. European Directive 2018/2001/EU

646. The 2020 goal of the European Directive 2009/28/EC on the promotion of the use of energy from renewable sources[381] read in Article 3(4): '[E]ach Member State shall ensure that the share of energy from renewable sources in all forms of transport in 2020 is at least 10% of the final consumption of energy in transport in that Member State.' The successor Directive 2018/2001/EU[382] in Article 3(1) now requests the Member States to collectively ensure that the share of energy from renewable sources in the Union's gross final consumption of energy in 2030 is at least 32%. As a specific requirement in respect of the transport sector and to 'mainstream the use of renewable energy in the transport sector', Article 25(1) of Directive 2018/2001/EU requires each Member State to 'set an obligation on fuel suppliers to ensure that the share of renewable energy within the final consumption of energy in the transport sector is at least 14% by 2030 (minimum share) in accordance with an indicative trajectory set by the Member State'.

647. While the focus of the EU for increasing renewable energy in the transport sector previously rested on the promotion of the use of biofuels, the EU now more and more tries to support electric vehicles using electricity from renewable energy as well as renewable liquid and gaseous transport fuels of non-biological origin. This could already be seen in Article 3(4)(c) of Directive 2009/28/EC: '[F]or the calculation of the electricity from renewable energy sources consumed by electric road vehicles, that consumption shall be considered to be 2.5 times the energy content of the input of electricity from renewable energy sources.' As a consequence, energy from renewable sources used in electric vehicles counted 2.5 times more towards the national targets for energy consumption of renewable sources than its

380. Verordnung über Anforderungen an eine nachhaltige Herstellung von Biokraftstoffen, Biokraftstoff-Nachhaltigkeitsverordnung, of 2 Dec. 2021 (BGBl. I p. 5126, 5143). For the similar Regulation on the Sustainability of Biomass used for Electricity Generation *see* below Part V, Ch. 5, s. 2.

381. Directive 2009/28/EC of the European Parliament and of the Council of 23 Apr. 2009 on the promotion of the use of energy from renewable sources and amending and subsequently repealing Directives 2001/77/EC and 2003/30/EC, OJ L 140 of 5 Jun. 2009, 16 et seq.

382. Directive 2018/2001/EU of the European Parliament and of the Council of 11 Dec. 2018 on the promotion of the use of energy from renewable sources, OJ L 328 of 21 Dec, 2018, 82 et seqq.

actual energy content would allow. In the revised Directive 2018/2001/EU, for the purpose of the minimum renewable energy share in the transport sector, the share of renewable electricity shall be considered to be four times its energy content when supplied to road vehicles and may be considered to be 1.5 times its energy content when supplied to rail transport (Article 27(2) of Directive 2018/2001/EU).

648. Importantly, the Directive 2018/2001/EU contains an overall 'cap' for the use of biofuels, bioliquids, and biomass fuels in Article 26(1). Accordingly, for calculations of the share of renewable energy sources under the Directive, the share of biofuels, bioliquids, and biomass fuels consumed in transport produced from food and feed crops 'shall be no more than one percentage point higher than the share of such fuels in the final consumption of energy in the road and rail transport sectors in 2020 in that Member State, with a maximum of 7% of final consumption of energy in the road and rail transport sectors in that Member State'.

649. The less euphoric approach of the EU towards the use of biofuels in the transport sector at least partly is due to increasing concerns on the sustainability of their use. To counteract these concerns, Directive 2009/28/EC and Directive 2018/2001/EU provide for compulsory sustainability requirements for the production of biofuels, bioliquids, and biomass fuels. In Germany these criteria and the certification system, which shall verify compliance, are regulated in the Biofuels-Sustainability Ordinance.

§2. Quota Obligations for Biofuels and other renewable Fuels under German Law

650. Before 2007, the use of biofuels has been promoted in Germany mainly with means of tax reductions. With the former Directive 2003/30/EC of 8 May 2003 on the promotion of the use of biofuels or other renewable fuels for transport, the European Communities wanted to achieve that Member States take care for a minimum share of biofuels and other renewable fuels on their markets. Member States were required to set 'national indicative targets'. 'Reference values' for these targets have been 2% calculated on the basis of energy content of all petrol and diesel for transport purposes placed on the markets by 31 December 2005, and 5.75% by 31 December 2010 (Article 3 paragraph 1 Directive 2003/30/EC).

651. With the Biofuels Quota Act of 2007, Germany introduced certain quota obligations for the share of biofuels within the transport sector.[383] These quota obligations went beyond the standard which was required by the former Directive 2003/30/EC.[384] While tax advantages for biofuels were reduced and mainly limited to pure biofuels, the biofuel quotas became the main measure for the support of biofuels.[385] The provisions have been implemented in the Federal Immissions Control

383. *See* for the legislative reasoning BT-Drs. 16/2709.
384. H.D. Jarass, 'Die neuen Regelungen zur Biokraftstoffquote', *ZUR* (2007): 518, 519.
385. BT-Drs. 17/2861, 2.

Act in sections 37a et seqq. These rules and in particular the concrete quotas have been changed in 2009.[386] The definition of biofuels is clarified under section 37b BImSchG in particular with a reference to, but several restrictions from the Biomass Ordinance.

652. Previously, the quota obligations in former section 37 paragraphs 3 and 3a BImSchG differentiated between a general quota, a specific quota for diesel, and a specific quota for petrol. Obligated parties placing diesel on the market had to ensure a share of diesel-replacing biofuels of at least 4.4% until 31 December 2014. Obligated parties placing petrol on the market had to ensure a share of petrol-replacing biofuels of at least 1.2% for 2007, at least 2% for 2008 and at least 2.8% for the years 2009 until 2014. The overall quota could be found in the third sentence of section 37 paragraph 3 BImSchG. Accordingly, the minimum share of biofuels in the total quantity of petrol and diesel placed on the market by an obligated party was 5.25% in 2009, and 6.25% from 2010 until 2014. These minimum shares of biofuels referred to the energy content of the fuels.

653. Importantly, the quota obligations have been transformed to GHG reduction obligations from 2015 onwards. From 2015 onwards, obligated parties have to place a minimum share of biofuels on the market, by which the share of GHG of the total quantity of petrol and diesel together with the biofuels is reduced by certain quotas (section 37a paragraph 4 BImSchG) compared to a reference value for fossil fuels. In 2021, these greenhouse gas reduction quotas have been increased, and a clear path of increasing greenhouse gas reduction quotas has been set out for the period 2020 to 2030.[387] Accordingly, the greenhouse gas reduction quotas amount to 6% from 2020 onwards, to 7% from 2022 onwards, and increase year by year up to a level of 25% from 2030 onwards. The GHG reduction obligations can also be met by using electricity from renewable energy sources in electric vehicles, or by utilizing renewable fuels of non-biological origin such as hydrogen generated with electricity from renewable energy sources. Details and conditions under which these fuels can be used are governed by two ordinances under the Federal Immissions Protection Act, 37. BImSchV and 38. BImSchV.

654. The mechanism of compliance with the biofuel quota obligations has been developed with a close link to the Energy Tax Law. Concepts of the Energy Tax Law have been adopted within the provisions on the biofuel quotas.[388] Anyone who – commercially or within the framework of business undertakings – markets fuels (petrol or diesel) subject to taxes under specific clauses of the Energy Tax Act needs to ensure that the total quantity of fuel placed on the market over one calendar year reaches the greenhouse gas reduction obligations according to the provisions

386. *See* BT-Drs. 16/11131.

387. Gesetz zur Weiterentwicklung der Treibhausgasminderungs-Quote of 24 Sep. 2021, BGBl. I p. 4458.

388. H.D. Jarass, *BImSchG,* 8th edn (München: C.H. Beck, 2010), s. 37a para. 4; M. Röckinghausen in: Landmann & Rohmer, *Umweltrecht* (München: C.H. Beck, March 2010), s. 37a BImSchG para. 1.

explained above (section 37a paragraph 1 BImSchG). The duty does not differentiate between several kinds of further utilization of the fuels.[389] Certain exceptions from the fulfilment of the biofuel quotas apply in particular for the German armed forces (*Bundeswehr*) as well as for the National Petroleum Stockpiling Agency. Obliged to ensure the biofuel quotas is the party who is liable to pay taxes within the meaning of the Energy Tax Act (section 37a paragraph 3 BImSchG). It is also possible to transfer the compliance with the quota obligations to a third party by a written contract.

655. Due to the growing concerns on sustainability of the use of biomass for the energy supply, Germany introduced sustainability criteria for the production of biofuels. The central mechanism of the Regulation on Requirements for a Sustainable Production of Biofuels (*Biokraft-NachV*) claims that biofuels only count towards the quota obligations in the Federal Immissions Control Act if the requirements of the Regulation are met and verified.[390] These requirements encompass conditions for the protection of natural habitats and for sustainable agriculture. Also, biofuels need to possess a certain potential for the reduction of GHGs. In the beginning, biofuels needed to account for a potential for the reduction of GHGs of 35%. This value increased to 50%, and is increased for newer installations to 60% and to 65%.[391] The implementation of the sustainability criteria renders a complex certification system necessary which is described in the regulation. The structures for certification have been set up and several private certification systems are registered for sustainability certification.

656. The biofuel quotas in the Federal Immissions Control Act must be seen together with the qualifications of fuels required by the Tenth Ordinance for the Implementation of the Federal Immission Control Act (Ordinance on the Property and the Marking of the Quality of Fuels, 10. BImSchV).[392] The allowable admixtures of biofuels to fossil fuels under this Ordinance have been raised. From January 2011 onwards, petrol can be offered with a share of up to 10% bioethanol. However, any person offering petrol of 'super' quality with more than 5% ethanol by volume is also be obliged to offer petrol with a maximum ethanol content of 5% by volume at the same point of sale, section 3 paragraph 2 of the 10. BImSchV. Consumers hesitated using the E10-petrol due to concerns on the compatibility with their cars. The severe problems in the market launch of E10 demonstrated that consumers must thoroughly be informed of the uses and potential drawbacks by industry and politics.

389. M. Röckinghausen in: Landmann & Rohmer, *Umweltrecht* (München: C.H. Beck, March 2010), s. 37a BImSchG para. 4.
390. Section 3 Biokraft-NachV.
391. *See* closer s. 6 Biokraft-NachV, also for the applicability of the higher values.
392. Verordnung über die Beschaffenheit und die Auszeichnung der Qualitäten von Kraftstoffen of 8 Dec. 2010 (BGBl. I p. 1849).

Part IV. Regulatory Framework Concerning Coal

657. Seen together, hard coal and lignite for a long time dominated the electricity generation in Germany, with a share of around 43% in 2009, 46% in 2011,[393] 35.4% in 2018,[394] and around 30% in 2021.[395] Their main relevance lies on electricity generation and the utilization in the steel industry. For the generation of heat in particular for use in households or the business sector, coal hardly plays a role.[396] Hard coal and lignite together have a share of around 23% (2010) respectively 25% (2012) and 22% (2018) in Germany's primary energy consumption.[397] In light of the nuclear phase-out that is envisaged by the end of 2022 in Germany, the importance of coal for electricity generation in Germany already increased. This is regarded critical given the aims of reductions in greenhouse gases pursued by the German *Energiewende*.

658. Most German statutory regulations apply to several energy sources. For example, the legal rules for the construction and operation of a coal-fired power plant in principle correspond with the rules applying for gas fired power plants. Hence, when looking at the regulatory framework regarding coal, the regulations already discussed above in the chapters on electricity and gas – in particular those on authorizations, permits, etc. – are also relevant. However, this part provides for some particularities applying for coal and the rules on the exploitation of coal under German mining law. A focus of this part is on the Coal-Fired Power Generation Termination Act (*Kohleverstromungsbeendigungsgesetz, KVBG*) which shall gradually reduce and terminate coal-fired power generation until 2038.

393. Federal Ministry of Economy and Technologies, *Energie in Deutschland, Trends und Hintergründe zur Energieversorgung in Deutschland* (August 2010), 21 and (February 2013), 19.
394. BMWi, Energiedaten: Gesamtausgabe, October 2019, slide 28.
395. Fraunhofer ISE, Nettostromerzeugung in Deutschland 2021: Erneuerbare Energien witterungsbedingt schwächer, available via www.ise.fraunhofer.de, last access 1 May 2022.
396. Federal Ministry of Economy and Technologies, *Energie in Deutschland, Trends und Hintergründe zur Energieversorgung in Deutschland* (August 2010), 22.
397. Federal Ministry of Economy and Climate Action, 'Primärenergieverbrauch nach Energieträgern', statistical data available via the webpage www.bmwi.de, updated 17 Dec. 2010 and 7 Aug. 2013; BMWi, Energiedaten: Gesamtausgabe, October 2019, slide 3.

Chapter 1. Production

659. The construction and operation of a (larger) facility which processes coal or makes use of coal as an energy source is only possible if the preconditions of the law on spatial planning are met, see section 1. Moreover, the construction and operation will – in most cases – be subject to a permit under the Federal Immissions Control Act (*BImSchG*, introduced in more detail above in Part II, Chapter 2). Section 2 of this part will briefly discuss facilities which might require a permit under the Federal Immissions Control Act with relation to coal. Section 3 is concerned with Carbon Capture and Storage (CCS). In section 4 it will be discussed that the Federal Immissions Control Act, as a general rule, does not contain explicit obligations with regard to climate protection. Section 5 sets out the rules of the Coal-Fired Power Generation Termination Act (*Kohleverstromungsbeendigungsgesetz, KVBG*) on a gradual reduction of coal-fired power generation until 2038.

§1. Spatial Planning

660. For the decision on the place of location for a larger facility (i.e., power plants), spatial planning of the *Bund*, the *Länder*, and the municipalities (*Gemeinden*) is of high importance. For coal-fired power plants, the relevance of spatial planning has been underlined by a decision of the higher administrative court Münster (*Oberverwaltungsgericht*). The court declared the land-use plan for a power plant of E.ON void, *inter alia* because the relevant land-use plan was not in accordance with other spatial planning decisions.[398]

661. Spatial planning may involve planning on European level as well as planning by *Bund*, *Länder*, or municipalities. The plans will become more detailed the lower the level of spatial planning is. At the same time, certain aims and planning principles may be determined on a higher level and become binding for the subsequent planning decision on lower levels.

662. The general rules on spatial planning are provided by the Spatial Planning Act (*Raumordnungsgesetz, ROG*).[399] According to the previous regulatory framework, the *Bund* was merely entitled to provide a framework with regard to spatial planning. After an amendment of the Basic Law (*Grundgesetz*), however, spatial planning now falls within the concurrent legislative competencies of the *Bund*.[400] That means that the *Bund* is in principle not restricted in regulating the matter. However, the *Länder* may with own legislation deviate from the rules provided by the *Bund*.[401]

---

398. OVG Münster, judgment of 3 Sep. 2009, 10 D 121/07.NE, *ZUR*, 2009, 597.
399. Raumordnungsgesetz of 22 Dec. 2008 (BGBl. I p. 2986).
400. Article 74 para. 1 no. 31 Basic Law, GG.
401. Article 72 para. 3 no. 4 Basic Law, GG.

663. The next levels of legislation on planning law are provided by the German *Länder*. The subsequent planning decisions may apply for the whole territory of a federal state as well as for certain regions. Practically, the spatial planning within the *Länder* is most important for energy-related projects.[402] In this respect it merits mentioning that an environmental impact assessment may be integrated in the spatial planning procedures.[403]

664. On different levels, spatial planning can provide for aims (*Ziele*) and planning principles (*Grundsätze*). According to section 3 number 2 ROG, 'aims' of spatial planning are binding demands in the form of textual or graphic specifications. It is important to note that a deviation from the aims of spatial planning may be possible in specific cases (section 6 ROG). This can be the case, for instance, if a respective plan explicitly foresees exceptions for specific cases (section 6 paragraph 1 ROG). 'Principles' of spatial planning are, on the contrary, guidelines which have to be taken into account by subsequent decisions (in particular when weighting different possibilities or in the context of discretionary decisions, section 3 number 3 ROG). A conflicting demand may in the process of weighting be more important than a principle of spatial planning, and thus prevail in the single case. Nevertheless, the principles play a decisive role for the subsequent levels of planning. There, principles have to be taken into account in the context of further planning decisions.

665. The most detailed plan is the land-use plan (*Bebauungsplan*) set up by the municipalities. While spatial planning in general merely provides for aims and principles which have to be taken into account by subsequent levels of planning, land-use plans set out detailed rules with respect to construction decisions in a certain area or with regard to a certain project. As a general rule, the land-use plan – contrary to other planning – has 'external effects' for individuals (residents, neighbours, etc.). The land-use plan forms the basis for the admissibility of concrete projects and the issuing of building permits, see sections 29 et seq. Construction Code (*Baugesetzbuch, BauGB*).[404]

666. Recent coal-fired power plant projects in Germany have often led to protests by environmental associations/organizations or citizens because of the environmental hazards involved and because of an increased awareness of the general public on the topics of climate change and GHG emissions. As will be explained below, the GHG emissions balance of a power plant is only of limited importance for the permit necessary for the installation under the Immissions Control Law. However, the above-mentioned judgment of the higher administrative court Münster demonstrated that climate protection can play an important role with regard to the law of spatial planning.[405]

402. G. Hermes in: J.P. Schneider & C. Theobald, *Recht der Energiewirtschaft*, 5th edn (München: C.H. Beck, 2021), s. 8 para. 14.
403. Closer G. Hermes in: J.P. Schneider & C. Theobald, *Recht der Energiewirtschaft*, 5th edn (München: C.H. Beck, 2021), s. 8 paras 30 et seqq.
404. Construction Code in the version of the publication of 3 Nov. 2017 (BGBl. I p. 3634).
405. OVG Münster, judgment of 3 Sep. 2009, 10 D 121/07.NE, *ZUR*, 2009, 597 (with comment of R. Klinger); subsequent BVerwG, decision of 16 Mar. 2010, 4 BN 66.09, *ZUR*, 2010, 311. *See* the

667. The higher administrative court Münster declared a land-use plan for a coal-fired power plant of E.ON next to the town of Datteln void. One main reason was the fact that the regional development plan for the Land North Rhine-Westphalia displayed another location for a power plant. Also, the court made reference to a state development programme. This programme set out a demand for an energy use which would preserve resources and protect the climate. This prominent example highlights that climate protection may play a role for power plant projects at the level of spatial planning. The court accentuated that the state planning aimed at a reduction of GHG and that the respective land-use plan allowing the project would not ensure fulfilment of this provision.[406] Moreover, the judgment relies on a range of other reasons. These include that the solution of problems resulting from the project provided for in the land-use plan may not be left nearly completely to solve for the licensing procedure under the Immissions Control Law. Another important issue for the court was the fact that the envisaged power plant should be constructed too close to residential zones. In future, more attention will need to be paid to the requirements of spatial planning and to the demands of planning law.[407]

§2. Necessity of a Permit under the Federal Immissions Control Act

668. The Fourth Ordinance for the Implementation of the Federal Immissions Control Act (Ordinance on Installations Requiring a Permit, *4. BImSchV*) stipulates for which facilities a BImSchG-permit is required. In this Ordinance, the Federal Government set up an exclusive catalogue of those facilities which require a permit under the Federal Immissions Control Act. The Fourth Federal Immissions Control Ordinance and in particular its annex have been revised by transposing Directive 2010/75/EU on industry emissions into national law, however with only few material changes.[408]

669. Relevant for large coal-fired power plants is number 1.1 of Annex 1 of the 4. BImSchV, see above Part II, Chapter 2, section 2. Further licensing requirements for the energy production using coal can be found in number 1.2 of Annex 1. Accordingly, installations for the generation of electricity, steam, hot water, process heat or hot waste gas *inter alia* by use of coal, coke including petroleum coke or coal briquettes, with a rated thermal input (*Feuerungswärmeleistung*) of more than 1 MW and less than 50 MW generally require a permit under the BImSchG.

670. As explained above, a simplified licensing procedure may apply for these facilities under number 1.2 Annex 1 to the 4. BImSchV.

---

comments of R. Verheyen, 'Die Bedeutung des Klimaschutzes bei der Genehmigung von Kohlekraftwerken und bei der Zulassung des Kohleabbaus', *ZUR* (2010): 403, 405.

406. OVG Münster, judgment of 3 Sep. 2009, 10 D 121/07.NE, *ZUR*, 2009, 597, 601.

407. *See* M. Vollmer, 'Kraftwerke vor Gericht – Nachbar- und Verbandsklagen gegen Immissionsschutz genehmigungen', *IR* (2011): 2.

408. J. Betensted & R. Grandjot & S. Waskow, 'Die Umsetzung der Richtlinie 2010/75/EU über Industrieemissionen (IE-Richtlinie) im Immissionsschutzrecht', *ZUR* (2013): 395 (396).

671. In numbers 1.10, 1.11, and 1.14 Annex to the 4. BImSchV, other facilities in need for a permit are mentioned: facilities for briquetting of lignite or hard coal, facilities for dry distillation especially of hard coal, lignite, wood, peat or pitch (except charcoal piles), and facilities for the gasification or liquefaction of coal or bituminous shale/slate.

672. The licensing procedures and material conditions of the Federal Immissions Control Act are explained above in Part II, Chapter 2, section 4.

§3. Carbon Capture and Storage

673. Directive 2009/31/EC of the European Parliament and of the Council of 23 April 2009 on the geological storage of carbon dioxide provides a framework for CCS in the Member States of the EU.[409] The CCS technology shall support combating climate change. The Directive highlights that the technology has to be used environmentally safe, see Article 1 of the Directive. Member States had to implement the regulations of the Directive by 25 June 2011, Article 39(1).

674. Even before the Directive entered into force, the German government presented a first draft version of a Statute on the Separation, Transport, and Permanent Storage of Carbon Dioxide on 1 April 2009. The parties of the government at that time, however, did not reach an agreement on the statute.[410] Since then, the advantages and disadvantages of CCS have been discussed intensively. On the one hand, the chance of reducing the emissions of coal-fired power plants is acknowledged. On the other hand, however, high development costs for the technology have been raised as a downside of CCS. Also, the environmental risks of the CCS technology and competing demands for the restricted available storage facilities have been mentioned.

675. It had been discussed whether CO_2 storage facilities can be explored on the basis of the mining law until an agreement on the CCS statute is reached.[411] The Energy Concept (see above Introduction, Chapter 6) highlighted the relevance of CCS for energy intensive industries and for fossil coal-fired power plants. Consequently, the concept sets out the intention to test CCS.[412]

676. Discussions and in particular reservations of several *Länder* against the legislative project have delayed the enacting of a CCS Act. In 2012, the Act on the

---

409. Directive 2009/31/EC of the European Parliament and of the Council of 23 Apr. 2009 on the geological storage of carbon dioxide and amending Council Directive 85/337/EEC, European Parliament and Council Directives 2000/60/EC, 2001/80/EC, 2004/35/EC, 2006/12/EC, 2008/1/EC and Regulation (EC) No. 1013/2006, OJ L 140 of 5 Jun. 2009, 114.
410. H.J. Koch & A. Braun, 'Aktuelle Entwicklungen des Immissionsschutzrechts', *NVwZ* (2010): 1199, 1201.
411. *See* Handelsblatt, Spezial Energie, of 31 Jan. 2011, 'Eignungstest für CO2-Lager', 5.
412. Energy Concept, BT-Drs. 17/3049, 9 et seq.

Demonstration of the Permanent Capture of CO_2 came into force.[413] The Act differentiates between the exploration of rock formations suitable for the permanent storage of carbon dioxide and the construction and operation of a carbon dioxide storage. While the exploration is subject to a permit, the construction and operation of a carbon dioxide storage requires a strict plan approval procedure and plan approval decision. Already at the time of enacting this law, observers doubted whether the CCS Act, given the fact of heavy opposition to CCS projects in Germany, will lead to a CCS storage installations really being built in Germany.[414] The only CCS project in Germany has been the pilot storage installation in Ketzin in which around 67,000 tonnes of CO_2 have been stored from 2008 to 2013.[415]

§4. Climate Protection under the Federal Immissions Control Act

677. Despite high public awareness of the topic, the CO_2-balance of a coal-fired power plant will, if at all, only play a minor role in the licensing process under the BImSchG. Instead, the Greenhouse Gas Emissions Trading Act (*Treibhausgas-Emissionshandelsgesetz, TEHG*) shall lead to reductions in CO_2 emissions by implementing the European emissions trading scheme (closer below Part VI).[416] The Federal Immissions Control Act refers to the TEHG and, in relation to installations falling within the scope of the TEHG, gives this statute precedence on the matter (section 5 paragraph 2 BImSchG).

678. Section 5 paragraph 2 BImSchG states in relation to installations falling within the scope of the TEHG that requirements on the limitation of GHG emissions under the BImSchG shall be admissible only if they serve the purpose of ensuring compliance with the obligation to prevent any harmful effects on the environment (see section 5 paragraph 1 sentence 1 BImSchG). The principle of protection in section 5 paragraph 1 number 1 BImSchG, however, refers to specific hazards mostly within a certain spatial area. Thus, this principle is of limited importance for combating climate change. Section 5 paragraph 2 sentence 2 BImSchG further provides that no energy efficiency requirements related to carbon dioxide emissions may be included in a BImSchG-permit that go beyond the requirements laid down in the GHG Emissions Trading Act.

679. The mere reference to the rules of the Greenhouse Gas Emissions Trading Act for the permit required under Federal Immissions Control Law hardly appears

---

413. Kohlendioxid-Speicherungsgesetz of 17 Aug. 2012 (BGBl. I p. 1726).

414. W. Fischer, 'Kein CCS in Deutschland trotz CCS-Gesetz?', STE Preprint (2012), available at www.fz-juelich.de (last access 1 May 2022).

415. Bundesministerium für Wirtschaft und Klimaschutz, CCU/CCS: Baustein für eine klimaneutrale und wettbewerbsfähige Industrie?, available at www.bmwi.de, last access 1 May 2022.

416. Gesetz über den Handel mit Berechtigungen zur Emission von Treibhausgasen, Treibhausgas-Emissionshandelsgesetz of 21 Jul. 2011 (BGBl. I p. 1475).

to be 'up to date'.[417] It contrasts with the increased awareness of the hazards of climate change. In particular, renewable energy factually could be given preference by demanding certain CO_2-emission reductions in the licensing procedure for a power plant. At least, CO_2-emissions need to be restricted to a minimum which can be achieved with efficient power plant technologies.

§5. Gradual Reduction of Coal-Fired Power Generation latest until 2038

680. Following political discussions and a report of the so-called coal commission (*Kohlekommission*) that has been introduced by the Federal Government,[418] Germany decided to gradually reduce and terminate coal-fired power generation until 2038. In the Coalition Agreement of 2021, the government further agreed to 'ideally' bring forward the phase-out of coal to 2030.[419] Therefore, in addition to the legislative status at the time at which this monograph is updated and which is explained in the following, amendments to bring forward the phase-out of coal are possible.

681. On 14 August 2020, the Act on the Reduction and Termination of Coal-Fired Power Generation (Coal-Fired Power Generation Termination Act, *Kohleverstromungsbeendigungsgesetz, KVBG*) entered into force.[420] The Coal-Fired Power Generation Termination Act provides for a gradual reduction of the coal-fired power generation in Germany up until 2038 against compensation for the operators. Section 1 paragraph 1 sentence 2 KVBG states the Act shall regulate the gradual and, as far as possible, steady reduction and termination of the generation of electrical energy through the use of coal in Germany. The reduction aims within the Act strive to achieve the following remaining net electrical capacity of coal-fired power plants on the electricity market: 1) in 2022, 15 gigawatt capacity for hard coal and 15 gigawatt capacity for lignite, 2) In 2030, 8 gigawatt capacity for hard coal and 9 gigawatt capacity for lignite, 3) latest in 2038, 0 gigawatt capacity for hard coal and 0 gigawatt capacity for lignite (*see* section 2 paragraph 2 KVBG).

682. The mechanisms in the Coal-Fired Power Generation Termination Act as to the reduction of coal-fired power generation differentiate between hard coal and lignite. For hard coal, initially a tender mechanism shall be used to determine which capacity is reduced at which point in time against which compensation payment. Subsequently, the reduction of coal-fired power generation based on hard coal shall be governed by the Act itself ('*gesetzliche Reduzierung*'). For lignite, there is no

---

417. Critical also S. Krohn in: M. Appel & M. Ohms & J. Saurer, *BImSchG* (Berlin: Erich Schmidt Verlag, 2021), § 5 paras 188 et seqq.
418. *See* Kommission Wachstum, Strukturwandel und Beschäftigung, Abschlussbericht, Jan 2019, www.bmwi.de last accessed 1 May 2022.
419. SPD/GRÜNE/FDP, Mehr Fortschritt wagen, Bündnis für Freiheit, Gerechtigkeit und Nachhaltigkeit, Koalitionsvertrag zwischen SPD, BÜNDNIS 90/DIE GRÜNEN und FDP, Dec. 2021.
420. Kohleverstromungsbeendigungsgesetz of 8 Aug. 2020 (BGBl. I p. 1818).

tender system in the beginning, but the reduction of coal-fired power generation based on lignite is governed by the Act itself.

683. The tender procedures for coal-fired power generation based on hard coal are organized by the Federal Network Agency (*BNetzA*). In case the operator is entitled to bid under the qualification criteria set out in the Coal-Fired Power Generation Termination Act, the operator in essence bids with a specific capacity of coal-fired power generation and a compensation amount which shall be claimed in case the capacity receives an award in the tender (the so-called hard coal addition, *Steinkohlezuschlag*, section 10 paragraph 1 KVBG).[421] In the tender publication, the Federal Network Agency publishes *inter alia* the tender volume and a maximum bid price that applies for this tender round, section 11 KVBG. The maximum bid prices reduce over time (section 19 KVBG). Within the selection process for the bids in a tender round, also the historic yearly carbon dioxide emissions per megawatt of the hard coal-fired power generation plant and statements of the transmission grid operators on aspects of system stability are taken into account (*see* section 18 paragraphs 3 and 4 KVBG). Then the Federal Network Agency issues awards to the bidders with the lowest code figures that have been calculated accordingly. Operators which have been awarded in the tender can claim the awarded hard coal addition against the Federal Republic of Germany, *see* section 23 KVBG. Where the reduction of coal-fired power generation based on hard coal is governed by the Act itself ('*gesetzliche Reduzierung*') which applies generally as of 2031 (but may apply earlier), the Federal Network Agency determines based on the further criteria defined in the Coal-Fired Power Generation Termination Act for which plant a reduction becomes effective at which point in time (*see* section 27 KVBG).

684. For coal-fired power generation based on lignite, Annex 2 to the KVBG sets out decommissioning dates for specific power plants. According to section 40 KVBG, the plant operators shall permanently decommission their lignite plants no later than the date specified in Annex 2. The dates in Annex 2 range from 2020 to 2038. Specific plants shall transfer first into a phased decommissioning ('*zeitlich gestreckte Stilllegung*'). The basis for the decommissioning path for lignite power plants are based on negotiations between the Federal Government and the operators and shall also be governed by contractual agreements.[422] Compensation payments for the operators may amount to 4.35 billion Euros (section 44 paragraph 1 KVBG).

421. S. Michaels & O. Däuper, 'Das Kohleausstiegsgesetz im Überblick – Welche Rechtsfragen bleiben offen?', *EnWZ* (2020): 291, 292.
422. S. Michaels & O. Däuper, 'Das Kohleausstiegsgesetz im Überblick – Welche Rechtsfragen bleiben offen?', *EnWZ* (2020): 291, 292.

Chapter 2. Exploitation

685. Nowadays, the vast majority of Germany's supply with hard coal originates from imports. The extraction of hard coal within Germany amounted to 142.3 million tonnes in 1960 and declined over 69.8 million tonnes in 1990 to 13.8 million tonnes in 2009, and to only 2.6 million tonnes in 2018.[423] From that time onwards, hard coal extraction in Germany has been ceased.[424]

686. The share of hard coal in the German electricity generation amounts to about 10% (2021).[425] Due to the decrease of domestic extraction of hard coal, most of the hard coal utilized origins from imports. The share of imported hard coal has continued rising in particular due to the lack of competitiveness of the German domestic hard coal extraction.

687. In contrast to this, lignite is extracted from domestic mines. Lignite exploitation amounted to 169.9 million tonnes in 2009 and to 166.3 million tonnes in 2018.[426] In 2021, around 20% of the electricity generation in Germany has been based on lignite.[427]

688. Historically, extraction of hard coal has been heavily subsidized in Germany to ensure competitiveness. The following section 1 on state subsidies will thus focus on the subsidies that have been available for hard coal extraction, and in particular on the cessation of these subsidies.

689. The exploration and exploitation of coal is subject to the mining law which will be explained in the second section below. This explanation aims at providing a more detailed introduction to the mining law in Germany which is also of relevance for the exploitation of oil and gas.

§1. State Subsidies for Domestic Hard Coal Production

690. The extraction of hard coal has been heavily subsidized in Germany. In 2008, the hard coal mining in Germany received financial aid in an amount of EUR

---

423. Federal Ministry of Economy and Climate Action, 'Einfuhr von Steinkohle in Deutschland', www.bmwi.de, last access: 28 Feb. 2022.
424. Federal Ministry of Economy and Climate Action, 'Kohle', available at www.bmwi.de, last access 26 Feb. 2022.
425. Fraunhofer ISE, Nettostromerzeugung in Deutschland 2021: Erneuerbare Energien witterungsbedingt schwächer, available via www.ise.fraunhofer.de, last access 1 May 2022.
426. Federal Ministry of Economy and Climate Action, 'Kohle', available at www.bmwi.de, last access 26 Feb. 2022.
427. Fraunhofer ISE, Nettostromerzeugung in Deutschland 2021: Erneuerbare Energien witterungsbedingt schwächer, available via www.ise.fraunhofer.de, last access 1 May 2022.

2 billion. At that time, the sector was the biggest recipient of subsidies in Germany. This financial aid constituted a share of 35.6% of all aids granted by the *Bund*, i.e., the Federal Republic of Germany.[428]

691. However, on 7 February 2007 the *Bund*, North Rhine-Westphalia and the Saarland agreed on ceasing the subsidies for hard coal by 2018. In the following, the provisions of the statute now governing the cessation of subsidies shall be introduced after a short description of the historic development of hard coal subsidies in Germany.

692. The subsidies for hard coal have been a subject of intensive politic discussions. By the proponents, arguments of security of supply and the sustainment of the coal sector and its workplaces in Germany have been brought forward as arguments. Opponents referred to the environmental problems caused by the coal industry. Also, it has been argued that instead of coal, renewable energy sources should be used which could contribute to securing energy supply. Subsidies for hard coal also strongly conflict with a competitive energy market and might restrict the use of renewable energy sources. In view of these reasons, the legislator decided for ceasing the subsidies for the hard coal sector.

I. Historic Development of Hard Coal Subsidies

693. Since the mid of the 1960s, Germany pursued the goal of sustaining a certain share of domestic hard coal for electricity generation. Main arguments for this decision have been the security of supply and (at a later stage) also the aim of securing the workplaces in the mining companies. The subsidies for the hard coal sector were granted on the basis of specific power generation statutes.[429]

694. Until 1995, the third of these power generation statutes (Statute on the Further Security of the Use of Community Coal in the Electricity Sector)[430] provided for a certain amount of buy-off in its first section. According to its second section, the additional costs have been granted on the basis of an equalization fund. The costs were effectively borne by the end consumers by a premium on their electricity costs, the so-called *Kohlepfennig*. This way of financing has been declared non-constitutional by the Federal Constitutional Court in 1994. The reasoning was that the *Kohlepfennig* would be a special contribution (*Sonderabgabe*) within the financial provisions of the German Basic Law (*Grundgesetz*) and, as such, would be not admissible.[431]

428. Federal Ministry of Finance, 'Einundzwanzigster Subventionsbericht', 'Bericht der Bundesregierung über die Entwicklung der Finanzhilfen des Bundes und der Steuervergünstigungen für die Jahre 2005–2008', available via the webpage www.bundesfinanzministerium.de, 5.
429. Leipelt in: W. Danner & C. Theobald, *Energierecht* (München: C.H. Beck, 66. Addition 2010), Steinkohle, B. Kommentar, para. 4.
430. Drittes Verstromungsgesetz in the version of the publication of 19.04.1990 (BGBl. I p. 917).
431. BVerfG, judgment of 11 Oct. 1994, 2 BvR 633/86, BVerfGE 91, 186.

695. Thus, in the fourth power generation statute, fixed amounts were provided for the financing of hard coal exploitation.[432] Until 2005, the subsidies were granted on the basis of a 'coal compromise' in 1997. During this time, the subsidies decreased to EUR 2.7 billion in 2005.[433] As a consequence, a process of restructuring the coal sector had to begin.

II. Cessation of Subsidies by the Hard Coal Funding Act in 2018

696. On the basis of the agreement in 2007, the Act on Financing of the Cessation of Subsidized Hard Coal Mining in the Year 2018 (Hard Coal Financing Act) has been adopted.[434] This Act declares in section 1 paragraph 1 that the subsidies for the hard coal mining will cease to exist in 2018. After intensive discussions in 2010, the Council of the EU agreed to withdraw the German hard coal subsidies (only) by 2018. The Hard Coal Financing Act was designed to ensure the finances for the selling of domestic hard coal until 2018 and to provide financial aid for the 'socially acceptable' process of restructuring the German hard coal sector (section 1 paragraph 2).

697. Section 3 provides for the maximum amount to be paid from the federal government budget.[435] These sums amounted to EUR 1,699,000,000 in 2009 and decreased to EUR 794,400,000 in 2019. For employees in the mining companies, financial aid may be granted under further conditions according to section 5. Remarkably, also after the 'cessation' of the subsidies in 2018, further financial aid for 'further existing obligations' can be granted (according to section 4 of the Hard Coal Financing Act).[436]

§2. Mining Law

698. The mining law in Germany is governed by the Federal Mining Law (*Bundesberggesetz*, hereinafter: *BBergG*).[437] It is accompanied by detailed provisions of the Federal States. In this section, the main features of admission under the Federal Mining Law will be explained with relevance to the hard coal and lignite sectors. Some more detailed ordinances and administrative regulations by the Federal States will be mentioned in this context.

---

432. Leipelt in: W. Danner & C. Theobald, *Energierecht* (München: C.H. Beck, 66. Addition 2010), Steinkohle, B. Kommentar, para. 7.
433. Federal Ministry of Economy and Technologies, 'Kohlepolitik', 'Die Steinkohle-Beihilfen', www.bmwi.de/BMWi/Navigation/Energie/kohlepolitik.html, last access: 18 Dec. 2009.
434. Gesetz zur Finanzierung der Beendigung des subventionierten Steinkohlebergbaus zum Jahr 2018, Steinkohlefinanzierungsgesetz of 20 Dec. 2007 (BGBl. I p. 3086).
435. For further maximum aids granted by North Rhine-Westphalia, *see* the information of the Federal Ministry of Economy and Climate Action, 'Kohle', on www.bmwi.de, last access: 1 May 2022.
436. Out of the federal government budget, a maximum amount of EUR 1,658,400,000 shall be available under s. 4 para. 1, which is further expanded under para. 3.
437. Bundesberggesetz of 13 Aug. 1980 (BGBl. I p. 1310).

699. After explaining the scope of the statute and the types of mineral resources regulated in the first paragraph, the mining rights available are to be explained under II. These mining rights alone, however, do not entitle its owner to conduct mining activities. All mining activities may only be performed on the basis of so-called operating plans (*Betriebsplan*) as set forth under sections 50 et seqq. BBergG (see below III.). At last, this section will provide an overview of the measures available for the mining supervision (*Bergaufsicht*) to control mining activities under IV.

I. Scope of the Federal Mining Law and Types of Mineral Resources

700. Section 2 BBergG together with the definitions in section 4 clarifies the scope of the mining law. Generally speaking, the mining law applies to the exploration, exploitation, and treatment of freely minable (*bergfreie Bodenschätze*) and freehold (*grundeigene Bodenschätze*) natural resources (section 2 paragraph 1 number 1 BBergG). The terms 'exploration' and 'exploitation' need to be understood rather broadly. For example, the exploitation also comprises the necessary preparatory as well as the subsequent works.[438]

701. Section 3 BBergG differentiates between freely minable resources (*bergfreie Bodenschätze*) and freehold resources (*grundeigene Bodenschätze*). Freehold resources are within the ownership of the owner of a property (section 3 paragraph 2 BBergG). As a consequence, exploitation does not require a specific mining right. The right to explore and exploit these resources in general results of the ownership on the property itself.[439]

702. The freely minable resources are listed in section 3 paragraph 3 BBergG and comprise *inter alia* hard coal and lignite, as well as gases (especially those which accrue while the coal is exploited). Taking account of its importance for battery production, in 2021 the status of lithium as freely minable resource has been clarified.[440] In contrast to the freehold resources, the ownership of a property does not extend to the freely minable resources (section 3 paragraph 2 sentence 2 BBergG). Instead, these resources are ownerless and may (contrary to section 958 of the Civil Law Code) only be acquired by means of a mining right (see the following paragraph). This provision is no expropriation of the property owner. Instead, it determines the content and the limit of the 'property' pursuant to Article 14 paragraph 1 sentence 2 of the Basic Law (GG).[441]

438. E. Kremer & P. Neuhaus, *Bergrecht* (Stuttgart: W. Kohlhammer, 2001), 18.
439. E. Kremer & P. Neuhaus, *Bergrecht* (Stuttgart: W. Kohlhammer, 2001), 17.
440. P. Schütte & M. Winkler, 'Aktuelle Entwicklungen im Bundesumweltrecht, Berichtszeitraum: 1.2.2021 bis 12.4.2021', *ZUR* (2021): 376, 379.
441. E. Kremer & P. Neuhaus, *Bergrecht* (Stuttgart: W. Kohlhammer, 2001), 16. Central statements of the Federal Constitutional Court to this clause can be found in the famous '*Naßauskiesungsentscheidung*', BVerfG, judgment of 15 Jul. 1981, 1 BvL 77/78, BVerfGE 58, 300.

II. Mining Rights

703. Those who want to explore or exploit freely minable resources, like hard coal and lignite, are required to have specific permits provided by the Federal Mining Law (section 6 BBergG). It needs to be emphasized that while these mining rights in principle allow for the exploration or exploitation, the mining itself may be conducted only if an operating plan has been accepted by the competent authority.

A. Exploration Licence

704. The exploration licence (*Erlaubnis*) under section 7 BBergG grants the exclusive right to explore mining resources, which are closer defined in the licence. Although the licence generally does not allow for exploitation, it allows its holder to exploit the resources required for the process of exploration. An exploration licence does not preclude parallel licences of exploration in a broader area or exploration for scientific purposes (section 7 paragraph 2 BBergG).

B. Production Licence

705. The production licence (*Bewilligung*) is provided for in section 8 BBergG. It grants the exclusive right to explore and exploit resources specified in the licence in a certain area/field and to gain ownership on these resources. Section 8 paragraph 1 numbers 2–4 BBergG grant additional rights, for example, for the construction and operation of certain facilities with the purposes of exploration and exploitation. The provisions for claims based on ownership in the German Civil Law Code are applicable on the right arising out of the production licence. Consequently, the holder of the production licence may bring forward an action for restitution of resources under section 985 of the Civil Law Code. He is also entitled to demand removal or omission of any acts impairing his right (section 1004 of the Civil Law Code). Like the exploration licence, the production licence also does not preclude parallel licences of exploration in a broader area or exploration for scientific purposes (section 8 paragraph 3 BBergG).

C. Mining Proprietorship

706. Section 9 BBergG provides for a third form of mining rights, the mining proprietorship (*Bergwerkseigentum*). The norm refers to the provisions on the production licence insofar as the rights resulting from the mining proprietorship are concerned. But it declares the right on properties pursuant to the German Civil Law Code applicable on this form of a licence. Thus, the mining proprietorship can be inscribed in the cadastral register and can be charged independent of the person of its owner. The specific security interests in land, like the mortgage (*Hypothek*) or the land charge (*Grundschuld*), can be applied for the mining proprietorship. This is important if it shall serve financing purposes.[442] Moreover, under section 94 of the Civil Law Code, essential parts of the property and thus of the mining proprietorship automatically belong to this right and cannot be separated from it. Again, the mining proprietorship does not preclude parallel licences of exploration in a broader area or exploration for scientific purposes (section 8 paragraph 3 in conjunction with section 9 paragraph 1 sentence 2 BBergG).

707. This form of a mining licence is thus more far-reaching than the production licence. However, it needs to be mentioned that the possession of a production licence for the specific resource and area/field is a prerequisite for gaining the mining proprietorship (section 13 number 1 BBergG). According to the LBEG of Lower Saxony, the mining proprietorship lacks practical importance as a newly granted licence.[443] The mining proprietorship may, however, play a role as an old right transferred by the clause of section 151 BBergG.[444]

D. Application for a Mining Right, Further Rights Based on a Licence

708. All mining rights are only granted upon application to the competent authority (section 10 BBergG). The Federal States issued certain requirements for the application of the mining rights.[445] Sections 11–13 BBergG provide grounds for denying a particular licence in an enumerative form. Consequently, if no ground for denying a licence exists, the administration needs to grant the licence. The applicant has a legal claim to demand the desired licence.

709. In cases of competing applications for a production licence in a certain field, the holder of an exploration licence enjoys preference (section 14 BBergG). The applicant holding an exploration licence needs to be informed by the authority in case other persons apply for a production licence for the field in question.

710. The exploration licence may be granted for up to five years, the production licence and the mining proprietorship for a maximum of fifty years. In practice, for these licences a period of twenty to thirty years will hardly be transgressed.[446] The BBergG also contains norms on the revocation of mining rights. Such a revocation is possible if facts occur under which the granting of the right needed to be denied (section 18 paragraph 1 BBergG). Moreover, the exploration licence generally needs

---

442. E. Kremer & P. Neuhaus, *Bergrecht* (Stuttgart: W. Kohlhammer, 2001), 25.
443. State Authority for Mining, Energy and Geology (LBEG) of Lower Saxony, 'Mining proprietorship', available at www.lbeg.niedersachsen.de/master/C50977955_N50943712_L20_D0_I31802357, last access: 1 May 2022. The LBEG provides some information on the Federal Mining Law in English and also offers certain translations of ordinances concerning the mining law. Also the terminology for the different kinds of mining rights in this paper has been taken from this webpage.
444. Sections 149 et seqq. BBergG regulate the perpetuation of old mining rights which existed before the BBergG came into force.
445. *See* State Authority for Mining, Energy and Geology (LBEG) of Lower Saxony, www.lbeg.niedersachsen.de/live/live.php?&article_id=928&navigation_id=569&_psmand=4, last access: 1 May 2022.
446. E. Kremer & P. Neuhaus, *Bergrecht* (Stuttgart: W. Kohlhammer, 2001), 33.

to be revoked if it is not utilized within a period of one year. The same applies for the production licence within a period of three years, or if the utilization of these licences has been interrupted for the particular period (section 18 paragraphs 2 and 3 BBergG).

711. Sections 42 et seq. BBergG contain more detailed rules concretizing the right to exploit resources granted by the mining rights. Here, it is stipulated more precisely which other resources might be exploited while exercising the rights of a (production) licence. Also, the ability to construct supporting facilities subsurface and to gain the resources resulting thereof are regulated. Under the conditions of section 47 BBergG, the owner of a licence may be entitled to use foreign mining openings (*Grubenbaue*) against a certain monetary participation in the costs of the construction. This norm is of practical importance for old mine shafts in which hard coal was exploited, and which shall now be used for the exploitation of methane.[447]

III. Operating Plans

712. Concrete mining activities can in general only begin on the basis of a so-called operating plan. This plan needs to be approved by the competent authority. Section 51 paragraph 1 sentence 1 BBergG states that all facilities for the exploration, exploitation, and processing may be constructed, operated, and shut down only on the basis of operating plans (*Betriebspläne*) proposed by the entrepreneur and approved by the competent authority. The procedure for operating plans is a combined licensing and supervision procedure.[448] The operating plans can take various forms according to the function they serve.

713. The duty to prepare operating plans for the undertakings enables the mining authorities to exercise a continuous supervision of the mining facilities. In supervising the facility, the mining authorities have a more effective and a more detailed control. Due to the general hazardousness of mining activities, this continuous and effective supervision is the central aim of the operating plans.

714. For the drawing and for the content of the operating plans, the Federal Mining Law often does not provide detailed specifications. It is thus the task of the operator to propose and to define the concrete project. Since he will often be in preliminary consultations with the competent authorities, the authorities can guide him during the drafting process and therefore exercise indirect influence on the plan proposed.[449]

---

447. E. Kremer & P. Neuhaus, *Bergrecht* (Stuttgart: W. Kohlhammer, 2001), 31.
448. U. Büdenbender, W. Heintschel von Heinegg & P. Rosin, *Energierecht I, Recht der Energieanlagen* (Berlin/New York: Walter de Gruyter, 1999), para. 470.
449. E. Kremer & P. Neuhaus, *Bergrecht* (Stuttgart: W. Kohlhammer, 2001), 47.

A. Framework Operating Plan

715. The competent authority may demand a so-called framework operating plan (*Rahmenbetriebsplan*) for a longer period which may be designed due to the circumstances of the particular case (section 52 paragraph 2 number 1 BBergG). These plans must contain general descriptions of the intended project, the planned technical performance, and the anticipated time.

716. Under the general rule of section 52 paragraph 2 number 1 BBergG, the competent authority enjoys discretion in demanding such framework operating plans. It will exercise this discretion in the affirmative, in particular if the proposed project requires an overall plan due to its duration (or size or complexity). The framework operating plan is in particular helpful for the operation if several detailed main and special operating plans are required under a connective framework. Operators can also hand in framework operating plans without being requested by the competent authority. These framework operating plans most often last for a period between five and twenty years.[450]

717. The competent authority is demanding a framework operation plan in case the project requires an environmental impact assessment (section 52 paragraph 2a BBergG). In these cases, the authority is bound to conduct a plan approval procedure (*Planfeststellungsverfahren*) and the framework operating plan is obligatory. The mining activities that are subject to an environmental impact assessment are governed by the Ordinance on the Environmental Impact Assessment for Mining Projects (*UVP-V Bergbau*).[451] Section 1 UVP-V Bergbau – which lists these mining projects – provides in its first number, *inter alia*, for the exploitation of hard coal and lignite (according to a closer defined size of the project).

718. In case of an obligatory framework operating plan, the plan approval procedure replaces the normal approval procedure for operating plans (section 57a paragraph 1 sentence 1 BBergG).[452] The legal effects of the plan approval may, insofar as interests of third parties and certain authorities are affected, extend to the admission and prolongation of main, special or final operating plans which are necessary to enforce the framework operating plan (section 57a paragraph 5 BBergG). This rule only applies to objections about which a decision has been taken or to objections about which a decision could have been made if the objection was raised in time.

450. E. Kremer & P. Neuhaus, *Bergrecht* (Stuttgart: W. Kohlhammer, 2001), 50.

451. Verordnung über die Umweltverträglichkeitsprüfung bergbaulicher Vorhaben, UVP-V Bergbau, of 13 Jul. 1990 (BGBl. I p. 1420).

452. The usual approval procedure for operating plans is explained below under E. For an overview on plan approval procedures *see* above Part I, Ch. 3, s. 1.

B. Main Operating Plan

719. The main operating plan (*Hauptbetriebsplan*) is mentioned rather briefly in section 52 paragraph 1 BBergG. This clause states that main operating plans need to be prepared for the construction and conduct of an operation for a period generally not exceeding two years. The second sentence specifies that also an intermission in the operation of up to two years needs to be regarded as conduct of an operation.

720. At least a main operating plan must be prepared for any mining activity which is subject to the duty to propose operating plans. This plan therefore forms the basis of any mining operation.[453] The content of the main operating plan is, however, not closely defined in the Federal Mining Law. As a general rule, the main operating plan needs to provide a comprehensive image of the planned mining activity.[454] The concrete content of the plan is specified by administrative regulations of the *Länder*.

721. As far as hard coal mining in North Rhine-Westphalia is concerned, the upper board of mines for North Rhine-Westphalia (*Landesoberbergamt*) specified the typical content of a main operating plan in the guidelines on the operating plan procedure. The main operating plan for hard coal mining has been structured in four main chapters. It should provide a 'general description on the state and development of the operation', a 'description on the technical state and development of the operation', legal norms and administrative decisions, as well as an overview on the special operation plans which come into consideration for certain parts of the operation.[455] The first part was further divided into information about the mining rights and daily situation, environmental protection, as well as work safety and health protection. Due to the second part, closely defined information on the activities above ground as well as underground needed to be provided.

C. Special Operating Plans

722. Special operation plans (*Sonderbetriebspläne*) need to be prepared for certain parts of the operation or for certain projects (section 52 paragraph 2 number 2 BBergG). These plans apply for parts and projects with an independent importance from the general mining activities, which are therefore not suitable for inclusion in the main operation plan.[456]

---

453. *See* U. Büdenbender, W. Heintschel von Heinegg & P. Rosin, *Energierecht I, Recht der Energieanlagen* (Berlin/New York: Walter de Gruyter, 1999), para. 472.
454. E. Kremer & P. Neuhaus, *Bergrecht* (Stuttgart: W. Kohlhammer, 2001), 55.
455. Landesoberbergamt Nordrhein-Westfalen, Richtlinien für die Handhabung des Betriebsplanverfahrens (BP-RL) of 31 Aug. 1999, Annex 1, Hauptbetriebsplan für den Steinkohlenbergbau. Available via the webpage of the Bezirksregierung Arnsberg, http://esb.bezreg-arnsberg.nrw.de/index.html, last access: 26 Feb. 2011.
456. E. Kremer & P. Neuhaus, *Bergrecht* (Stuttgart: W. Kohlhammer, 2001), 57.

723. In particular for the hard coal mining in North Rhine-Westphalia, a detailed system of special operating plans had been developed.[457] A good overview on the diverse special operating plans possibly demanded is provided by the guidelines on the operating plan procedure of the upper board of mines for North Rhine-Westphalia.[458] Accordingly, special operating plans might *inter alia* be necessary for the following parts of the operation or for the following projects: disposal of specific mining wastes; exploration drilling and geophysical examination works; construction and operation of certain facilities like pressure vessels, crane installations, mining railroads, facilities for the storage; filling or transport of combustible fluids or fluids hazardous to water; all construction projects above ground, as demolition works above ground, backfilling of open pits; exposures of the mining on the surface properties (underground), utilization of residues as stowage (underground), construction of mine opening (underground).

724. Special operating plans on exposures of the mining on the surface properties might be necessary as a consequence of a judgment of the Federal Administrative Court, the so-called Moers-Kappelen-Judgment.[459] Accordingly, the interests of the surface property owners need to be taken into account in the approval of operating plans. The owners also have the right to be heard in the proceedings. Before this judgment, the legal protection for third parties was interpreted narrowly and they were generally required to tolerate any detriments evoking out of the mining activities (they were given the opportunity to ask for damages but not to intervene the activities themselves). However, legal protection for third parties under the Federal Mining Law is still tailored rather narrowly.[460]

D. Final Operating Plan

725. An operating plan is also required for the cessation of the operation (section 53 BBergG). This final operating plan (*Abschlussbetriebsplan*) applies for the definite cessation of operations and in general also for a cessation of more than two years. It can also apply in case of a utilization of the mine not pursuing the original

457. Closer described by E. Kremer & P. Neuhaus, *Bergrecht* (Stuttgart: W. Kohlhammer, 2001), 58 et seq.
458. *See* Landesoberbergamt Nordrhein-Westfalen, Richtlinien für die Handhabung des Betriebsplanverfahrens (BP-RL) of 31 Aug. 1999, Annex 1, Hauptbetriebsplan für den Steinkohlenbergbau, para. 4.
459. BVerwG, judgment of 16 Mar. 1989, 4 C 36/85, *BVerwGE*, 81, 329; B. Stüer, 'Abschlussbetriebsplanung für den Braunkohletagebau Ost – Bergrechtliche Nachsorgepflichten', *LKV* (2002): 12, 17; E. Kremer & P. Neuhaus, *Bergrecht* (Stuttgart: W. Kohlhammer, 2001), 59. The operating plans concerned with exposures of the mining on the surface areas have been created after the judgment of the Federal Administrative Court and are now generally applied in hard coal mining.
460. B. Stüer, 'Abschlussbetriebsplanung für den Braunkohletagebau Ost – Bergrechtliche Nachsorgepflichten', *LKV* (2002): 12, 16.

purpose.[461] With the final operating plan, the areas are released from the regime of mining law and put under the control of the general laws (construction, environmental, planning).[462]

726. The final operating plan needs to contain a precise description of the technical performance and duration of the intended cessation. Moreover, section 53 BBergG refers to most of the provisions of section 55 BBergG and therefore to the preconditions for an approval of an operating plan. These conditions are only applicable with the proviso of third persons' protection from any hazards for life and health also after cessation of operation (section 55 paragraph 2 BBergG). Recultivation of the surface area and complete removal of any installations in the areas of continental shelf and coastal waters also need to be ensured. Thus, for the cessation of an operation the general requirements for the approval of an operating plan apply. However, the particularities of a cessation need to be taken into account.[463]

727. Section 2 paragraph 1 number 2 BBergG states that the Federal Mining Law is applicable for recultivation 'during and after exploration, exploitation, and treatment'. As a consequence, already during the operation of a mine, certain precautionary measures need to be taken to ensure the recultivation after cessation.[464] An orderly condition of the surface is achieved if it is prepared for another reasonable use.[465] This duty of recultivation was of high relevance during the recent years, in particular for the lignite mining above ground. Many lignite open cast mines needed to be recultivated, for example, by flooding the remaining holes. Recultivation may also still be necessary due to the fact that the former German Democratic Republic, without taking environmental protection sufficiently into account, supplied its energy demand to a high percentage by lignite.[466]

E. Approval of Operating Plans

728. The entrepreneur must hand in the operating plan for approval to the competent authority before beginning of the intended works (section 54 paragraph 1 BBergG). This duty also applies for a prolongation, supplement or modification of the plan. The decision on approving the operating plan has to be taken in the affirmative in case the conditions of section 55 BBergG are fulfilled.

461. G. Boldt & H. Weller, *Bundesberggesetz, Kommentar* (Berlin: Walter de Gruyter, 1984), s. 53 para. 2; E. Kremer & P. Neuhaus, *Bergrecht* (Stuttgart: W. Kohlhammer, 2001), 64.
462. B. Stüer, 'Abschlussbetriebsplanung für den Braunkohletagebau Ost – Bergrechtliche Nachsorgepflichten', *LKV* (2002): 12.
463. B. Stüer, 'Abschlussbetriebsplanung für den Braunkohletagebau Ost – Bergrechtliche Nachsorgepflichten', *LKV* (2002): 12, 13.
464. G. Boldt & H. Weller, *Bundesberggesetz, Kommentar* (Berlin: Walter de Gruyter, 1984), s. 2 para. 21.
465. G. Boldt & H. Weller, *Bundesberggesetz, Kommentar* (Berlin: Walter de Gruyter, 1984), s. 55 para. 45.
466. B. Stüer, 'Abschlussbetriebsplanung für den Braunkohletagebau Ost – Bergrechtliche Nachsorgepflichten', *LKV* (2002): 12.

729. The entrepreneur needs to comply with the preconditions pursuant to section 55 paragraph 1 BBergG. These conditions decide upon which requirements may be demanded of a certain mining operation in a specific case, and they are also decisive for the mining supervision. The provisions in section 55 BBergG are thus referred to as the 'material core' of the BBergG.[467]

730. The entrepreneur needs first of all to be in possession of the necessary mining right (number 1). Moreover, he and the person in charge with the conduct of the mining activity need to be reliable, and either the entrepreneur or the person in charge with the conduct of the mining needs to possess the necessary technical qualification and physical ability (number 2).

731. Number 3 requires necessary precaution against hazards for life and health and requires the protection of material goods as well as of employees and third persons in the operation. Requirements for the security, health protection, and environmental protection are further specified in the Mining Regulation for all Mining Activities (*Allgemeine Bundesbergverordnung, ABBergV*).[468]

732. Also, the mining activity must not have a detrimental impact on the preservation of resources if the preservation lies within the public interest (number 4). With this clause, aspects of the sustainability of mining have been codified, demanding in particular to avoid a 'predatory exploitation' of natural resources. A later possibility to exploit other resources economically needs to be taken into account.[469]

733. The surface area must be protected in the interest of personal safety and of the public traffic (number 5). Wastes need to be disposed of properly (number 6), and the necessary precaution for a later recultivation of the surface needs to be taken (number 7). Further duties are contained in the remaining numbers 8–13. Material preconditions concerning nature protection or Immissions Control Law may also be of relevance.[470]

734. Section 54 paragraph 2 BBergG requires a participation of any authorities or municipalities concerned by the measures proposed in the operating plan. Due to the law of the *Länder*, a further participation of the municipalities may arise. The general procedural provisions are contained in the Administrative Procedure Codes of the *Länder* (see section 5 BBergG). The simple approval procedure is contrasted by the plan approval procedure which is necessary for obligatory framework operating plans.[471]

---

467. G. Boldt & H. Weller, *Bundesberggesetz, Kommentar* (Berlin: Walter de Gruyter, 1984), s. 55 para. 1.
468. Allgemeine Bundesbergverordnung of 23 Dec. 1995 (BGBl. I p. 1466).
469. E. Kremer & P. Neuhaus, *Bergrecht* (Stuttgart: W. Kohlhammer, 2001), 230.
470. BVerwG, judgment of 16 Mar. 1989, 4 C 36/85, *BVerwGE*, 81, 329; *see* E. Kremer & P. Neuhaus, *Bergrecht* (Stuttgart: W. Kohlhammer, 2001), 253 et seq.
471. *See* the remarks on this procedure above A.

735. The procedure ends with the approval of the operating plan in written form. It may be subject to further conditions if they are necessary to ensure compliance with the material provisions (section 36 of the Administrative Procedure Code). If necessary, it may also be required to provide a security to assure fulfilment of certain preconditions (section 56 paragraph 2 BBergG). Operating plans under section 52 BBergG may be prolonged, supplemented or modified (section 52 paragraph 4 sentence 2 BBergG).

IV. Mining Supervision

736. The competencies for the authorities in charge with the supervision of mining activities are listed in the fifth part of the Federal Mining Law (*Bergaufsicht*). These norms provide classic police authority instruments for these authorities. They are entitled, for instance, to demand the necessary information for performing the mining supervision (in particular from persons in possession of a mining right, section 70 paragraph 1 BBergG). Moreover, they are entitled to conduct examinations and to enter the factory and business premises as well as certain other installations. If a mining activity is conducted without an approved operating plan (or in another illegal manner), operations can be prohibited by means of section 72 BBergG.

737. A general norm under which the authority may order 'measures for the enforcement of the provisions of Federal Mining Law' is contained in section 71 paragraph 1 sentence 1 BBergG. The second sentence allows taking measures that go beyond the requirements which have been drawn up in an operating plan. However, this is only allowed if such measures are necessary to protect life, health or material goods of employees or third persons.

Chapter 3. Transport

738. The requirements for electric wires, by which electricity generated from coal can be supplied to end consumers, are explained above in Part I, Chapter 3.

Chapter 4. Distribution

739. Rules applying for the distribution of electricity generated from coal are explained above in Part I, Chapter 4.

Chapter 5. Consumption

740. Rules applying for the consumption of electricity generated from coal are explained above in Part I, Chapter 5.

Part V. Regulatory Framework on Renewable Energy

741. There is an urgent need to reduce greenhouse gas emissions of energy production. Renewable energy has received substantial support in Germany, in particular, the Renewable Energy Sources Act (*Erneuerbare-Energien-Gesetz, EEG*) fostered the increased use of renewable energy for electricity generation. The basic model of the Renewable Energy Sources Act relies on granting priority grid access and financial support for the feed-in of electricity from renewable sources into the grid. This regulatory mechanism has been copied by a range of other countries. In Germany, the Act has been amended several times and now stipulates for much more specific rules concerning the support for renewable energy. Whereas originally renewable energy installations have been supported by fixed tariffs provided in the EEG, the financial support for larger renewable energy installations is determined through procurements by tender now.

742. This part will focus on the provisions of the Renewable Energy Sources Act. Also in other energy sectors such as the heat and fuel sectors, regulatory mechanisms aim to increase the share of renewable energy. The provisions for the heat sector will be briefly explained below (Chapter 7), and the provisions seeking to increase renewable energy in the transport sector have been introduced above Part III, Chapter 5 already. The share of renewable energy in the heat and transport sector still is much lower than in the electricity sector, which is a severe concern in regard to combatting climate change and security of supply. In all areas, it is necessary to focus efforts on rapidly reducing greenhouse gas emissions and fostering security of supply by employing renewable energy sources.

Chapter 1. Introduction

743. The promotion of renewable energy in Germany – particularly in the electricity sector – has experienced a real boost over the past decades. Wind parks, photovoltaics, and biomass power plants are no longer a far and distant future in German energy policy; they are becoming the prevailing energy source for electricity generation in Germany. The feed-in tariff system has been largely successful in increasing the percentage of renewable energies for electricity generation. The share of renewable energies in the electricity generation reached 26.5% in 2014 and 45% in 2020.[472] Generally speaking, there is a wide consensus regarding the promotion of renewable energy between the political parties in Germany. However, starting in end of 2012, an intensive debate on the increase in energy prices begun. The increase in electricity prices has mainly been discussed in the context of support for renewable energies, though the factual reasons are much more complex. Against this background, amendments of the EEG since then tried to strike a balance between fostering the expansion of renewable energy sources and cost and consumer price efficiency.

744. In particular by introducing direct marketing requirements and tender procedures for larger renewable energy installations, a closer orientation of renewable energy on the market has been promoted.[473] The commercial viability of renewable energy is a necessary objective, also since so far the feed-in tariffs for renewable energy have been paid by the end consumers. It must be noted that the long-standing competitive disadvantage of renewable energy resulted not only out of technical reasons, but to a large extent also out of the external costs of the non-renewable energy production which are not internalized.[474] Moreover, other energy sources often benefit from direct or indirect promotion measures too. As long as these drawbacks for renewable energy are not repealed, they will require additional promotion to ensure their development.

745. The feed-in support model for renewable energy was developed in Germany and has since been applied in several other countries. It can safely be said that the feed-in support system has been the most successful promotional tool for renewable energy. This is demonstrated in particular by taking account of the steadily growing rates of renewable energy sources in the energy mix in Germany. Renewable energy also receives a lot of attention in the scientific community, and there is an extensive amount of judicial literature on the topic, from commentaries to special journals on new forms of energy.

---

472. Bundesnetzagentur / Bundeskartellamt, *Monitoringreport 2021*, Dec 2021, pp. 56–58, available at www.bundesnetzagentur.de.

473. *See* already the Energy Concept, 'Energiekonzept für eine umweltschonende, zuverlässige und bezahlbare Energieversorgung', BT-Drs. 17/3049, 4, and the main points for the reform of the EEG 2014, 21 Jan. 2014 http://www.bmwi.de/DE/Themen/energie,did=617196.html accessed 1 Feb. 2014.

474. The aim of reducing the costs of energy supply also by incorporating external long-term effects is explicitly mentioned in the aims of EEG in its first section.

746. Several countries in the EU have used quota systems as an alternative model for the promotion of renewable energy. However, the majority of the Members States rely on a system of financial feed-in support.[475] One main reason for the success of the feed-in model is the high grade of investment security offered to producers.

747. This being said, the feed-in models are developed further to ensure market integration and cost efficiency of the renewable energy build-out. Due to the increasing share of renewable energy in the energy mix, detrimental effects on the environment by renewable energy also need to be minimized. In this context, the sustainability requirements for the production of biomass through a rather complicated certification system in a Biomass Sustainability Ordinance can be mentioned.

748. Following political discussion on the appropriate support levels, for instance feed-in tariffs for electricity from photovoltaic installations already have been cut in 2010 and 2012 to a higher extent as has been aimed at originally. However, it needs to be noted that the reduction of feed-in tariffs only concerns new installations. Installations with an earlier commissioning are still supported by the tariffs granted, depending on the date of their commissioning. This guarantees significant investment security to the operators. For newer installations, obligations on direct marketing and participation in tender procedures may apply.

749. The construction and operation of installations for the production of energy from renewable sources is not governed by the Renewable Energy Sources Act. For the construction and operation of the plants, the general planning, building and immission control laws apply. Either the Federal Immissions Control Act or the construction law stipulates the administrative approval procedures. Since these statutes are described in another context, the chapters on the different kinds of renewable energy sources will highlight only particularities for certain plants. A specific legal regime applies for construction and operation of offshore wind installations.

§1. Facts and Figures

750. In 2009, the electricity generation from renewable sources increased nearly by a factor of 5 to a level of 93 TWh compared to 1990.[476] In 2020, electricity generation from renewable energy sources amounted to 236.6 TWh.[477] Electricity generated from renewable sources thus reached a share of 15.6% in gross electricity generation in 2009, and of 45% in gross electricity generation in 2020.

---

475. W. Lehnert & J. Vollprecht, 'Neue Impulse von Europa: Die Erneuerbare-Energien-Richtlinie der EU', *ZUR* (2009): 307, 311.
476. Federal Ministry of Economy and Technologies, *Energie in Deutschland, Trends und Hintergründe zur Energieversorgung in Deutschland* (August 2010), 34.
477. Bundesnetzagentur / Bundeskartellamt, *Monitoringreport 2021*, Dec 2021, p. 57 et seq., available at www.bundesnetzagentur.de.

751. Renewable energy reached a share of 10.3% in 2009, 12.7% in 2012, and 16% in 2021 in the total final energy consumption.[478] In contrast to the relatively high expansion of renewable energy in the electricity sector, this shows that the heat and transport sector still are largely dependent on fossil energy sources. The share of renewable energy sources in the final energy consumption for heat and cold amounted to around 15% in 2020, and the share of renewable energy sources in the final energy consumption in the transport sector amounted to only around 7% in 2020.[479] This shows the need of massive efforts to increase the share of renewable energy also in these other sectors.

§2. Development of the Renewable Energy Sources Act

752. Support for small plants generating electricity from renewable sources started with the Cartel Law as governed by the Act against Restraints of Competition (*GWB*).[480] Undertakings with a dominant position on the market were not allowed to constrain small undertakings in the utilization of electricity generated in own plants unreasonably. The jurisdiction took the 'principle of avoided costs' as an orientation to determine the remuneration for the feed-in of the generated electricity, leading to a case-by-case examination on how to calculate the relevant remuneration.[481]

753. The main legislative step to promote the electricity generation from renewable sources was the enacting of the Electricity Feed-In Statute (*Stromeinspeisungsgesetz*) in 1990. This statute regulated the duty of energy supply companies to take off electricity generated from renewable sources and to pay for this electricity in accordance with the rules for calculating the remuneration.

754. Although several amended versions of the Renewable Energy Sources Act entered into force since that time, the basic mechanism provided by the Stromeinspeisungsgesetz is the central promotion measure until today. The Stromeinspeisungsgesetz was replaced by the Act on Granting Priority to Renewable Energy Sources (*EEG 2000*) in the year 2000. In the first few years of its existence, this new statute initiated a rapid increase of renewable energy sources in the electricity sector. New versions of the Renewable Energy Sources Act have been enacted with

---

478. Federal Ministry for the Environment, *Erneuerbare Energien in Zahlen* (June 2010), available at: www.erneuerbare-energien.de, 9; Federal Ministry for the Environment, 'Erneuerbare Energien 201 0', provisional data, 23 Mar. 2011. AGEE-Stat, Erneuerbare Energien in Zahlen, December 2013; Umweltbundesamt, Primärenergieverbrauch, statistical data available via the webpage www.umweltbundesamt.de, last access 6 Mar. 2022.
479. Umweltbundesamt, Anteil erneuerbarer Energien in den Sektoren Strom, Wärme und Verkehr, table available via the webpage www.umweltbundesamt.de, last access 6 Mar. 2022.
480. The Competition Law is explained in Part VII.
481. M. Altrock, V. Oschmann & C. Theobald, *EEG*, 4th edn (München: C.H. Beck, 2013), Einführung, paras 5–12.

the *EEG 2004*, the *EEG 2009*, the *EEG 2012*, the *EEG 2014*, the *EEG 2017*, and the *EEG 2021*. At the time this update is made, a draft *EEG 2023* is under discussion.

755. The following Chapter 2 of this monograph will refer to and explain the provisions of the EEG 2021, but for some sections also refer to previous provisions of the EEG. This will be the case in particular where important mechanisms of support for renewable energies shall be explained, even if they have changed with the amended version of the Act.

§3. European Law on Renewable Energy

756. The promotion of renewable energy is fostered by the EU in the light of combating climate change and diversifying the energy mix. The framework for this promotion is set out in particular in the Directive on the Promotion of the Use of Energy from Renewable Sources which shall be introduced in I. below. One important consideration for national support schemes for renewable energy is whether they classify as state aid under EU law. In this context, the decision of the European Court of Justice in the case *PreussenElektra* as well as the subsequent ECJ decision on the EEG 2012 shall be discussed below under II.

I. European Directive on the Promotion of the Use of Energy from Renewable Sources

757. Directive 2001/77/EC[482] already demanded a promotion of electricity from renewable sources from the Member States, but it *inter alia* did not involve all sectors of renewable energy production. With Directive 2009/28/EC on the Promotion of the Use of Energy from Renewable Sources, the European Community set itself a target for 2020 of at least a 20% share of energy from renewable sources in the Community's gross final consumption of energy (Article 3(1) of Directive 2009/28/EC).[483] The revised Directive 2018/2001/EU[484] in Article 3(1) requests the Member States to collectively ensure that the share of energy from renewable sources in the Union's gross final consumption of energy in 2030 is at least 32%. Most provisions of Directive 2018/2001/EU had to be transposed into national laws of the Member

482. Directive 2001/77/EC of the European Parliament and of the Council of 27 Sep. 2001 on the promotion of electricity from renewable energy sources in the internal electricity market. Directive 2009/28/EC also repeals Directive 2003/30/EC of the European Parliament and of the Council of 8 May 2003 on the promotion of the use of biofuels or other renewable fuels for transport, OJ L 123, 17 May 2003, 42.

483. Directive 2009/28/EC of the European Parliament and of the Council of 23 Apr. 2009 on the promotion of the use of energy from renewable sources and amending and subsequently repealing Directives 2001/77/EC and 2003/30/EC, OJ L 140 of 5 Jun. 2009, 16 et seq.

484. Directive 2018/2001/EU of the European Parliament and of the Council of 11 Dec. 2018 on the promotion of the use of energy from renewable sources, OJ L 328 of 21 Dec, 2018, 82 et seqq.

States by 30 June 2021, Article 36(1). The main provisions of the Directive shall be briefly explained since they are relevant to the German Law on renewable energy.

A. Goals for Renewable Energy in the Energy Mix

758. Directive 2009/28/EC provided compulsory targets for the share of energy from renewable sources for each Member State (Article 3(1) in conjunction with Annex I to the Directive). The target set for 2020 for the share of renewable energy within the gross final consumption of energy in Germany amounted to 18% (as a comparison: France: 23%, United Kingdom: 15%).

Article 3(1) of the revised Directive 2018/2001/EU sets out a common goal of at least a 32% share of energy from renewable sources in the Union's gross final consumption of energy in 2030, applying for all Member States collectively. To achieve this goal, Article 3(2) of the Directive requests Member States to set national contributions to meet the binding overall Union target collectively with the other Member States. Also, from 1 January 2021, according to Article 3(4) of the Directive the share of energy from renewable sources in each Member State's gross final consumption of energy shall not be lower than the baseline share shown in the third column of the table in Part A of Annex I. For Germany, this baseline for 2020 amounts to 18%, taken up the value set out by the predecessor Directive.

B. Flexibility of the Member States in Choosing the Support Mechanism

759. The EU takes the different capacity and potential of its Member States in the field of renewable energy into account, as well as the various promotion measures used by the Member States.[485] Directive 2018/2001/EU, like the predecessor Directive 2009/28, does not oblige Member States to use a certain support scheme to promote renewable energy. Article 4(1) of the revised Directive instead states the Member States 'may' apply support schemes to reach the EU goal on renewable energy and the Member States' contribution. Therefore, the choice of promotion measures principally remains within the discretion of the Member States.[486]

760. However, the Directive does contain certain requirements for the promotion of energy from renewable sources and therefore in respect of the design of the national support schemes. Article 4(2) and (3) Directive 2018/2001/EU are concerned with market integration of renewable energy, and with the impacts of support schemes on the energy markets. Accordingly, '[s]upport schemes for electricity from renewable sources shall provide incentives for the integration of electricity

485. *See* Recital 22 of the Directive. The term 'support scheme' is defined in Art. 2 Nr. 5 of the Directive.

486. Also under the former Directive 2001/77/EC, the Member States were entitled to choose between several promotion measures, *see* P. Salje, *EEG*, 5th edn (Köln: Carl Heymanns Verlag, 2009), Einführung, para. 99.

from renewable sources in the electricity market in a market-based and market-responsive way, while avoiding unnecessary distortions of electricity markets as well as taking into account possible system integration costs and grid stability'. Article 4(3) continues that '[s]upport schemes for electricity from renewable sources shall be designed so as to maximise the integration of electricity from renewable sources in the electricity market and to ensure that renewable energy producers are responding to market price signals and maximise their market revenues'. The following sentence contains a specific requirement for direct support schemes in which support shall be granted in the form of a market premium (*inter alia* sliding or fixed). Further, 'Member States shall ensure that support for electricity from renewable sources is granted in an open, transparent, competitive, non-discriminatory, and cost-effective manner', Article 4(4). While this sentence does not mention tendering procedures explicitly, the following sentence states that Member States may exempt small-scale installations and demonstration projects from such.

761. Article 6(1) of the Directive requires the Member States to ensure that the 'level of, and the conditions attached to, the support granted to renewable energy projects are not revised in a way that negatively affects the rights conferred thereunder and undermines the economic viability of projects that already benefit from support'. This shall limit the Member States in retroactively changing support schemes for existing installations, and thereby securing financial stability for operators. The Directive in Article 15 also stipulates certain standards for the national administrative procedures for the admission of renewable energy plants. Such administrative procedures shall be 'proportional and necessary' (Article 13(1)). Under lit. a) of Article 13(1), this clause also demands that the administrative procedures shall be 'streamlined and expedited'. Germany already implemented measures to speed up the planning procedures for infrastructure projects[487] and adopted such measures particularly in the energy sector.[488]

C. Cooperation of Member States

762. The Directive does not specify which promotion mechanism for renewable energy the Member States must use; but it does offer opportunities for the cooperation of the Member States in reaching their national renewable energy targets. In Recital 22 it is stated that the 'Directive should facilitate cross-border support for renewable energy without affecting national support schemes'. Moreover, the Directive wants to open up the possibility to let renewable energy-based electricity, imported from outside the Union, count towards the national targets.

---

487. Gesetz zur Beschleunigung von Planungsverfahren für Infrastrukturvorhaben of 17 Dec. 2006, BGBl. I 2006, 2833.
488. *See* the Statute on the Expansion of Energy Lines, Energieleitungsausbaugesetz (EnLAG) of 21 Aug. 2009 (BGBl. I p. 2870).

763. These measures are facilitated by Articles 8–13 of the Directive. Article 8 allows for statistical transfers of a specified amount of energy from renewable sources from one Member State to another Member State. Such a transfer need not be followed by any physical transfer of energy. This might therefore create a market for such transfers between the Member States.[489]

764. Articles 9 and 10 allow for joint projects for the production of energy from renewable sources between Member States. The Member States notify the proportion or amount of renewable energy which is to be regarded as counting towards the renewable energy share of another Member State (Article 9(2)).

765. Common projects are also possible between a Member State and a third country, however, only under the restrictive conditions of Articles 11 and 12 of the Directive. Article 13 even allows the Member States to set up joint support schemes for renewable energy or to partly coordinate their national support schemes.

D. Sustainability Requirements for Biomass Used as a Renewable Energy Source

766. Directive 2009/28/EC introduced sustainability requirements for certain types of biomass used for the generation of energy which are continued with Directive 2018/2001/EU. The basic mechanism is that energy from biofuels, bioliquids, and biomass fuels shall only count towards the Union target for renewable energy and only be eligible for financial support if the biomass used is produced in accordance with a closer defined sustainability standard (Article 29(1) of the Directive). Accordingly, Member States must implement the requirements in their national support schemes. Member States generally will render the support granted for renewable energy under their promotion measures dependent on the compliance with the sustainability requirements.

767. The introduction of sustainability standards for biomass for the generation of energy has been a response to the growing concerns on the detrimental impacts on the environment which an uncontrolled production of biomass could have.[490] Accordingly, Recital 69 of Directive 2009/28/EC stated:

> The increasing worldwide demand for biofuels and bioliquids, and the incentives for their use provided for in this Directive, should not have the effect of encouraging the destruction of biodiverse lands.

---

489. *See* to the predecessor Directive C. Ringel & C. Bitsch, 'Die Neuordnung des Rechts der Erneuerbaren Energien in Europa', *NVwZ* (2009): 807; W. Lehnert & J. Vollprecht, 'Neue Impulse von Europa: Die Erneuerbare-Energien-Richtlinie der EU', *ZUR* (2009): 307, 312.

490. *See* closer Sachverständigenrat für Umweltfragen, *Klimaschutz durch Biomasse, Sondergutachten* (Berlin: Erich Schmidt Verlag, July 2007).

768. Directive 2018/2001/EU contains essentially three main criteria for the sustainability of biomass for the energy generation. First, biofuels, bioliquids, and biomass fuels need to achieve minimum greenhouse gas emission savings (Article 29(10)). Second, biofuels, bioliquids and biomass fuels may not be made from raw material obtained from land with high biodiversity value. Which areas fall within this category is further defined by Article 29(3). Third, biofuels, bioliquids, and biomass fuels produced from agricultural biomass shall not be made from raw material obtained from land with high carbon stock (Article 29(4)). Further, the Directive provides for requirements for harvesting operations as well as land-use, land-use change, and forestry (LULUCF) criteria.

769. The Directive provides complex and detailed regulations for determining the sustainability of energy from biofuels, bioliquids, and biomass fuels, which will require a certification system in order to verify compliance. Article 30 of Directive 2018/2001/EU sets out a framework for how compliance with the sustainability and greenhouse gas emissions saving criteria shall be verified. This still leaves a lot of leeway for the Commission and Member States to detail the compliance mechanisms.

II. ECJ Decisions on PreussenElektra and EEG 2012

770. The compatibility of the promotion mechanism for renewable energy as stipulated in the German Electricity Feed-In Statute (*Stromeinspeisungsgesetz*, subsequently replaced by the *EEG*) with the law of the European Communities was already questioned by a number of authors before the decision of the European Court of Justice in *PreussenElektra*. Particular focus of these doubts was whether the statute complies with the provisions on state aid and on the free movement of goods in the Treaty on the European Communities. As will be explained in more detail below, the feed-in statutes guarantee the producers of electricity from renewable sources a take-off of the electricity produced and, initially, remuneration according to fixed tariffs. The Court's ruling on the state aid issue helps to understand how this promotion mechanism has been regarded in legal terms.[491]

771. In PreussenElektra, the European Court of Justice has been questioned in a preliminary ruling whether the rules on the payment for electricity as provided by the German *Stromeinspeisungsgesetz* constitute state aid according to the rule now contained in Article 107 TFEU. As a general rule, this article declares 'any aid granted by a Member State or through state resources in any form whatsoever which distorts or threatens to distort competition by favouring certain undertakings or the production of certain goods' incompatible with the common market.

491. Also, the compatibility with the rules on free movement of goods has been affirmed by the European Court of Justice. The Directive on Renewable Energy by the European Communities is nowadays the more specific regulation clarifying the relation to the free movement of goods and guaranteeing compliance, if the conditions of the Directive are fulfilled. *See also* Case C-573/12.

772. The European Court of Justice does not disregard the fact that the mechanism of the feed-in tariffs under the German Electricity Feed-In Statute provides an economic advantage to the producers of electricity from renewable sources. However, the Court emphasizes that under its jurisdiction only advantages 'granted directly or indirectly through state resources' have been considered as 'aid' within the meaning of (now) Article 107 TFEU.[492] In line with its earlier interpretation, the Court rules:

> In this case, the obligation imposed on private electricity supply undertakings to purchase electricity produced from renewable energy sources at fixed minimum prices does not involve any direct or indirect transfer of State resources to undertakings which produce that type of electricity.
>
> Therefore, the allocation of the financial burden arising from that obligation for those private electricity supply undertakings as between them and other private undertakings cannot constitute a direct or indirect transfer of State resources either.[493]

773. The Court concluded that the promotion mechanism under the German Electricity Feed-In Statute can therefore not be regarded to be state aid within the frame of (now) Article 107 TFEU. Although this interpretation might be considered as narrow, it offers a clear guideline to the application of the state aid provisions. It also provides a distinction from other legal measures enacted to support certain technologies or industries with an economic advantage which is not granted directly or indirectly through state resources. Other rules like the rules on the free movement of goods still may be applicable for a control of the specific support mechanism. This might explain the court's ruling as well.

774. In 2013, the question of the compatibility of the Renewable Energy Sources Act with EU law arose again. The European Commission opened a formal procedure to examine whether the partial exemption of energy intensive industries from the EEG surcharge (*EEG-Umlage*) constitutes state aid. The Commission has been of the opinion that the feed-in tariffs and also the market premium granted under the EEG 2012 would be state aid within the terms of Article 107 TFEU.[494] With judgment of 10 May 2016, the General Court of the European Union affirmed the position of the Commission and ruled that the Commission was correct in finding that the EEG 2012 involves state resources and therefore constitutes state aid.[495]

---

492. European Court of Justice, Case C-379/98, judgment of 13 Mar. 2001, *PreussenElektra v. Schleswag*, para. 58.
493. European Court of Justice, Case C-379/98, judgment of 13 Mar. 2001, *PreussenElektra v. Schleswag*, paras 59 and 60.
494. *See* European Commission, press release 'Staatliche Beihilfen: Kommission eröffnet eingehende Prüfung der Förderung stromintensiver Unternehmen durch Teilbefreiung von EEG-Umlage', 18 Dec. 2013; decision of the Commission, C(2013) 4424 final; Commission Decision (EU) 2015/1585 of 25 Nov. 2014 in State aid proceedings SA. 33995 (2013/C).
495. General Court of the European Union, Case T-47/17, judgment of 10 May 2016, *Federal Republic of German v. European Commission*.

775. However, Germany appealed this decision, emphasizing that the Renewable Energy Sources Act (in line with the decision in *PreussenElektra*) would not constitute state aid. On 28 March 2019, the European Court of Justice set aside the judgment of the General Court of the European Union and annulled the Commission Decision.[496] In essence, the ECJ reasoned that the General Court failed to establish that Germany held a power of disposal over the funds generated by the EEG surcharge, and also failed to establish that Germany exercised public control over the TSOs responsible for managing the funds.[497] In this decision, the ECJ *inter alia* relies on the EEG surcharge representing 'any difference between the price obtained by the TSOs on the spot market of the EEG electricity exchange' which the TSOs can pass on to the electricity suppliers, but that electricity suppliers are not required to pass on the amounts of the EEG surcharge to end consumers (although in practice that generally is what happens on a contractual basis).[498] While the public authorities monitor the proper implementation of the EEG 2012 and the EEG surcharge in particular, there would be no public control over the funds generated by the EEG surcharge.[499]

776. The judgments of the European Court of Justice demonstrate that the support mechanism for renewable energy can be, and has been structured in a way that it does not fall within the state aid rules of the TFEU. This being said, it must be noted that Germany subsequently changed the way in which the EEG surcharge is being financed. The EEG surcharge under the revised EEG 2021 is partly covered by the state budget (see closer below Chapter 2 §6). In light of this development, Germany has notified the rules of the EEG 2021 for state aid approval to the European Commission.[500] Since the support under the Renewable Energy Sources Act due to the changes likely will be treated as state aid, the guidelines of the European Commission on state aid measures will be of high relevance for its justification.

§4. Political support for Renewable Energy and further Development of the EEG

777. The goal of future expansion of renewable energy has been stated clearly in the wording of the German Energy Concept 2010.[501] According to the German Energy Concept 2010, conventional energy sources shall gradually be replaced by renewable energy sources. The goal of the German Energy Concept 2010 was that

496. European Court of Justice, Case C-405/16 P, judgment of 28 Mar. 2019, *Federal Republic of German v. European Commission.*
497. European Court of Justice, Case C-405/16 P, judgment of 28 Mar. 2019, *Federal Republic of German v. European Commission,* para. 73.
498. *Ibid*, para. 70.
499. *Ibid*, para. 80.
500. Closer information on the state aid approval by the European Commission can be found on www.bmwi.de/Redaktion/DE/FAQ/EEG-2021/faq-beihilferechtlichen-genehmigung-eu-kommission.html, last accessed 1 May 2022.
501. Whereas the Energy Concept also aimed to extend the running-times of nuclear power stations, *see* closer above Introduction, Ch. 6.

the share of renewable energy sources in the gross final consumption of energy raises to 18% until 2020. At the time of the German Energy Concept 2010, the Federal Government aimed at a 'development path' of 30% share of renewable energy until 2030, 45% until 2040, and 60% until 2050. Within the electricity generation, the share of renewable energy sources was intended to raise to 35% by 2020, 50% by 2030, 65% by 2040, and 80% by 2050.[502]

778. The cost of support for renewable energy has been in the focus of public debate in and from 2013. Two aspects are of great importance in order to understand why renewables' support costs have been widely discussed: first, the mechanism for allocating the costs of the support for renewable energies in the electricity sector was modified in 2010. In the new system, an 'EEG surcharge' (*EEG-Umlage*) must be paid by all electricity supply companies which, in turn, demand this EEG surcharge from the end consumers on a contractual basis. This EEG surcharge seems to render visible the costs for support of renewables. The amount of the EEG surcharge has increased from 3.592 cent/kWh (in 2012) to 5.277 cent/kWh (in 2013), 6.240 cent/kWh (in 2014), 6.405 cent/kWh (in 2019), and 6.756 cent/kWh (in 2020).[503] Following political measures, the EEG surcharge has been stabilized at a level of 6.500 cent/kWh in 2021, and due to significant changes in market prices, the amount of the EEG surcharge decreased to 3.723 cent/kWh in 2022.

779. The increase in EEG surcharge in 2013 alarmed politicians. At the beginning of 2013, the Federal Minister for the environment and the Federal Minister for the economy published their ideas on an 'electricity price cap' (*Strompreisbremse*).[504] These proposals were mainly made with a view of achieving a short-term reduction of the EEG surcharge. However, these proposals have not been adopted by the legislator.

780. It can well be said that the EEG surcharge does not reveal the costs of renewable energy only. In particular, it has been stressed by proponents of renewable energy that spot market prices have been reduced by the large amount of renewable energy in the system which – following the EEG balancing mechanism – are sold, to a great extent, at the spot market of the electricity exchange. In turn, prices for electricity on the spot market go down (so-called merit-order-effect). The low income for the electricity from renewable energy sources has added to the high amounts of the EEG surcharge.[505] This even leads to lower prices for the selling of

---

502. Energy Concept, BT-Drs. 17/3049, 2.
503. For closer information on the amount of the EEG surcharge *see* the webpage of the transmission grid operators www.netztransparenz.de.
504. BMU/BMWi, Energiewende sichern – Kosten begrenzen, Gemeinsamer Vorschlag zur Dämpfung der Kosten des Ausbaus der Erneuerbaren Energien', 13 Feb. 2013.
505. Öko-Institut, 'EEG-Umlage und die Kosten der Stromversorgung für 2014 – Eine Analyse von Trends, Ursachen und Wechselwirkungen', June 2013; Peter Becker, 'Der (wahre) Strompreis: Das unbekannte Wesen', [2012] ZNER p. 563. *See also* the legislative reasoning to the EEG 2014, BT-Drs.18/1304, p. 139 to 143. Partially different view: Monopolkommission, Sondergutachten 65, Energie 2013: Wettbewerb in Zeiten der Energiewende, p. 13.

renewable energy – it has been said that this mechanism leads to the renewables compromising their own market price. Moreover, costs for the EEG surcharge for household customers increased due to larger exemptions for industry having been broadened through the EEG 2012.

781. Following the debate on electricity prices, the legislator introduced a far-reaching amendment of the EEG in 2014. The coalition from CDU/CSU and SPD agreed on an 'expansion corridor' for renewable energies in the electricity sector of 40% to 45% in 2025 and 55% to 60% in 2035. This expansion corridor was intended to foster the growth of renewable energy while giving other participants of the energy industry planning reliability.[506] The introduction of an expansion corridor is remarkable in particular since the EEG 2012 provided for minimum goals for the expansion of renewable energy sources instead. The EEG aimed at an increase in the installed capacity of onshore wind energy plants of 2.500 MW annually, from offshore wind energy plants of overall 6.500 MW in 2020 and 15.000 MW in 2030, from photovoltaic installations of 2.500 MW annually and from biomass installations of only up to 100 MW annually. Not surprisingly, these expansion corridors have been controversial. The legal consequence of the expansion paths has been the calculation of the degression, i.e., the percentage by which the support granted by the EEG is reduced (or in rare circumstances increased) annually. Depending on whether the path of expansion is complied with, exceeded or undercut, this percentage was adjusted according to sections 26 to 31 EEG 2014. With the EEG 2014, direct marketing became coercive for larger new EEG installations. Also, tender procedures for renewable energy installations have been tested in a 'pilot project' for stand-alone photovoltaic installations. The introduction and scope of the tender procedures and their specific design have been subject to political debate. This has become visible already by the *Bundesrat* (the representation of the German *Länder*) taking a more cautious approach towards tender procedures in the legislative proceedings. The *Bundesrat* expressed general concerns on tender procedures for the support of smaller and medium EEG installations in particular and requested at least an adequate phase with technology specific projects and an analysis of the results.[507]

782. The EEG 2017 further built on these principles. The main amendment with the EEG 2017 has been the introduction of tender procedures to determine the amount of support for larger renewable energy installations. The Guidelines on State aid for environmental protection and energy 2014–2020 of the European Commission required, as a general rule subject to exceptions, that from 1 January 2017 financial support for electricity from renewable energy sources is granted in a competitive bidding process on the basis of clear, transparent, and non-discriminatory

506. Legislative reasoning, BT-Drs. 18/1304, pp. 131 et seq.
507. BR-Drs. 157/14 (Beschluss), p. 2.

criteria.[508] Accordingly, in the course of the EEG 2017 amendment, tender procedures have been introduced for larger onshore, offshore, solar, and biomass installations.[509] For the installations covered by the tender procedures, the support levels therefore are determined by the bidding process in the respective tender. Besides this, in particular for smaller installations and for the energy sources not covered by the tender requirement, financial support has been still available based on support values set by the legislator in the EEG itself. The EEG 2021 amendment built on the principles of the EEG 2017 and will be described in the following.

783. In the Coalition Agreement 2021,[510] the Social Democratic Party (SPD), the Greens (Bündnis 90/Die Grünen), and the Free Democratic Party (FDP) set ambitious targets in transforming and modernizing Germany on the path to climate neutrality. The aim for the expansion of photovoltaics are 200 GW until 2030, for onshore wind energy 2% of the total area at land shall be assigned, and the capacities for offshore wind shall be substantially increased to at least 30 GW in 2030, 40 GW in 2035, and 70 GW in 2045. The parties stated that 80% of the gross electricity consumption in 2030 shall be covered from renewable energy sources. The yearly tender amounts shall be adjusted accordingly.

784. At the time this update is being made, the legislator intends to implement a far-reaching amendment of the Renewable Energy Sources Act with an EEG 2023 as well as interim changes. This amendment shall increase the expansion goals for renewable energy substantially, and is to be seen both in the light of the urgent need to combat climate change, as well as the Ukraine-war which made the necessity for security of supply apparent. The EEG 2023 shall set the goal to make the national electricity generation virtually greenhouse gas neutral until 2035. Under an increased expansion goal for renewable energy, at least 80% of gross electricity consumption shall derive from renewable energy sources in 2030. This would equal around 600 TWh of electricity from renewable energy sources in 2030. To reach these goals, the expansion paths and tender volumes in particular for wind energy and solar energy shall be increased accordingly. The level of tender volumes for onshore wind shall be increased to 10 gigawatts per year, with the aim of having an installed onshore wind capacity of 115 gigawatts in 2030. The level of tender volumes for solar energy shall be increased to 22 gigawatts per year, with the aim of reaching 215 gigawatts installed capacity in 2030.[511] With a separate amendment of the Offshore Wind Energy Act, the expansion goals for offshore wind installations shall be increased substantially to at least 30 gigawatts by 2030, 40 gigawatts by

---

508. European Commission, Guidelines on State aid for environmental protection and energy 2014–2020, 28.6.2014, 2014/C 200/01, para. 126.
509. *See* J. Vollprecht & M. Altrock, 'Die EEG-Novelle 2017: Von Ausschreibungen bis zuschaltbare Lasten', *EnWZ* (2016): 387 et seqq.; H. Kahl, M. Kahles & T. Müller, 'Neuordnungen im EEG 2017', *ER* (2016): 187 et seqq.
510. SPD/GRÜNE/FDP, Mehr Fortschritt wagen, Bündnis für Freiheit, Gerechtigkeit und Nachhaltigkeit, Koalitionsvertrag zwischen SPD, BÜNDNIS 90/DIE GRÜNEN und FDP, Dec. 2021.
511. Entwurf eines Gesetzes zu Sofortmaßnahmen für einen beschleunigten Ausbau der erneuerbaren Energien und weiteren Maßnahmen im Stromsektor, BT-Drs. 20/1630, p. 2.

2035, and 70 gigawatts by 2045.[512] To accelerate the build-out of renewables, the amendment of the Renewable Energy Sources Act shall provide that the use of renewable energies is in the overriding public interest and contributes to public security.[513]

512. Entwurf eines Zweiten Gesetzes zur Änderung des Windenergie-auf-See-Gesetzes und anderer Vorschriften, BT-Drs. 20/1634, p. 1.
513. BT-Drs. 20/1630, p. 2, 137.

Chapter 2. Overview of the German Renewable Energy Sources Act (EEG)

785. In the following chapter, the Act on Granting Priority to Renewable Energy Sources (Renewable Energy Sources Act, EEG)[514] will be explained. This chapter focuses on key mechanism of the EEG, and on the version of the EEG 2021[515]. But it also shows some development lines and provisions of earlier versions of the EEG. The growing complexity of the promotion of electricity from renewable sources and its legal framework can be seen already by the increasing number of legal provisions in the Act, amounting to sixty-six in the EEG 2012 and around 200 in the EEG 2021, compared to only five in the German Electricity Feed-In Statute of 1990, the '*Stromeinspeisungsgesetz*'. Moreover, the EEG 2021 contains five annexes and is accompanied by a number of legal ordinances.

786. This chapter describes the regulatory mechanism of the Renewable Energy Sources Act. An overview of the Act and of the relevant provisions for all installations generating electricity from renewable sources will be provided. Also, the equalization scheme of the Renewable Energy Sources Act will be briefly explained. This mechanism governs the further handling and equalization of costs of the amounts of electricity taken off and remunerated by grid operators. The subsequent chapters of this part deal with the several renewable energy sources. They briefly give an overview on the necessary administrative permits as well as on selected specific characteristics for financial support under the EEG.

§1. Aims of the Renewable Energy Sources Act, Scope of Application

787. For the gross electricity supply, section 1 paragraph 2 of the EEG 2021 sets an aim of 65% share of renewable energy in 2030. The previous goal of the EEG 2012 for 2020 has been a share of renewables of at least 35%. The aims pursued by the EEG are listed in the first paragraph of section 1 EEG 2021:

> The purpose of this Act is to enable the energy supply to develop in a sustainable manner in particular in the interest of mitigating climate change and protecting the environment, to reduce the costs of the energy supply to the economy not least by including long-term external effects, to conserve fossil energy resources and to promote the further development of technologies to generate electricity from renewable energy sources.[516]

514. Erneuerbare-Energien-Gesetz of 21 Jul. 2014 (BGBl. I p. 1066), as amended.
515. Last amendment to EEG considered here is made with Art. 11 of the Act of 16 Jul. 2021 (BGBl. I p. 3026).
516. Translations of the Act are often taken from an unofficial translation offered by the Federal Ministry for the Environment, available at: www.bmwi.de, whereas the latest translation available has been for the EEG 2017.

788. Thus, the Renewable Energy Sources Act does not only refer to climate and environmental protection, it also mentions other motives for the support of renewable energy. Interestingly, the Act particularly refers to external long-term effects of fossil energy sources. It therefore points out that the costs for renewable energy are considerably lower if these effects are taken into account. Security of supply could be added to the list in section 1 EEG 2021 as a further motivation, since renewable energy sources are generally available within Germany and thus add to the security of supply.

789. In section 1 paragraph 3 EEG 2021, a long-term goal for the expansion of renewable energy has been added. Accordingly, the aim of the EEG is also to ensure that all electricity generated or consumed within the territory of the Federal Republic of Germany, including the German Exclusive Economic Zone (federal territory), is generated in a greenhouse gas-neutral manner before 2050.

790. Section 2 of the EEG adds principles of market integration, direct marketing, and assessing the level of financial support, as a general rule, on basis of tender proceedings.

§2. Regulatory Mechanism: Grid Connection, Take-Off and Payment Obligations, Equalization Scheme

791. The Renewable Energy Sources Act relies on compulsory grid connection of installations generating electricity from renewable sources, on compulsory take-off of the electricity produced and on financial support in the form of market premium or fixed tariffs for the electricity fed-in by grid operators. The rules on grid connection of installations using renewable energy sources and on the take-off of the electricity produced are provided by part 2 of the EEG 2021. Part 3 EEG 2021 contains rules on the financial support by market premium or feed-in tariffs. It provides for general rules on the remuneration, including provisions on tender procedures for financial support and the direct marketing of electricity, as well as for specific conditions and concrete support values for specific renewable energy sources. Direct marketing of electricity from renewable sources shall support in bringing renewable energy closer to the markets, and tender procedures are aiming at reducing the overall costs for support of renewables.

792. The central statutory obligations of grid operators in respect of renewable energy installations can be found in sections 8, 11, and 19 EEG 2021. Section 8 paragraph 1 EEG 2021 obliges grid operators to immediately and as a priority to connect installations generating electricity from renewable energy sources to their grid system. Under section 11 paragraph 1 EEG 2021, grid operators shall immediately and as a priority physically take-off, transmit, and distribute the entire available quantity of electricity from renewable energy sources. Finally, section 19 paragraph 1 EEG 2021 obliges grid operators to pay financial support to installation operators pursuant to further clauses for specific renewable energy sources. Financial support can be granted in the form of a market premium in case the installations are marketed in the form of direct marketing, or – in particular for older installations or smaller new installations – by feed-in tariffs. Financial support is paid for electricity generated in installations exclusively using renewable energy sources.

793. Thus, the Renewable Energy Sources Act introduces civil law obligations between installation operators and grid operators.[517] Instead of using direct state aid measures to support operators of installations generating electricity from renewable sources, the German legislator provided for private claims of installation operators against grid operators. Section 7 EEG 2021 clarifies that the Act sets forth statutory obligations between the parties. Grid operators may not make the fulfilment of their obligations under the EEG conditional upon the conclusion of a contract (section 4 paragraph 1 EEG 2021). Contracts between the grid operator and the operator of the renewable energy facility are not prohibited. However, the clause clearly states that the duties of the grid operator under the Renewable Energy Sources Act must be fulfilled, independent of the fact whether any contract is concluded between the parties.

794. Nevertheless, grid operators and installation operators in some cases conclude contracts to arrange the feed-in of electricity in practice. Such contracts are, for instance, 'grid connection contracts' or 'feed-in contracts'.[518] However, due to the statutory obligations set forth by the Renewable Energy Sources Act, the conclusion of contracts is not necessary. Even more, section 4 paragraph 2 EEG 2012 allows for deviations from the provisions of the EEG only under further conditions. The underlying idea is that the Renewable Energy Sources Act – through the equalization scheme – affects all final electricity consumers.

795. The equalization scheme in Part 4 of the Renewable Energy Sources Act governs the manner in which the electricity taken off and remunerated by the grid operators is used. It also foresees how the costs are equalized between grid operators and passed on to electricity supply companies and finally to the final electricity consumers. This equalization scheme works in several steps. The first step is the take-off and remuneration of electricity from renewable energy sources by the grid operator. In the next step, the grid operator delivers the electricity to the upstream transmission system operator and receives payments in accordance with the EEG. Hereinafter, the transmission system operators equalize the quantities of electricity among themselves. Under the Renewable Energy Ordinance (*Erneuerbare-Energien-Verordnung, EEV*),[519] transmission system operators are obliged to market the electricity from renewable sources. They may demand proportionate

517. Grid operators are operators of grid systems of all voltages for general electricity supply, s. 3 no. 36 EEG.
518. *See* in more detail P. Salje, *EEG*, 6th edn (Köln: Carl Heymanns Verlag, 2013), s. 4 paras 8 et seq.
519. Erneuerbare-Energien-Verordnung of 17 Feb 2015 (BGBl. I S. 146).

compensation for their charges (so-called EEG surcharge, *EEG-Umlage*) from electricity supply companies that supply final consumers with electricity. The electricity supply companies generally pass the costs of the EEG surcharge via the electricity rates on to the final consumers of electricity, but this is not further regulated by the EEG itself.

§3. Grid Connection and Take-Off of Electricity From Renewable Sources

796. The privileged grid connection of installations generating electricity from renewable energy sources is one of the central pillars of the Renewable Energy Sources Act. Under the clause in section 8 paragraph 1 EEG 2021, these installations enjoy a priority and immediate grid connection. This clause obliges grid operators to:

> connect installations to generate electricity from renewable energy sources and from mine gas without delay and as a priority to the place in their grid system which is appropriate in terms of the voltage level and which is the shortest linear distance to the site of the installation if this or a different grid system does not have a technically and economically more suitable connection point.

797. This clause provides for the general rules to determine the grid connection point of the installation generating electricity from renewable sources. The importance of the grid connection point can best be understood with a view on the sharing of costs for the grid connection between installation operators and grid operators. As a general rule, the installation operator is obliged to bear the costs associated with connecting installations generating electricity from renewable energy sources to the grid connection point (section 16 paragraph 1 EEG 2021). However, costs of optimizing, boosting, and expanding the grid system need to be borne by the grid operator (section 17 EEG 2021). Therefore, the grid connection point generally draws the line between the costs for the grid connection and the expansion of the grid. It is therefore central in determining whether it is the installation operator or the grid operator who is in charge of these costs.

798. First, the grid needs to be technically suitable for the connection. However, a different voltage level or an insufficient capacity need not hinder the connection. Instead, a duty of the grid operator to expand the grid may exist (section 8 paragraph 4 in conjunction with section 12 EEG 2021). Grid operators may be obliged to immediately optimize, boost, and expand their grid systems in order to guarantee the purchase, transmission, and distribution of the electricity generated from renewable energy sources. Installation operators may even have a claim against grid operators on the expansion of their grids if the installation for generation of electricity from renewable sources is not yet constructed. But in this case the construction needs to be sufficiently concretized.

799. The obligation to expand the grid does not exist if the expansion of the grid would be economically unreasonable (section 12 paragraph 3 EEG 2021). According to the legislative reasoning, the expansion is economically reasonable if the costs of the expansion do not exceed 25% of the costs of the construction of the installation.[520] In determining what is economically reasonable, other criteria may also apply.

800. In case of small installations (maximum capacity of 30 kW), located on a plot of land where there already is a connection to the grid system, the pre-existing grid connection point is deemed to be the most suitable connection point (section 8 paragraph 1 sentence 2 EEG 2021). Generally, the 'house connection point' is in these cases considered to be the correct connection point.

801. For other installations, the point in the shortest linear distance from the location of the installation is the 'starting point' in determining the grid connection point. The addition 'if this or a different grid system does not have a technically and economically more suitable connection point' is essential in this context. In the jurisdiction of the Federal Court of Justice, this restriction has been interpreted in favour of an economical consideration to find the overall economically most feasible variant. Accordingly, in a so-called comparison of variants, the most economical variant needs to be determined.[521] The relevant costs for this comparison of variants include all costs related to linking the facility to the connection point. Whether these costs are considered as grid connection or grid expansion costs is not decisive at this point. If there is a connection point that is economically more feasible than the point closest to the installation, this must be proven by the grid operator.

802. Paragraphs 2 and 3 of section 8 EEG 2021 contain rights to choose a more suitable connection point for both the installation operator and the grid operator. These clauses therefore provide for a certain degree of flexibility in the determination of the connecting point. Accordingly, the installation operator as well as the grid operator is entitled to choose another grid connection point than the point that resulted from the above-mentioned comparison of variants. A judgment of the Federal Court of Justice in 2012 helped clarifying the relation between the general rule and the elective rights.[522] Section 8 paragraph 2 EEG does not give an election right to the installation operator if the additional costs resulting from this for the grid system operator are not inconsiderable. The grid operator has to bear the resulting incremental costs (section 16 paragraph 2 EEG 2021) if he chooses to assign a different grid connection point.

520. *See* the reasoning to the EEG 2004, BT-Drs. 15/2864, 34.
521. BGH, judg. of 18 Jul. 2007 – VIII ZR 288/05, NJW-RR 2007, 1645, 1647 et seq.; judg. of 1 Oct. 2008 – VIII ZR 21/07, ZNER 2008, 370; judg. of 10 Oct. 2012 – VIII ZR 362/11, ZNER 2012, 612.
522. BGH judg. of 10 Oct. 2012 – VIII ZR 362/11, ZNER 2012, 612.

803. Until 2011, the procedure for the determination of the grid connection point was regulated only briefly. Section 5 paragraph 5 EEG 2009 merely stipulated that those interested in feeding in electricity and grid operators must submit the necessary documentation to each other (upon request and within eight weeks) to test and verify the grid compatibility. For this, the required grid system data is particularly important.

804. However, a more detailed definition of the grid connection procedure has been coming into force with an Act to transpose Directive 2009/28/EC into national law.[523] The grid connection procedure since then, generally speaking, works in two steps.[524] In the first step according to section 8 paragraph 5 EEG 2021, grid system operators shall, 'without delay after receiving a grid system connection request, provide those interested in feeding in electricity with a precise timetable for processing the grid system connection request'. The timetable needs to contain the procedural steps involved in processing the grid system connection request and the information required to enable the grid system operators to determine the grid connection point or conduct planning on the expansion of the grid. In the second step, after receiving the necessary information, the grid operators have (without delay, but in no more than eight weeks) to provide more detailed information. This information entails a timetable for immediately establishing the grid connection, all information required in order to test the grid connection point and a comprehensible and detailed estimate of the costs likely to be incurred by the installation operators by virtue of the grid connection.

805. The grid operator must render grid connection possible 'immediately'. Although the necessary planning procedures or grid expansion measures can take some time, the grid operator must avoid any undue delay. Installation operators are entitled to demand provisional measures by civil courts under eased conditions (section 83 EEG 2021) to safeguard the grid connection, but also to comply with other central obligations under the EEG. The claims may be brought forward even before the installation is constructed.

806. The Renewable Energy Sources Act differentiates between the connection to the grid in section 8 EEG 2021 and the compulsory physical take-off provided for in section 11 EEG 2021. Under section 11 paragraph 1 EEG 2021, grid operators are obliged to 'without delay and as a priority physically purchase, transmit and distribute the entire available quantity of electricity from renewable energy sources and from mine gas'. It is important to note that this obligation can also exist if the installation is connected to a grid that is not designed for general electricity supply (section 11 paragraph 2 EEG 2021). In these cases, the electricity generated by the installation is physically fed into this grid structure and physically consumed by the

523. Act on Transposition of Directive 2009/28/EG (Europarechtsanpassungsgesetz Erneuerbare Energien – EAG EE) of 12 Apr. 2011 (BGBl. I p. 619).
524. H. Thomas, 'Probleme von Netzanschluss und Netzanschlussverfahren für EEG-Anlagen in der jüngeren Rechtsprechung des BGH', *ZNER* (2013): 348.

connection users of the grid. The feed-in into the grid for general supply is, however, conducted on commercial and accounting terms. The electricity is therefore virtually fed into the grid for general supply. Consequently, the operator of the grid for general supply must in principle pay the financial support for this electricity as if it were physically fed into his grid.

807. It is also worth noting that the claims for priority grid connection in section 8 EEG 2021 and physical take-off of electricity from renewable energy sources in section 11 EEG 2021 do not require that the specific installation is also eligible for financial support under the EEG. In particular, a successful participation in a tender procedure is not required for an installation operator to raise its claim for grid connection. Therefore, the claims for grid connection and physical take-off of electricity from renewable energy sources also will be relevant for installations that market electricity outside the financial support regime of the EEG, particularly under Power Purchase Agreements.

§4. Financial Support under the EEG

808. Payments under the EEG can be granted essentially in two forms: as market premium or as feed-in tariff. Larger renewable energy installations are required to be marketed in the so-called direct marketing. In the direct marketing, installation operators need to market the electricity generated in the installation to a third party and therefore receive a market price for the electricity. In addition, operators have a claim against the grid operator for payment of a market premium (*Marktprämie*) for the electricity produced. The installation operators thus have two income streams: market prices and market premium. In contrast, in the form of marketing with feed-in tariff support, the electricity is made available to the responsible grid operator which pays feed-in tariffs in respect of the electricity volume.

809. Separate from the question in which form financial support is granted is the question how the level of financial support is determined. For larger installations covered by the tender requirements, the support levels are determined by the bidding process in the respective tender. In the tender, the so-called relevant value (*anzulegender Wert*) as the base value for the financial support is determined. Besides this, in particular for smaller installations and for the energy sources not covered by the tender requirement, financial support has been still available based on support values set by the legislator in the EEG itself. In these other cases, the EEG sets out the relevant value for financial support itself, whereas the applicable relevant value will depend on the commissioning date of the installation in particular.

I. Tender Procedures

810. With the introduction of tender procedures, and for the renewable energy installations subject to the tender requirement, a claim for financial support does only exist for installation operators which successfully participated in the tender process. Whereas previously the legislator set the support level for renewable energy installations, and the operators' demand determined how much capacity has been built, in the system of tender procedures the state specifies the volume of renewable energy expansion (at least the maximum build-out per tender round), but the installation operators determine the support level by means of their bids in the tender.[525] According to the central provision for tenders in section 22 paragraph 1 EEG, the Federal Network Agency shall determine the entitled parties and the relevant value for financial support for electricity from onshore wind energy installations, solar installations, biomass installations, and offshore wind energy installations by tender.

811. The tender requirements vary between the different renewable energy sources. In the case of onshore wind energy installations, section 22 paragraph 2 EEG generally requires an award issued in a tender procedure for the entitlement to financial support under the EEG. The entitlement also exists for electricity generated with an installed capacity that exceeds the awarded capacity by up to 15%. Further, the provision foresees two exemptions from the tender requirement. Onshore wind installations with an installed capacity of up to and including 750 kW are under section 22 paragraph 2 sentence 2 Nr. 1 EEG generally exempted from the tender requirement. Under Nr. 2, pilot onshore wind energy installations with an installed capacity totalling to 125 MW a year are excluded from the tender requirement as well. Pilot onshore wind energy turbines mean the first two onshore wind energy installations of a type, subject to further material and registration requirements laid out in section 2 Nr. 37 EEG.

812. For offshore wind installations, section 22 paragraph 5 EEG generally foresees that the entitlement to financial support requires that an award issued by the Federal Network Agency in a tender is effective. Pilot offshore wind energy installations in line with the Offshore Wind Energy Act (*WindSeeG*) are exempted from the tender requirement.

813. Also solar installations with an installed capacity of up to and including 750 kW are exempted from the tender requirement. Otherwise, a successful participation in a tender is necessary for claiming financial support for electricity generated with solar installations (section 22 paragraph 3 EEG). The threshold value shall be increased from 750 kW to 1,000 kW with the EEG 2023 amendment.[526]

814. In case of biomass installations, new installations are exempted from the tender requirement only up to an installed capacity of up to 150 kW. Also, biomass installations with a commissioning date prior to 1 January 2017 are allowed to participate in tender procedures under further conditions, *see* section 39g EEG. In case of such existing biomass installations, the threshold of 150 kW for exemptions does not apply.

525. H. Kahl, M. Kahles & T. Müller, 'Neuordnungen im EEG 2017', *ER* (2016): 187, 188.
526. BT-Drs. 20/1630, p. 137.

815. Highly important for the expansion of renewable energy installations is the volume of capacity that is subject to each of the tender rounds. These respective volumes are set out in sections 28 et seqq. EEG for onshore wind, solar, and biomass installations, and in the Offshore Wind Energy Act for offshore wind installations. Also since due to mechanism in the EEG the volume for the tenders may be modified, the Federal Network Agency shall announce the tenders within the scope of the EEG on its website at the earliest eight weeks and at the latest five weeks before the respective bid deadline for the respective form of energy.[527] Further, the Federal Network Agency publishes the awards granted in a tender.

816. The requirements for a bid in the tender, and the tender procedures are set out in sections 30 et seqq. EEG. Further, specific requirements for a participation in a tender are set out in sections 36 et seqq. EEG and in the Offshore Wind Energy Act for the specific types of renewable energy installations (some of these requirements are introduced below in the chapters on each energy source). Generally speaking, important information to be included in the bid is the bid capacity and the bid in cent per kWh (section 30 paragraph 1 Nrs 4 and 5 EEG). Also, bidders need to provide a security, which generally can be provided either in the form of a guarantee (*Bürgschaft*) issued by a bank or a credit insurer or by depositing the required amount, section 31 paragraph 3 EEG.

II. Administratively set Support Levels

817. In sections 40 et seqq. EEG, the Act also sets out relevant values (*anzulegende Werte*) for financial support of renewable energy installations. The relevant values depend on the different types of renewable energy and often differentiate between the capacities of the installation in threshold values. For example, the particular support values for financial support for electricity generated from hydro-energy distinguish between a rated capacity of up to 500 kW, up to 2 MW, up to 5 MW, up to 10 MW, up to 20 MW, up to 50 MW, and above 50 MW. According to section 23d EEG, where the support value is set out in line with the rated capacity or the installed capacity, the entitlement for financial support shall be determined for solar installations or wind energy installations in each case on a pro-rata basis in line with the installed capacity of the installation in relation to the respective threshold value to be applied, and in all other cases on a pro-rata basis in line with the rated capacity of the installation.

818. It is important to note that the calculation of the concrete support values is often orientated on the rated capacity rather than the installed capacity.[528] Section 3 number 6 EEG defines the rated capacity as the 'ratio of the total kilowatt-hours generated in the calendar year in question to the total number of full hours for that

527. *See* www.bundesnetzagentur.de/DE/Fachthemen/ElektrizitaetundGas/Ausschreibungen/start.html, last access 17 Mar. 2022.
528. H. Loibl, in: C. Germer & H. Loibl, *Energierecht, Handbuch*, 2nd edn (Berlin: Erich Schmidt Verlag, 2007), 458.

calendar year less the number of full hours prior to the generation of the first electricity from renewable energy sources in the installation and after final decommissioning of the installation'.

819. For facilities commissioned after specific points in time set out in the EEG, the relevant values for financial support may be reduced pursuant to different mechanisms set out in sections 40 et seqq. EEG for each of the renewable energy sources ('degression'). This means that from a specific point in time onwards, another relevant value applies in respect of new renewable energy installations. The once calculated relevant values in respect of a specific existing installation, however, apply for the entire period during which financial support is paid under the EEG.

820. Consequently, this means that the relevant values calculated for a certain point in time in which the installation is commissioned apply for the whole duration of financial support (generally for twenty years). That is why the term 'commissioning' defined in section 3 number 30 EEG is of high importance for the amount of financial support. Installation operators may prefer to reach an earlier year of commissioning in case this results in a higher financial support level and is therefore financially more interesting.

821. The amount by which levels of financial support are reduced for new installations differs depending on the type of renewable energy source used. Also, it is important to note that the result of the tender procedures also may play a role in the development of support values for new installations which are determined by statute. For instance in the case of onshore wind, the average of bid values of the highest bid awarded in previous tender procedures impacts the calculation of the support values also for such new installations which do not fall under a tender requirement.

III. Financial Support – Market Premium or Feed-in Tariff

822. From the EEG 2014 onwards, the main instrument for financial support towards renewable energy installations is not anymore the feed-in tariff. Instead, installation operators, as a general principle subject to exceptions in particular for small installations, shall be coerced to direct market the electricity generated in the renewable energy installation and to gain a market price for the electricity. In this form of direct marketing (*Direktvermarktung*), the grid operators are obliged to pay a market premium (*Marktprämie*) in case the conditions of the Renewable Energy Sources Act are complied with. This market premium is paid by grid operators for every kWh, in addition to the market price (which is paid by the direct marketer).

The installation operators thus have two income streams: market prices and market premium. The market premium is intended to balance the additional costs of renewable energy generation.[529]

823. Direct marketing of the electricity generated in the renewable energy installation has become coercive for new installations from the EEG 2014 onwards in several steps.[530] For electricity from installations with a commissioning date prior to 1 January 2016, a feed-in tariff could be claimed if the installed capacity of the installation is 500 kW as a maximum. This capacity limit has been reduced to 100 kW for electricity from installations with a commissioning date after 31 December 2015.

824. According to section 21 paragraph 1 Nr. 1 EEG 2021, only electricity from installations with an installed capacity of up to 100 kW whose support value has been determined by the EEG (and not by tender procedures) can be eligible for a feed-in tariff (*Einspeisevergütung*). Installation operators which claim the feed-in tariff must make available to the grid operator all of the electricity generated in this installation which is not consumed in the immediate vicinity of the installation and is fed through a grid system (section 21 paragraph 2 Nr. 1 EEG 2021). With this provision, the legislator wanted to avoid that installation operators sell the generated electricity directly on the market themselves in times of high market prices, and use the minimum tariffs of the EEG merely in case the market prices are low.[531] In contrast to installations which are marketed in the form of direct marketing, installations with feed-in tariff support may not participate in the balancing energy market with this installation (section 21 paragraph 2 Nr. 2 EEG 2021).

825. All installations above the threshold of 100 kW generally need to be marketed in the form of direct marketing with market premium if a financial support under the EEG shall be claimed. However, a feed-in tariff exceptionally may also be demanded for electricity from larger installations under section 21 paragraph 1 Nr. 2 EEG 2021. However, the values that form the basis for this tariff is reduced by 20% compared to the support level that would apply in case of direct marketing (*see* section 53 paragraph 3 EEG 2021). Therefore, this further feed-in tariff shall merely provide a safeguard that also installations for which direct marketing is coercive can return to a (significantly lower) support by feed-in tariffs 'if anything goes wrong'. From the investor point of view and even more from the perspective of a

529. For a detailed review *see* G. Wustlich & D. Müller, 'Die Direktvermarktung von Strom aus erneuerbaren Energien im EEG 2012 – Eine systematische Einführung in die Marktprämie und die weiteren Neuregelungen zur Marktintegration' *ZNER* (2011): 380; W. Lehnert, 'Markt- und Systemintegration der Erneuerbaren Energien: Eine rechtliche Analyse der Regeln zur Direktvermarktung im EEG 2012', *ZUR* (2012): 4; T. Schomerus & A. Henkel, 'Die Marktprämie im EEG 2012 – eine erste Zwischenbilanz' *ER* (2012): 13; H. Thomas, 'Das EEG 2012 – Eine Darstellung nach Anspruchsgrundlagen', *NVwZ-Extra* (11/2012), 1.

530. *See* legislative reasoning, BT-Drs. 18/1304, pp. 133 et seq.

531. Reasoning of the Federal Government, BT-Drs. 16/8148, 49 (to s. 17 EEG).

financing institution, the possibility to opt for a feed-in tariff instead of the market premium in case of problems with the marketing of the electricity may nevertheless be of high relevance.

826. Installation operators also have the possibility to market the electricity from renewable energy installations without receiving any financial support in the other form of direct marketing (*sonstige Direktvermarktung*), section 21a EEG 2021. This becomes increasingly important for installations that shall be marketed via power purchase agreements.

827. Financial support may also be available in form of a landlord-to-tenant supply premium (*Mieterstromzuschlag*). This financial support can be claimed for electricity from solar installations with a total installed capacity of up to 100 kW which are installed on or in a residential building and supplied to a final consumer. Further, the electricity must be consumed within this building or in residential buildings or ancillary facilities in a direct spatial relationship with this building without being fed through a grid for general supply (section 21 paragraph 3 EEG).

828. As a further alternative within the direct marketing of green energy, previous versions of the EEG contained a possibility of direct marketing of electricity from renewable energy sources by the green electricity privilege. This mechanism led to a reduction of the EEG surcharge for electricity suppliers that reached a high percentage of green energy in their portfolio. The general idea of this privilege was that electricity suppliers with a high share of renewable energy within their portfolio are already promoting the use of renewable energy sources and therefore can be partly exempted from the EEG surcharge. A main condition to be fulfilled was that at least 50% of the electricity must come from renewable energy sources. With the EEG amendment 2014, the privilege has been withdrawn.[532] A main reason was that the European Commission assumed this privilege could be incompatible with rules of the Treaty on the Functioning of the EU in its decision to open an in-depth inquiry concerning the EEG on 18 December 2013.

IV. Important Preconditions for Financial Support under the EEG

829. The obligation of grid operators to grant financial support in the form of market premium or feed-in tariff (or a landlord-to-tenant supply premium) is stipulated in section 19 paragraph 1 EEG. The provision requires that in the installation exclusively renewable energy sources (or mine gas) are utilized. Under this 'principle of exclusivity' (*Ausschließlichkeitsprinzip*), only installations using renewable energy sources that are not blended with fossil fuels can be eligible for financial

532. *See* BT-Drs. 18/1304, pp. 134 et seq.

support. The principle, however, does not prohibit utilizing several types of renewable energy sources in a single installation.[533] It is also subject to a number of exceptions.

830. Technical and operational requirements for installation operators are provided in section 9 EEG. As long as an installation operator does not fulfil certain of these requirements, the operator might not be entitled to claim financial support (section 52 paragraph 2 Nr. 1 EEG). By setting these technical minimum requirements, the legislator aims at an enhanced technical design of installations to foster their integration into the energy markets. As the number of installations that generate electricity from renewable sources grows, the technical preconditions have become increasingly strict.

831. Under section 9 paragraphs 1 and 2 EEG, installation operators may be required to equip installations with a technical facility to reduce output by remote control in the event of grid overload, and to call up the current electricity feed-in at any given point in time. The grid operator must have access to these facilities. These technical facilities have initially been introduced in conjunction with the feed-in management under the EEG, which has now been replaced by the redispatch regime under the EnWG. Under restrictive conditions, grid operators can exceptionally curtail the output of renewable energy installations (see above Part I, Chapter 1, § 1, III.).

832. For photovoltaic installations, technical requirements may apply also for small installations. Operators of photovoltaics with a capacity up to 25 kW may decide whether they use technical facilities to reduce output by remote means in the event of grid overload or limit the maximum effective capacity fed-in at the grid connection point with the grid system to 70% of the installed capacity (section 9 paragraph 2 Nr. 3 EEG). For biogas installations, specific further technical requirements may apply according to section 9 paragraph 5 EEG, aiming at limiting the CO_2 emissions of the biogas plant.

833. Additional requirements apply in case of direct marketing and claiming the market premium for electricity generated in an installation. In case of direct marketing of electricity, the installations need to maintain technical devices with which the direct seller or another person to whom the electricity is sold are able at all times to call up the current level of feed-in, and to curtail the feed-in by remote control (section 10b paragraph 1 Nr. 1 EEG). Also, rights need to be granted to the direct seller or to the other person to whom the electricity is sold to call up the current level of feed-in and to curtail the feed-in quantity by remote control to an extent which is necessary for a needs-based feed-in of the electricity and which is not proven to be excluded under the obligations imposed under licensing law (section

533. Reasoning of the Federal Government, BT-Drs. 16/8148, 49; P. Salje, *EEG*, 6th edn (Köln: Carl Heymanns Verlag, 2013), s. 16 para. 13.

10b paragraph 1 Nr. 2 EEG). In case a market premium shall be claimed, the installation operator further needs to grant the grid operator the right to label the electricity as 'electricity from renewable energy sources or from mine gas, financed from the EEG surcharge', and, as a general rule, the electricity shall be balanced in a balancing or sub-balancing group in which only electricity from renewable energy sources or from mine gas sold in the direct marketing form of the market premium is balanced (section 20 EEG).

834. The EEG also contains several provisions to cover energy storage in the context of renewable energy. Section 19 paragraph 3 EEG allows that financial support under the Renewable Energy Sources Act can also be claimed if electricity has been stored in between.[534] But in case of an intermediate storage of electricity from renewable sources, financial support can only be claimed for the amount of electricity that is fed into the grid resulting from the storage process, section 19 paragraph 3 sentence 2 EEG.[535] Moreover, the amount of remuneration available depends on the amount that could have been claimed without intermediate storage of the electricity, section 19 paragraph 3 sentence 3 EEG. This does not equal the initial amount of renewable electricity since conversion and storage losses occur. These storage losses are not compensated.[536] For the electricity fed into the grid from the storage installation, the remuneration rates under the EEG for the renewable energy sources that are 'stored' apply. That means that if wind energy is stored by a storage installation, the electricity fed into a grid for general supply is remunerated with the rates that would have applied for the wind energy installation at the beginning of the process. It therefore might make more economic sense for the operator of the renewable energy plant to feed the electricity directly into the grid to claim the renewable energy remuneration rate.[537] However, depending on the use case of the specific storage installation, for instance in connection with direct marketing of electricity or to increase own consumption of electricity, commercially interesting storage applications enabled by the provisions in the EEG can be found.

V. The Installation and Treatment of Several Installations

835. The definition and application of the term 'installation' has been the subject of controversial debates throughout the development of the Renewable Energy

534. *See* BT-Drs. 17/6071, p. 123.
535. This was also the general opinion on the earlier clause on energy storage in the Renewable Energy Sources Act 2009, *see* reasoning to the EEG 2009, BT-Drs. 16/8148, S. 49; *Lehnert* in: Altrock/Oschmann/Theobald, EEG, 3. Ed. 2011, s. 16 paras 40 et seq.; *Ekardt* in: Frenz/Müggenborg, EEG, 2nd, edn, 2011, s. 16 para. 19; *Wieser*, ZUR 2011, 240 (242); *Sailer*, ZNER 2011, 249 (251). For the changes with the EEG 2012 *see Sailer*, ZNER 2012, 153 (157 et seq.); *Lehnert/Vollprecht*, ZNER 2012, 356 (365).
536. *Sailer*, ZNER 2012, 153 (158); *Valentin/von Bredow*, ET 12/2011, 99 (103); *Thomas*, ZNER 2011, 608 (610).
537. *Thomas*, ZNER 2011, 608 (612); *Bösche/Ponder/Thomas*, RELP 2012, 159 (169).

Sources Act. A particular reason is the question of whether several plants, respectively generators, need to be considered as one installation for the purposes of calculation of the financial support under the EEG. This plays a role in particular if installations are promoted by feed-in tariffs, and if feed-in tariffs vary according to capacity ranges of the installations. In such cases, the question of whether or not to regard several plants as one installation plays quite a decisive role for the operator. By 'splitting up' installations into several smaller plants with lower capacities, installation operators in the past have tried to gain a more favourable remuneration for the electricity generated.

836. While the question on when to consider several installations as one was debated under the term 'installation' in the older versions of the EEG, the Renewable Energy Sources Act now contains a particular provision by which several installations can be treated as one for the calculation of financial support (section 24 paragraph 1 EEG):

> Accordingly, several installations shall be classified as one installation, notwithstanding ownership, and solely for specific purposes of determining the financial support and the requirement to participate in tenders for the latest generator commissioned, where
>
> 1. they are located on the same plot of land, the same building, the same commercial site or are otherwise in direct spatial proximity,
> 2. they generate electricity from the same kind of renewable energy source,
> 3. the electricity generated in them is financially supported in accordance with the rated capacity or the installed capacity of the installation, and
> 4. they were commissioned within a period of twelve consecutive calendar months.

837. This clause provides more precise criteria to determine when several installations must be considered as one. The respective classification as one installation, however, only applies for the specific purposes mentioned above. Any abuse of achieving higher feed-in tariffs by splitting up installations shall be avoided by this provision.[538] The term 'installation' is, on the contrary, defined in section 3 number 1 EEG as 'any facility generating electricity from renewable energy sources or from mine gas, whereby in the case of solar installations each module shall be an independent solar installation'. Thus, one clause of the Renewable Energy Sources Act is dedicated to the term 'installation'. Another separate clause deals with the question of whether several installations are to be considered as one in the context of financial support for electricity generated in these installations.

838. In particular for biomass installations, the Federal Court of Justice clarified the term 'installation' in a judgment in 2013. It decided that section 3 number 1 EEG

538. Reasoning of the Federal Government, BT-Drs. 16/8148, 50; V. Oschmann in: M. Altrock, V. Oschmann & C. Theobald, *EEG,* 4th edn (München: C.H. Beck, 2013), s. 19 para. 5.

2009 provides for a wide definition of an installation. Several block heat and power plants constructed in local vicinity and connected to one fermenter would therefore be regarded as one installation also by terms of section 3 number 1 EEG.[539] As a consequence, it is for these installations not decisive whether the above-mentioned conditions of section 24 EEG are also fulfilled. The said installations are also by the general definition of an installation united to be only one installation.

839. A legislator wanting to promote the use of renewable energy by a feed-in statute will have to pay special attention to the interpretation of the term 'installation'. In particular, this definition should take the several functions the term must fulfil into account. In addition to the question of calculation of financial support/feed-in tariffs, the term 'installation' will play a role in, for example, determining when an installation is (newly) commissioned or whether the installation complies with certain (environmental) criteria.

§5. Equalization Scheme

840. The costs of the support for electricity generated from renewable energy sources are allocated through a nationwide equalization scheme, which can be found in part 4 of the Renewable Energy Sources Act. This scheme allows for the financial support paid by the grid operators to be passed on to the upstream transmission system operator, and then to the electricity supply companies and finally to the end consumers of electricity.[540] This equalization scheme ensures that the burdens of the financial support granted under the EEG are distributed equally within Germany and that no regional differences can develop.[541] Exceptional rules apply in particular to electricity-intensive companies.

841. The equalization scheme works in several steps; the first step is the financial support of electricity from renewable energy sources by the responsible grid operator. In the case of financial support with feed-in tariff, the grid operator also takes off the electricity from the renewable energy installation. In contrast, in the form of direct marketing with market premium, the grid operator only pays the market premium, but the installation operator markets the electricity itself. In the second step, the grid operator delivers any electricity it has taken off in the form of feed-in tariff support to the upstream transmission system operator (section 56 EEG). According to section 57 EEG, the grid operator receives compensation for the payments made to the installation operators in accordance with the provisions of the EEG from the upstream transmission system operator (this covers any financial support payments made by the grid operators, both in the form of feed-in tariff support as well as in the form of market premium). Avoided charges for the use of

539. BGH, judg. of 23 Oct. 2013, VIII ZR 262/12.

540. *See* for more detail M. Altrock in: M. Altrock, V. Oschmann & C. Theobald, *EEG,* 4th edn (München: C.H. Beck, 2014), s. 34; A. Schäfermeier in: J. Reshöft, *EEG,* 3rd edn (Baden-Baden: Nomos, 2009), s. 34 et seq.

541. Federal Ministry of Economy and Technologies, *Energie in Deutschland, Trends und Hintergründe zur Energieversorgung in Deutschland* (August 2010), 35.

the grid system according to the Regulation on Fees for the Access to Electricity Supply Grids (*StromNEV*) may be deducted from these compensation payments.

842. In the third step, the transmission system operators equalize the quantities of electricity and the financial compensation paid among themselves. They have to determine the overall quantity of electricity they have taken off and paid for in the previous calendar year, as well as the electricity volume for which they have compensated for the market premium and received the right to label the electricity as 'electricity from renewable energy sources or mine gas'. Moreover, they have to determine the percentage share of this quantity in relation to the total quantity of electricity that was delivered to the end consumers in each area by electricity supply companies. This calculation forms the basis for a claim to sell electricity to and receive financial compensation payments from other transmission system operators. This claim is for transmission system operators who had to take off quantities, or pay compensation payments, greater than the average share.

843. In the fourth step, electricity supply companies that deliver electricity to end consumers originally have been obliged to take off and pay for the share of electricity purchased and paid for by their regular transmission system operator. This take-off and payment has been based on a profile that must approximate the actually purchased quantity of electricity. However, this mechanism has been modified by the Regulation on the Further Development of the Equalization Scheme (hereinafter: *AusglMechV*),[542] and subsequently by the Renewable Energies Ordinance *(Erneuerbare-Energien-Verordnung, EEV)*.[543] Accordingly, transmission system operators are no longer obliged to deliver the electricity to downstream electricity supply companies. These electricity supply companies are not obliged to take off and pay for the electricity from the transmission system operators. Instead, transmission system operators must market the electricity from renewable sources (which they receive from the form of feed-in tariff support) on the spot market of an electricity stock exchange, section 2 EEV. Therefore, they sell the electricity from renewable sources at the spot market of the electricity stock exchange. Transmission system operators may demand proportionate compensation for their costs of marketing the electricity and of paying financial support for renewable energy installations (so-called EEG surcharge, *EEG-Umlage*) from electricity supply companies that supply end consumers. This *EEG-Umlage* compensates for the gap (if any) between revenue from the marketing of the electricity from renewable sources compared to the feed-in tariffs and market premium payments which transmission system operators must pay to the grid operators in the equalization scheme or directly to installation operators under the EEG.

---

542. Verordnung zur Weiterentwicklung des bundesweiten Ausgleichsmechanismus of 17 Jul. 2009 (BGBl. I p. 2101). *See* closer M. Altrock & A. Eder, 'Verordnung zur Weiterentwicklung des EEG-Ausgleichsmechanismus (AusglMechV): Eine erste kritische Betrachtung', *ZNER* (2009): 128; A. Rostankowski, 'Die Ausgleichsmechansmus-Verordnung und der Ausbau Erneuerbarer Energien', *ZNER* (2010): 125.

543. Erneuerbare-Energien-Verordnung of 17 Feb. 2015 (BGBl. I p. 146).

844. Generally speaking, the EEG surcharge must be paid by any electricity supplier delivering electricity to end consumers (section 60 paragraph 1 EEG). However, the EEG provides for several exemptions from and reductions of the EEG surcharge. Due to the levels which the EEG surcharge had reached, these exemptions/reductions became of high relevance.

845. Electricity supply companies, whose total quantity of electricity supply consisted of at least 50% renewable energy, under the EEG 2009 did not have to pay the EEG surcharge.[544] This required that this share of electricity should in principle be eligible for compensation in accordance with the feed-in tariffs of the Renewable Energy Sources Act. This privilege, however, has been abolished entirely.

846. Practically important limitations of the EEG surcharge apply to certain electricity-intensive enterprises and rail operators. Limitations also may apply for transport companies with electrically powered busses, companies in the electrochemical production of hydrogen and for shore power systems for seagoing vessels. Electricity-intensive enterprises that are allocated to a sector listed in Annex 4 to the EEG can apply for a significant reduction of the EEG surcharge under sections 63 and 64 EEG under further conditions, which *inter alia* relate to a minimum electricity consumption at a consumption point and the intensity of the electricity costs of the undertaking.

847. Other important limitations of the EEG surcharge exist for self-consumption of electricity, see sections 61 et seqq. EEG. While previously self-consumption has been largely exempted from EEG surcharge, from the EEG 2014 onwards EEG surcharge in principle also was due for self-consumption of electricity. Exceptions applied, however, for existing installations. Also, for self-consumption from a renewable energy installation, only an EEG surcharge of 40% applied, section 61b EEG. In limited cases, like in particular self-consumption from small installations (installed capacity of 10 kW under section 61a Nr. 4 EEG, 30 kW under section 61b paragraph 2 EEG), no EEG surcharge may be payable at all. The Federal Court of Justice decided that self-consumption requires a strict personal identity: it must be the same (natural or judicial) person who – in a legal sense – operates the installation and consumes the electricity.[545] A main criterion here is that the installation operator factually takes over the operational risk of running the electricity-generating installation.[546] Obviously, this poses quite a high threshold for making use of this privilege in practice.

848. Finally, electricity supply companies can pass on the costs of the EEG-allocation to final electricity consumers using the electricity rates. This step is not further governed by a specific clause of the Renewable Energy Sources Act.

544. *See* s. 3 para. 6 AusglMechV in conjunction with s. 37 para. 1 sentence 2 EEG.
545. BGH, ZNER 2010, p. 67.
546. Volker Oschmann in: Martin Altrock/Volker Oschmann/Christian Theobald, EEG, 4. ed. 2013, s. 3 para. 48.

849. The EEG surcharge under the revised EEG 2021 already is partly covered by the state budget as revenues from the national emissions trading (see below Part VI, Chapter 2, §3) shall be used to reduce the level of the EEG surcharge.[547] In light of this development, Germany had notified the rules of the EEG 2021 for state aid approval to the European Commission.

850. From 1 July 2022 onwards, the EEG surcharge payable by electricity supply companies shall be reduced to zero. In an interim step for the second half of 2022, this is governed by an Act to reduce the costs from the EEG surcharge passed by the German parliament.[548] In the permanent solution to reduce the EEG surcharge to zero from 2023 onwards, the need of financing the equalization scheme shall be covered by the 'Energy and Climate Fund'. In particular, revenues from the national fuel emissions trading shall be utilized. In this context, several energy-related surcharges shall be combined in a new Energy Surcharges Act (*Energie-Umlagen-Gesetz*).[549]

851. This is a remarkable change to the way Germany has organized financing of the support for renewable energy in the electricity sector. The legislator expects that this will facilitate own consumption and other business models for which the previous system (and amount) of the EEG surcharge has been an obstacle.[550] Due to the state (partly) financing the EEG account, the legislator treats the support with the EEG now as state aid falling under the state aid control of the European Commission.[551]

---

547. B. Scholtka & F. Frizen, 'Die Entwicklung des Energierechts im Jahr 2020'. *NJW* (2021): 906, 907.
548. Gesetz zur Absenkung der Kostenbelastungen durch die EEG-Umlage und zur Weitergabe dieser Absenkung an die Letztverbraucher, BT- Drs. 20/1025.
549. BT-Drs. 20/1630, p. 4 et seq.
550. BT-Drs. 20/1630, p. 5.
551. BT-Drs. 20/1630, p. 140.

Chapter 3. Wind Energy

852. The electricity generation from wind energy is a central pillar of the German energy transition. It has enjoyed high growth rates over the past years, and it now constitutes a substantial share of total electricity production in Germany. At the end of 2009, the total installed capacity of wind power plants in Germany amounted to 25,730 MW. In 2012, it reached 30,869 MW onshore and 435 MW offshore.[552] In 2020, the installed capacity increased to 54.4 GW onshore and 7.75 GW offshore.[553] The electricity generated by wind power reached 37.8 TWh in 2009 and 49.9 TWh in 2012.[554] In 2020, it amounted to 103.7 TWh onshore and 27.3 TWh offshore.[555] The total share of wind energy in electricity generation amounted to 6% in 2009 and to 8.3% in 2012.[556] In 2020, the share of wind energy in the gross electricity consumption in Germany amounted to 23.7%.[557] Due to the rapid growth of wind energy, the administrative courts have been occupied with a number of litigations on the construction of wind power plants. Some legal aspects surrounding the construction of wind power plants will therefore be explained in the first section, followed by a section further explaining specific rules on wind energy plants in the Renewable Energy Sources Act and Offshore Wind Energy Act. The Renewable Energy Sources Act does not determine the planning and construction law for installations generating electricity from renewable sources. Instead of a specific law, the general planning and construction law applies.

§1. Construction of Wind Energy Plants

853. Different licensing procedures and material conditions apply to onshore and offshore wind power plants.

I. Onshore Wind Energy Plants

854. Larger onshore wind power plants are subject to a licence under the Federal Immissions Control Act (BImSchG), which provides for a comprehensive licensing procedure (see above in Part 2, Chapter 2). The 4. BImSchV in number 1.6 of the Annex 1 regulates that wind power plants with an overall height of more

552. AGEE-Stat, Erneuerbare Energien in Zahlen, December 2013.
553. Federal Ministry for Economic Affairs and Climate Action, Erneuerbare Energien, available at www.bmwi.de, last access 13 Apr. 2022.
554. Federal Ministry for the Environment, 'Erneuerbare Energien in Zahlen', Internet-Update, 15 Dec. 2010, available on www.erneuerbare-energien.de, last access: 3 Jan. 2011, 6. AGEE-Stat, Erneuerbare Energien in Zahlen, December 2013.
555. Federal Ministry for Economic Affairs and Climate Action, Erneuerbare Energien, available at www.bmwi.de, last access 13 Apr. 2022.
556. Federal Ministry of Economy and Technologies, *Energie in Deutschland, Trends und Hintergründe zur Energieversorgung in Deutschland* (August 2010), 19. AGEE-Stat, Erneuerbare Energien in Zahlen, December 2013.
557. Federal Ministry for Economic Affairs and Climate Action, Erneuerbare Energien, available at www.bmwi.de, last access 13 Apr. 2022.

than 50 m require a permit according to the simplified licensing procedure of the Federal Immissions Control Act (and according to the formal procedure in the case of twenty or more wind turbines).[558] Such wind power plants must be licensed under the Federal Immissions Control Act with the effects of such a licence as the concentration effect (see above in Part 2, Chapter 2, section 2). A special permitting provision has been created to deal with repowering, section 16b BImSchG.

855. Smaller wind power plants are subject to the general construction law as stipulated in the Construction Code (*Baugesetzbuch, BauGB*).[559] They require a building permit according to the construction laws of the *Länder*. Since the licence under the Federal Immissions Control Act also comprises material requirements of other statutes, wind power plants licensed under the BImSchG must fulfil the important conditions of sections 29 et seqq. BauGB as well. These conditions are also applicable to projects directly authorized under the construction law.

856. The Construction Code provides the general rules governing the admissibility of construction projects in sections 29 et seqq. BauGB. Wind power plants are often constructed in a so-called undeveloped outskirt area (*Außenbereich*). They are therefore often not subject to a land-use plan (*Bebauungsplan*), in which certain areas for specific constructions are generally disclosed. In the undeveloped outskirt area, construction projects are only admissible under the restrictive conditions of section 35 BauGB. This norm generally pursues the aim of keeping this area free of construction, which shall be concentrated in the areas designated in land-use plans and within built-up areas. However, section 35 paragraph 1 BauGB privileges certain construction projects in the undeveloped outskirt area. These projects are therefore also permitted in this area, but on the condition that the project is not in conflict with public interests.

857. The fact that the legislator from 1997 onwards decided to include any projects 'intended for research, development or use of wind or water-powered energy sources' as a privileged project in (now) section 35 paragraph 1 number 5 BauGB has been a major boost for the promotion of (onshore) wind energy. Wind power plants are therefore generally considered to be privileged projects allowable in the undeveloped outskirt area. As mentioned before, being classified as a privileged project does not automatically result in admissibility of a project. Admissibility remains subject to the condition of public interests not opposing the project. For example, public interests may oppose the project if the project contravenes provisions in the preparatory land-use plan (*Flächennutzungsplan*), see section 35 paragraph 3 number 1 BauGB.

558. In an earlier version of the 4. BImSchV up to 2005, the licensing requirement under the Immissions Protection Act applied to 'wind farms' with at least three wind power plants. Until a judgment of the Federal Administrative Court of 30 Jun. 2004, 4 C 9.03, it has been highly disputed how the term 'wind farm' needs to be interpreted if the plants of several operators, only regarded together, reached the threshold of three wind power plants, *see* H. Loibl in: C. Germer & H. Loibl, *Energierecht, Handbuch*, 2nd edn (Berlin: Erich Schmidt Verlag, 2007), 467 et seq. A transitory provision has been implemented in s. 67 para. 9 BImSchG.

559. Construction Code in the version of the publication of 3. Nov. 2017 (BGBl. I p. 3634).

858. A practically relevant clause with regard to wind power plants is the so-called plan reservation in section 35 paragraph 3 sentence 3 BauGB. Accordingly, public interests, as a general rule, conflict with a project also where it has been designated for some other location by means of provisions in a preparatory land-use plan or within the aims of regional development. Due to this clause, the municipalities may allocate *inter alia* so-called priority areas (*Vorranggebiete*) for the use of wind energy, so that these areas can in general be used for construction and operation of wind power plants. Wind power plants outside these areas, however, will then generally be in conflict with public interests. These areas thus allow a location planning for wind energy plants by the municipalities.

859. This clause has been subject to a number of court proceedings in the recent past, which clarify when the municipalities may make use of this instrument.[560] The courts decided in particular that a mere 'obstruction planning' (*Verhinderungsplanung*), being an allocation of practically useless priority areas with the intention to avoid basically any use of wind energy in the area of the municipality, would be not sufficient.[561] While the municipalities are not required to provide the best possible locations for wind energy plants, they are obliged to regard the decision of the legislator in section 35 paragraph 1 number 5 BauGB and allow wind power plants in the undeveloped outskirt area. If they want to exclude wind energy plants from certain parts of their area, this may only be done on the basis of a conclusive spatial planning concept for their whole area. On the contrary, they may not use the effect of section 35 paragraph 3 sentence 3 BauGB as a means to factually obstruct wind energy.[562] The municipalities thus do not enjoy unlimited discretion in deciding about the priority areas.[563]

860. Public interests also might conflict with the project if it may cause or may be exposed to harmful environmental impacts according to section 35 paragraph 3 number 3 BauGB. Possibly harmful immissions caused by wind power plant are controlled in this clause.[564] The immissions of wind power plants have been subject to a number of court decisions over the past years.

861. As far as noise protection is concerned, wind power plants basically need to comply with the technical requirements as stipulated in the Technical Instructions on Noise Protection (*Technische Anleitung zum Schutz gegen Lärm, TA*

560. For an overview *see* the references of H. Loibl, in: C. Germer & H. Loibl, *Energierecht, Handbuch,* 2nd edn (Berlin: Erich Schmidt Verlag, 2007), 482 et seq.
561. P. Salje, *EEG,* 5th edn (Köln: Carl Heymanns Verlag, 2009), Einführung para. 133; H. Loibl, in: C. Germer & H. Loibl, *Energierecht, Handbuch,* 2nd edn (Berlin: Erich Schmidt Verlag, 2007), 484.
562. BVerwG, judgment of 24 Jan. 2008, 4 CN 2.07, *UPR,* 2008, 264 et seq.
563. From a systematic perspective, it is of importance that the preparatory land-use plan generally does not impose direct legal effects for citizens. However, through the norm of s. 35 para. 3 sentence 3 BauGB, it creates some immediate legal effects for citizens.
564. If the wind power plant is subject to a licence under the Federal Immissions Control Act, the obligation not to cause harmful immissions results of s. 5 para. 1 no. 1 BImSchG.

Lärm).[565] This technical instruction provides a number of immission limit values for noises, depending on the planning area in which the noise pollution takes place. It also differentiates between limit values both inside and outside buildings. The TA Lärm also regulates how noise pollution is measured. Under the jurisdiction of the Federal Administrative Court, the TA Lärm is treated as a norm-concretizing administrative regulation, with the result that the immission protection values are directly applicable. Courts in general must use these values when determining whether immissions caused by a wind power plant are harmful.[566]

862. Other judgments treated optical effects of wind power plants, in particular the possible shadow impact of such a plant on a neighbouring property. The existence of a wind power plant itself and the possible negative impact on the open landscape may, generally speaking, not be regarded as an 'immission', since they do not cause any effect on the environment in a manner that is listed in section 3 paragraph 2 BImSchG. These effects thus do not constitute an 'immission' under the definition of this term. As far as the shadow impact is concerned, the jurisdiction – in the absence of scientific evidence on negative impacts of shadowing on human health – developed a 'conservative rule of thumb' to decide whether a shadow impact needs to be tolerated by a neighbour or not. Accordingly, residential buildings may not be impacted by the shadow of wind power plants for longer than 30 hours per year and 30 minutes per day.[567]

863. Under section 35 paragraph 3 number 5 BauGB, public interests also conflict with the project if, for instance, the project has an impact on nature conservation, the preservation of the countryside or if it deforms the overall appearance of the locality or the landscape. Wind power plants need to comply with the requirements arising out of the nature protection law. Under the building law as stipulated in the legislation of the Länder, wind power plants in particular may need to comply with compulsory distance spaces to neighbouring buildings.

864. Concerning the licensing procedure, wind power plants may have to conduct an environmental impact assessment under the Environmental Impact Assessment Statute (*UVPG*).[568] Such an environmental impact assessment is obligatory for wind parks with twenty or more wind power plants (and a height of at least 50m), number 1.6.1 of the Annex 1 to the Environmental Impact Assessment Statute. For

565. Sixth general administrative regulation to the Federal Immissions Control Act (Sechste Allgemeine Verwaltungsvorschrift zum Bundes-Immissionsschutzgesetz, Technische Anleitung zum Schutz gegen Lärm – TA Lärm of 26 Aug. 1998, GMBl No. 26/1998 503).
566. BVerwG, judgment of 29 Aug. 2007, BVerwG 4 C 2.07.
567. OVG Lüneburg, judgment of 15 Mar. 2004, 1 ME 45/04, *ZNER*, 2004, 311.
568. Gesetz über die Umweltverträglichkeitsprüfung, in the version of the publication of 18 Mar. 2021 (BGBl. I p. 540).

wind parks with three to five wind power plants, a site-related preliminary examination, for wind parks with six to nineteen wind power plants, a general preliminary examination on whether an environmental impact assessment is necessary must be conducted, see numbers 1.6.2 and 1.6.3 of the Annex 1 to the Environmental Impact Assessment Statute.[569]

II. Offshore Wind Energy Plants

865. On 1 January 2017, the Offshore Wind Energy Act (*Windenergie-auf-See-Gesetz, WindSeeG*)[570] came into force. This Act comprises rules for planning and permitting as well as for financial support of offshore wind installations which have previously been regulated in several other statutes.

866. According to section 3 number 11 of the Offshore Wind Energy Act, an offshore wind installation (*Windenergieanlage auf See*) is any wind-powered installation that has been erected at least three nautical miles seawards from the shoreline. The legal situation concerning permitting of offshore wind installations differs depending on whether the respective installations are located in the Exclusive Economic Zone (EEZ, *Ausschließliche Wirtschaftszone*, AWZ) or in the territorial sea. Thus, the permitting regime for offshore wind installations is linked with the different areas set out by the United Nations Convention on the Law of the Sea (UNCLOS, also called the Law of the Sea Convention). The sea areas are divided into various areas according to the provisions of the UNCLOS.

867. The territorial sea belongs to the sovereign territory of the respective coastal state; therefore, it is the national law of the coastal state that applies without limitations in this area. Accordingly, for wind power plants installed within the 12-Miles-Zone, the licensing procedures and requirements explained above apply, since these areas form a part of the national territory.[571] Additional requirements may result out of the Water Resources Act (*WHG*) as well as out of statutes governing the safety of shipping.

868. In contrast to the aforementioned wind power plants constructed within the territorial sea, wind power plants constructed within the Exclusive Economic Zone, defined as the area outside the 12-Miles-Zone but within a distance of 200 miles, are subject to special norms. In this zone, the coastal state has under Article 56 paragraph 1 lit. a of the UNCLOS *inter alia* sovereign rights for the 'economic exploitation and exploration of the zone, such as the production of energy from the water, currents, and winds'.

---

569. *See* closer also to the effects on the licensing procedure under the BImSchG U. Prall in: M. Altrock, V. Oschmann & C. Theobald, *EEG,* 4rd edn (München: C.H. Beck, 2013), s. 29.
570. Windenergie-auf-See-Gesetz of 13 Oct. 2016 (BGBl. I p. 2258, 2310).
571. G. Hermes in: J.P. Schneider & C. Theobald, *Recht der Energiewirtschaft,* 5th edn (München: C.H. Beck, 2021), s. 8 para. 71; H. Loibl in: Germer & Loibl, *Energierecht*, 469 et seq.

869. A detailed regime for the planning of locations for converter and transformer platforms as well as for the routes and corridors for power lines has been implemented. Previously, this spatial planning has been set out in the Federal Spatial Offshore Grid Plan (*Bundesfachplan Offshore*) as well as in a special plan for the offshore grid connection lines, the Offshore Grid Development Plan (*Offshore-Netzentwicklungsplan*). With the Offshore Wind Energy Act, however, the number of relevant plans should be reduced. The new planning instrument is the Site Development Plan (*Flächenentwicklungsplan*). Planning of the grid connection lines has been integrated into the general planning regime for high voltage grids to ensure synchronization with the grid expansion at land.[572]

870. The construction and operation of offshore wind installations in the Exclusive Economic Zone is subject to a plan approval (*Planfeststellung*), section 45 et seqq. WindSeeG. Seated in Hamburg, the Federal Maritime and Hydrographic Agency (*Bundesamt für Seeschifffahrt und Hydrographie*, hereinafter: BSH) is the competent authority to grant approval for wind power plants in the Exclusive Economic Zone.[573] The first German offshore wind field 'Alpha Ventus', which lies 45 kms off the island Borkum and contains twelve wind power plants, was constructed in 2009. Over 1,000 wind energy installations are operational in the North Sea and Baltic Sea now. To accelerate planning procedures, for centrally pre-surveyed areas the plan approval procedure shall be replaced by a plan approval permit (*Plangenehmigung*) with an amendment to the WindSeeG in the legislative proceedings at the time this update is being made.[574]

871. Until 2012, another form of permit was required for the construction and erection of new (offshore) installations as well as for any substantial alteration of the installations and their operation. The approval used to be an 'obligatory decision' (*gebundene Entscheidung*), meaning that the Federal Maritime and Hydrographic Agency as the competent authority did not have any discretion to decide whether or not to issue a permit. The permit had to be issued if the requirements were fulfilled.[575] Following an amendment of the Offshore Installation Ordinance (*Seeanlagenverordnung, SeeAnlV*) in 2012, the construction and operation of offshore installations as well as substantial changes became subject to a plan approval

572. G. Hermes in: J.P. Schneider & C. Theobald, *Recht der Energiewirtschaft*, 5th edn (München: C.H. Beck, 2021), s. 8 para. 73.
573. The BSH offers information about the approval procedure for wind power plants in the Exclusive Economic Zone in English on its webpage www.bsh.de . It also provides a list of all approved wind farm projects.
574. Entwurf eines Zweiten Gesetzes zur Änderung des Windenergie-auf-See-Gesetzes und anderer Vorschriften, BT-Drs. 20/1634, p. 4.
575. Schmälter, in: W. Danner & C. Theobald, *Energierecht* (München: C.H. Beck, 67. Addition 2010), s. 3 SeeAnlV para. 1.

procedure, initially governed by section 2 SeeAnlV.[576] With some modifications, the permitting regime based on plan approval procedures has been continued with the Offshore Wind Energy Act.[577]

872. A plan approval procedure follows another scheme for decisions than the normal conditional administrative norms. The plan approval is an instrument for the planning administration, leaving an area of discretion to include all the diverse interests affected by the project and to bring them as close to an optimal balance as possible. If granted, the plan approval comprises all permits and licensing procedures which are required for the realization of a project (so-called concentration effect). In the case of offshore wind, this has particular relevance for decisions of the Federal Agency for Nature Conservation.[578] Section 48 paragraph 4 WindSeeG contains important preconditions for a plan approval decision. These requirements comprise, *inter alia*, that the safety and the easiness of the traffic shall not be impaired, and that the marine environment is not endangered.

873. The Federal Maritime and Hydrographic Agency is the responsible authority for the plan approval procedure and the final decision. Section 45 paragraph 3 WindSeeG declares sections 72–78 of the Administrative Procedure Act (*Verwaltungsverfahrensgesetz, VwVfG*) applicable for the plan approval procedure (unless the WindSeeG does not set out other provisions).

874. Concerning the cable connection of offshore wind turbines in the territorial sea, it is important to note that section 43 Sentence 1 number 2 EnWG requires for a plan approval procedure (*Planfeststellungsverfahren*) to be conducted.

875. Sections 17a et seqq. EnWG contain regulations about the grid connection of offshore wind installations. These rules are explained in more detail above in Part I Chapter 2 section 2 III. Under German law, the transmission grid operators are obliged to construct and operate the grid connection for offshore wind turbines. With an amendment of the EnWG in 2012, stipulating a complete system change for the grid connection of offshore wind turbines, the German legislator tried to solve substantial practical difficulties that became visible in creating the first grid connections. Under the modified regime, while the transmission grid operator is still obliged to install and operate the grid connection, this follows a much more detailed planning procedure. Of high importance are also rules on liability for grid connections that have not been constructed in due time.

576. *See* in more detail W. F. Spieth/M. Uibeleisen, 'Neues Genehmigungsregime für Offshore-Windparks', *NVwZ* (2012): 321; L. Zabel, 'Die Novelle der Seeanlagenverordnung – Auswirkungen auf die Zulassung von Offshore-Windparks und Netzanschlussvorhaben', *NordÖR* (2012): 263 et seq.

577. S. Plicht, 'Gesetz zur Entwicklung und Förderung der Windenergieanlagen auf See', *EnWZ* (2016): 550, 554.

578. L. Zabel, 'Die Novelle der Seeanlagenverordnung – Auswirkungen auf die Zulassung von Offshore-Windparks und Netzanschlussvorhaben', *NordÖR* (2012): 263, 264.

§2. Support under the Renewable Energy Sources Act and Offshore Wind Energy Act

876. For onshore and offshore wind energy installations, the entitlement and amount of financial support, as a general rule, is determined in tender procedures according to the rules in the Renewable Energy Sources Act and the Offshore Wind Energy Act.

I. Onshore Wind Energy Plants

877. Onshore wind energy installations generally require an award issued in a tender procedure for the entitlement to financial support under the EEG (section 22 paragraph 2 EEG). The entitlement also exists for electricity generated with an installed capacity that exceeds the awarded capacity by up to 15%. Further, the provision foresees two exemptions from the tender requirement. Onshore wind installations with an installed capacity of up to and including 750 kW are under section 22 paragraph 2 sentence 2 Nr. 1 EEG generally exempted from the tender requirement. Under Nr. 2, pilot onshore wind energy installations with an installed capacity totalling up to 125 MW a year are excluded from the tender requirement as well. Pilot onshore wind energy turbines mean in particular the first two onshore wind energy installations of a type, subject to further material and registration requirements laid out in section 2 Nr. 37 a) EEG.

878. The volume for onshore wind capacity that shall be subject to a tender is specified in section 28 EEG. For instance, the tender volume for 2023 shall amount to 3,000 MW capacity to be installed, and the tender volume for 2024 shall amount to 3,100 MW capacity to be installed. The volume is tendered on specific tender dates which generally shall be 1 February, 1 May, and 1 September of a year. Additional dates may apply for volumes that have not been awarded. The tender volumes may be adjusted in particular to reflect volumes which have not been awarded, or in case it is expected that no sufficient volumes will be available for participation in the tender.

879. With an amendment to the EEG under discussion at the time of this update, the level of tender volumes for onshore wind shall be increased to 10 gigawatts per year (see section 28 of the draft EEG 2023), with the aim of having an installed onshore wind capacity of 115 gigawatts in 2030 (the installed capacity in 2022 amounts to around 56 gigawatts).[579] The tender dates shall be modified as well.

880. Besides the general requirements for a bid in the tender, sections 36 et seqq. EEG set out specific requirements that need to be adhered to for a bid for onshore wind energy. In particular, onshore wind installations for which a bid in the tender shall be made must have received the permits under the Federal Immissions Protection Act four weeks prior to the tender date, section 36 paragraph 1 Nr. 1 EEG.

579. BT-Drs. 20/1630, p. 2, 28, 192.

Also, the installations must be notified as permitted to the register four weeks prior to the tender date. The amount of security to be provided for a bid for onshore wind installations shall be determined by multiplying the bid volume with 30 Euros per kilowatt capacity to be installed, section 36a EEG.

881. Section 36b EEG sets out a maximum support value for the tender procedures. The maximum value decreases over time.

882. To enable onshore wind projects of citizen energy associations, section 36g EEG contains favourable rules for such associations under further conditions set out in the provision. In case a citizen energy association meets the requirements and its bid is awarded in a tender procedure, deviating from the general pay-as-bid structure, the relevant bid value shall be the bid value of the highest awarded bid in the same tender round, section 36g paragraph 3 EEG. With the draft EEG 2023 amendment, more citizen energy projects shall be exempted from the tender requirement, but limited to wind projects up to 18 MW and solar projects up to 6 MW.[580]

883. It is important to note that the relevant value for financial support will be derived from the value awarded in the tender by applying a correction value that shall account for the different wind conditions among the locations, section 36h EEG. This mechanism shall allow comparable bids to be made in the tender procedures, but also that locations throughout Germany can be used for the expansion of onshore wind. The model of a reference yield is meant to avoid that excessive financial support is granted to electricity from wind energy plants in high-wind locations, while providing an incentive for the construction of wind energy plants inland.[581] This mechanism shall be developed further with the EEG 2023 amendment to facilitate using sites in southern Germany.[582]

884. For onshore wind energy installations for which support levels are still set administratively by the EEG, the support level shall be derived from the bid values of the highest bid still awarded on the bid dates for onshore wind turbines in the year prior to the previous year, section 46 paragraph 1 EEG. Contrary to other renewable energy installations promoted under the EEG, the support values for onshore wind energy plants do not differentiate between the installation capacities, but again it does take the output of the installation due to the wind conditions on the concrete location into account.

II. Offshore Wind Energy Plants

885. For offshore wind installations, section 22 paragraph 5 EEG generally foresees that the entitlement to financial support requires that an award issued by the

580. BT-Drs. 20/1630, p. 138.
581. *See* W. Frenz in: W. Frenz & H.J. Müggenborg & T. Cosack & B. Hennig & T. Schomerus, *EEG*, 5. Ed. (Berlin: Erich Schmidt Verlag, 2018), s. 36h para. 1.
582. BT-Drs. 20/1630, p. 138.

Federal Network Agency in a tender is effective. Pilot offshore wind energy installations in line with the Offshore Wind Energy Act (*WindSeeG*) are exempted from the tender requirement.

886. Details on the tender volumes, specific tender requirements, and tender procedure are set out in the Offshore Wind Energy Act. This Act generally aims to increase the installed capacity of offshore wind turbines connected to the grid from 2021 to a total of 20 gigawatts by 2030 and to a total of 40 gigawatts by 2040 (section 1 paragraph 2 WindSeeG). With a statutory amendment in the legislative proceedings at the time this update is being made, the expansion goals for offshore wind installations shall be increased substantially to at least 30 gigawatts by 2030, at least 40 gigawatts by 2035, and at least 70 gigawatts by 2045.[583]

887. Besides the Offshore Wind Energy Act, provisions of the Renewable Energy Sources Act remain relevant for offshore wind installations, for instance in relation to claiming financial support with market premium in the form of direct marketing.

888. The Offshore Wind Energy Act essentially differentiates between tender procedures for existing projects which are commissioned from 1 January 2021 onwards, and tender procedures for offshore wind installations on pre-surveyed areas in the so-called central model which are commissioned from 1 January 2026 onwards.[584] For the existing projects for which a certain status of project development had been reached already at the time the new Offshore Wind Energy Act was adopted (*see* section 26 paragraph 2 WindSeeG), tenders have been performed with the bid dates 1 April 2017 and 1 April 2018. A particularly remarkable result of both tender rounds has been that in both procedures the lowest bid made and awarded had a bid value of 0 cents.[585]

889. From 2021 onwards, the Federal Network Agency tenders for pre-surveyed areas. For such pre-surveyed areas, it is within the responsibility of the Federal Network Agency to conduct certain investigations and to provide bidders with information relevant for the tender procedure (see sections 9 and 11 WindSeeG). This

583. Entwurf eines Zweiten Gesetzes zur Änderung des Windenergie-auf-See-Gesetzes und anderer Vorschriften, BT-Drs. 20/1634, p. 1.

584. *See* S. Plicht, 'Gesetz zur Entwicklung und Förderung der Windenergieanlagen auf See', *EnWZ* (2016): 550, 551 et seq.; M. Böhme & J. Bukowski, 'Auswirkungen der 0-Cent-Ausschreibungen, Nach welchen Differenzierungskriterien soll künftig der Zuschlag erteilt werden?', *EnWZ* (2019): 243, 244.

585. *See* for the tender results the information provided by the Federal Network Agency, Ausschreibungen für bestehende Projekte nach § 26 WindSeeG, https://www.bundesnetzagentur.de/DE/Beschlusskammern/BK06/BK6_72_Offshore/Ausschr_best_Projekte/Ausschr_best_Projekte.html?nn=729642, last accessed 21 Apr. 2022; *see* on further consequences also M. Böhme & J. Bukowski, 'Auswirkungen der 0-Cent-Ausschreibungen, Nach welchen Differenzierungskriterien soll künftig der Zuschlag erteilt werden?', *EnWZ* (2019): 243.

comprises in particular that examinations of the marine environment shall be carried out and documented, that a preliminary exploration of the subsoil shall be carried out and documented and that reports shall be produced on the wind and oceanographic situation of the site (section 10 paragraph 1 WindSeeG).

890. Besides the general requirements for a bid in the tender, sections 20 et seqq. WindSeeG in conjunction with the EEG set out specific requirements that need to be adhered to for a bid for offshore wind energy. In particular, a security needs to be provided, and section 22 WindSeeG sets out maximum support values for the tender procedures.

891. For the construction and commissioning of offshore wind installations, sections 59 et seqq. WindSeeG set out implementation deadlines as well as sanctions in case of non-compliance with the implementation deadlines.

892. To reach the substantially increased goals which shall be introduced for offshore wind installations, and in light of previous tender results, with a current amendment to the WindSeeG two separate tender designs shall be introduced for centrally pre-surveyed areas and for areas without such central pre-survey.[586]

586. Entwurf eines Zweiten Gesetzes zur Änderung des Windenergie-auf-See-Gesetzes und anderer Vorschriften, BT-Drs. 20/1634, p. 3 et seq.

Chapter 4. Hydropower

893. Electricity generation from hydropower installations accounted for a share of 3.3% in the final electricity consumption in 2009 and 3.6% in 2012.[587] In Germany, around 7,700 hydropower plants amount to an installed capacity of altogether 5.340 MW (2009) and 5.607 MW (2012). The electricity generation from these plants amounted to 19,094 GWh in 2009 and 21,577 GWh in 2012.[588] The share of electricity generation from hydropower installations in the gross electricity production amounted to 3.3% in 2021.[589]

894. The electricity generated by hydropower installations continues to be financially supported on the basis of administratively set support values provided in the Renewable Energy Sources Act. No requirement to participate in tender procedures has been introduced in relation to hydropower installations.[590]

895. The relevant support values (*anzulegende Werte*) for electricity generated from hydropower plants in section 40 EEG differentiate between the capacities of the plant. The relevant values under section 40 paragraph 1 numbers 1 to 3 EEG apply to smaller hydropower plants with a capacity of maximum 5 MW. The values vary according to the capacity of the plant. For hydropower installations with a capacity over 5 MW, financial support may be granted pursuant to section 40 paragraph 1 numbers 4 to 7 EEG, which differentiates further according to the capacity of the installation.

896. Under certain conditions, financial support under the EEG can also be claimed for electricity generated in hydropower installations, if these were commissioned prior to 1 January 2009 and modernized with an increase in generation capacity since 31 December 2016 (see section 40 paragraph 2 and 3 EEG). Thus, electricity from older installations may also be remunerated according to the support values under subsequent provisions of the EEG. A similar approach could be found in section 23 paragraph 2 and 3 EEG 2012.

897. An entitlement for financial support for hydropower installations exists only if the installation has been erected in a spatial relationship to a wholly or partially existing dam installation or a dam installation which is primarily to be constructed for purposes other than the generation of electricity from hydropower, or without a complete transversal structure (section 40 paragraph 4 EEG).

---

587. Federal Ministry for the Environment, 'Erneuerbare Energien in Zahlen', Internet-Update, 15 Dec. 2010, available on www.erneuerbare-energien.de, last access: 8 Jan. 2011, 7; AGEE-Stat, Erneuerbare Energien in Zahlen, December 2013.
588. AGEE-Stat, Erneuerbare Energien in Zahlen, December 2013.
589. DESTATIS, Bruttostromerzeugung in Deutschland, www.destatis.de, last access 21 Apr. 2022.
590. T. Schomerus and L. Reins in: W. Frenz & H.J. Müggenborg & T. Cosack & B. Hennig & T. Schomerus, *EEG*, 5. Ed. (Berlin: Erich Schmidt Verlag, 2018), s. 40 para. 1.

898. Thus, through ecological criteria (which have varied in earlier versions of the EEG), the Renewable Energy Sources Act pursues environmental goals by rendering financial support for hydropower installations dependent on the fulfilment of environmental standards.

Chapter 5. Biomass

899. Altogether, the share of electricity generation from all types of biomass reached 4%–5% in 2009 and over 6% in 2012.[591] In 2021, the share of biomass in gross electricity production reached 7.8%.[592] In order to correctly assess the importance of biomass for energy consumption, its share in the heat and fuel sector must also be taken into account. In 2009, around 92% of the heat generated from renewable sources came from biomass in Germany.[593] In 2021, the overall share of biomass in consumption of heat generated from renewable energy sources still amounted to around 86%.[594] In the fuel sector in 2009 and 2012, biomass reached a share of around 5.5% of total fuel consumption.[595] In 2019, the share of biomass in fuel consumption for transport purposes amounted to around 5%.[596] However, this chapter focuses on the electricity generation from biomass that is supported by the Renewable Energy Sources Act (for the heat sector see below Chapter 7, for the fuel sector see above Part III, Chapter 5, section 2).

900. The use of biomass for energy consumption can in principle be carbon neutral. Only the CO_2 that was stored when the organic material was growing is emitted in the process of energy generation. Also, the use of biomass as energy source supports the restructuring process of agriculture. Easy storage and the capacity to be used in all energy sectors, particularly transport, are considerable advantages of bioenergy. However, legal incentives for the use of biomass must not counteract the overall goal of CO_2-reductions and not incentivize biomass production that harms the environment. The government undertook measures to demand a certain GHG reduction potential, starting with liquid biofuels. Moreover, certain ecological criteria for the use of biomass must be fulfilled, as prescribed by sustainability requirements that apply since 1 January 2011.

§1. Construction of Biomass Power Plants

901. Biomass power plants will be subject to either the general construction law or to the Immissions Control Law. In case the conditions of the relevant statutes are

591. Federal Ministry for the Environment, 'Erneuerbare Energien in Zahlen', Internet-Update, 15 Dec. 2010, available on www.erneuerbare-energien.de, last access: 8 Jan. 2011, 7. AGEE-Stat, Erneuerbare Energien in Zahlen, December 2013.
592. DESTATIS, Bruttostromerzeugung in Deutschland, www.destatis.de, last access 21 Apr. 2022.
593. Federal Ministry for the Environment, 'Entwicklung der Erneuerbaren Energien in Deutschland im Jahr 2009', slide show of 15 Dec. 2010, available on www.erneuerbare-energien.de, last access: 9 Jan. 2011.
594. Umweltbundesamt, Erneuerbare Energien in Zahlen, www.umweltbundesamt.de, last access 21 Apr. 2022.
595. Federal Ministry for the Environment, 'Erneuerbare Energien in Zahlen', Internet-Update, 15 Dec. 2010, available on www.erneuerbare-energien.de, last access: 8 Jan. 2011, 7. AGEE-Stat, Erneuerbare Energien in Zahlen, December 2013.
596. Fachagentur Nachwachsende Rohstoffe, Aktuelle Marktsituation, Kraftstoffabsatz in Deutschland, https://biokraftstoffe.fnr.de, last access 1 May 2022.

fulfilled, the operators are entitled to demand a licence. The administrative authority generally does not have the discretion to deny a licence if the applicant is in compliance with the conditions, in accordance with the relevant norms.

902. A licence subject to the Federal Immissions Control Act (*BImSchG*) for the biomass power plant itself may be necessary, in particular under the numbers 1.15, 1.16, 8, and 9.36 in the Annex 1 to the Ordinance on Installations Requiring a Permit (*4. BImSchV*). Biomass power plants can also be constructed as auxiliary facilities to an existing facility subject to a licence under the Immissions Control Law. In this case, the competent authority must be notified under section 15 BImSchG. In case of major alterations, a licensing under section 16 BImSchG must be undertaken.[597]

903. Biomass power plants can qualify as privileged projects in 'undeveloped outskirt areas'. According to construction law, they can therefore more easily be constructed in these areas.[598] Allowing biomass fired power plants to qualify as privileged projects in the undeveloped outskirt area also promotes a structural change in the agriculture.[599] The energetic utilization of biomass by section 35 paragraph 1 number 6 BauGB is, however, only privileged under certain further requirements. In particular, the installation needs to be located within the framework of a facility that serves agricultural or forestry activities, or that is used for market-gardening purposes or cattle breeding. Moreover, the privilege only applies if the capacity of a biogas production plant does not exceed 2.3 million standard cubic metres of biogas per year, and the rated thermal input of other plants does not exceed 2 MW. For these reasons, the privilege plays a role for certain biomass installations only.

904. The Federal Administrative Court clarified that the privilege under section 35 paragraph 1 number 6 BauGB also applies if an agricultural holding that operates a biogas facility produces biomass exclusively for the purpose of energy generation.[600] Earlier judgments granted the privilege only in case the biogas facility serves as an auxiliary installation in relation to the agricultural holding.[601]

905. A project that is classified as privileged in the undeveloped outskirt area may still not be in conflict with public interest. Compliance with regional development plans may play a role here too. The duty to avoid harmful immissions is key here. In particular, the immission limit values of the TA Luft and TA Lärm must be

597. H. Loibl & C. Heigl in: C. Germer & H. Loibl, *Energierecht, Handbuch*, 2nd edn (Berlin: Erich Schmidt Verlag, 2007), 503 et seq.

598. *See* above Ch. 3, s. 1. The material preconditions of the construction law also need to be fulfilled for a licence under the Immissions Control Law.

599. P. Salje, *EEG*, 5th edn (Köln: Carl Heymanns Verlag, 2009), Einführung para. 135.

600. BVerwG, judgment of 11 Dec. 2008, 7 C 6.08.

601. With regard to the legal requirement of being used 'within the framework' of a facility serving agricultural or forestry activities, *see* the references at M. Maslaton, 'Die Entwicklung des Rechts der Erneuerbaren Energien 2007/2008', *LKV* (2009): 152, 157.

respected. Limit values for smell nuisances are governed in specific administrative regulations (so-called Smell Nuisances Guideline, *Geruchsimmissionsrichtlinie, GIRL*).

906. The Council Regulation number 1069/2009 laying down health rules as regards animal by-products and derived products not intended for human consumption may demand other material requirements in relation to biogas plants, and so can the Waste Law. Also, an environmental impact assessment may need to be conducted, see number 8.4 of the Annex 1 to the Environmental Impact Assessment Statute.

§2. Financial Support under the Renewable Energy Sources Act

907. Which substances are regarded as biomass within the scope of the Renewable Energy Sources Act is governed by the Biomass Ordinance (*Biomasseverordnung, BiomasseV*).[602] This Ordinance and the Renewable Energy Sources Act according to section 2 paragraph 1 BiomasseV define biomass as fuels made of phytomass and zoomass, including 'products, by-products, residues, and waste from phytomass and zoomass whose energy content comes from phytomass and zoomass'. A non-exclusive catalogue in the second paragraph further specifies this general definition. The third paragraph declares that certain substances should be regarded as biomass whether or not the general conditions of paragraph 1 are fulfilled. Section 3 BiomasseV then clarifies that certain substances like fossil fuels and products and by-products made from fossil fuels are not regarded as biomass.

908. In principle, only installations generating electricity from biomass exclusively can demand financial support under the EEG. However, this so-called exclusivity principle is subject to a number of exceptions. For example, section 44c paragraph 1 Nr. 2 EEG allows for the use of quantities of vegetable oil methyl ester as a start-up, priming, and supporting fuel.

909. Under previous versions of the EEG, the feed-in tariffs available from the Renewable Energy Sources Act strongly supported the increase of the share of electricity generated from biomass in the German energy mix. A basic remuneration has been granted for any electricity generated from biomass. Above that, a complex system of bonuses specified by several Annexes to the EEG tried to foster the use of innovative technologies, energy crops, and combined heat and power generation. A so-called technology bonus has been available for plants that use innovative technologies (technology bonus), another bonus has been available for electricity from energy crops (bonus for electricity from energy crops), and a third bonus has applied for electricity from biomass generated in combined heat and power generation (CHP bonus). The conditions and the additional payment for the specific bonus were

602. Verordnung über die Erzeugung von Strom aus Biomasse of 21 Jun. 2001 (BGBl. I p. 1234). An English version (from which the subsequent translation has been taken) has been provided by the Federal Ministry for the Environment on the webpage www.bmu.de, last access: 16 Jan. 2011.

stipulated in Annexes 1–3 of earlier versions of the Renewable Energy Sources Act. All these bonuses could apply cumulatively; a single plant could therefore be entitled to several of these bonuses and thereby significantly increase the minimum remuneration (see the 2. Ed. of this monograph for a more detailed explanation of these bonuses).

910. The EEG 2012 changed this system of feed-in tariffs significantly. The EEG 2014 again led to material changes and has restricted the use of biomass as energy source significantly.

911. Following the introduction of tender procedures, also new biomass installations with an installed capacity above 150 kW are subject to a tender requirement if financial support shall be claimed. Biomass installations with a commissioning date prior to 1 January 2017 are allowed to participate in tender procedures under further conditions, *see* section 39g EEG. In case of such existing biomass installations, the threshold of 150 kW for exemptions does not apply.

912. The tender volume for biomass installations shall amount to 600 MW capacity to be installed per calendar year, section 28b paragraph 2 EEG. The volume may be adjusted according to criteria set out in that provision.

913. Besides the general requirements for a bid in the tender, sections 39 et seqq. EEG set out specific requirements that need to be adhered to for a bid for biomass installations. In particular, a security needs to be provided, and section 39b EEG sets out maximum support values for the tender procedures which decrease over time.

914. Specific requirements that must be met for existing biomass installations to participate in tender procedures are provided in section 39g EEG. In particular, the previous claim for financial support in respect of these installations may only exist for a maximum of eight years at the time of the tender procedure.

915. For biomass installations for which support levels are still set administratively by the EEG, the support level is set in section 42 EEG.

916. The Renewable Energy Sources Act further promotes a flexible energy production in biomass installations to use their potential of shifting production to times of high demand. To foster flexibility, sections 50 et seqq. EEG grant a flexibility addition or premium under further conditions that shall reflect flexible operation capacity.

917. With the EEG amendment 2023, the support for biomass installations shall even further be focused on highly flexible peak installations to use the ability of storing energy in form of bioenergy. Biomethane shall in future only be usable in highly flexible power plants that generate electricity for no more than 10% of the hours in a year.[603] Also, new biomass and cogeneration installations shall be also laid out for a future use of hydrogen (H2-ready).[604]

918. Section 44b paragraph 4 EEG basically allows to feed-in biogas ('biomethane') into a gas network and to withdraw it at another point of the network. This gas is deemed to be biomethane within the scope of the Renewable Energy Sources Act. This fiction requires that the thermal equivalent of the withdrawn quantity of such gas at the end of a calendar year corresponds to the quantity of gas from biomass fed into the gas network elsewhere. Also, mass balance system must be used for the whole transport and supply of gas. In essence, this clause allows biogas to be fed into the gas network and to utilize it for the generation of electricity and heat at a location where heat is demanded (heat sink).[605] Rules in the Regulation on the Access to Gas Supply Grids (GasNZV) further promote biogas to be fed into the gas grid (see above Part 2, Chapter 5, §4).

§3. Sustainability Requirements for Biomass

919. In the light of growing sustainability concerns on the use of biomass in the energy supply, Germany introduced sustainability criteria for the production of liquid biofuels in the electricity sector. The Ordinance on requirements for a sustainable production of bioliquids for electricity generation (Biomass-Electricity-Sustainability Ordinance, *BioSt-NachV*) sets out these sustainability requirements, as well as a certification system to demand compliance with these conditions.[606] For larger installations, with an amendment of the BioSt-NachV end 2021, the scope of the Ordinance has been expanded to also include solid and gaseous biomass.[607]

920. The central mechanism of this Ordinance is that financial support under the EEG for electricity generated from bioliquids and from gaseous and solid fuels produced from biomass can only be claimed when the plant complies with the requirements of the BioSt-NachV. In essence, these requirements comprehend the protection of natural habitats and sustainable agricultural management, a certain potential of the bioliquids to reduce GHG emissions, and the application for registration of the installation in the market master data register (see section 3 paragraph 1 BioSt-NachV). Pursuant to section 4 BioSt-NachV, the relevant biomass may not

603. BT-Drs. 20/1630, p. 138.
604. BT-Drs. 20/1630, p. 3 et seq.
605. A. Rostankowski & J. Vollprecht in: M. Altrock, V. Oschmann & C. Theobald, *EEG*, 4rd edn (München: C.H. Beck, 2013), s. 27c para. 2, 13 et seqq.
606. Verordnung über Anforderungen an eine nachhaltige Herstellung von Biomasse zur Stromerzeugung, Biomassestrom-Nachhaltigkeitsverordnung of 2 Dec. 2021 (BGBl. I p. 5126). For more detail *see* J. Vollprecht, 'Die neue Biomassestrom-Nachhaltigkeitsverordnung: Auswirkungen auf die Vergütung von Strom nach dem EEG', *IR* (2010): 28.
607. J. Vollprecht & P. Schwarz, 'Die Biomassestrom-Nachhaltigkeitsverordnung in (ziemlich) neuem Gewand', *IR* (2022): 53.

be obtained from land with high biodiversity value, the definition of which is further defined in the clause. Moreover, areas with high above-ground or underground carbon stock may not be used for the production of biomass, according to section 4 paragraph 3 BioSt-NachV.

921. Section 6 BioSt-NachV demands that the use of bioliquids achieves a certain reduction in GHG emissions. Initially, the GHG emission savings had been at a level of at least 35%. This value increased to at least 50% by 1 January 2017. For an interface commissioned after 6 October 2015 and until 31 December 2020, the required level is at least 60%. For interfaces commissioned from 1 January 2021, the level is at 65%. The level for new installations using gaseous and solid fuels is at minimum 70%, and for installations commissioned from 1 January 2026 at 80%, section 6 paragraph 2 BioSt-NachV.

922. The implementation of the sustainability criteria requires a complex certification system, which is described in the Ordinance. Under section 7 BioSt-NachV, installation operators must prove to the grid operator that the requirements for the financial support according to the BioSt-NachV have been fulfilled. Certain forms of proofs can be used to prove compliance with the sustainability requirements; these are listed in section 10 BioSt-NachV. They are generally issued by 'interfaces', particularly operations and operational sites that receive biomass from the operations that cultivate and harvest such biomass, and oil mills (see the more detailed definition in section 2 paragraph 29 BioSt-NachV). The proofs are issued based on mass balance systems according to section 13 BioSt-NachV.

Chapter 6. Solar Energy

923. Constituting 8.7% of gross electricity production in 2021, the share of solar energy reached a significant part within the renewable energies used for electricity supply.[608] Solar energy enjoyed enormous growing rates during the recent years. New photovoltaic installations with a total capacity of 3,800 MW have been installed in Germany in 2009.[609] In 2010, installations with a capacity of more than 7,000 MW have been commissioned.[610] In 2020, the total capacity of new photovoltaic installations amounted to around 4,800 MW.[611] The total installed capacity of photovoltaics amounted to 53,720 MW end of 2020.[612]

924. Solar energy installations have initially been promoted by a 100,000-roof-programme, now the support of these installations comes mainly from financial support under the Renewable Energy Sources Act.[613] The feed-in tariffs under the Renewable Energy Sources Act have been favourable and considerably higher than for other energy sources, and they have been the cornerstones of the remarkable increase. This means that solar energy also accounts for a large share of the costs related to the EEG. In 2010, the Energy Concept of the Federal Government pointed out that solar energy would generate 9% of the electricity supported by the EEG, but would account for 40% of the total costs.[614] Due to significant cost reductions for photovoltaic installations, new installations however require much lower levels of financial support, or can even be realized on the basis of power purchase agreements or as decentral projects for own consumption outside the financial support regime of the Renewable Energy Sources Act.

925. The legislator took the at that time high costs of solar energy promotion into consideration by cutting the feed-in tariffs for electricity from photovoltaics[615] in mid-2010 (the so-called photovoltaics amendment) and by another photovoltaic amendment in mid-2012.[616] The reduction of tariffs for installations commissioned in the subsequent years (degression) has been remarkably high and depended on the

608. DESTATIS, Stromerzeugung 2021: Anteil konventioneller Energieträger deutlich gestiegen, available at www.destatis.de, last access 23 Apr. 2022.
609. Federal Ministry for the Environment, 'Erneuerbare Energien in Zahlen', Internet-Update, 15 Dec. 2010, available on www.erneuerbare-energien.de, last access: 8 Jan. 2011, 6.
610. Press release of the Federal Ministry for the Environment No. 008/11 of 20 Jan. 2011.
611. Bundesnetzagentur / Bundeskartellamt, *Monitoringreport 2021*, Dec 2021, p. 87, available at www-.bundesnetzagentur.de.
612. Bundesnetzagentur / Bundeskartellamt, *Monitoringreport 2021*, Dec 2021, p. 87.
613. *See* closer for the development of the rules V. Oschmann in: M. Altrock, V. Oschmann & C. Theobald, *EEG*, 4rd edn (München: C.H. Beck, 2013), s. 32.
614. Energy Concept, BT-Drs. 17/3049, 4.
615. In Germany, installations generating electricity from solar radiation are mainly photovoltaic installations which are thus subsequently referred to, although the EEG refers to all 'installations generating electricity from solar radiation'.
616. Act of 11 Aug. 2010 (BGBl. I p. 1170). Gesetz zur Änderung des Rechtsrahmens für Strom aus solarer Strahlungsenergie und zu weiteren Änderungen im Recht der erneuerbaren Energien of 17 Aug. 2012 (BGBl. I p. 1754).

absolute growth rates of photovoltaic installations. The more photovoltaic installations are commissioned in general during one year, the higher the degression rate for photovoltaic installations has been calculated. Moreover, the Federal Ministry for the Environment found a compromise with representatives of the solar energy industry to cut the tariffs for electricity from solar energy also in mid-2011, in addition to the regular degression which applies every year.[617] It was difficult to find an appropriate balance between the reduction in tariffs so as to curb costs imposed on final consumers, and the goal not to cause excessive hardship for the solar energy industry that was developed with the support of the EEG.

926. It is also to be seen against these discussions on the cost side for promotion of solar energy that photovoltaic installations have been the first for which tender procedures have been introduced in Germany. All larger photovoltaic installations are subject to tender procedures now, or can be realized based on power purchase agreements or own consumption 'outside the EEG'. For smaller photovoltaic installations, financial support under administratively set support values in the EEG still is available.

§1. Construction Law for Photovoltaic Installations

927. Solar energy facilities installed on the roof of a house or on its outside surface are subject to construction law. However, most of the *Länder* exempted solar energy facilities from the necessity to apply for a permit under their Construction Law Statute.[618] The installations must nevertheless fulfil the material requirements of construction law. This applies for the stability requirements as stipulated in the construction law of the *Länder*, as well as for the requirements of the Planning Law under sections 29 et seq. BauGB. Designations for solar energy may be expressly provided in the land-use plans. However, even if certain areas are not designated, solar panels will often be admissible as attendant facilities under section 14 of the BauNVO.[619] Section 14 paragraph 3 BauNVO favours solar energy installations by stating that they are to be viewed as generally admissible attendant facilities even if the generated energy is completely or predominantly fed into the public grid.

928. Under section 35 paragraph 1 BauGB, no privilege for open area solar panels exists within the undeveloped outskirt area. In this area, solar panels may therefore only be constructed under restrictive conditions of public interests not being affected (section 35 paragraph 2 BauGB).[620] Consequently, in practice open area

---

617. Press release of the Federal Ministry for the Environment No. 008/11 of 20 Jan. 2011.
618. C. Germer & H. Loibl, *Energierecht, Handbuch,* 2nd edn (Berlin: Erich Schmidt Verlag, 2007), 526.
619. H. Loibl in: C. Germer & H. Loibl, *Energierecht, Handbuch,* 2nd edn (Berlin: Erich Schmidt Verlag, 2007), 527.
620. M. Maslaton, 'Die Entwicklung des Rechts der Erneuerbaren Energien 2007/2008', *LKV* (2009): 152, 154.

photovoltaic plants are mainly built based on a land-use plan that expressly designates an area for their installation. This is also a result of the fact that financial support under the Renewable Energy Sources Act is only available under certain planning conditions. These conditions can be fulfilled by construction of open area solar panels within the area of a land-use plan in particular (see closer below section 3). However, alternatives for construction in other areas exist as well.

929. A privileged project in the undeveloped outskirt area, however, is the use of solar radiation energy in, on and on roof and exterior wall surfaces of buildings, if the installation is structurally subordinate to the building (section 35 paragraph 1 Nr. 8 BauGB).

§2. Installations Attached to or on Top of Buildings under the EEG

930. For the financial support for solar energy, the Renewable Energy Sources Act differentiates between panels attached to or on top of buildings, and other panels. Solar installations with an installed capacity of more than 750 kW need to participate in a tender procedure to be able to claim financial support under the EEG (section 22 paragraph 3 EEG). In respect of the tender procedures, the EEG differentiates between solar installations of the first segment which are open area solar installations, and solar installations on constructions which are not buildings, and solar installations of the second segment which are solar installations attached to or on top of buildings.

931. Separate tender rounds are conducted for solar installations of the first segment and solar installations of the second segment. The tender volume for solar installations of the second segment usually is much lower than within the first segment (*see* section 28a EEG).

932. For tenders within the second segment of solar installations, besides the general requirements for a bid in the tender, sections 38c et seqq. EEG set out specific requirements that need to be adhered to for a bid for solar installations attached to or on top of buildings. Each bid may not exceed an installed capacity of 20 MW, section 38c paragraph 2 EEG. Also, a security in a specific form (*Projektsicherungsbeitrag*) needs to be provided (section 38d EEG). Section 38e EEG sets out maximum support values for the tender procedures which decrease over time.

933. If installations do not fall under a tender requirement, financial support can be claimed pursuant to the support values set in section 48 EEG. This financial support is particularly relevant for solar installations attached to or on top of buildings. Smaller solar installations are exempted from the tender requirement, and therefore continue to claim financial support on basis of administratively set support values in the EEG.

934. An installation that generates electricity from solar radiation and is attached to or constructed on top of a building can benefit from financial support, whereas the amount of the support value is dependent on its capacity. A higher support value applies for the installed capacity up to 10 kW, and also the support value for the installed capacity up to 40 kW is higher than the support value which applies for installed capacity up to 750 kW (section 48 paragraph 2 EEG).

935. Importantly, support values for solar installations with later commissioning dates are reduced each month by the degression pursuant to section 49 EEG. The monthly degression is also to avoid a high number of commissionings prior to a reduction in tariffs. The concrete amount of support values are determined by the Federal Network Agency in dependence of the past expansion rates of photovoltaic installations. The current tariffs can be found on the webpage of the Federal Network Agency.[621]

936. The question of the commissioning date is of importance from the financial perspective of the investors, especially for photovoltaic installations. In section 3 number 30 EEG, the term 'commissioning' has been defined as 'the first time an installation is put into operation, following the establishment of operational readiness'. The interpretation of this definition has been the subject of intensive debates. Due to shortages on the market, in particular the necessity of power inverters for commissioning of photovoltaic installations has been problematic.

937. In particular the Clearingstelle EEG argued for a rather early understanding of the point in time of the commissioning. According to its advice, a photovoltaic installation shall be commissioned when it has generated electricity for the first time and this electricity is dissipated (consumed) outside the installation. In consequence of this interpretation, the mere illumination of a light bulb would be enough to qualify for a commissioning.[622] This advice has found broad application in practice. However, the decisions of the Clearingstelle EEG are legally not binding.

938. With the EEG 2012, the legislator reacted regarding the question of commissioning of photovoltaic installations. According to the enhanced definition, the commissioning now requires that the installation is fixed in place there were it shall permanently be located. Also, it must be equipped with the accessories necessary to generate alternating current.

939. The financial support under section 48 paragraph 2 EEG applies to photovoltaic installations that are attached to or placed on top of a building or noise barriers exclusively. Section 3 number 23 EEG clarifies that the term 'building' comprises 'roofed building structures which can be independently used and entered by humans and are primarily designed for the purpose of protecting humans, animals or objects'. This designated primary purpose of protecting humans, animals or objects has been subject of a number of court decisions. Courts had to analyse cases

621. www.bundesnetzagentur.de.
622. Clearingstelle EEG, *Advice (Hinweis)*, no. 1 (2010) of 25 Jun. 2010, available on: www.clearingstelleeeg.de, last access: 9 Jan. 2011.

in which the building and the photovoltaic installations were constructed simultaneously in particular. Installations attached to or on top of a building (outside the tender procedures) benefit from a higher support value than regular open area (photovoltaic) installations, which provides owners with an economic incentive to claim their installation was built on top of a building. Courts will however continue to verify whether the construction of a photovoltaic installation was the predominant purpose of the building structure.

940. A self-consumption privilege which existed under the EEG 2009 has been abolished with the EEG 2012. Due to the level of electricity supply prices, self-consumption is attractive even without any bonus. For the installation operator, utilizing the self-generated electricity generally makes more economic sense since the electricity costs saved are higher than the financial support he would receive in case of feed-in. Photovoltaics therefore often play a role in decentral energy solutions.

§3. Open Area Installations under the EEG

941. Open area installations and solar installations on constructions which are not buildings with an installed capacity of more than 750 kW are generally subject to a tender requirement. They can participate in the tenders in the first segment of solar installations. For tenders within the first segment of solar installations, besides the general requirements for a bid in the tender, sections 37 et seqq. EEG set out specific requirements that need to be adhered to for a bid for open area installations and solar installations on constructions which are not buildings. In particular, a security needs to be provided, and section 37b EEG sets out maximum support values for the tender procedures. From 1 January 2022, the maximum support values generally are oriented towards tender results in previous tender rounds. In case of a successful bid, installation operators can claim issuance of a payment entitlement (sections 38, 38a EEG).

942. Importantly, open area installations are only promoted on specific categories of sites which are listed in section 37 paragraph 1 Nr. 2 EEG. Only if installations shall be constructed in a category listed in this provision, a bid in a tender round can be made. Important categories of sites on which solar installations may qualify for financial support are the following: sites which had already been sealed by the time when the decision to adopt or amend a land-use plan was taken, sites which were being used as a conversion area used for commercial, transport, housing or military purposes at the time when the decision to adopt or amend a land-use plan was taken, sites which ran alongside motorways/railway lines (at a distance of up to 200 metres with an at least 15 metres free corridor) at the time when the decision to adopt or amend a land-use plan was taken, sites which are located within an area covered by a land-use plan that was adopted pursuant to section 30 of the Federal Building Code prior to 1 September 2003 and has not since been amended to allow for the erection of a solar installation, sites which have been designated as a commercial or industrial area in a zoning plan that was adopted before 1 January 2010 under further conditions. Also farmland and grassland – which for a long time was not eligible within the site criteria – may be used for solar sites under further criteria if the land is located in a closer defined disadvantaged area.

943. If installations do not fall under a tender requirement, financial support can be claimed pursuant to the support values set in section 48 EEG.

944. But again, section 48 paragraph 1 EEG renders financial support dependent on certain conditions ensuring that only certain areas are used for the construction and operation of photovoltaic installations. These site specific criteria are overlapping with the criteria for sites for which bids can be made within the first segment, but the site criteria are not identical.

945. In practice, open area installations are often constructed in an area for which a land-use plan exists that designates areas for the utilization of solar energy. As a consequence, the related conditions of section 48 paragraph 1 Nr. 3 EEG are of high importance to solar energy projects with an installed capacity up to 750 kW for which a claim for financial support shall be made outside the tender procedures.

946. After the first photovoltaics amendment restricted the possibility of using certain green areas for solar installations, the use of 'areas of conversion' has become particularly attractive to installation operators. Without a closer definition within the Renewable Energy Sources Act, the interpretation of the term 'areas of conversion' has been intensively discussed.[623] The Clearingstelle EEG particularly took the environmental damage caused by the economic, transport, housing or military use into account, which would argue in the affirmative for an area of conversion.[624] The use of environmentally degraded areas is certainly a central intention of the legislator. However, particular areas used for military purposes may, at least in parts, have high environmental value. In these cases the general nature protection law applies; nevertheless, questions on the classification as area of conversion still have to be answered.

947. Moreover, the operator must be in compliance with the other conditions of the EEG as well if he wishes to obtain remuneration under the EEG.

948. With the EEG amendment 2023, special forms of photovoltaic installations – photovoltaics on agricultural areas, floating photovoltaics, and photovoltaics on parking spaces – shall be integrated into the tenders for open area installations.[625]

623. LG Gießen, judgment of 1 Apr. 2008, *IR*, 2008, 138; A. Große, 'Zum Begriff der Konversionsflächen im EEG', *ZNER* 7 (2010): 235 et seq.; C. Bönning, 'Zum Begriff der Konversionsfläche', *Sonne Wind & Wärme* 10 (2010): 166 et seq.

624. Clearingstelle EEG, *Recommendation (Empfehlung)*, no. 2 (2010) of 1 Jul. 2010, available on www.clearingstelle-eeg.de, last access: 24 Apr. 2022.

625. BT-Drs. 20/1630, p. 3.

Chapter 7. Renewable Energy Sources in the Heat Sector

949. In the heat sector the use of Renewable Energy has previously been supported by the Act on the Promotion of Renewable Energy in the Heat Sector (hereinafter: *EEWärmeG*).[626] The Act aimed at increasing the share of renewable energy in the final energy consumption for heat (space heat, cooling and process heat and hot water) to 14% by 2020 (section 1 paragraph 2 EEWärmeG). On one hand, the Act relied on an obligation to use renewable energy in the heat sector, pursuant to part 2 EEWärmeG. On the other hand, the *Bund* provided financial support for the use of renewable energy under part 3 EEWärmeG.

950. In 2020, the law on saving energy and using energy from renewable sources has been unified in the Building Energy Act (*Gebäudeenergiegesetz, GEG*).[627] As far as use of renewable energy sources is concerned, the Building Energy Act builds upon, and further develops principles from the previous Act on the Promotion of Renewable Energy in the Heat Sector.

951. The Building Energy Act aims at using energy as sparingly as possible in buildings, and increasing the share of renewable energy for heat, cold, and electricity in the operation of buildings. It contains several requirements in relation to newly constructed buildings that shall foster low energy buildings and a reduction of energy demand.

952. In line with the predecessor legislation, the Building Energy Act in particular obliges owners of newly constructed buildings to cover a certain share of the energy demand for heat and cold with renewable energy sources (section 10 paragraph 2 Nr. 3 and sections 34–45 GEG).

953. The obligation to cover a certain share of the energy demand with renewable energy sources can be fulfilled using different renewable energy sources. These sources require different shares to cover the energy demands according to sections 34–45 GEG. Accordingly, the obligation to cover the energy demand with renewable energy can be complied with if solar radiation covers at least 15% of the energy demand for heat and cold (section 35 paragraph 1 GEG). The use of gaseous biomass meets the obligation if at least 30% of the energy demand is covered by this source in case a cogeneration installation is used (section 40 paragraph 2 sentence 2 GEG). In case a gas boiler is used, 50% of the energy demand must be covered by gaseous biomass. If liquid or solid biomass is used instead, 50% of the energy demand is required (sections 38 and 39 GEG). The same percentage is required for the use of geothermal energy and ambient heat (section 37 GEG).

---

626. Gesetz zur Förderung Erneuerbarer Energien im Wärmebereich, Erneuerbare-Energien-Wärmegesetz, of 07 Aug. 2008 (BGBl. I p. 1658).
627. Gebäudeenergiegesetz vom 8. August 2020 (BGBl. I S. 1728).

954. Importantly, so far the obligation to cover a certain share of the energy demand with renewable energy sources applies only to owners of newly constructed buildings. However, for existing public buildings, obligations for a use of renewable energy sources may apply in case of major renovations, section 52 GEG.

955. A Market Incentive Programme has been another pillar under the Renewable Energy Heat Act to promote installations generating renewable heat by two means: first, investment grants for the construction or the expansion of certain kinds of installations have been available on application to the Federal Office of Economics and Export Control (BAFA). Second, preferential tariffs for the investment into certain installations could be granted by the KfW Bankengruppe. Based on the statutory basis in the Renewable Energy Heat Act, detailed provisions and also more detailed requirements for the financial support have been set forth in guidelines on the promotion of measures for the utilization of renewable energies in the heat market.

956. Also under the revised Building Energy Act, financial support for measures of energy efficiency and using renewable energy play a decisive role, see sections 89 et seqq. GEG. However, promotion means within the central programme heating with renewable energy have been stopped end of 2020,[628] so that the continuance of specific support programmes is under political debate.

957. The Building Energy Act also replaced the previous framework that was in place on energy saving in buildings and energy efficient installation engineering within buildings, previously governed by the Energy Saving Act (*EnEG*)[629] and the Regulation on the Energy-Saving Heat Protection and Energy-Saving Systems Engineering of Buildings (*EnEV*).[630] This legislation originally resulted from the energy crisis in the 1970s.[631] It has been amended in 2013 to transform the requirements resulting of Directive 2010/31/EU on the energy performance of buildings. But it already foresaw that from 2021 on, new buildings shall in principle be constructed as 'nearly zero-energy building' (section 2a EnEG).

958. The Building Energy Act now requires to construct buildings as 'lowest energy building' (*Niedrigstenergiegebäude*, section 10 paragraph 1 GEG). This requires that the total energy demand of the building needs to remain within certain maximum values provided in the Building Energy Act, that energy losses for heating and cooling are avoided upon further provisions, and that the already mentioned obligations to cover a share of the energy demand of the building with renewable energy sources are met with (section 10 paragraph 2 GEG).

---

628. *See* BAFA, Programmende „Heizen mit Erneuerbaren Energien" am 31.12.2020, www.bafa.de, last access 1 May 2022.
629. Energieeinsparungsgesetz in the version of the publication of 1 Sep. 2005 (BGBl. I p. 2684).
630. Energieeinsparverordnung of 24 Jul. 2007 (BGBl. I p. 1519).
631. Christiane Nill-Theobald & Christian Theobald, *Grundzüge des Energiewirtschaftsrechts,* 2nd edn (München: C.H. Beck, 2008), 487.

959. Moreover, Part 5 of the GEG also sets forth rules on the issuance and use of an 'energy pass' for buildings.

Part VI. Interaction between Energy Law and Environmental Law

960. Various environmental law provisions and regulations have been adopted during the past decades and a large number of new provisions have been introduced into German law in the course of the implementation of European Directives. Almost all environmental regulations can potentially be relevant for the energy sector. Nature Protection law and the designation of protected sites, for instance, can be relevant for planning decisions and the choice of a specific site for an installation or the planning of overhead lines. Immissions Control Law, Water Law, and Legislation on Waste, Soil Protection, and Industrial Safety are relevant for the construction and operation of almost all installations. Moreover, an operator might possibly face environmental liability *inter alia* according to the 1990 Environmental Liability Act or the 2007 Environmental Damages Act.[632]

961. It is not possible to provide a comprehensive overview of all relevant statutes, provisions, and of all interrelations of energy law and environmental law in this publication. However, a short overview of the relevant statutory sources shall be given, see Chapter 1. Chapter 2 refer to regulations on emissions trading which are of particular importance for the energy sector. Chapter 3 explains the German Cogeneration Act, while Chapter 4 refers to the German law on energy efficiency.

---

632. With regard to environmental liability in Germany, *see* M. Petersen, *Umweltschadensgesetz*, Kommentar (Köln: Carl Heymanns Verlag, 2013). For information in English, *see* M. Petersen, 'The Environmental Liability Directive – Extending Nature Protection in Europe', *Environmental Law Review* 11 (2009): 5.

Chapter 1. Overview of Relevant Statutory Sources

962. Instead of one single regime comprehensively regulating environmental law in Germany, German environmental law rather consists of a somewhat fragmented system of different regulations and provisions which refer to environmental law in different ways.[633] Of particular relevance are the following regulations:

Federal Immissions Control Act (*Bundes-Immissionsschutzgesetz, BImSchG*) and several Immissions Control Ordinances
Federal Nature Conservation Act (*Bundesnaturschutzgesetz, BNatSchG*)
Laws on Nature Conservation of the Federal States (*Landesnaturschutzgesetze*)
Federal Water Resources Act (*Wasserhaushaltsgesetz, WHG*)
Water Acts of the Federal States (*Landeswassergesetze*)
Federal Soil Protection Act (*Bundes-Bodenschutzgesetz, BBodSchG*)
Federal Soil Protection and Contamination Ordinance (*Bundes-Bodenschutz- und Altlastenverordnung, BBodSchV*)
Environmental Impact Assessment Act (*Gesetz über die Umweltverträglichkeitsprüfung, UVPG*)
Act for the Promotion of Closed Substance Cycle Management and Ensuring Environmentally Compatible Waste Disposal (*Kreislaufwirtschaftsgesetz, KrWG*)
Environmental Liability Act (*Umwelthaftungsgesetz, UmweltHG*)
Environmental Damages Act (*Umweltschadensgesetz, USchadG*)
Environmental Information Act (*Umweltinformationsgesetz, UIG*)
Environmental Appeals Act (*Umweltrechtsbehelfsgesetz, UmwRG*) etc.

963. German environmental law has been developed over many years and the fact that the provisions are scattered across many different laws has been criticized frequently. There are environmental laws which refer to different sectors and focus on specific environmental issues such as air quality control, noise protection, waste management, nature protection, soil protection, environmental liability, etc., but there is no comprehensive regulation of environmental law in a single statute.

964. Against this background it has been advocated that a comprehensive Environmental Code should be adopted in order to harmonize and simplify German environmental law. However, after heated discussions and various attempts to adopt such an Environmental Code, the efforts have so far not led to a result.[634] The latest attempt to adopt an Environmental Code failed at the end of 2009. But, following

---

633. For detailed information about German environmental law, *see*, for instance, Landmann & Rohmer et al., *Umweltrecht*, 96th edn (München: C.H. Beck, 2022); S. Schlacke, *Umweltrecht*, 8th edn (Baden-Baden: Nomos Verlagsgesellschaft, 2021).
634. For information in English, *see* 'Environmental Code' on the webpage of the umweltbundesamt: www.umweltbundesamt.de, last accessed 1 May 2022.

the aforementioned discussions concerning the adoption of an Environmental Code, at least some environment-related regulations such as the Federal Nature Conservation Act and the Federal Water Resources Act have been amended substantially.[635]

635. H.J. Müggenborg & A. Hentschel, 'Neues Wasser- und Naturschutzrecht', *NJW* (2010): 961; H.P. Michler & F. Möller, 'Änderungen der Eingriffsregelung durch das BNatSchG 2010', *NuR* (2011): 81; M. Gellermann, 'Naturschutzrecht nach der Novelle des Bundesnaturschutzgesetzes', *NVwZ* (2010): 73; M. Kotulla, 'Das novellierte Wasserhaushaltsgesetz', *NVwZ* (2010): 79.

Chapter 2. Emissions Trading

§1. Background

965. German legislation on climate change and emissions trading has been strongly influenced by legislation on international and EU level. Therefore, a short overview of the most important steps for addressing climate change on the international and the EU level will be presented first.

966. In 1992, the United Nations Framework Convention on Climate Change (UNFCCC)[636] came into force which sets out an overall framework for intergovernmental efforts to handle the challenge posed by climate change. With 195 Parties, the Convention enjoys near-universal membership. The Convention aims to stabilize GHG concentrations in the atmosphere at a level that will prevent a further climate change by human interferences.[637]

967. Since the provisions of the UNFCCC were not sufficient to reach the goals agreed upon therein, the Kyoto Protocol[638] was adopted in 1997. The protocol entered into force on 16 February 2005. The protocol is an internationally binding legal framework which focuses on the reduction and stabilization of GHG Emissions. The EU and its Member States ratified the Kyoto Protocol in 2002 and are therefore bound by its provisions. While the Convention encourages industrialized countries to stabilize GHG emissions, the protocol commits them to do so. The protocol's first commitment period started in 2008 and ended in 2012.

968. Under the Kyoto Protocol, countries shall meet their targets primarily through national measures. However, there have been three global market-based mechanisms:

(1) Emissions trading.
(2) Clean development mechanism (CDM).
(3) Joint implementation (JI).

969. To ensure the agreed targets are complied with, the Kyoto Protocol *inter alia* set out an emissions management system. This works on the principle that for each tonne of GHG emitted, industrialized countries must be in possession of an internationally recognized emissions certificate. The Kyoto Protocol stipulates that each industrial country is assigned a defined quantity of certificates (Assigned Amount Units, AAUs) that entitle it to emit a certain volume of GHGes. The limitation of certificates shall create incentives for technological innovation or changes in fuel to bring down emissions.

---

636. United Nations Framework Convention on Climate Change (New York, 9 May 1992).
637. For more information, *see* the information provided on the webpage of the United Nations Framework Convention on Climate Change, available at http://unfccc.int
638. Kyoto Protocol to the United Nations Framework Convention on Climate Change (Kyoto, 11 Dec. 1997).

970. Aside from trading in AAUs, there are the project-based mechanisms Joint Implementation and CDM. With the Joint Implementation Mechanism, industrialized countries are credited with emission reductions attained by investing in other industrialized countries. The reduction can then be traded as Emission Reduction Units (ERU). The CDM focuses on infrastructure improvements in developing and emerging economies. By participating in the project-based mechanisms JI and CDM, further emission certificates can be earned.

971. Towards the end of the first commitment period of the Kyoto Protocol, the parties tried to negotiate and to ratify a new international framework. After unsuccessful negotiations in 2009 in Copenhagen, Denmark, the 2010 climate conference in Cancún, Mexico, managed to achieve at least some first compromises and concessions. Following the 2011 United Nations Climate Change Conference in Durban, South Africa, an agreement to extend the protocol to 2020 and to set a date of 2015 for the development of a successor document was reached on 8 December 2012 at the end of the United Nations Climate Change Conference in Doha, Qatar.

972. On 12 December 2015, the Paris Agreement has been adopted by 196 Parties. The Paris Agreement aims at holding the increase in global average temperature to 'well below 2° C, and to pursue efforts to limit the temperature increase to 1.5° C above pre-industrial levels. To achieve this aim, the Paris Agreement works with a system of nationally determined contributions which each party shall prepare, communicate, and maintain. For more information on the international level, see the information provided on the webpage of the UNFCCC.[639]

973. In the EU, the EU's Emissions Allowance Trading Scheme commenced operation on 1 January 2005, governed by Directive 2003/87/EC.[640] It constitutes the world's largest emissions trading scheme and is viewed as the most important climate protection measure in the European Union.[641] The Directive was followed by the so-called Linking Directive,[642] which enhanced the EU ETS in 2004.

974. There have been further developments of the EU ETS[643] – for example, the adoption of Directive 2008/101/EC which includes aviation activities in the scheme for GHG emission allowance trading[644] and the adoption of Directive 2009/29/

639. http://unfccc.int
640. Directive 2003/87/EC of the European Parliament and of the Council of 13 Oct. 2006 establishing a Scheme for Greenhouse Gas Emission Allowance Trading within the Community and amending Council Directive 96/61 (2003) OJ L275/32.
641. C. Kreuter-Kirchhof, 'Emissionshandel und Erneuerbare Energien Richtlinie, Instrumente zur Umsetzung der Klimaschutzstrategie der EU', *ZUR* (2019): 396, 398.
642. Directive 2004/101/EC of the European Parliament and of the Council of 27 Oct. 2004 amending Directive 2003/87/EC establishing a Scheme for Greenhouse Gas Emission Allowance Trading within the Community, in Respect of the Kyoto Protocols Project Mechanisms (2004) OJ L338/18.
643. W. F. Spieth / M. Hamer. 'Die neuen Zuteilungsregelungen für Industrieanlagen in der dritten Phase des europäischen Emissionshandelssystems', *NVwZ* (2011): 920.
644. Directive 2008/101/EC of the European Parliament and of the Council of 19 Nov. 2008 amending Directive 2003/87/EC so as to include aviation activities in the scheme for greenhouse gas emission allowance trading within the Community (2009) OJ L8/3; for more information *see* M.

EC.[645] For information about latest developments, see information provided on the webpage on the European Commission.[646]

975. Last but not least, the EC Registry Regulation[647] can be mentioned, which establishes a Union Registry for the trading period of the emissions trading scheme which commenced on 1 January 2013.

§2. German Legislation on Emissions Trading

976. The basic regulation for the implementation of the Emissions Trading Directive is the German Greenhouse Gas Emissions Trading Act (TEHG).[648] In 2004, it laid – in connection with further legislation – the legal framework for the trade in emission certificates in Germany. Pursuant to section 1 TEHG, the purpose of the Act is to create a basis for trading emission certificates in a community-wide trading system in order to contribute to a cost-effective reduction of GHGs to global climate protection. The Linking Directive has been implemented by the German Project-Based Mechanisms Act (ProMechG).[649]

977. The activities listed in Annex 1 Part 2 of the TEHG require a permit pursuant to section 4 paragraph TEHG. Within the activities, many larger industrial plants that emit greenhouse gases are covered. Also included are larger energy production units based on fossil fuels.

978. Pursuant to section 7 paragraph 1 TEHG, every operator of an installation subject to emissions trading must dispense the emission allowances corresponding to the emissions caused in the previous year. Emissions allowances can be bought and sold via emissions trading, and greenhouse gas emissions thus receive a price.

979. National Allocation Plans (NAP), the Allocation Acts (Gesetz über den nationalen Zuteilungsplan für Treibhausgas-Emissionsberechtigungen in der Zuteilungsperiode 2005–2007; Gesetz über den nationalen Zuteilungsplan für

---

Petersen, 'The Legality of the EU's Stand-Alone Approach to the Climate Impact of Aviation: The Express Role Given to the ICAO by the Kyoto Protocol', *Review of European Community and International Environmental Law (RECIEL)* 17 (2008): 196.

645. Directive 2009/29/EC of the European Parliament and of the Council of 23 Apr. 2009 amending Directive 2003/87/EC so as to improve and extend the greenhouse gas emission allowance trading scheme of the Community (2009) OJ L 140.
646. European Commission, EU Emissions Trading Scheme, http://ec.europa.eu, last accessed 1 May 2022.
647. Commission Regulation (EU) No. 389/2013 of 2 May 2013 establishing a Union Registry pursuant to Directive 2003/87/EC of the European Parliament and of the Council, Decisions No. 280/2004/EC and No. 406/2009/EC of the European Parliament and of the Council and repealing Commission Regulations (EU) No. 920/2010 and No. 1193/2011.
648. Gesetz über den Handel mit Berechtigungen zur Emission von Treibhausgasen (Treibhausgas-Emissionshandelsgesetz) of 8 Jul. 2004 (BGBl. I S. 1578), amended fundamentally in 2011 (BGBl. I. S. 1475).
649. Projekt-Mechanismen-Gesetz of 22 Sep. 2005 (BGBl. I S. 2826).

Treibhausgas-Emissionsberechtigungen in der Zuteilungsperiode 2008–2012[650]) and the Allocation Ordinances (Verordnung über die Zuteilung von Treibhausgas-Emissionsberechtigungen in der Zuteilungsperiode 2005–2007; Verordnung über die Zuteilung von Treibhausgas-Emissionsberechtigungen in der Zuteilungsperiode 2008–2012; Verordnung über die Zuteilung von Treibhausgas-Emissionsberechtigungen in der Handelsperiode 2013 bis 2020[651]) specified the allocation rules and the amounts of allowances to be allocated to participating companies in Germany from 2005 to 2020.

980. The Allocation Acts provided the legal basis for the implementation of the allocation plan, defining the total amount of emissions allowances, and the rules by which they had to be distributed to the participating installations in the energy sector. The Allocation Ordinances were the implementation regulations that contained detailed obligations for individual allocations and the verification of allocation applications by installation operators. From the third trading period, emission allowances in principle shall be auctioned (Article 10 of Directive 2003/87/EC).[652] However, free allocation of allowances – which has been subject of debate – also continues in the fourth trading period starting on 1 January 2021, albeit to a decreasing extent.

981. The competent national authority is the German Emissions Trading Authority (*Deutsche Emissionshandelsstelle – DEHSt*) at the Federal Environment Agency.[653]

§3. Fuel Emissions Trading Act (BEHG)

982. From 2021 onwards, the Fuel Emissions Trading Act (*Brennstoffemissionshandelsgesetz, BEHG*) creates a system of national emissions trading in addition to the European emissions trading scheme.[654] Companies that bring heating oil, liquid or natural gas, coal, petrol or diesel on the market must acquire and dispense allowances for the emission volume that is attributable to them as a result of bringing the fuels on the market. This is intended to achieve CO_2 pricing also outside the EU Emissions Trading Scheme (so-called non-ETS sector). Double counting with the European emissions trading system is to be avoided.

983. The new national emissions trading system (nEHS) started in 2021 with a fixed price system. After the *Bundestag* and *Bundesrat* agreed on an increase of the initial fixed prices, the fixed price is to be 25 euros per tonne in 2021, rising to a

650. Zuteilungsgesetz 2012 of 7 Aug. 2007 (BGBl. I S. 1788).
651. Zuteilungsverordnung 2020 of 26 Sep. 2011 (BGBl. I S. 1921).
652. C. Kreuter-Kirchhof, 'Emissionshandel und Erneuerbare Energien Richtlinie, Instrumente zur Umsetzung der Klimaschutzstrategie der EU', *ZUR* (2019): 396, 398 et seq.
653. For information, *see* www.dehst.de.
654. Brennstoffemissionshandelsgesetz of 12 Dec. 2019 (BGBl. I p. 2728).

fixed price of 55 euros per tonne by 2025 (see section 10 BEHG). Initially, therefore, the price for fuel emissions will not be formed on a market, but will be determined by regulation.[655]

984. From 2026, a market-based price mechanism for the emission rights covered by the BEHG shall begin through auctioning. Whether the BEHG will achieve the envisaged steering effect is subject of critical debate.[656]

655. I. Zenke & C. Telschow, 'CO_2-Bepreisung durch nationalen Emissionshandel', *EnWZ* (2020): 157, 158 et seq.

656. *See* I. Zenke & C. Telschow, 'CO_2-Bepreisung durch nationalen Emissionshandel', *EnWZ* (2020): 157, 162 et seq.; C. Franzius, 'Auf dem Weg zum Klimaschutzgesetz', *EnWZ* (2019): 435, 439.

Chapter 3. Cogeneration

985. Electricity generated through cogeneration in Germany reached a share of 19% of total electricity production in 2019 and has thereby increased during recent years.[657] Cogeneration is promoted by a special statute, the Cogeneration Act (*Kraft-Wärme-Kopplungsgesetz, KWKG 2020*).[658] This statute has similar aims and methods as the Renewable Energy Sources Act. Before this Act was implemented, cogeneration was only supported by the prohibition of abusive practices under competition law. As a result, remuneration for cogeneration was only available according to the principle of 'avoided costs'.[659]

986. The Cogeneration Act aims at increasing the net electricity generation of cogeneration to 110 terawatt hours by 2020 and to 120 terawatt hours by 2025, section 1 paragraph 1 KWKG. Cogeneration is defined in section 2 Nr. 13 KWKG as the simultaneous conversion of energy into electricity and useful heat in a stationary technical facility. The statute regulates the take-off and remuneration for electricity generated through cogeneration in plants which run on hard coal, lignite, waste, waste heat, biomass, gaseous or fluid combustibles (section 1 paragraph 2 Nr. 1 KWKG). The costs of the promotion of cogeneration by the KWKG are allocated through an equalization scheme.

987. The duty of the grid operator to connect cogeneration plants to their grid and to grant priority access to the electricity fed-in is stipulated in section 3 KWKG. By implementing the duty of this priority take-off in 2009, the legislator further equated cogeneration plants with electricity generation from renewable energy sources.[660]

988. Operators of cogeneration plants with an electrical cogeneration capacity of more than 100 kW must market the electricity generated through cogeneration directly or consume it themselves, section 4 paragraph 1 KWKG. Therefore, similar to the Renewable Energy Sources Act, the Cogeneration Act now generally requires direct selling of electricity from larger cogeneration installations in the market to foster market integration. Direct marketing exists if the electricity is supplied to a third party, whereas a third party may also be an end consumer.

989. If no obligation to sell electricity on the market exists, operators of cogeneration installations can request from the grid operator to take off the electricity from cogeneration. In this case, the grid operator has to pay a usual price for the

657. Umweltbundesamt, Kraft-Wärme-Kopplung (KWK) im Energiesystem, www.umweltbundesamt.de, last accessed 1 May 2022.
658. Gesetz für die Erhaltung, die Modernisierung und den Ausbau der Kraft-Wärme-Kopplung, Kraft-Wärme-Kopplungsgesetz, of 21 Dec. 2015 (BGBl. I S. 2498).
659. P. Salje, *EEG*, 5th edn (Köln: Carl Heymanns Verlag, 2009), Einführung para. 20.
660. F. Buchmann & M. Hirschmann, 'Die Novelle des KWK-Gesetzes', *RdE* (2009): 204, 206.

electricity which is an average price for base load electricity in the preceding quarter at the European Energy Exchange (EEX) in Leipzig, section 4 paragraph 3 KWKG.

990. Electricity generated through cogeneration may receive a certain payment addition as further detailed in sections 5 et seqq. KWKG. Only the share of the electricity generated through cogeneration is promoted by the KWKG. The eligibility for the payment is subject to a number of preconditions, and differs upon the installed capacity of the cogeneration installation.

991. Importantly, one precondition to receive financial support under the KWKG is an approval of the cogeneration installation by the Federal Office for Economic Affairs and Export Control (BAFA) under section 10 KWKG.

992. Cogeneration installations can also fall under the promotion mechanism of the Renewable Energy Sources Act. In order to avoid double promotion, the Cogeneration Act does not apply if the electricity produced by cogeneration is remunerated under the Renewable Energy Sources Act (section 1 paragraph 3 KWKG).

Chapter 4. Energy Efficiency

993. The German legislator transformed the earlier European Directive 2006/32/EC on energy end-use efficiency and energy services by adopting a Statute on Energy Services and other Energy Efficiency Measures (hereinafter: *EDL-G*).[661] The European Framework on energy efficiency has been developed further with the EU Energy Efficiency Directive 2012/27/EU[662] and Directive 2018/2002/EU.[663]

994. The EDL-G aims at increasing the efficiency of energy use by final customers in Germany and to achieve cost-effectiveness by means of energy services and other energy efficiency measures (section 3 paragraph 1 sentence 1 EDL-G). To pursue this aim, the Federal Government shall identify certain goals for energy savings pursuant to section 3 paragraph 1 sentence 2 EDL-G.

995. In essence, the Statute on Energy Services and other Energy Efficiency Measures tries to develop a market for energy-saving products and services in order to comply with these energy-saving goals. How this market shall be incentivized and how it shall work in practice is not described in detail. Section 3 paragraph 2 EDL-G merely provides that the energy-saving goals must be met by 'economic and appropriate measures'. In particular, the necessary mechanisms, incentives, and general framework for energy efficiency measures will be constituted and the preconditions for the development of a market for energy services and other energy efficiency measures shall be set up. The public authorities will set an example by fostering the use of energy efficiency measures, and thus incentivize the use of energy efficiency measures of other market participants.

996. The main duty applying to private market participants is an information obligation under section 4 EDL-G. Accordingly, energy suppliers must inform their final customers every year about the effectiveness of energy efficiency measures. They must also inform them about the available offers exercised by energy service providers and providers of energy efficiency measures in particular. Moreover, the Federal Office of Economics and Export Control will also serve the purpose of a Federal Office for Energy Efficiency.[664] *Inter alia*, this Office keeps a list of suppliers of energy efficiency services and other energy efficiency measures.

661. Gesetz über Energiedienstleistungen und andere Energieeffizienzmaßnahmen of 4 Nov. 2010 (BGBl. I p. 1483).
662. Directive 2012/27/EU of 25 Oct. 2012 on energy efficiency, amending Directives 2009/125/EC and 2010/30/EU and repealing Directives 2004/8/EC and 2006/32/EC.
663. Directive 2018/2002/EU of 11 Dec. 2018 amending Directive 2012/27/EU on energy efficiency, L 328/210.
664. *See* closer www.bfee-online.de, last access: 1 May 2022.

997. The Statute on Energy Services and other Energy Efficiency Measures has been criticized for its lack of concrete binding obligations.[665] More demanding obligations have been withdrawn in the legislative process. Indeed, the mere information obligation in particular is in contrast with the important role of energy efficiency. For energy efficiency in the buildings sector see above Part V, Chapter 7.

665. C. Thole & M. Kachel, 'Zahnloser Tiger Energieeffizienzgesetz – Handlungsspielräume für Energieversorgungsunternehmen', *IR* (2010): 122 et seq..

Part VII. Interaction between Energy Law and Competition Law

998. The Competition Law applying on the German energy sector derives from European and German law. Competition law – next to the law of regulation – plays an important role in the attempt to create competitive energy markets. This part provides an overview of the relevant statutory sources,[666] gives brief information of the relevant provisions under European Law and describes some aspects of the application of the German GWB on the energy sector in Germany.

666. All legal sources are also available on the webpage of the Federal Competition Authority, the Bundeskartellamt, www.bundeskartellamt.de.

Chapter 1. Overview of the Relevant Statutory Sources

999. Under European Law, the central norms are provided by Articles 101 and 102 of the TFEU (ex-Articles 81 and 82 EC Treaty). These norms belong to the primary European Law and have thus binding effect also upon all citizens and undertakings. Council Regulation (EC) No. 1/2003 of 16 December 2002 on the implementation of the rules on competition laid down in Articles 81 and 82 of the Treaty further specifies the rules of (now) Articles 101 and 102 TFEU.

1000. As far as merger control is concerned, the central statutory source is the Council Regulation (EC) No. 139/2004 of 20 January 2004 on the control of concentrations between undertakings (hereinafter: EC Merger Regulation). Also, these provisions have direct binding effects since they are issued in the form of a regulation.

1001. The central German statute for the Competition Law, as far as cartels, abusive practices, and merger control are concerned, is the GWB.[667] This statute contains a ban on cartels in its section 1 GWB. Sections 19 et seqq. GWB prohibit abusive practices, and sections 35 et seqq. GWB provide rules on merger control.

1002. The Federal Competition Authority, the *Bundeskartellamt*, issued Guidelines on the setting of fines. The *Bundeskartellamt* also established a lenience programme under which it can grant cartel participants, who contribute to uncovering a cartel, a waiver or a reduction of fines.[668] Administrative charges which may be applied are governed by the Regulation on the administrative charges by competition authorities (*KartKostV*).[669]

1003. For the protection of fair competition and thus concerning the behaviour of participants *within* the market, the German Act against Unfair Competition (*UWG*) applies.[670] This statute is not further treated in this part.

---

667. Gesetz gegen Wettbewerbsbeschränkungen in the version of the publication of 26 Jun. 2013 (BGBl. I p. 1750, 3245).
668. *See inter alia* Bundeskartellamt, Bundeskartellamt publishes new guidelines on its leniency programme and the setting of fines, available at www.bundeskartellamt.de, last accessed 1 May 2022.
669. Verordnung über die Kosten der Kartellbehörden of 16 Nov. 1970 (BGBl. I p. 1535).
670. Gesetz gegen den unlauteren Wettbewerb, in the version of the publication of 3 Mar. 2010 (BGBl. I p. 254).

Chapter 2. Overview of European Competition Law with Regard to the Energy Sector

1004. Like for other sectors, the competition rules of the EU play an important role with regard to the energy sector. This is also true for energy companies whose activities deal (also) in the interstate trade. Consequently, the provisions on competition in the TFEU may be applicable. With the aim of liberalizing the energy markets, the European Commission has made increased use of the competition rules on the energy markets.

1005. Articles 101 and 102 TFEU are applicable on electricity and gas undertakings.[671] Belonging to the primary law of the EU, Articles 101 and 102 TFEU are directly applicable on private undertakings. The articles regulate with direct binding effect which forms of cartels and abusive practices are forbidden. Exceptions may arise from Article 106 paragraph 2 TFEU for undertakings entrusted with the operation of services of general economic interest.

§1. Ban on Cartels, Article 101 TFEU

1006. Article 101 TFEU prohibits unlawful coordination of the market behaviour of independent companies in the horizontal as well as in the vertical relationship to other undertakings. Its first paragraph reads:

> The following shall be prohibited as incompatible with the internal market: all agreements between undertakings, decisions by associations of undertakings and concerted practices which may affect trade between Member States and which have as their object or effect the prevention, restriction or distortion of competition within the internal market, and in particular those which:
>
> a) directly or indirectly fix purchase or selling prices or any other trading conditions;
> b) limit or control production, markets, technical development, or investment;
> c) share markets or sources of supply;
> d) apply dissimilar conditions to equivalent transactions with other trading parties, thereby placing them at a competitive disadvantage;
> e) make the conclusion of contracts subject to acceptance by the other parties of supplementary obligations which, by their nature or according to commercial usage, have no connection with the subject of such contracts.

671. ECJ, judgment of 27 Apr. 1994, C-393/92, ECR. 1994, I-1477– *Almelo*; I. Van Bael & J.F. Bellis, *Competition Law of the European Community*, 4th edn (The Hague: Kluwer Law International, 2005), 1369; V. Emmerich, *Kartellrecht*, 11th edn (München: C.H. Beck, 2008), s. 39 para. 8; Kundan in: W. Danner & C. Theobald, *Energierecht* (München: C.H. Beck, 67. Addition 2010), II WettR B 1 para. 3.

1007. The second paragraph declares any agreements or decisions void which are prohibited by these material conditions. Article 101 paragraph 3 TFEU provides for highly practical exemptions from the general ban on cartels.

1008. Article 101 paragraph 1 TFEU comprises agreements, decisions, and concerted practices. In general, these terms are defined broadly. Their common feature is a form of coordinated behaviour. An agreement exists if the parties have expressed their common will to conduct on the market in a specific way.[672] It is not relevant what form this agreement has, or whether the agreement is a valid contract under national law.

1009. One-sided actions without any (implied) consent of the other party cannot be viewed as an agreement, but may need to be examined under the conditions of Article 102 TFEU.[673] Moreover, agreements within concerns, in particular between the holding company and its subsidiaries, are principally excluded from the ban on cartels in Article 101 TFEU. In this case, the companies form a unit in a way that they cannot exercise a separate will in their market behaviours. According to the European Court of Justice, relations within an economic unit cannot amount to an agreement or a concerted practice. Instead, the subsidiary in this case does not freely determine its conduct but carries out the instructions of the parent company.[674]

1010. The Regulation 1/2003 is of central relevance for the concrete application and procedure in cases falling under Article 101 (and Article 102) TFEU. Before, agreements with an impact on the competition could be announced to the state authorities and allowed for under certain conditions. Under the Regulation 1/2003, however, any measure falling under the conditions of Article 101 paragraph 3 EC is automatically exempted from the prohibition according to paragraph 1 by law.

§2. Prohibition of Abusive Practices, Article 102 TFEU

1011. Article 102 TFEU does not prohibit the achievement of a dominant position in the market. Instead, this dominant position of an undertaking is a prerequisite for the application of this article.

1012. The first paragraph of Article 102 TFEU reads:

> Any abuse by one or more undertakings of a dominant position within the internal market or in a substantial part of it shall be prohibited as incompatible with the internal market in so far as it may affect trade between Member States.

---

672. T. Lettl, *Kartellrecht* (München: C.H. Beck, 2005), para. 54, with further references on the jurisdiction.
673. T. Lettl, Kartellrecht (München: C.H. Beck, 2005), para. 56.
674. ECJ, judgment of 24 Oct. 1996, C-73/95 P, para. 16 – *Viho Europe BV v. Commission*.

1013. The second paragraph provides for particular examples for abusive practices. Contrary to Article 101 TFEU, Article 102 TFEU does not provide for any possibility of exemptions.

1014. The European Court of Justice defines the dominant position as a position 'of economic strength enjoyed by an undertaking which enables it to prevent effective competition being maintained on the relevant market by giving it the power to behave to an appreciable extent independently of its competitors, customers, and ultimately of its consumers'.[675] Determining the relevant market is thus of high importance for the application of the provision.

§3. Merger Control

1015. The rules on merger control shall safeguard a market structure which enables free competition. The relevant statutory source is Council Regulation (EC) No. 139/2004 of 20 January 2004 on the control of concentrations between undertakings (hereinafter: EC Merger Regulation).

1016. As an example, the acquisition of the gas business of two subsidiaries of MOL (MOL MWT and MOL Storage) by E.ON was approved only subject to conditions and obligations. To counter anticompetitive effects in the Hungarian gas and electricity markets, E.ON offered remedies. These remedies would result in an ownership unbundling of the gas production and transmission activities retained by MOL. It would also cover the commercial activities acquired by E.ON.[676]

675. ECJ, Case C-27/76, para. 66 – *United Brands Company and United Brands Continentaal BV v. Commission*.
676. *See* the European Press Release IP/05/1658 of 21 Dec. 2005.

Chapter 3. Act against Restraints of Competition (GWB)

1017. Until 1998, the public utility industry had been exempted from the application of central provisions of the German Act against Restraints of Competition (*GWB*).[677] Instead, a system of regional monopolies existed. The energy supply companies concluded 'demarcation contracts' (*Demarkationsverträge*) which, together with concession contracts, ensured this system of separate areas of supply. The demarcation contracts were concluded between energy supply companies with each other as well as between energy supply companies and municipalities. It was argued that the division of areas of supply would be necessary for a secure and cheap energy supply. Merely with a special supervision of energy companies, the cartel authorities were able to exercise a control.[678]

1018. This was changed in 1998. Since then, the clauses of the German GWB generally have been applicable on energy companies. This chapter introduces the provisions of this Act on cartels, on abusive practices as well as on merger control.

§1. Relationship between GWB and EnWG

1019. Liberalization led to the amendments of the EnWG described above, and made the energy industry subject to an intensified regulation. Thus, the relation between regulation and application of competition law needed to be clarified. The relationship between the rules of the EnWG and the GWB is governed by the clauses in section 111 EnWG and section 130 paragraph 3 GWB.

1020. Section 111 paragraph 1 sentence 1 EnWG declares that sections 19, 20, and 29 GWB are not applicable insofar as the EnWG or regulations based on the EnWG provide for explicitly exclusive rules. The provisions in part 3 of the EnWG and in the subsequent regulations are such exclusive rules (section 111 paragraph 2 EnWG). As a result, particularly the rules on grid connection and grid access of the EnWG are reserved for the regulatory authorities and not subject to supervision of the cartel authorities. Particularly for the topic of grid fee regulation, the EnWG needs to be considered as the 'special' Act.[679]

1021. However, this still leaves the cartel authorities a wide scope of competencies with regard to the energy sector, particularly in the fields of sales and supply of energy. The competencies of the cartel authorities comprise the supervision on prices of electricity and gas, the control of energy supply companies and the merger

677. The exemptions were provided in ss 103/103a of the former GWB.
678. For the historic development *see* V. Emmerich, *Kartellrecht*, 11th edn (München: C.H. Beck, 2008), s. 39 paras 13 and 30 with further references.
679. F. Hölscher in: G. Britz, J. Hellermann & G. Hermes, *EnWG, Energiewirtschaftsgesetz*, 3rd edn (München: C.H. Beck, 2015), s. 111 para. 1.

control. Also, insofar the European Commission does not take a decision, the national cartel authorities may be competent for the application of European competition law.[680]

§2. Prohibition of Agreements Restricting Competition

1022. The German GWB has been amended in 2005 with the aim to design the ban on cartels basically identical with (now) Article 101 TFEU. The material provision of section 1 GWB is since then mainly identical with Article 101 paragraph 1 TFEU. In effect, this will even more render the interpretation of the German ban on cartels identical with the European interpretation.[681]

1023. Section 1 GWB reads:

> Agreements between undertakings, decisions by associations of undertakings and concerted practices, which have as their object or effect the prevention, restriction or distortion of competition, shall be prohibited.[682]

§3. Prohibition of Abusive Practices

1024. The general prohibition of an abusive exploitation of a dominant position is contained in section 19 paragraph 1 GWB. Accordingly, any 'abuse of a dominant position by one or several undertakings is prohibited'. Section 18 GWB defines in which cases an undertaking has a dominant position in the market.

1025. More concrete examples for an abusive exploitation are provided in section 19 paragraph 2 GWB. In practice, these examples are generally examined first in order to determine an abusive behaviour on the market. If none of these case groups is relevant for the facts of the case, the behaviour can still be prohibited under the general terms of the first paragraph.

1026. Section 19 paragraph 2 number 4 GWB incorporates the essential-facility-doctrine[683] by stating that an abuse of a dominant position exists in particular if the dominant undertaking:

> refuses to supply another undertaking with such a good or commercial service for adequate consideration, in particular to grant it access to data, networks or other infrastructure facilities, and if the supply or the granting of access is

680. F. Hölscher in: G. Britz, J. Hellermann & G. Hermes, *EnWG, Energiewirtschaftsgesetz,* 3rd edn (München: C.H. Beck, 2015), s. 111 paras 10–15.
681. F. Ekey, *Grundriss des Wettbewerbs- und Kartellrechts* (Heidelberg: C.F. Müller, 2006), para. 468.
682. Translations of the provisions of the GWB have been taken from a translation offered by the Bundeskartellamt, available via www.bundeskartellamt.de.
683. Kundan in: W. Danner & C. Theobald, *Energierecht* (München: C.H. Beck, 67. Addition 2010), II WettR B 1 paras 4 and 9.

objectively necessary in order to operate on an upstream or downstream market and the refusal threatens to eliminate effective competition on that market, unless there is an objective justification for the refusal.

1027. With the aim of combating abusive practices in the energy sector, the legislator provided a special norm particularly for the price control in the energy sector in section 29 GWB. The norm reads:

> An undertaking, which is a supplier of electricity or pipeline gas (public utility company) on a market in which it, either alone or together with other public utility companies, has a dominant position, is prohibited from abusing such position by
>
> 1. demanding fees or other business terms which are less favorable than those of other public utility companies or undertakings in comparable markets, unless the public utility company provides evidence that such deviation is objectively justified, with the reversal of the burden of demonstration and proof only applying in proceedings before the competition authorities, or
> 2. demanding fees which unreasonably exceed the costs.
>
> Costs that would not arise to the same extent if competition existed must not be taken into consideration in determining whether an abuse within the meaning of sentence 1 exists. §§19 and 20 remain unaffected.

1028. With the task to enforce this provision, the *Bundeskartellamt* set up a special decision division to combat the abuse of dominant market positions by suppliers of gas and electricity in 2008.

§4. Merger Control

1029. This section will provide a brief overview on the merger control under the GWB, with a focus on relevant concentrations in the energy markets.

I. Principles of Merger Control

1030. According to section 36 paragraph 1 GWB, the general rule of German Merger Law is that a concentration which significantly restricts effective competition, in particular which is expected to create or strengthen a dominant position, shall be prohibited by the *Bundeskartellamt*. However, this general prohibition does not apply under specific circumstances, in particular if the undertakings concerned prove that the concentration will also lead to improvements of the conditions of competition and that these improvements will outweigh the disadvantages of dominance.

Section 35 GWB clarifies on which undertakings the rules on merger control will apply. Due to its first paragraph (but also see the further provisions in the subsequent paragraphs) this is the case:

if in the last business year preceding the concentration

1. the combined aggregate worldwide turnover of all the undertakings concerned was more than EUR 500 million, and
2. the domestic turnover of at least one undertaking concerned was more than EUR 50 million and that of another undertaking concerned was more than EUR 17.5 million.

1031. Section 35 paragraph 3 GWB clarifies that the merger control under the provisions of the GWB is not applicable where the European Commission has exclusive jurisdiction pursuant to Council Regulation (EC) No. 139/2004.

1032. Section 37 GWB defines what constitutes a 'concentration'. Concentrations need to be notified to the *Bundeskartellamt* pursuant to section 39 GWB. This duty applies for the undertakings participating in the concentration, and in certain cases also for the seller. The notification needs to provide the cartel authority with detailed information on the concentration. The *Bundeskartellamt* has the right to demand certain further information.

1033. If a further examination of the concentration is necessary, the *Bundeskartellamt* will enter into a 'main examination proceeding'. It will notify the undertaking thereof within a deadline of one month after receipt of the complete notification. In case the *Bundeskartellamt* exceeds this deadline, it may not prohibit the concentration (section 40 paragraph 1 GWB). The *Bundeskartellamt* will decide within the main examination proceedings whether the concentration is prohibited or cleared (section 40 paragraph 2 GWB). This generally needs to be done within a deadline of five months after receipt of the notification.

1034. Despite the merger control provisions, the concentration of REW and VEW to RWE and of Veba and Viag to E.ON have been allowed. The European Commission allowed the merger of Veba and Viag subject to conditions.[684] In examining the concentration of RWE and VEW, the *Bundeskartellamt* was aware of the strong market position of the 'duopol' of RWE and E.ON, which would be the result of the concentration. It therefore approved the merger of RWE and VEW only subject to comprehensive obligations.[685] Nevertheless, RWE and E.ON subsequently had high market shares in the relevant German energy market. Thus, in the following the *Bundeskartellamt* assessed critically further envisaged participations of

684. European Commission, OJ Nr. L 188 of 10 Jul. 2001 – *VEBA/VIAG.*
685. Bundeskartellamt, decision of 3 Jul. 2000, B8-309/99 – *RWE/VEW.*

RWE and E.ON with local and regional suppliers.[686] The *Bundeskartellamt* formulated a general presumption that the dominant position of these two companies in principle would be strengthened by *any* further participation.[687]

1035. Further material transactions have been announced from E.ON and RWE in March 2018 (E.ON/RWE Deal). E.ON acquired the majority shareholding of RWE in Innogy SE, and took over the electricity and gas sales activities as well as the distribution grid activities from Innogy. RWE received a minority shareholding in E.ON as well as a large share of the renewable energy generation of E.ON and participations in nuclear power stations. The E.ON/RWE Deal has been assessed and cleared in several procedures from European Commission and *Bundeskartellamt.*[688]

II. Ministerial Authorizations

1036. As an exception to the prohibition of concentration, the so-called ministerial authorization in section 42 GWB, became of high relevance for the German energy sector. This norm allows the Federal Minister of Economics and Energy to authorize a concentration which has been prohibited by the *Bundeskartellamt.* The underlying idea is that the net benefits of a concentration for the public may in a particular case outweigh the detrimental effect of such a concentration. Section 42 paragraph 1 sentence 1 GWB reads:

> The Federal Minister of Economics and Energy shall, upon application, authorize a concentration prohibited by the Bundeskartellamt if, in a specific case, the restraint of competition is outweighed by advantages to the economy as a whole following from the concentration, or if the concentration is justified by an overriding public interest.

1037. According to section 42 paragraph 1 sentence 3 GWB, such an authorization may be granted only 'if the scope of the restraint of competition does not jeopardize the market economy system'. Despite this restriction, the Minister of Economics and Technology two times approved the concentration of E.ON and Ruhrgas in 2002, which had been prohibited by the *Bundeskartellamt* before. This authorization strengthened the already dominating position of E.ON on the energy

686. Christiane Nill-Theobald & Christian Theobald, *Grundzüge des Energiewirtschaftsrechts,* 2nd edn (München: C.H. Beck, 2008), 204; V. Emmerich, *Kartellrecht,* 11th edn (München: C.H. Beck, 2008), s. 34 paras 38 and 54.

687. Bundeskartellamt, decision of 12 Sep. 2003, B8-Fa-21/03 – *E.ON/Stadtwerke Eschwege*; *see also* BGH, decision of 11 Nov. 2008, KVR 60/07, *NJW-RR*, 2009, 264; V. Emmerich, *Kartellrecht,* 11th edn (München: C.H. Beck, 2008), s. 34 para. 38; Christiane Nill-Theobald & Christian Theobald, *Grundzüge des Energiewirtschaftsrechts,* 2nd edn (München: C.H. Beck, 2008), 215.

688. *See* in more detail H. Hoch & C. Theobald, Schneider & C. Theobald, *Recht der Energiewirtschaft,* 5th edn (München: C.H. Beck, 2021), s. 6 paras 51–55.

markets. Therefore, the ministerial authorization has been criticized in legal observance as well as in the public discussion, pointing out the detrimental effect which it would have on competition in the energy markets.[689]

§5. Cartel Authorities, Sanctions and Measures

1038. The competent national authorities are the *Bundeskartellamt*, the Federal Ministry of for Economic Affairs and Climate Action, and the cartel authorities foreseen by the German *Länder*. Generally speaking, the *Bundeskartellamt* exercises the functions and powers assigned to the cartel authority by the Act against Restraints on Competition if the effect of the restrictive or discriminatory conduct or of a competition rule extends beyond the territory of a *Land*. If mainly the territory of a single *Land* is affected, the cartel authority of the *Land* is competent.

1039. The *Bundeskartellamt* is an independent competition authority with its seat in Bonn. It is organized in thirteen Decision Divisions (*Beschlussabteilungen*) which often control specific sectors. The Decision Divisions are autonomous and do not take any instructions in their decision procedure. All decisions of the divisions are taken by majority. The Decision Division particularly relevant for the energy sector is the Eighth Decision Division which deals with gas, electricity, and district heating as well as mineral oil, water, coal mining, and electro technology.[690]

1040. The *Bundeskartellamt* focuses on combating serious restrictions on competition by so-called hardcore cartels. It also founded a special unit for combating cartels (*Sonderkommission Kartellbekämpfung*, SKK). Moreover, the *Bundeskartellamt* provided a lenience programme. Under this programme persons and companies, who help in uncovering a cartel or prove its existence, may be exempted from penalties which otherwise would apply because of their involvement in the cartel.

1041. Under section 32 GWB, the cartel authorities may require the undertakings or associations of undertakings to end any infringement of a provision of the GWB, as well as any infringement of Article 101 or 102 TFEU. The cartel authority may impose all measures which are necessary to end the infringement effectively. The measures need to be proportional.

1042. Sections 32a–32e GWB provide for further competencies of the cartel authorities. For instance, they might order interim measures. The clauses also allow declaring commitments of undertakings binding for these undertakings. The cartel authority will then (under certain reservations) not exercise its power to take measures under section 32 GWB or to take interim measures. Under section 32d GWB, the cartel authority may in certain cases even withdraw the benefit granted by a block exemption regulation.

---

689. V. Emmerich, *Kartellrecht*, 11th edn (München: C.H. Beck, 2008), s. 34 para. 54 and s. 35 para. 3.
690. The organization chart can be found on the webpage of the *Bundeskartellamt*, www.bundeskartellamt.de.

1043. The administrative fines proceedings are stipulated in sections 81 et seqq. GWB. Section 81 GWB contains possible administrative fines for a range of breaches against the provisions of the GWB. The cartel authority may impose a fine in case of breaches of the material provision of Articles 101 and 102 TFEU and of sections 1 and 19–21 GWB. Also several violations against procedural requirements of the GWB, like duties of notification and disclosure, may entitle the cartel authority to impose fines.

1044. Section 33 GWB provides civil claims of affected parties in case of violation against any provision of the GWB, as well as Article 101 or 102 TFEU or a decision taken by the cartel authority. Parties can be entitled to raise claims for injunction as well as for damages.

1045. In case of an intentional or negligent violation of the mentioned substantial provision, the cartel authority may also order the 'skimming off' of the economic benefit (*Vorteilsabschöpfung*, section 34 GWB). It can require the undertaking to pay an amount of money corresponding to the economic benefit. Also certain associations may initiate this procedure (section 34a GWB), however, only with the aim to oblige the undertaking to pay the economic benefit gained to the federal budget.

§6. Monopolies Commission

1046. With its assessments, the Monopolies Commission (*Monopolkommission*) is of high relevance for the energy sector. The task of this Commission is to advise the government in the field of competition and regulation, and to assess the situation of concentrations in Germany, pursuant to the German Act against Restraints on Competition.[691] For this purpose, the Monopolies Commission prepares every two years an opinion assessing the situation and the foreseeable development of business concentration.

691. The Monopolies Commission has five members who are appointed for a term of four years by the Federal President on a proposal by the Federal Government.

Selected Bibliography

Altrock, M., V. Oschmann & C. Theobald. *EEG*. 2nd edn. München: C.H. Beck, 2008, 3rd edn, 2011 and 4rd edn, 2013.

Appel, M. & M. Ohms & J. Saurer, *BImSchG*. Berlin: Erich Schmidt Verlag, 2021.

Appel, M. 'Neues Recht für neue Netze – das Regelungsregime zur Beschleunigung des Stromnetzausbaus nach EnWG und NABEG'. *UPR* (2011): 406.

Bandulet, M., W. Elsenbast & M. Krug. 'Wettbewerbsprobleme und aktuelle Regulierungsansätze im deutschen Gasmarkt'. *InfrastrukturRecht* (2010): 245 et seq.

Baur, J.F., P. Salje & M. Schmidt-Preuß. *Regulierung in der Energiewirtschaft*. Köln: Carl Heymanns Verlag, 2011.

Becker, P. 'Das Energiekonzept der Bundesregierung'. *ZNER* (2010): 531.

Böhme, M. & J. Bukowski, 'Auswirkungen der 0-Cent-Ausschreibungen, Nach welchen Differenzierungskriterien soll künftig der Zuschlag erteilt werden?'. *EnWZ* (2019): 243.

Boldt, G. & H. Weller. *Bundesberggesetz, Kommentar*. Berlin: Walter de Gruyter, 1984.

Britz, G., J. Hellermann & G. Hermes. *EnWG, Energiewirtschaftsgesetz*. 3rd edn. München: C.H. Beck, 2015.

Büdenbender, U., W. Heintschel von Heinegg & P. Rosin. *Energierecht I, Recht der Energieanlagen*. Berlin/New York: Walter de Gruyter, 1999.

Byok, J. 'Neuabschluss und Verlängerung von Konzessionsverträgen – Anforderungen an Bekanntmachung und Durchführung des Auswahlverfahrens'. *RdE* (2008): 268.

Cameron, P.D. 'The Internal Market In Energy: Harnessing the New Regulatory Regime'. *European Law Review* 30 (2005): 634.

Corino, C. *Energy Law in Germany and its Foundations in International and European Law*. München: C.H. Beck, 2003.

Danner, W. & Ch. Theobald. *Energierecht*. München, C.H. Beck.

Däuper, O. *Gaspreisbildung und europäisches Kartellrecht*. München: C.H. Beck, 2003.

Däuper, O. & D. Couval. 'Die Ölpreisbindung aus kartellrechtlicher (Markt-)Sicht'. *ZNER* (2010): 224.

De Wyl, C., J. Eder & T.C. Hartmann. *Netzanschluss- und Grundversorgungsverordnungen*. Frankfurt a.M.: VWEW Energieverlag, 2008.

Durner, W. 'Die aktuellen Vorschläge für ein Netzausbaubeschleunigungsgesetz (NABEG) – Bewertung der Verfassungsmäßigkeit und des Beschleunigungspotentials'. *DVBl* (2011): 853.

Selected Bibliography

Durner, W. 'Die "Bundesfachplanung" im NABEG – Dogmatischer Standort, Bindungswirkung, Prüfprogramm und infrastrukturpolitische Modellfunktion'. *DVBl* (2013): 1564.

Ekey, F. *Grundriss des Wettbewerbs- und Kartellrechts.* Heidelberg: C.F. Müller, 2006.

Emmerich, V. *Kartellrecht.* 11th edn. München: C.H. Beck, 2008.

Energy Concept. 'Energiekonzept für eine umweltschonende, zuverlässige und bezahlbare Energieversorgung'. BT-Drs. 17/3049.

Federal Ministry of Economy and Technologies. *Energie in Deutschland, Trends und Hintergründe zur Energieversorgung in Deutschland* (Februar 2013).

Franzius, C., 'Auf dem Weg zum Klimaschutzgesetz'. *EnWZ* (2019): 435.

Frenz, W., *Klimaschutzrecht.* Berlin: Erich Schmidt Verlag, 2021.

Frenz, W. & H.J. Müggenborg & T. Cosack & B. Hennig & T. Schomerus, *EEG,* 5. Ed. Berlin: Erich Schmidt Verlag, 2018.

Gellermann, M. 'Naturschutzrecht nach der Novelle des Bundesnaturschutzgesetzes'. *NVwZ* (2010): 73.

Gerland, G. & T. Helm. 'Übergang zum Übertragungsmodell (Ownership Unbundling) bei Energieversorgungsunternehmen – Wege aus dem Pachtmodell?'. *Betriebs-Berater* (2008): 192–196.

Germer, C. & H. Loibl. *Energierecht, Handbuch.* 2nd edn. Berlin: Erich Schmidt Verlag, 2007.

Grigoleit, K. J. & C. Weisensee. 'Das neue Planungsrecht für Elektrizitätsnetze'. *UPR* (2011): 401.

Große, A. 'Zum Begriff der Konversionsflächen im EEG'. *ZNER* 7 (2010): 235.

Henneke, H.G. & K. Ritgen. *Kommunales Energierecht.* Wiesbaden: Kommunalund Schul-Verlag, 2010.

Hermeier, G. 'Die Zuständigkeitsverteilung bei der Regulierung des grenzüberschreitenden Stromhandels – Mehr Binnenmarkt durch mehr Zentralisierung?'. *Recht der Energiewirtschaft* (2007): 249–255.

Holznagel, B. & J. Nagel. 'Verfahrensbeschleunigung nach dem Energieleitungsausbaugesetz – Verfassungsrechtliche Grenzen und Alternativen'. *DVBl* (2010): 669–677.

Holznagel, B. & P. Schumacher. 'ERGEGplus – Wieder der Versuch der Einführung eines europäischen Regulierers durch die Hintertür'. *Recht der Energiewirtschaft* (2007): 225–232.

Holznagel, B. & R. Schütz. *Anreizregulierungsverordnung.* München: C.H. Beck, 2nd ed. 2019.

Jacobs, D. 'The German *Energiewende* – History, Targets, Policies and Challenges'. *RELP* (2012): 223.

Jarass, H.D. *BlmSchG.* 8th edn. München: C.H. Beck, 2010.

Jarass, H.D. 'Die neuen Regelungen zur Biokraftstoffquote'. *ZUR* (2007): 518.

Kahl, H., M. Kahles & T. Müller, 'Neuordnungen im EEG 2017'. *ER* (2016): 187.

Kahle, C. 'Die Eigentumsrechtliche Entflechtung (Ownership Unbundling) der Energieversorgungsnetze aus europarechtlicher und verfassungsrechtlicher Sicht'. *Recht der Energiewirtschaft* (2007): 293–299.

Kennedy, D. 'Merger in the English Electricity Industry'. *Energy Policy* 25 (1997): 393.

Kirch, T., 'Die Netzanbindung von Windenergieanlagen auf See im Küstenmeer', *IR* (2021):, 221.

Kirschnick, S. & D. Krappitz, 'Kernpunkte des Strommarktes 2.0 für Vertrieb, Erzeuger und Netzbetreiber'. *IR* (2016): 266.

Klahm, R. & C. Fabritius, 'Das Aus für die normative Regulierung'. *ER* (2021): 238.

Koch, H.J. & A. Braun. 'Aktuelle Entwicklungen des Immissionsschutzrechts'. *NVwZ* (2010): 1199.

Kommission Wachstum, Strukturwandel und Beschäftigung, Abschlussbericht, January 2019, <www.bmwi.de> last accessed 19 February 2021.

Kotulla, M. 'Das novellierte Wasserhaushaltsgesetz'. *NVwZ* (2010): 79.

Kremer, E. & P. Neuhaus. *Bergrecht.* Stuttgart: W. Kohlhammer, 2001.

Kreuter-Kirchhof, C., 'Emissionshandel und Erneuerbare Energien Richtlinie, Instrumente zur Umsetzung der Klimaschutzstrategie der EU'. *ZUR* (2019): 396.

Krumrey, H. 'Kein neuer Kurs bei der Energie'. *Energiewirtschaftliche Tagesfragen* (2009), Heft 12, 4.

Kühling J. & R. Pisal. 'Die Umsetzung der EU-Entflechtungsvorgaben im EnWG 2011'. *Energiewirtschaftliche Tagesfragen* (2012): 127.

Kühne, G. & C. Brodowski. 'Das neue Energiewirtschaftsrecht nach der Reform 2005'. *NVwZ* (2005): 850.

Kühne, G. & B. Scholtka. 'Das neue Energiewirtschaftsrecht'. *Neue Juristische Wochenschrift* (1998): 1905–1906.

Landmann & Rohmer (ed.). *Umweltrecht.* München: C.H. Beck.

Lange, K.W. 'Verbraucherschutz im neuen EnWG'. *RdE* (2012): 41.

Lecheler, H. & J. Gundel. 'Ein weiterer Schritt zur Vollendung des Energie-Binnenmarktes: Die Beschlunigungs-Rechtsakte für den Binnenmarkt für Strom und Gas'. *Europäische Zeitschrift für Wirtschaftsrecht* (2003): 625.

Leidinger, T. *Energieanlagenrecht.* Stuttgart: Boorberg, 2007.

Lehnert, W. & J. Vollprecht. 'Neue Impulse von Europa: Die Erneuerbare-Energien-Richtlinie der EU'. *ZUR* (2009): 307 et seq.

Lehnert, W. 'Markt- und Systemintegration der Erneuerbaren Energien: Eine rechtliche Analyse der Regeln zur Direktvermarktung im EEG 2012'. *ZUR* (2012): 4.

Lettl, T. *Kartellrecht.* München: C.H. Beck, 2005.

Loibl, H., et al. *Biogasanlagen im EEG.* 4th edn. Berlin: Erich Schmidt Verlag, 2016.

Mayen, T. & U. Karpenstein. 'Eigentumsrechtliche Entflechtung der Energieversorgungsnetze – Verfassungs- und gemeinschaftsrechtliche Aspekte des Eigentumsschutzes'. *Recht der Energiewirtschaft* (2008): 33–45.

Michaels, S. & O. Däuper, 'Das Kohleausstiegsgesetz im Überblick – Welche Rechtsfragen bleiben offen?'. *EnWZ* (2020): 291.

Michler, H.P. & F. Möller. 'Änderungen der Eingriffsregelung durch das BNatSchG 2010'. *NuR* (2011): 81.

Moench, C. & M. Ruttloff. 'Netzausbau in Beschleunigung'. *NVwZ* (2011): 1040.

Monopolies Commission, Special Report. *Strom und Gas 2009 – Energiemärkte im Spannungsfeld von Politik und Wettbewerb.* BT-Drs. 16/14060.

Müggenborg, H.J. & A. Hentschel. 'Neues Wasser- und Naturschutzrecht'. *NJW* (2010): 961.
Petersen, M. *Umweltschadensgesetz*, Kommentar. Köln: Carl Heymanns Verlag, 2013.
Petersen, M. 'The Environmental Liability Directive – Extending Nature Protection in Europe'. *Environmental Law Review* 11 (2009): 5.
Petersen, M. 'The Legality of the EU's Stand-Alone Approach to the Climate Impact of Aviation: The Express Role Given to the ICAO by the Kyoto Protocol'. *Review of European Community and International Environmental Law* 17 (2008): 196.
Petersen, M. 'Restructuring the Electricity Sector in the EU and Russia'. *European Energy and Environmental Law Review* 18 (2009): 171.
Plicht, S., Gesetz zur Entwicklung und Förderung der Windenergieanlagen auf See. *EnWZ* (2016): 550.
Reck, H.J. 'Pflichten der Kommunen bei auslaufenden Konzessionsverträgen in der Energieversorgung'. *KommJur* (2009): 401.
Ringel, C. & C. Bitsch. 'Die Neuordnung des Rechts der Erneuerbaren Energien in Europa'. *NVwZ* (2009): 807 et seq.
Rostankowski, A. 'Die Ausgleichsmechansmus-Verordnung und der Ausbau Erneuerbarer Energien'. *ZNER* (2010): 125.
Ruge, R. 'Die neue Anreizregulierungsverordnung (ARegV) – Systemwechsel bei der Regulierung der Netzentgelte im Energiebereich'. *DVBl* (2008): 956 et seq.
Sachverständigenrat für Umweltfragen. *Klimaschutz durch Biomasse, Sondergutachten.* Berlin: Erich Schmidt Verlag, July 2007.
Säcker, F.J. (ed.). *Berliner Kommentar zum Energierecht.* vol. 1. 2nd edn. Frankfurt am Main: Verlag Recht und Wirtschaft, 2010.
Salje, P. *EEG.* 5th edn. Köln: Carl Heymanns Verlag, 2009 & 6th edn. 2012.
Schalast, C. 'Das EU-Energiepaket 2007 – Wettbewerb, Binnenmarkt und Umweltschutz'. *InfrastrukturRecht* (2007): 75.
Schiffer, H.W. *Energiemarkt Deutschland.* 10th edn. Köln: TÜV Media, 2008.
Schirmer, B. 'Das Gesetz zur Beschleunigung des Ausbaus der Höchstspannungsnetze'. *DVBl* (2010): 1349.
Schlacke, S. *Umweltrecht.* 8th edn. Baden-Baden: Nomos Verlagsgesellschaft, 2021.
Schneider, J.P. & C. Theobald. *Recht der Energiewirtschaft.* 2nd edn. München: C.H. Beck, 2008 & 4th edn. 2013 & 5th edn. 2021.
Scholtka, B. & F. Frizen, 'Die Entwicklung des Energierechts im Jahr 2020'. *NJW* (2021): 906.
Scholtka, B. & J. Martin, 'Die Entwicklung des Energierechts im Jahr 2016'. *NJW* (2017): 932.
Scholtka, B. & L. Keller-Herder, Die Entwicklung des Energierechts im Jahr 2019, *NJW* (2020): 890
Scholtka, B. & S. Helmes. 'Energiewende 2011 – Schwerpunkte der Neuregelungen im Energiewirtschafts- und Energieumweltrecht'. *NJW* (2011): 3185.
Schomerus, T. & A. Henkel. 'Die Marktprämie im EEG 2012 – eine erste Zwischenbilanz'. *ER* (2012): 13.

Schomerus, T. 'Die Umsetzung von Art. 7 Energieeffizienz-Richtlinie 2012/27/EU in nationales Recht'. *ER* 2013, 184 et seq.

Schütte, P. & M. Winkler, 'Aktuelle Entwicklungen im Bundesumweltrecht, Berichtszeitraum: 1.2.2021 bis 12.4.2021'. *ZUR* (2021): 376.

Sellner, D., O. Reidt & M.J. Ohms. *Immissionsschutzrecht und Industrieanlagen.* 3rd edn. München: C.H. Beck, 2006.

Sellner, D. & F. Fellenberg. 'Atomausstieg und Energiewende 2011 – das Gesetzespaket im Überblick'. *NVwZ* (2011): 1025.

Spieth, W.F. & M. Hamer. 'Die neuen Zuteilungsregelungen für Industrieanlagen in der dritten Phase des europäischen Emissionshandelssystems'. *NVwZ* (2011): 920.

Spieth, W.F. & M. Uibeleisen. 'Neues Genehmigungsregime für Offshore-Windparks'. *NVwZ* (2012): 321.

Storr, S. 'Die Vorschläge der EU-Komission zur Verschärfung der Unbundling-Vorschriften im Energiesektor'. *Europäische Zeitschrift für Wirtschaftsrecht* (2007): 233.

Nill-Theobald, Christiane & Christian Theobald. *Grundzüge des Energiewirtschaftsrechts.* 3rd edn. München: C.H. Beck, 2013.

Theobald, Ch. 'Auslaufende Konzessionsverträge Strom und Gas: Was ist seitens der Kommunen zu tun?'. *DÖV* (2009): 356.

Theobald, C. & T. Gey-Kern. 'Das dritte Energiebinnenmarktpaket der EU und die Reform des deutschen Energiewirtschaftsrechts 2011'. *EuZW* (2011): 896.

Thole, C. & M. Kachel. 'Zahnloser Tiger Energieeffizienzgesetz – Handlungsspielräume für Energieversorgungsunternehmen'. *IR* (2010): 122 et seq.

Thomas, H. 'Probleme von Netzanschluss und Netzanschlussverfahren für EEG-Anlagen in der jüngeren Rechtsprechung des BGH'. ZNER (2013): 348.

Thomas, H. 'Das EEG 2012 – Eine Darstellung nach Anspruchsgrundlagen'. *NVwZ-Extra* (11/2012), 1.

Tudway, R. *Energy Law & Regulation in the European Union.* London: Sweet & Maxwell, 1999.

Vollprecht, J. 'Die neue Biomassestrom-Nachhaltigkeitsverordnung: Auswirkungen auf die Vergütung von Strom nach dem EEG'. *IR* (2010): 28.

Vollprecht, J. & P.Schwarz, 'Die Biomassestrom-Nachhaltigkeitsverordnung in (ziemlich) neuem Gewand'. *IR* (2022): 53.

Vollprecht, J. & M. Altrock, 'Die EEG-Novelle 2017: Von Ausschreibungen bis zuschaltbare Lasten'. *EnWZ* (2016): 387.

Weise, M. & C. de Wyl & T.C. Hartmann. 'Gescheiterte Großkraftwerksprojekte und Verfall der Reservierungsgebühr'. *Energiewirtschaftliche Tagesfragen* (2011): 83.

Weyer, H. & T. Iversen, 'Grundzüge des Redispatch 2.0'. *RdE* (2021): 1.

Wustlich, G. & D. Müller. 'Die Direktvermarktung von Strom aus erneuerbaren Energien im EEG 2012 – Eine systematische Einführung in die Marktprämie und die weiteren Neuregelungen zur Marktintegration'. *ZNER* (2011): 380.

Selected Bibliography

Zabel, L. 'Die Novelle der Seeanlagenverordnung – Auswirkungen auf die Zulassung von Offshore-Windparks und Netzanschlussvorhaben'. *NordÖR* (2012): 263.

Zenke, I. & C. Telschow, 'CO_2-Bepreisung durch nationalen Emissionshandel'. *EnWZ* (2020): 157.

Index

The numbers here refers to paragraphs numbers.

Index

Index

Made in United States
North Haven, CT
04 November 2026

21727459R00176